SUPERMAN BEYOND

MAN OF TOMORROW

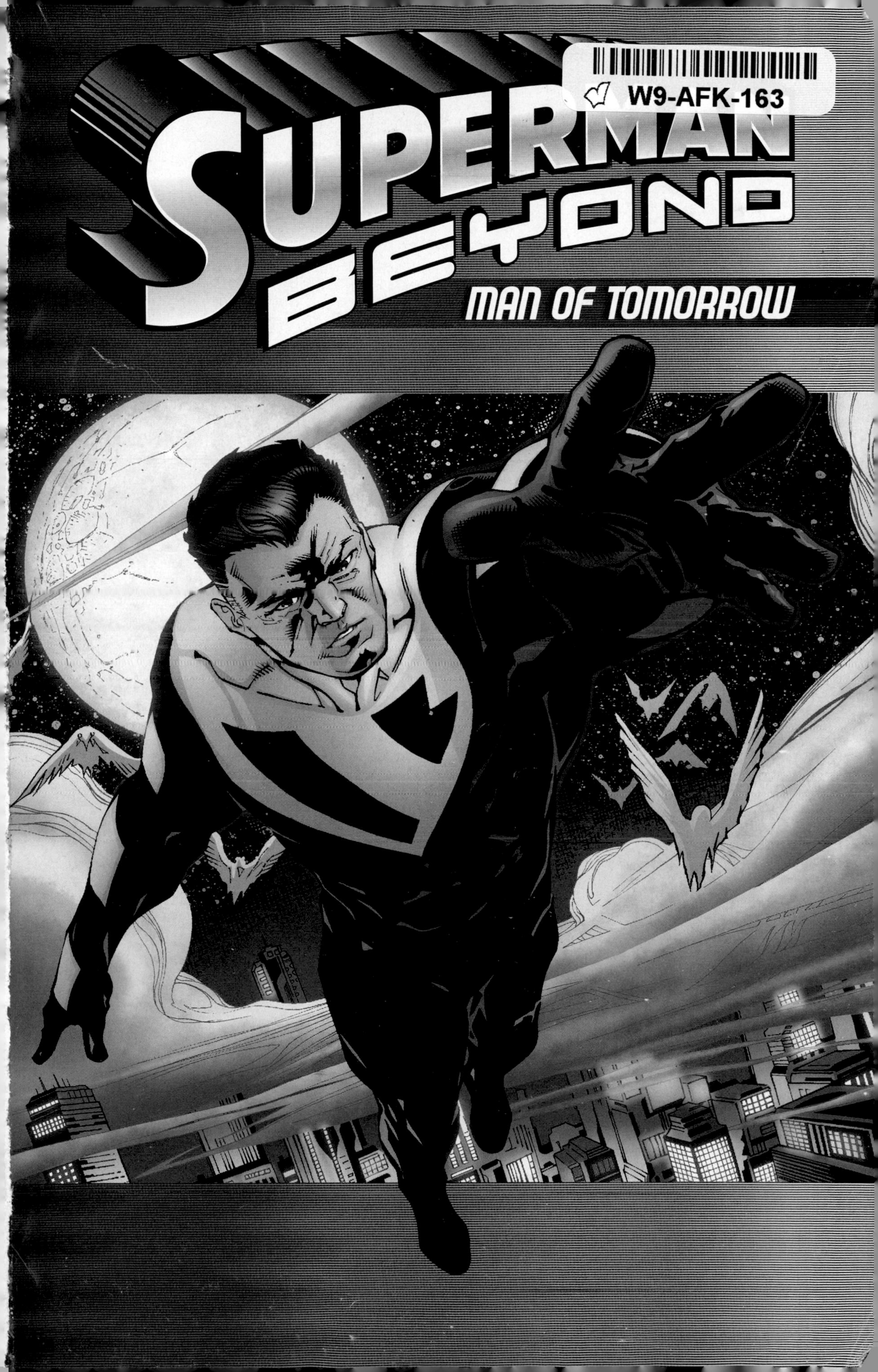

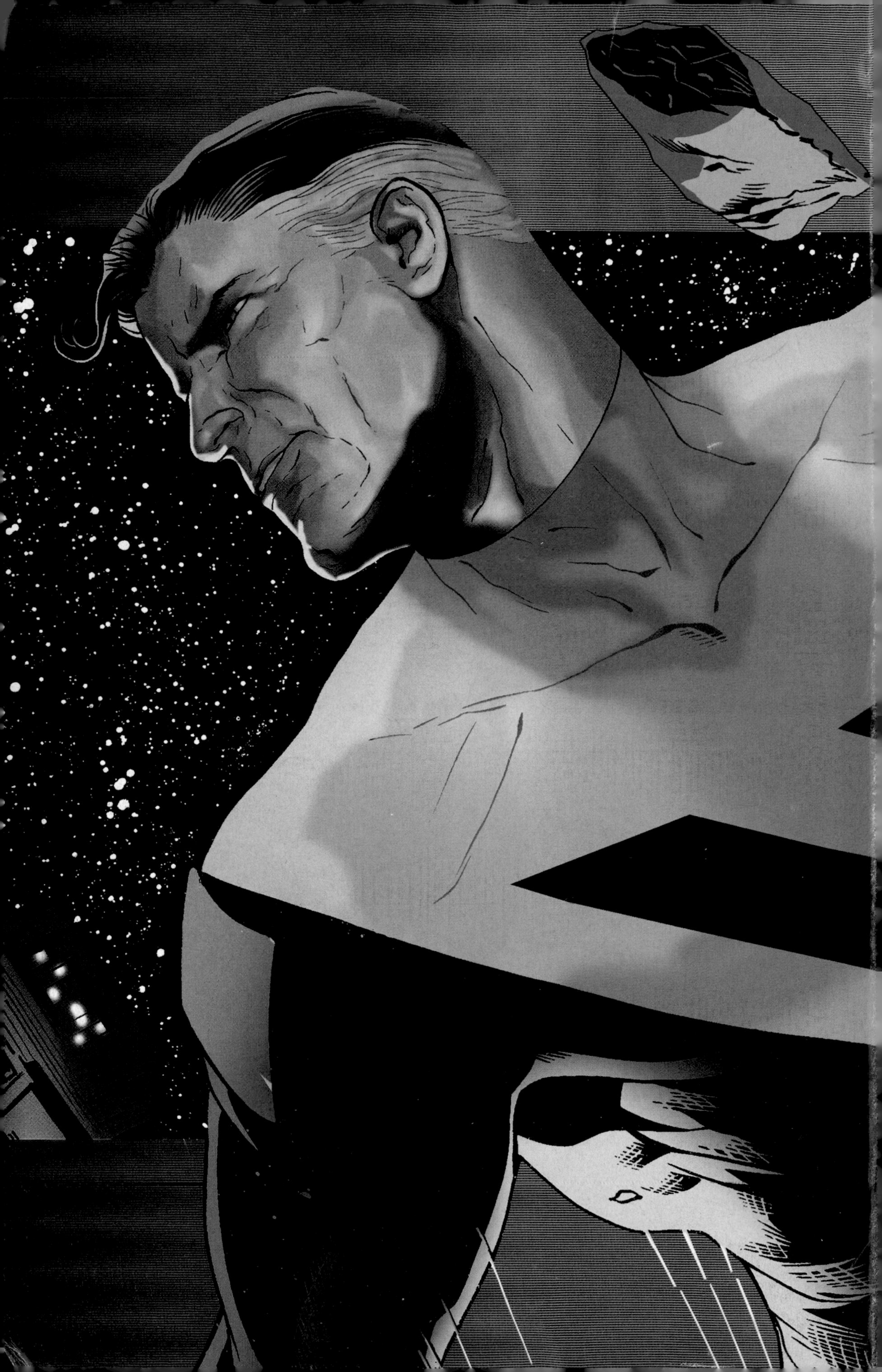

SUPERMAN BEYOND

MAN OF TOMORROW

J.T. KRUL · PAUL LEVITZ
TOM DEFALCO · RON FRENZ
WRITERS

HOWARD PORTER · JOHN LIVESAY
RENATO GUEDES · JOSÉ WILSON
TOM DEFALCO · RON FRENZ · SAL BUSCEMA
ARTISTS

RANDY MAYOR · RENATO GUEDES · CHRIS BECKETT
TONY AVIÑA · CARRIE STRACHAN
COLORISTS

SAIDA TEMOFONTE · STEVE WANDS · DAVE SHARPE
LETTERERS

HOWARD PORTER & JOHN LIVESAY
COLLECTION COVER ARTISTS

SUPERMAN CREATED BY JERRY SIEGEL AND JOE SHUSTER
BY SPECIAL ARRANGEMENT WITH THE JERRY SIEGEL FAMILY
BATMAN CREATED BY BOB KANE

Kwanza Johnson
Ben Abernathy
Eddie Berganza
Alex Antone Editors – Original Series
Sarah Litt
Rex Ogle Assistant Editors – Original Series
Robin Wildman Editor
Robbin Brosterman Design Director – Books
Curtis King Jr. Publication Design

Bob Harras Senior VP – Editor-in-Chief, DC Comics

Diane Nelson President
Dan DiDio and **Jim Lee** Co-Publishers
Geoff Johns Chief Creative Officer
John Rood Executive VP – Sales, Marketing & Business Development
Amy Genkins Senior VP – Business & Legal Affairs
Nairi Gardiner Senior VP – Finance
Jeff Boison VP – Publishing Planning
Mark Chiarello VP – Art Direction & Design
John Cunningham VP – Marketing
Terri Cunningham VP – Editorial Administration
Alison Gill Senior VP – Manufacturing & Operations
Hank Kanalz Senior VP – Vertigo & Integrated Publishing
Jay Kogan VP – Business & Legal Affairs, Publishing
Jack Mahan VP – Business Affairs, Talent
Nick Napolitano VP – Manufacturing Administration
Sue Pohja VP – Book Sales
Courtney Simmons Senior VP – Publicity
Bob Wayne Senior VP – Sales

SUPERMAN BEYOND: MAN OF TOMORROW
Published by DC Comics. Cover and compilation Copyright ©
2013 DC Comics. All Rights Reserved. Originally published in single
magazine form in SUPERMAN BEYOND 0, SUPERMAN BEYOND DIGITAL
CHAPTERS 1-10, SUPERMAN/BATMAN ANNUAL 4 Copyright © 2010,
2011, 2012 DC Comics. All Rights Reserved. All characters, their distinctive
likenesses and related elements featured in this publication are trademarks
of DC Comics. The stories, characters and incidents featured in this
publication are entirely fictional. DC Comics does not read or accept
unsolicited ideas, stories or artwork.

DC Comics, 1700 Broadway, New York, NY 10019
A Warner Bros. Entertainment Company.
Printed by RR Donnelley, Salem, VA. 6/14/13
Second Printing.
ISBN: 978-1-4012-3823-0

Library of Congress Cataloging-in-Publication Data

Krul, J. T.
    Superman Beyond : Man of Tomorrow / J.T. Krul, Howard Porter.
      pages cm
    "Originally published in single magazine form in Superman Beyond 0, Superman
Beyond Digital Chapters 1-10, Superman/Batman Annual 4."
    ISBN 978-1-4012-3823-0
    1. Graphic novels. I. Porter, Howard, illustrator. II. Title. III. Title: Man of Tomorrow.
    PN6728.S9K78 2013
    741.5'973—dc23

                                        2012048550

SUSTAINABLE
FORESTRY
INITIATIVE

Certified Chain of Custody
At Least 20% Certified Forest Content
www.sfiprogram.org
SFI-01042
APPLIES TO TEXT STOCK ONLY

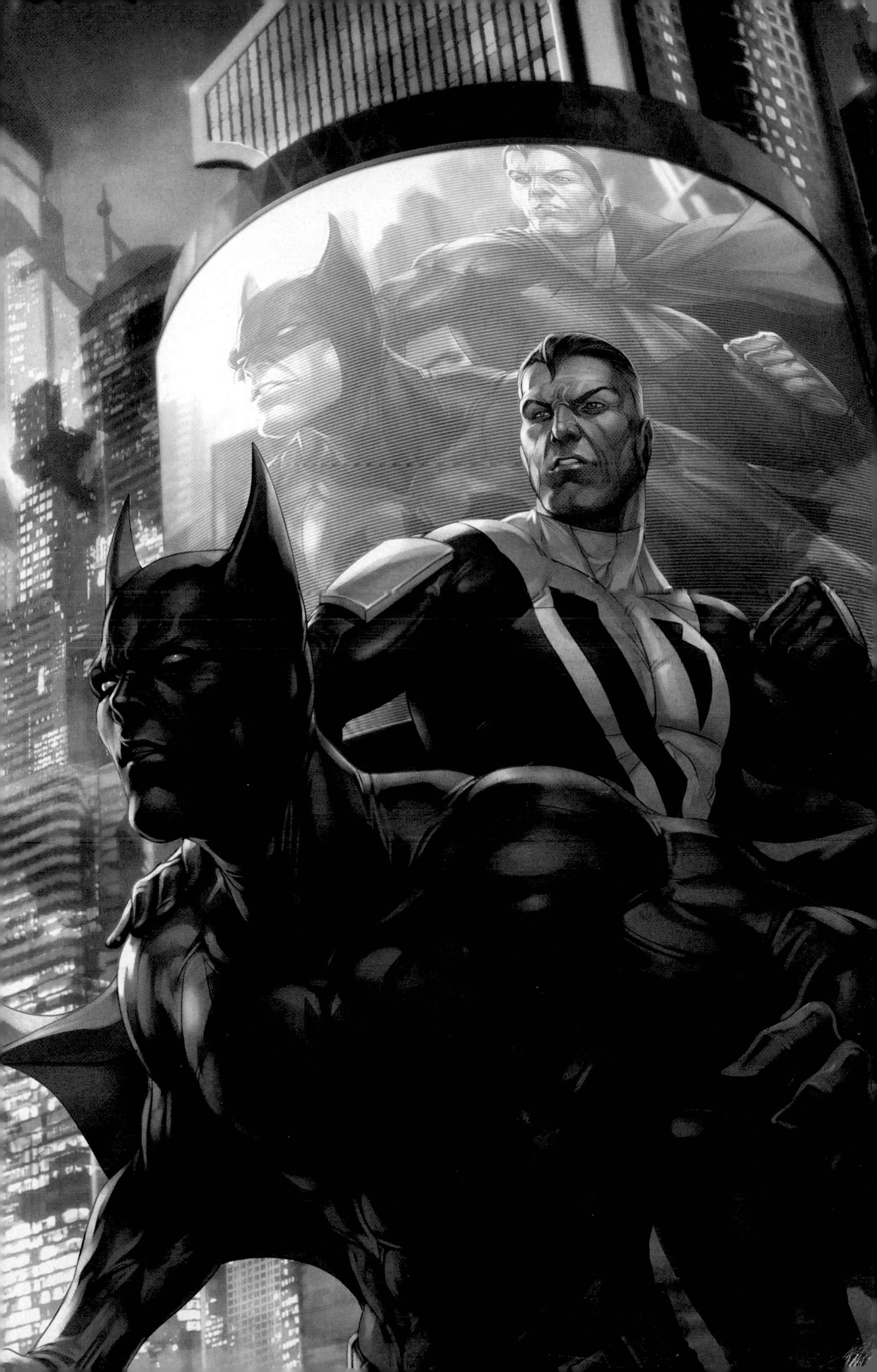

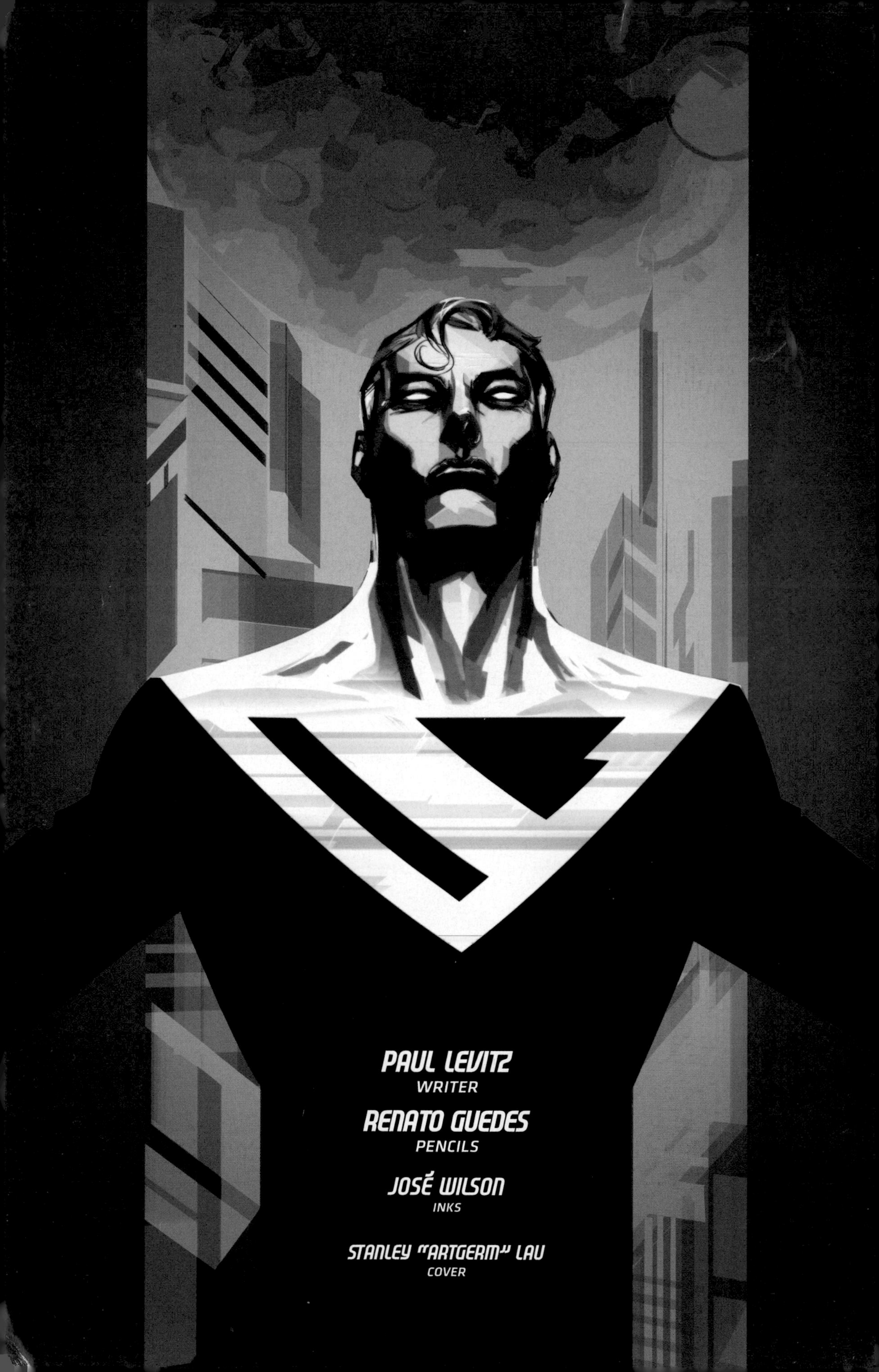

PAUL LEVITZ
WRITER

RENATO GUEDES
PENCILS

JOSÉ WILSON
INKS

STANLEY "ARTGERM" LAU
COVER

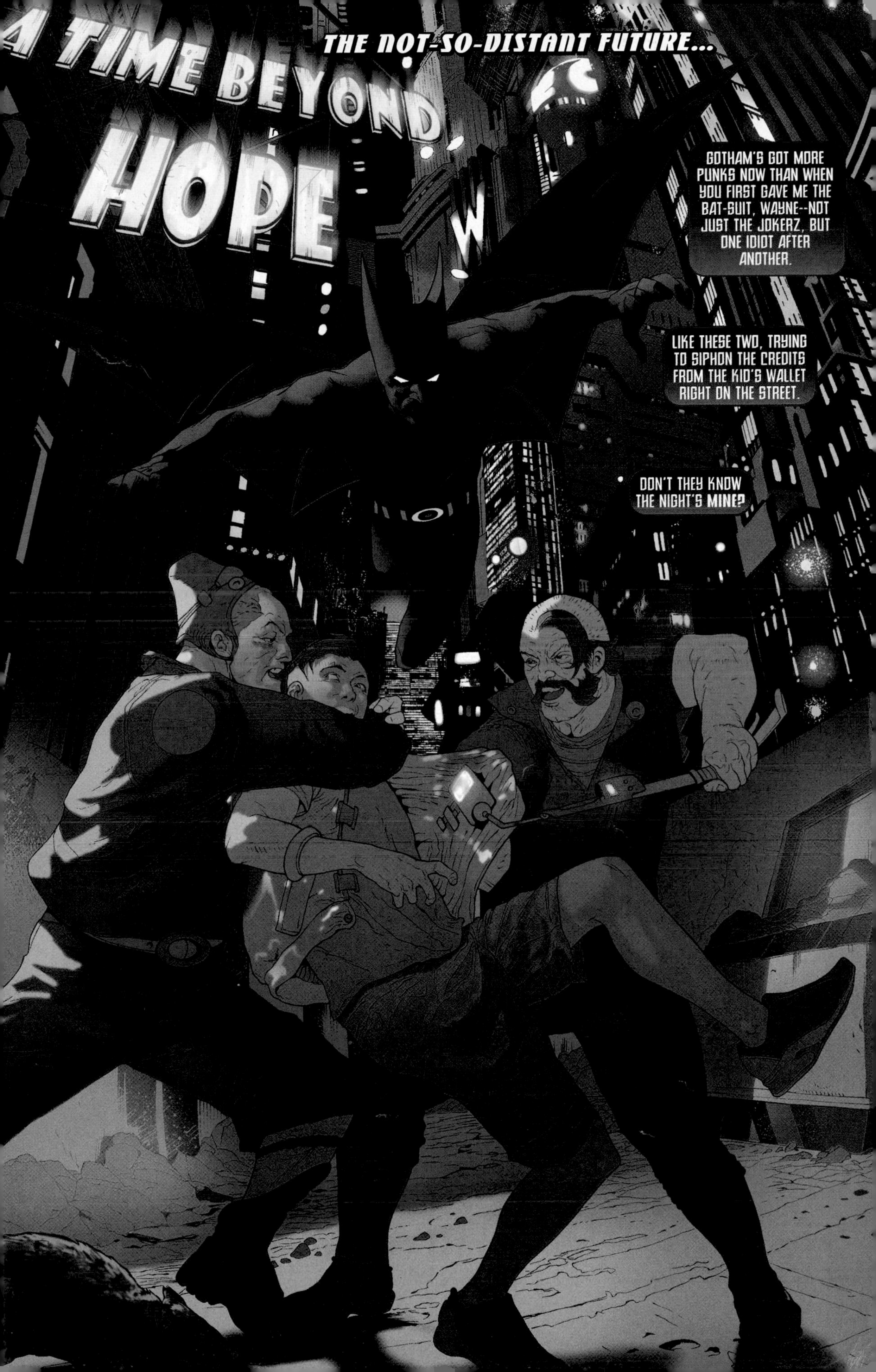
A TIME BEYOND HOPE
THE NOT-SO-DISTANT FUTURE...
GOTHAM'S GOT MORE PUNKS NOW THAN WHEN YOU FIRST GAVE ME THE BAT-SUIT, WAYNE--NOT JUST THE JOKERZ, BUT ONE IDIOT AFTER ANOTHER.
LIKE THESE TWO, TRYING TO SIPHON THE CREDITS FROM THE KID'S WALLET RIGHT ON THE STREET.
DON'T THEY KNOW THE NIGHT'S **MINE**?

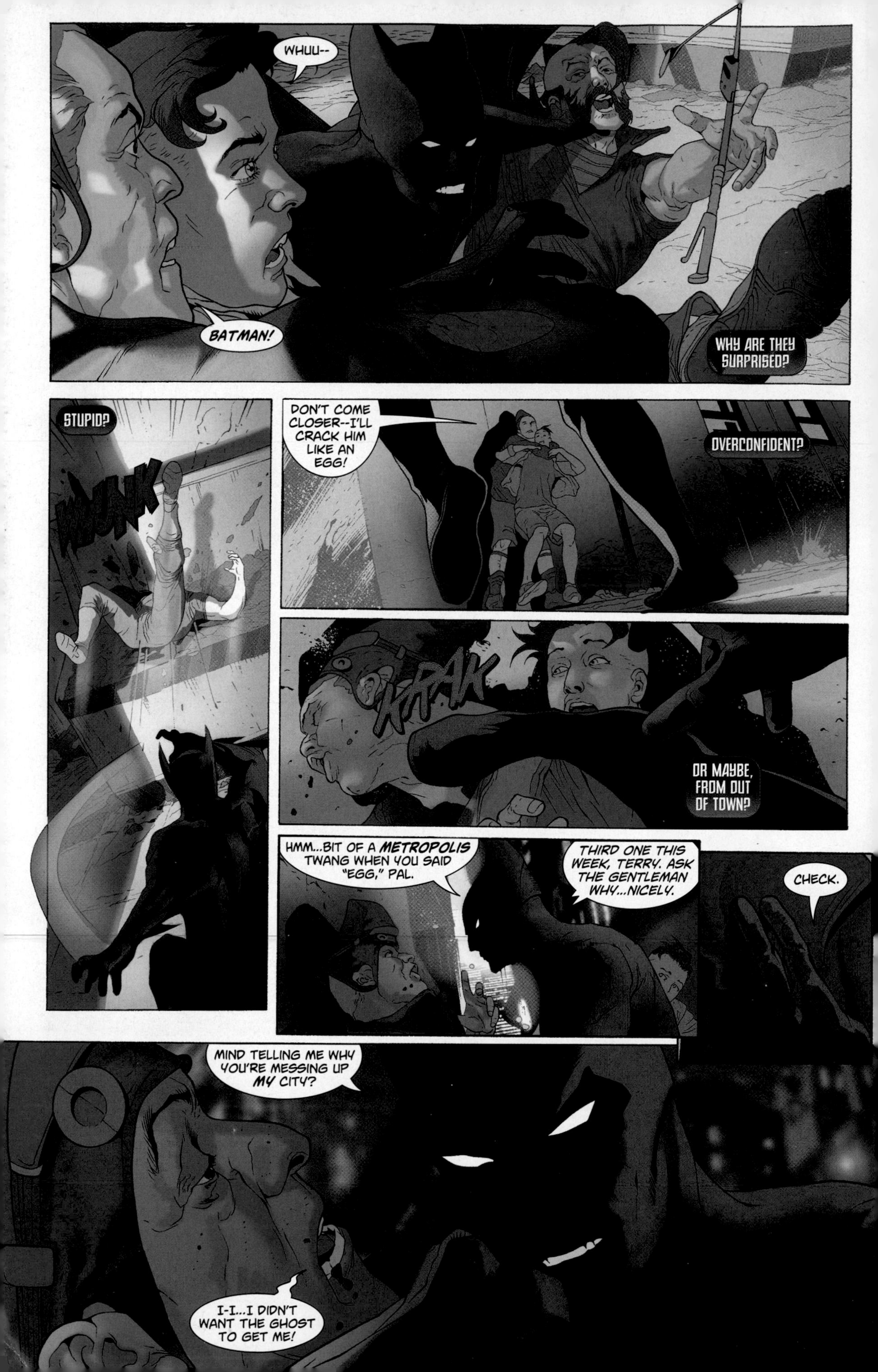
WHUU--
BATMAN!
WHY ARE THEY SURPRISED?
STUPID?
WUNK
DON'T COME CLOSER--I'LL CRACK HIM LIKE AN EGG!
OVERCONFIDENT?
KRAK
OR MAYBE, FROM OUT OF TOWN?
HMM...BIT OF A METROPOLIS TWANG WHEN YOU SAID "EGG," PAL.
THIRD ONE THIS WEEK, TERRY. ASK THE GENTLEMAN WHY...NICELY.
CHECK.
MIND TELLING ME WHY YOU'RE MESSING UP MY CITY?
I-I...I DIDN'T WANT THE GHOST TO GET ME!

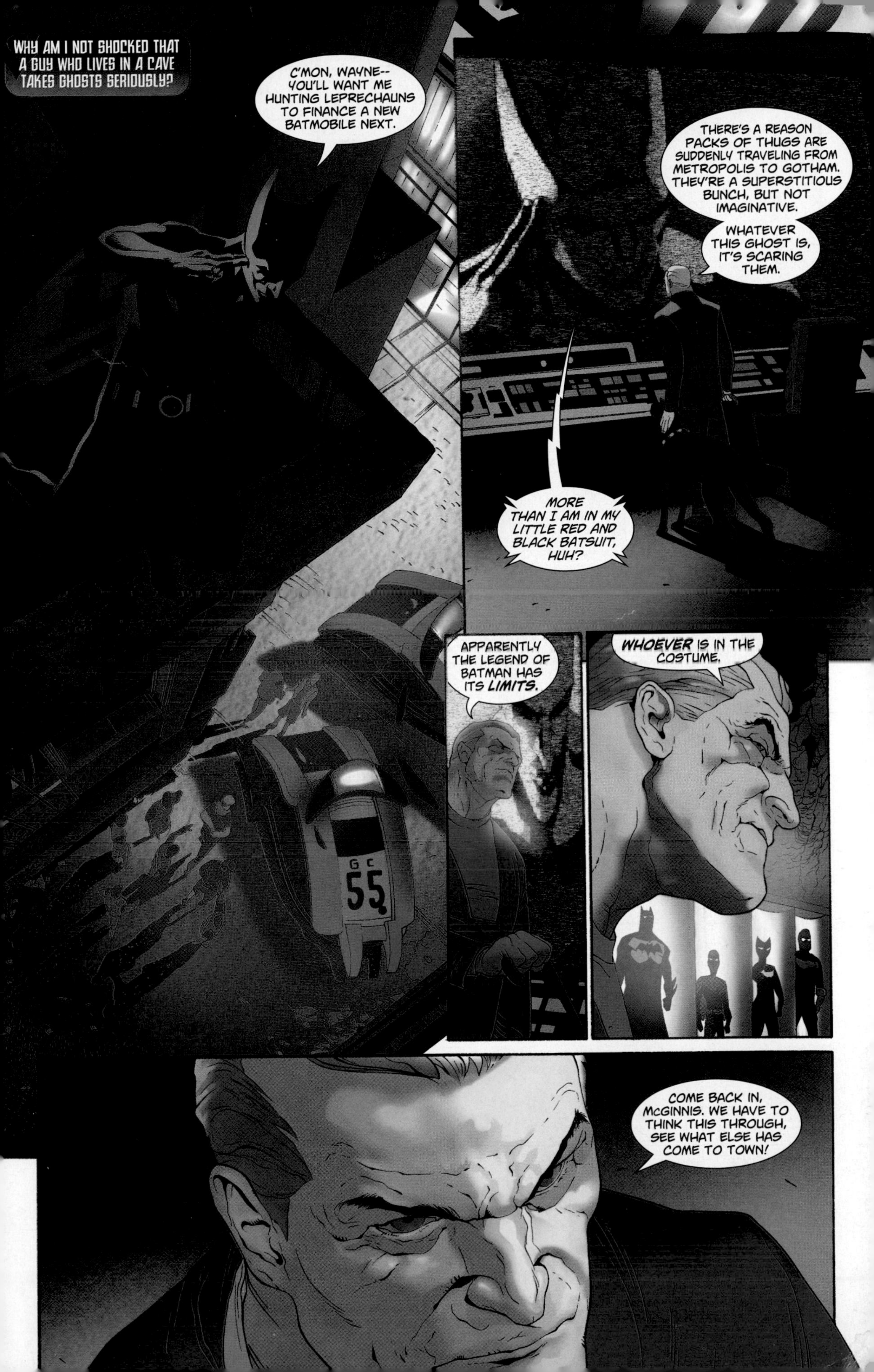
WHY AM I NOT SHOCKED THAT A GUY WHO LIVES IN A CAVE TAKES GHOSTS SERIOUSLY?
C'MON, WAYNE-- YOU'LL WANT ME HUNTING LEPRECHAUNS TO FINANCE A NEW BATMOBILE NEXT.
THERE'S A REASON PACKS OF THUGS ARE SUDDENLY TRAVELING FROM METROPOLIS TO GOTHAM. THEY'RE A SUPERSTITIOUS BUNCH, BUT NOT IMAGINATIVE.
WHATEVER THIS GHOST IS, IT'S SCARING THEM.
MORE THAN I AM IN MY LITTLE RED AND BLACK BATSUIT, HUH?
GC 55
APPARENTLY THE LEGEND OF BATMAN HAS ITS LIMITS.
WHOEVER IS IN THE COSTUME.
COME BACK IN, McGINNIS. WE HAVE TO THINK THIS THROUGH, SEE WHAT ELSE HAS COME TO TOWN!

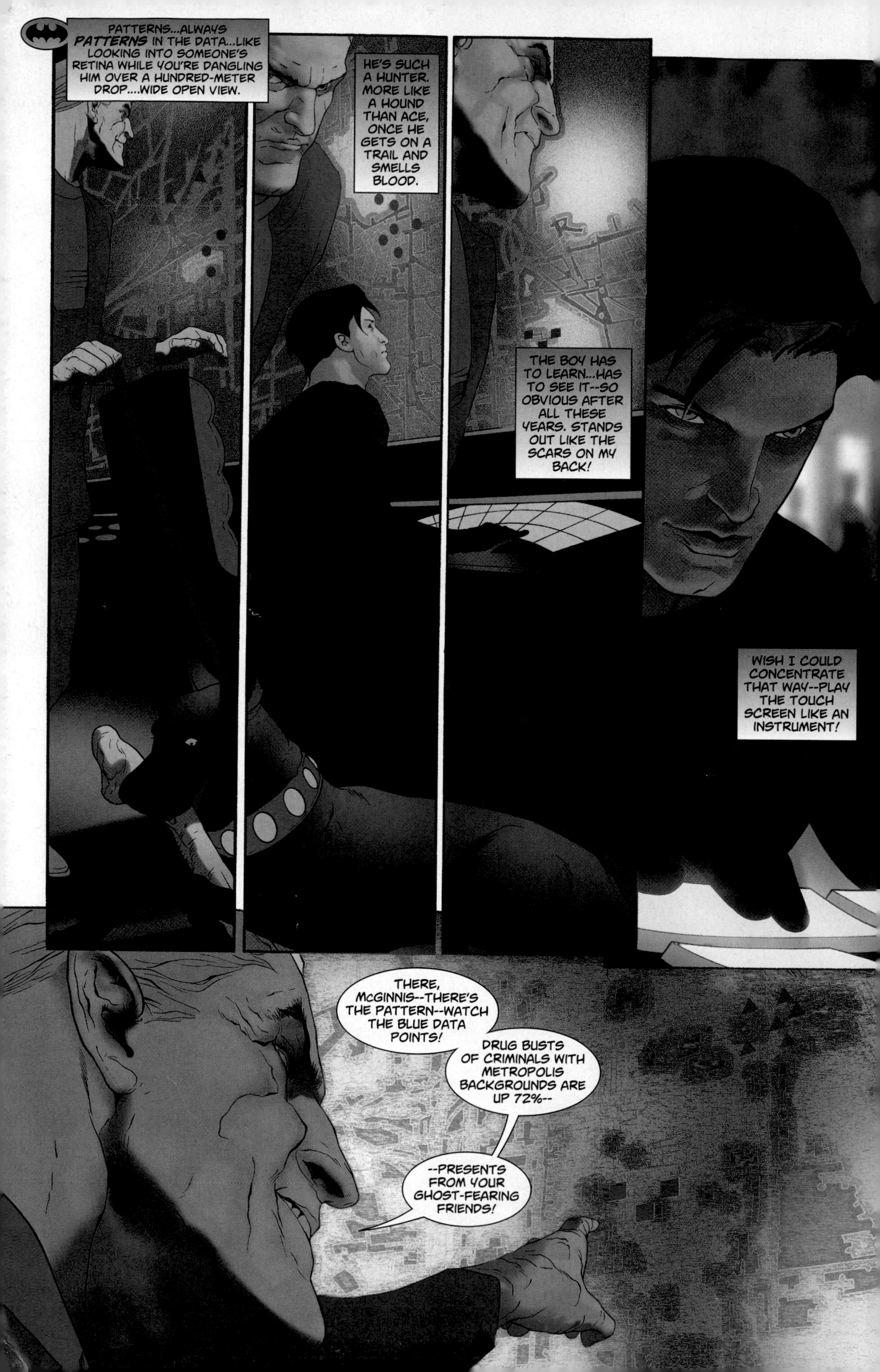
PATTERNS...ALWAYS PATTERNS IN THE DATA...LIKE LOOKING INTO SOMEONE'S RETINA WHILE YOU'RE DANGLING HIM OVER A HUNDRED-METER DROP....WIDE OPEN VIEW.
HE'S SUCH A HUNTER. MORE LIKE A HOUND THAN ACE, ONCE HE GETS ON A TRAIL AND SMELLS BLOOD.
THE BOY HAS TO LEARN...HAS TO SEE IT--SO OBVIOUS AFTER ALL THESE YEARS. STANDS OUT LIKE THE SCARS ON MY BACK!
WISH I COULD CONCENTRATE THAT WAY--PLAY THE TOUCH SCREEN LIKE AN INSTRUMENT!
THERE, McGINNIS--THERE'S THE PATTERN--WATCH THE BLUE DATA POINTS!
DRUG BUSTS OF CRIMINALS WITH METROPOLIS BACKGROUNDS ARE UP 72%--
--PRESENTS FROM YOUR GHOST-FEARING FRIENDS!

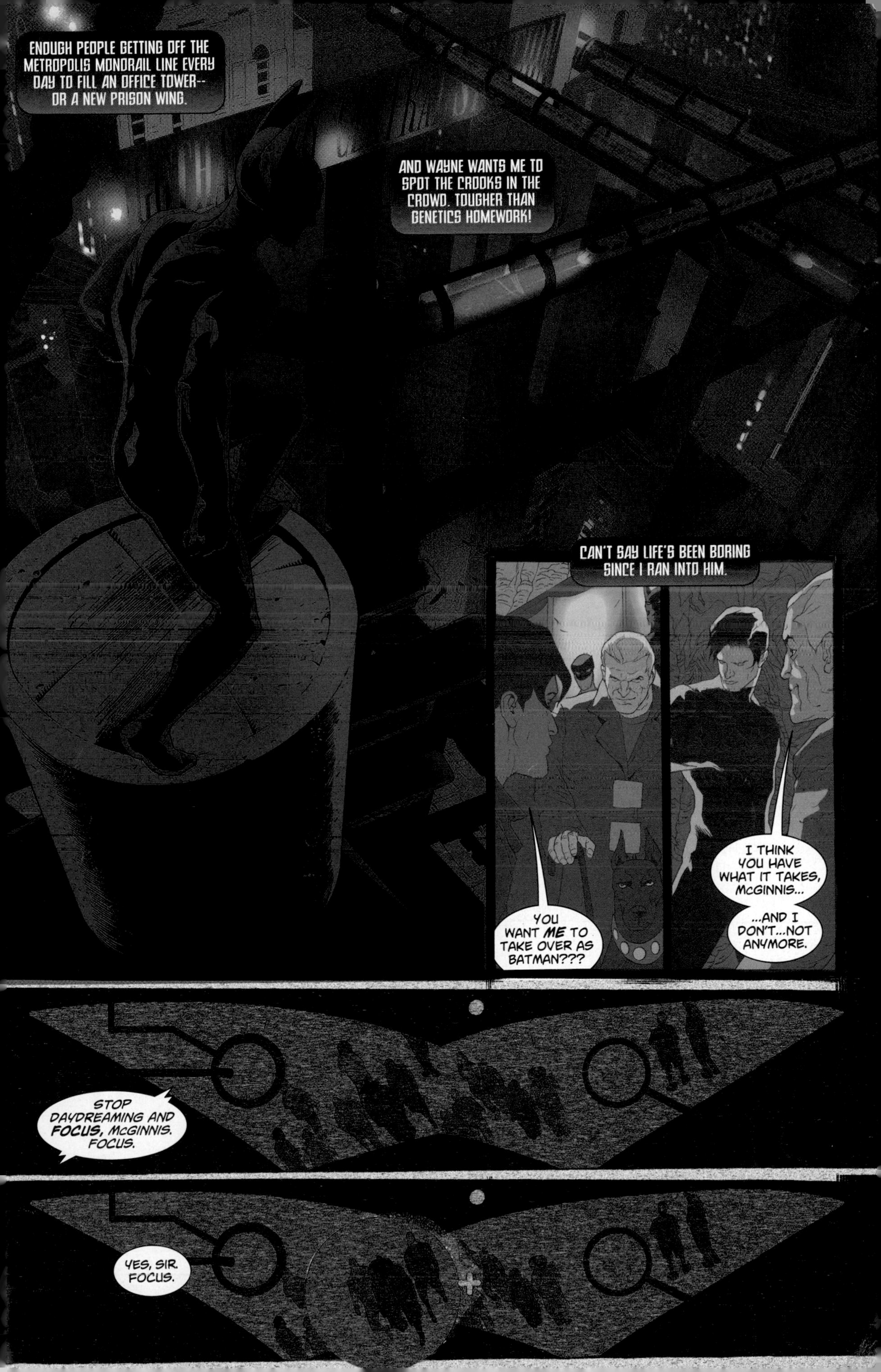

ENOUGH PEOPLE GETTING OFF THE METROPOLIS MONORAIL LINE EVERY DAY TO FILL AN OFFICE TOWER--OR A NEW PRISON WING.
AND WAYNE WANTS ME TO SPOT THE CROOKS IN THE CROWD. TOUGHER THAN GENETICS HOMEWORK!
CAN'T SAY LIFE'S BEEN BORING SINCE I RAN INTO HIM.
YOU WANT ME TO TAKE OVER AS BATMAN???
I THINK YOU HAVE WHAT IT TAKES, McGINNIS...
...AND I DON'T...NOT ANYMORE.
STOP DAYDREAMING AND FOCUS, McGINNIS. FOCUS.
YES, SIR. FOCUS.

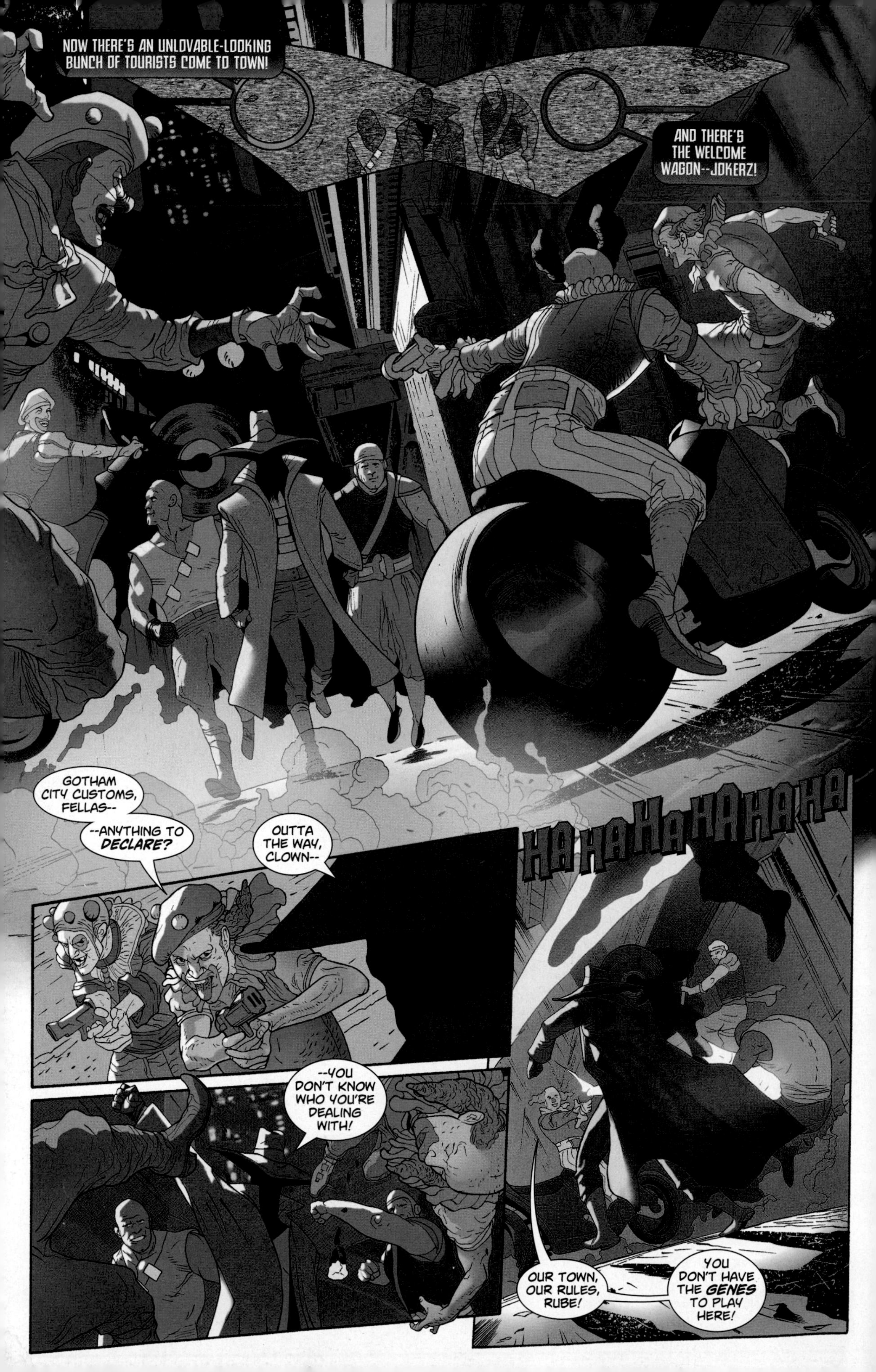
NOW THERE'S AN UNLOVABLE-LOOKING BUNCH OF TOURISTS COME TO TOWN!
AND THERE'S THE WELCOME WAGON--JOKERZ!
GOTHAM CITY CUSTOMS, FELLAS--
--ANYTHING TO DECLARE?
OUTTA THE WAY, CLOWN--
HA HA HA HA HA HA HA HA
--YOU DON'T KNOW WHO YOU'RE DEALING WITH!
OUR TOWN, OUR RULES, RUBE!
YOU DON'T HAVE THE GENES TO PLAY HERE!

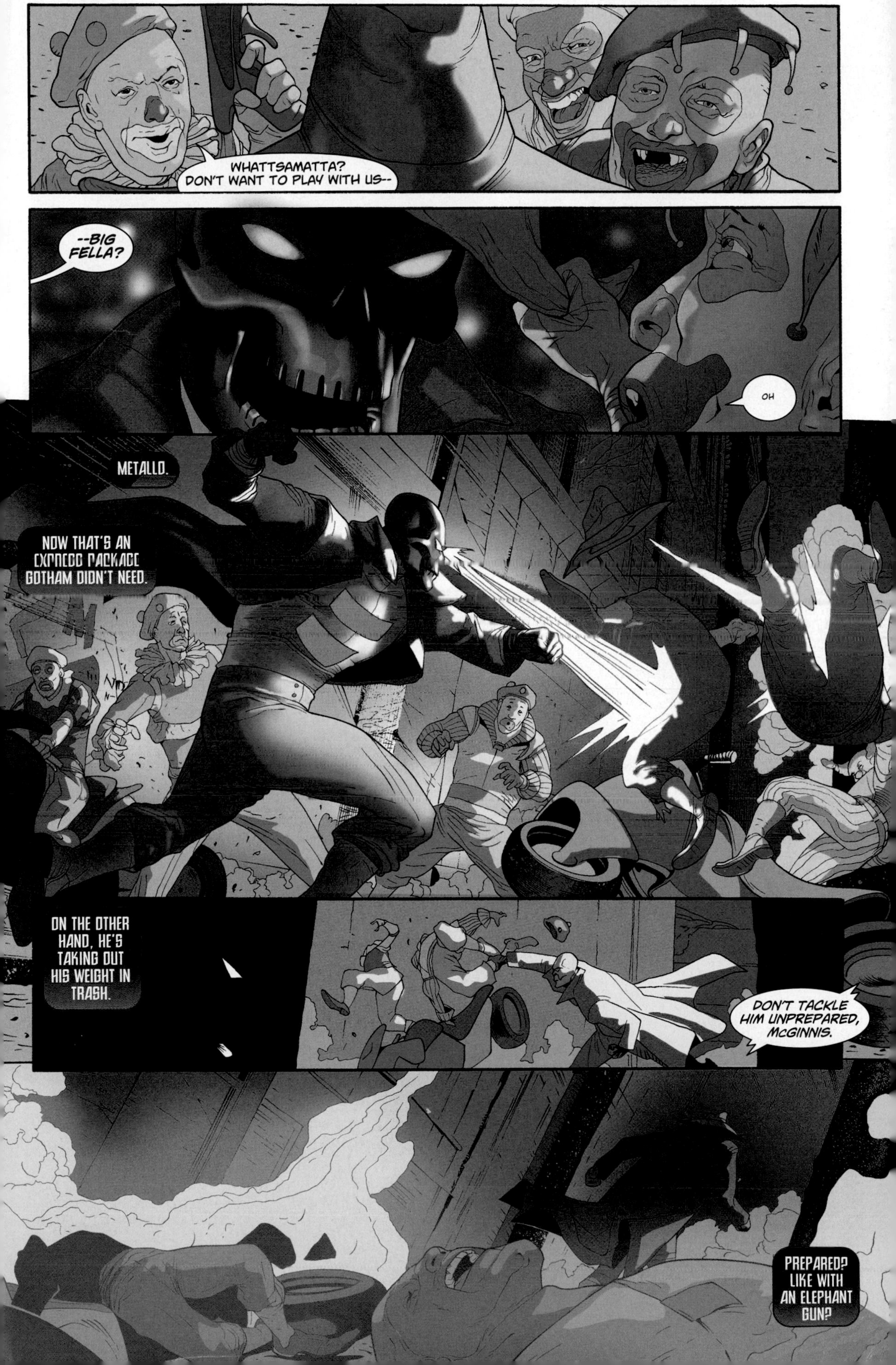
WHATTSAMATTA? DON'T WANT TO PLAY WITH US--
--BIG FELLA?
OH
METALLO.
NOW THAT'S AN EXPRESS PACKAGE GOTHAM DIDN'T NEED.
ON THE OTHER HAND, HE'S TAKING OUT HIS WEIGHT IN TRASH.
DON'T TACKLE HIM UNPREPARED, McGINNIS.
PREPARED? LIKE WITH AN ELEPHANT GUN?

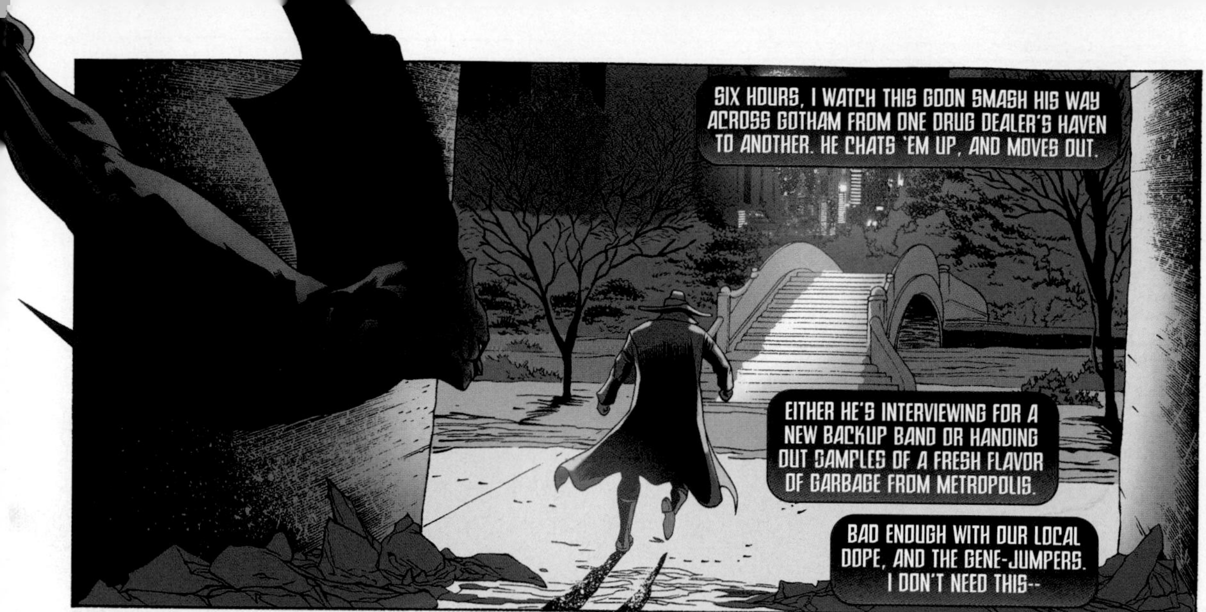
SIX HOURS, I WATCH THIS GOON SMASH HIS WAY ACROSS GOTHAM FROM ONE DRUG DEALER'S HAVEN TO ANOTHER. HE CHATS 'EM UP, AND MOVES OUT.
EITHER HE'S INTERVIEWING FOR A NEW BACKUP BAND OR HANDING OUT SAMPLES OF A FRESH FLAVOR OF GARBAGE FROM METROPOLIS.
BAD ENOUGH WITH OUR LOCAL DOPE, AND THE GENE-JUMPERS. I DON'T NEED THIS--

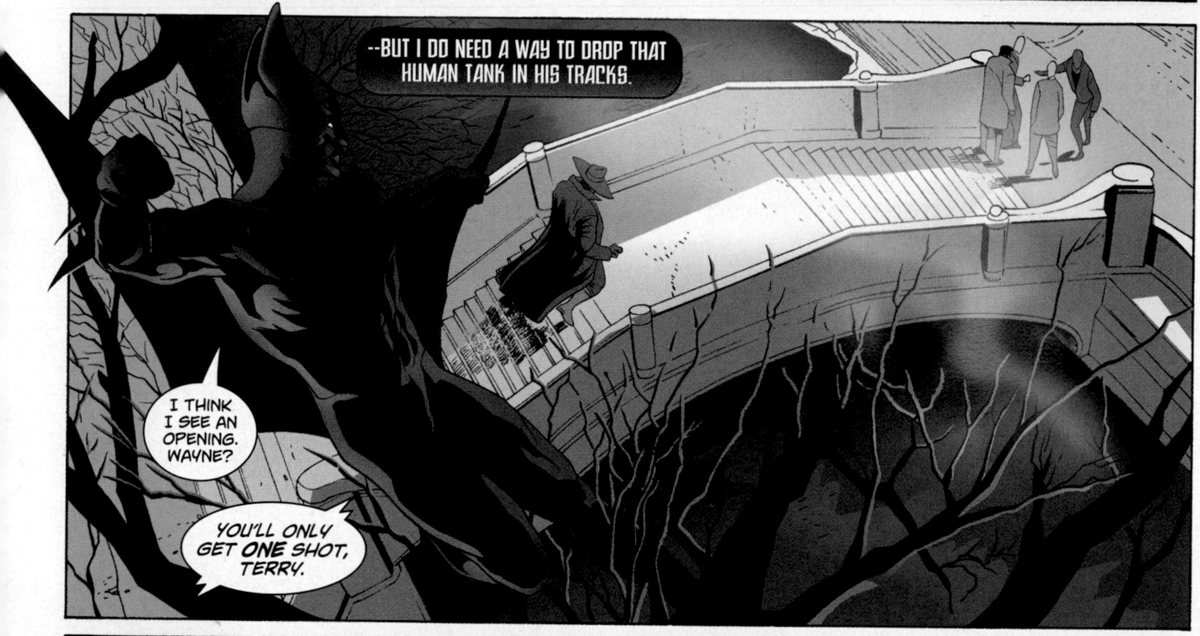
--BUT I DO NEED A WAY TO DROP THAT HUMAN TANK IN HIS TRACKS.
I THINK I SEE AN OPENING. WAYNE?
YOU'LL ONLY GET ONE SHOT, TERRY.

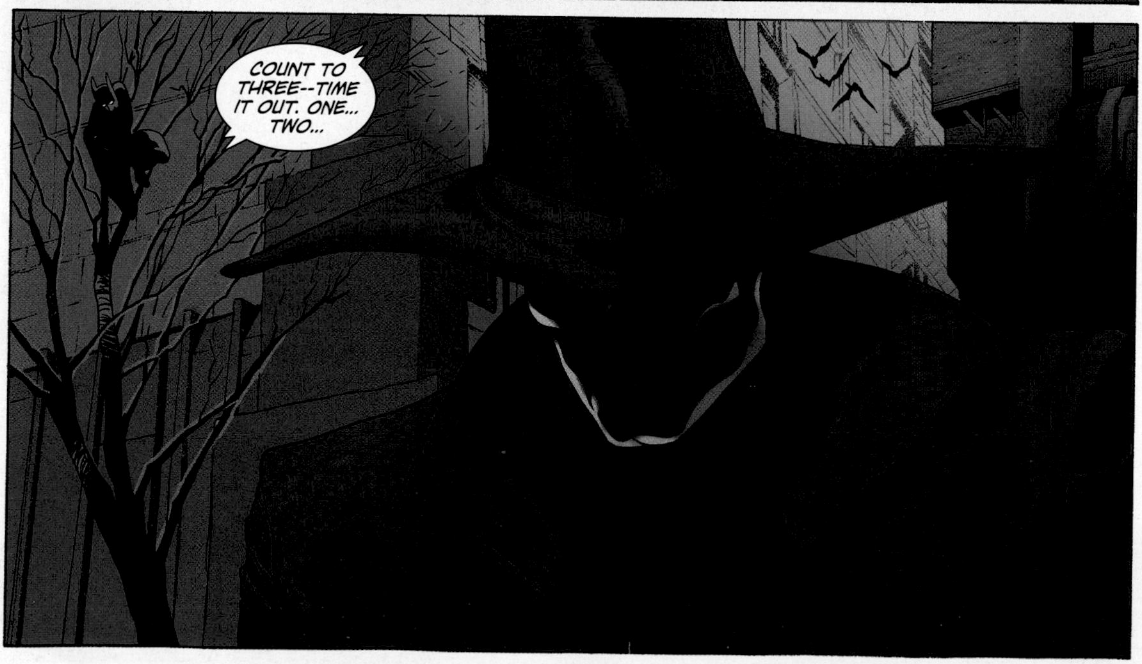
COUNT TO THREE--TIME IT OUT. ONE... TWO...

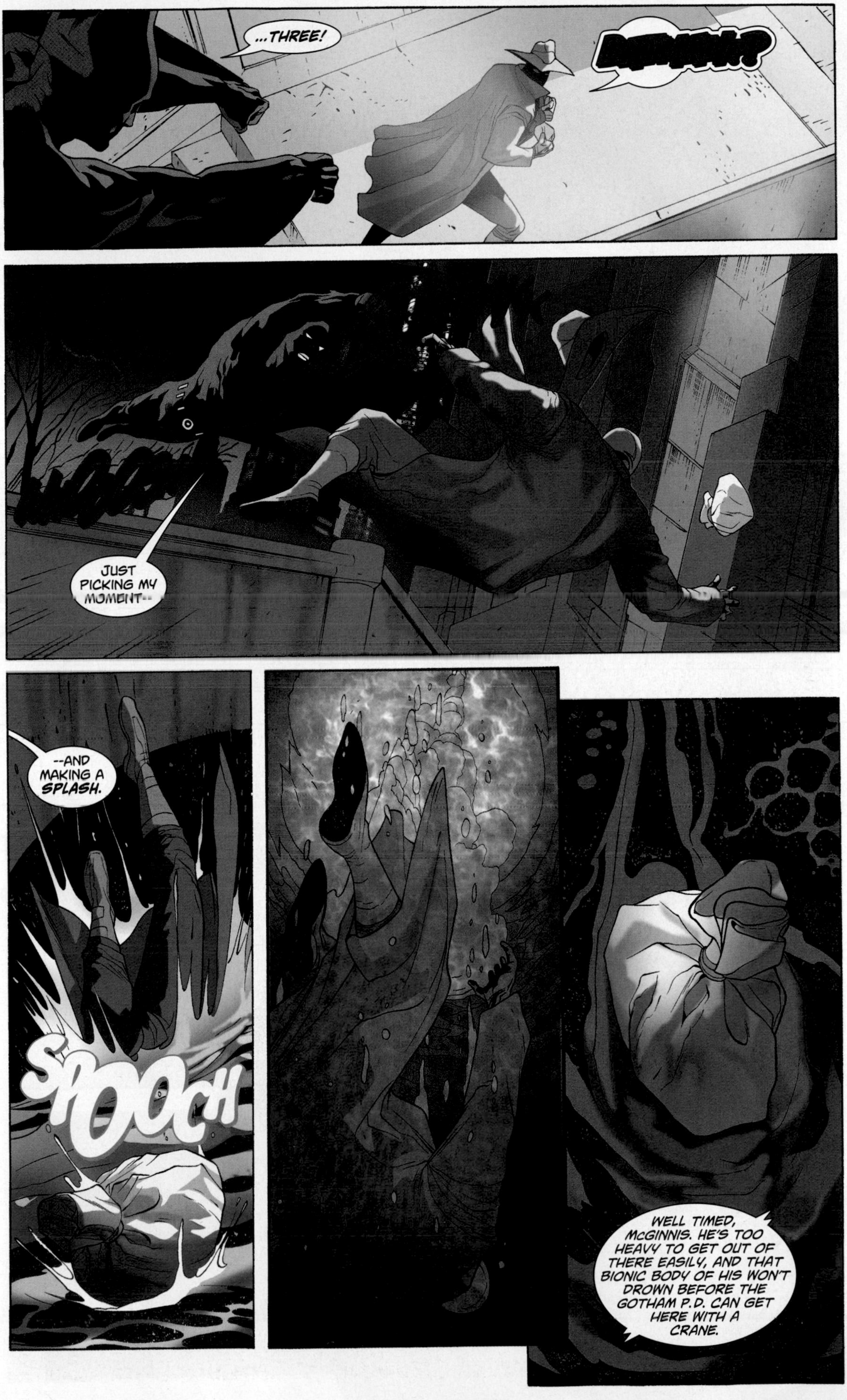
...THREE!
JUST PICKING MY MOMENT--
--AND MAKING A SPLASH.
SPOOCH
WELL TIMED, McGINNIS. HE'S TOO HEAVY TO GET OUT OF THERE EASILY, AND THAT BIONIC BODY OF HIS WON'T DROWN BEFORE THE GOTHAM P.D. CAN GET HERE WITH A CRANE.

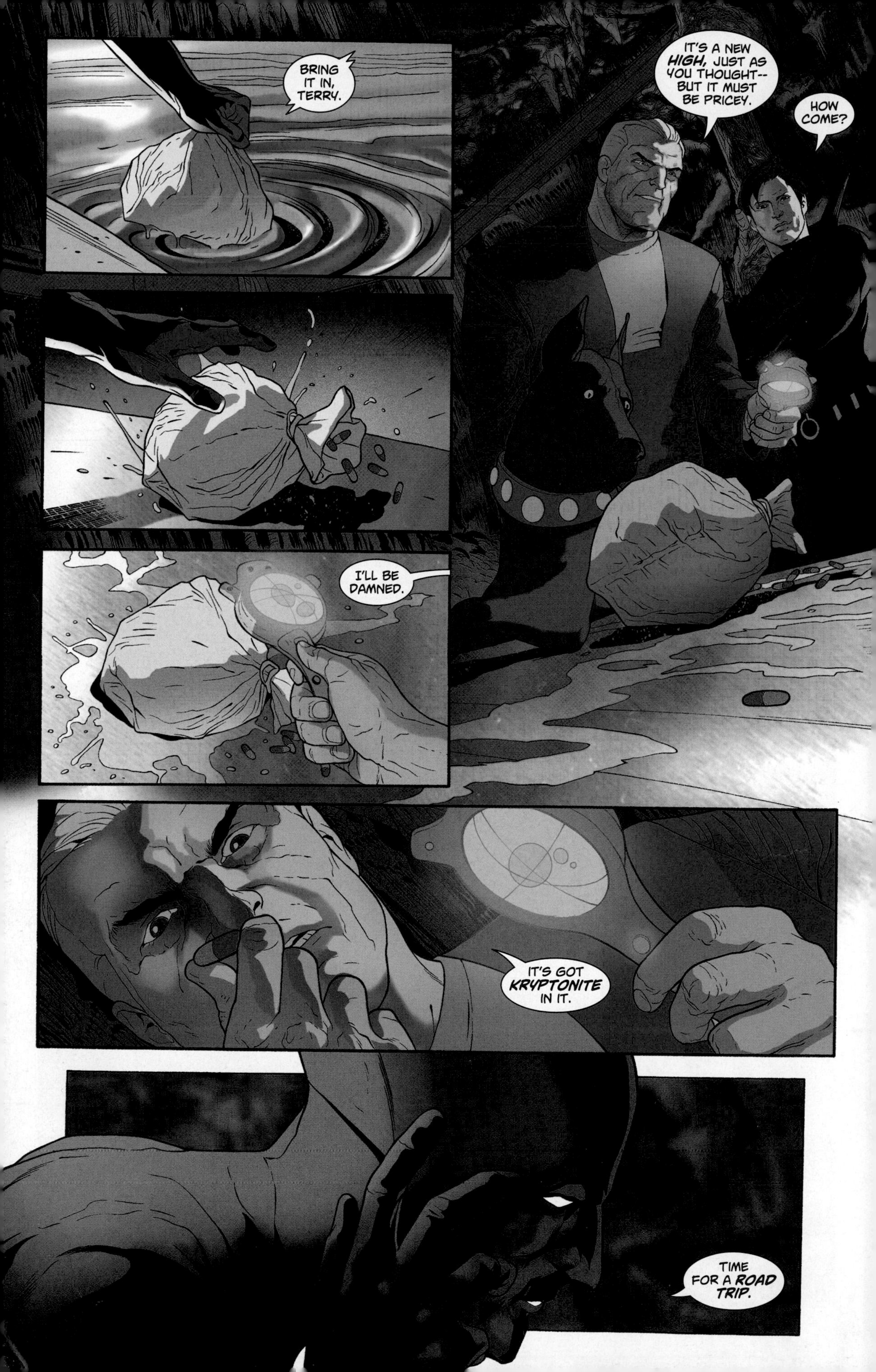
BRING IT IN, TERRY.
IT'S A NEW HIGH, JUST AS YOU THOUGHT-- BUT IT MUST BE PRICEY.
HOW COME?
I'LL BE DAMNED.
IT'S GOT KRYPTONITE IN IT.
TIME FOR A ROAD TRIP.

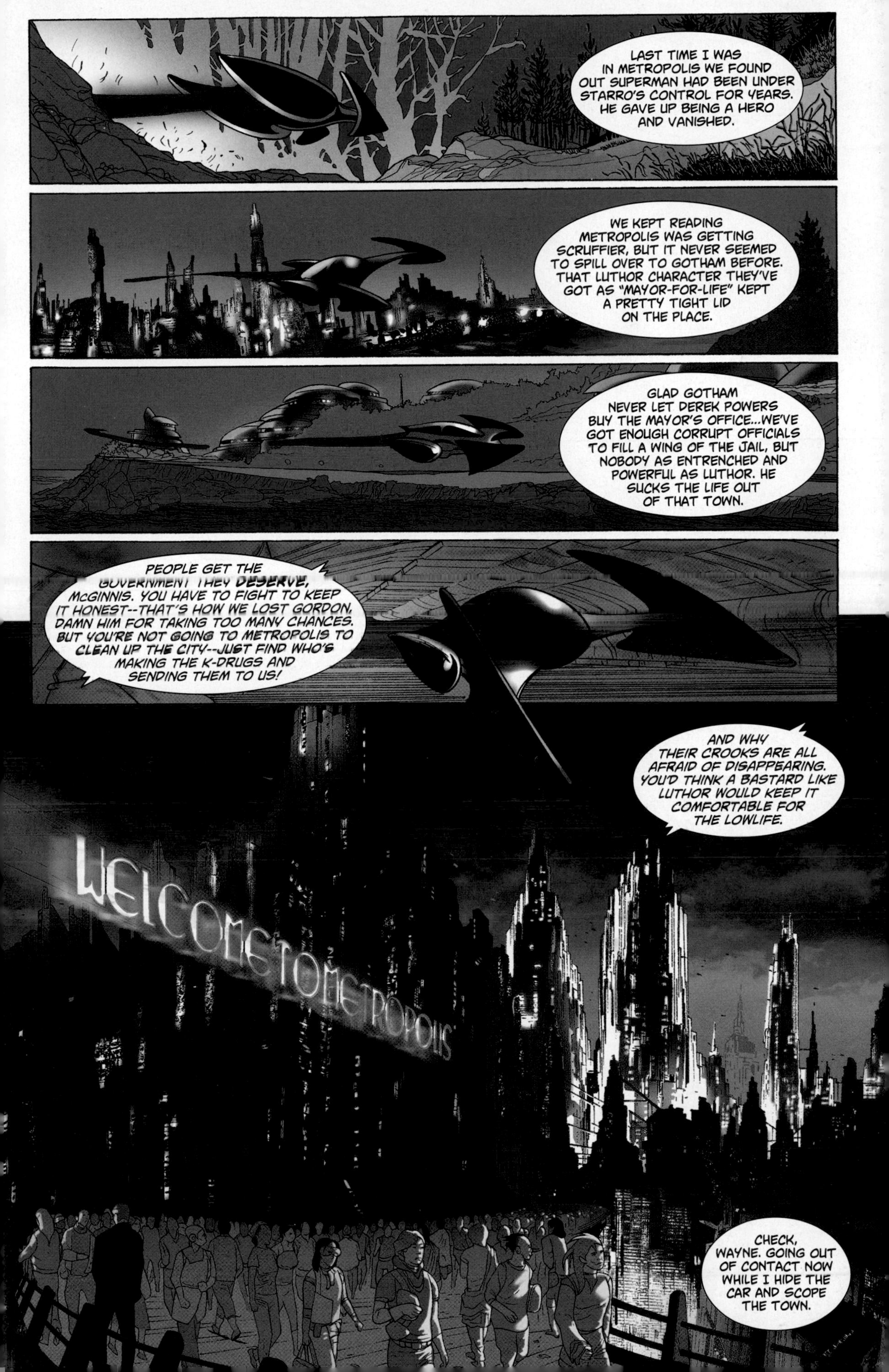
LAST TIME I WAS IN METROPOLIS WE FOUND OUT SUPERMAN HAD BEEN UNDER STARRO'S CONTROL FOR YEARS. HE GAVE UP BEING A HERO AND VANISHED.
WE KEPT READING METROPOLIS WAS GETTING SCRUFFIER, BUT IT NEVER SEEMED TO SPILL OVER TO GOTHAM BEFORE. THAT LUTHOR CHARACTER THEY'VE GOT AS "MAYOR-FOR-LIFE" KEPT A PRETTY TIGHT LID ON THE PLACE.
GLAD GOTHAM NEVER LET DEREK POWERS BUY THE MAYOR'S OFFICE...WE'VE GOT ENOUGH CORRUPT OFFICIALS TO FILL A WING OF THE JAIL, BUT NOBODY AS ENTRENCHED AND POWERFUL AS LUTHOR. HE SUCKS THE LIFE OUT OF THAT TOWN.
PEOPLE GET THE GOVERNMENT THEY DESERVE, McGINNIS. YOU HAVE TO FIGHT TO KEEP IT HONEST--THAT'S HOW WE LOST GORDON, DAMN HIM FOR TAKING TOO MANY CHANCES. BUT YOU'RE NOT GOING TO METROPOLIS TO CLEAN UP THE CITY--JUST FIND WHO'S MAKING THE K-DRUGS AND SENDING THEM TO US!
AND WHY THEIR CROOKS ARE ALL AFRAID OF DISAPPEARING. YOU'D THINK A BASTARD LIKE LUTHOR WOULD KEEP IT COMFORTABLE FOR THE LOWLIFE.
WELCOME TO METROPOLIS
CHECK, WAYNE. GOING OUT OF CONTACT NOW WHILE I HIDE THE CAR AND SCOPE THE TOWN.

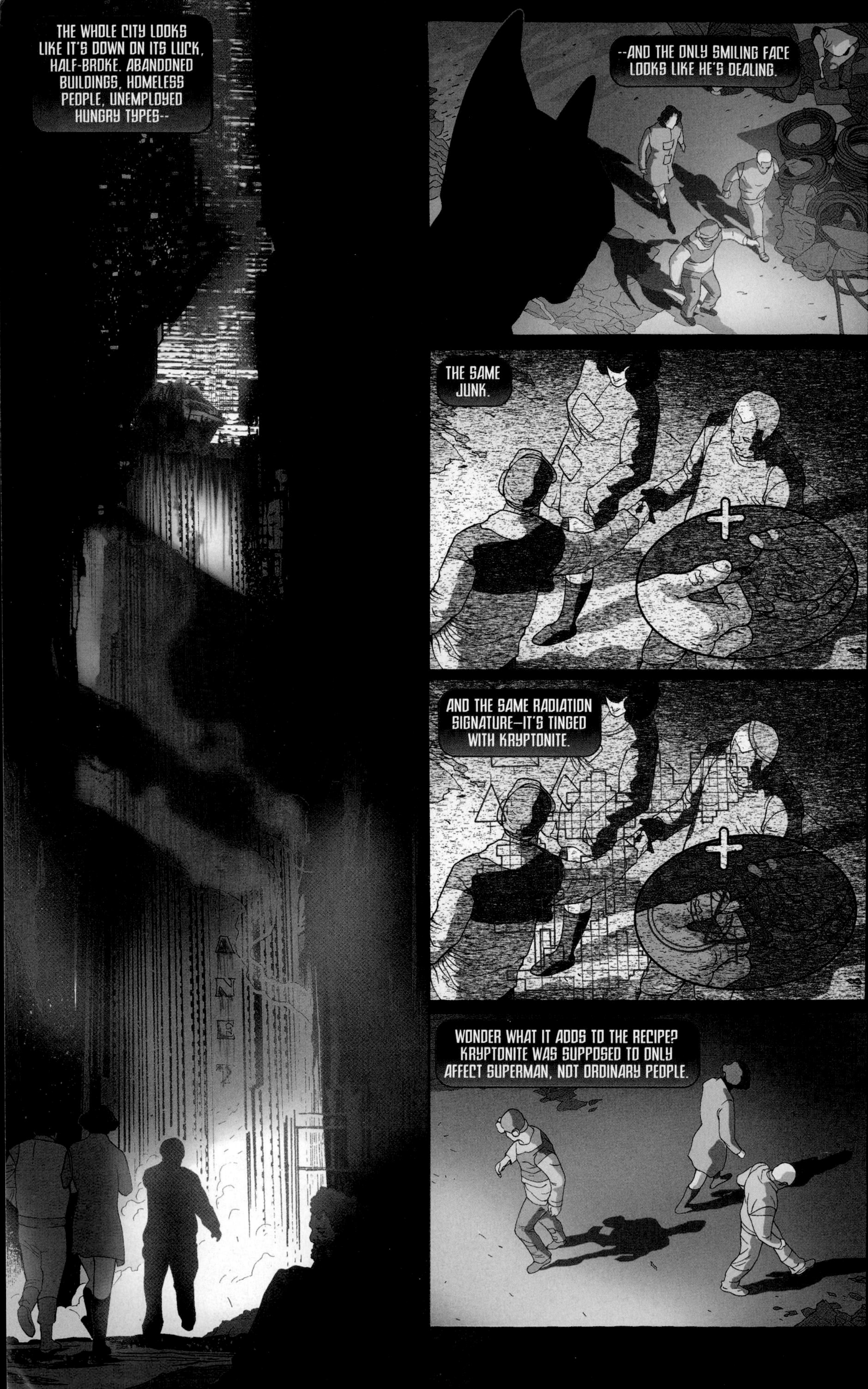
THE WHOLE CITY LOOKS LIKE IT'S DOWN ON ITS LUCK, HALF-BROKE. ABANDONED BUILDINGS, HOMELESS PEOPLE, UNEMPLOYED HUNGRY TYPES--
--AND THE ONLY SMILING FACE LOOKS LIKE HE'S DEALING.
THE SAME JUNK.
AND THE SAME RADIATION SIGNATURE—IT'S TINGED WITH KRYPTONITE.
WONDER WHAT IT ADDS TO THE RECIPE? KRYPTONITE WAS SUPPOSED TO ONLY AFFECT SUPERMAN, NOT ORDINARY PEOPLE.

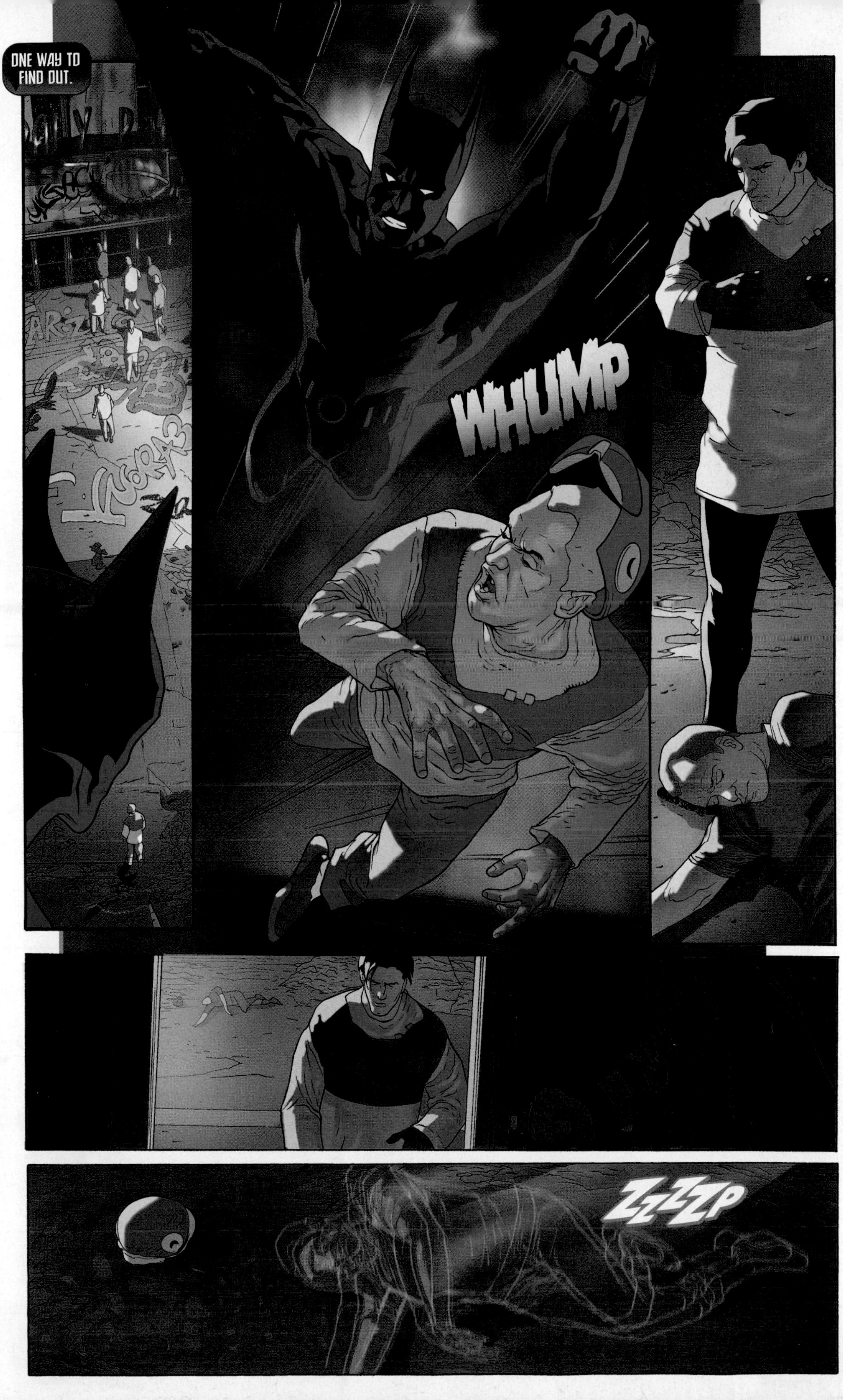
ONE WAY TO FIND OUT.
WHUMP
ZZZZP

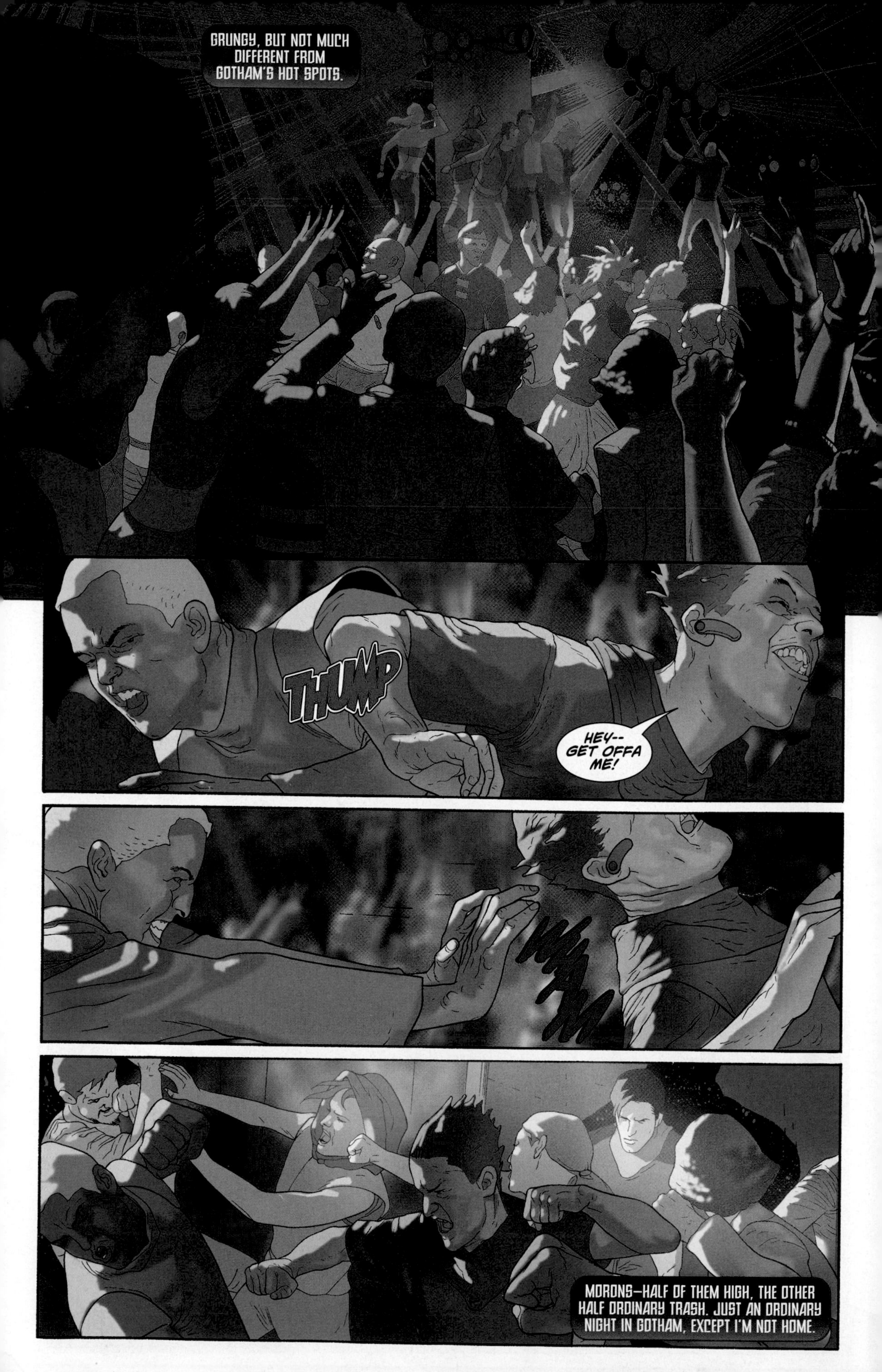
GRUNGY, BUT NOT MUCH DIFFERENT FROM GOTHAM'S HOT SPOTS.
THUMP
HEY-- GET OFFA ME!
MORONS—HALF OF THEM HIGH, THE OTHER HALF ORDINARY TRASH. JUST AN ORDINARY NIGHT IN GOTHAM, EXCEPT I'M NOT HOME.

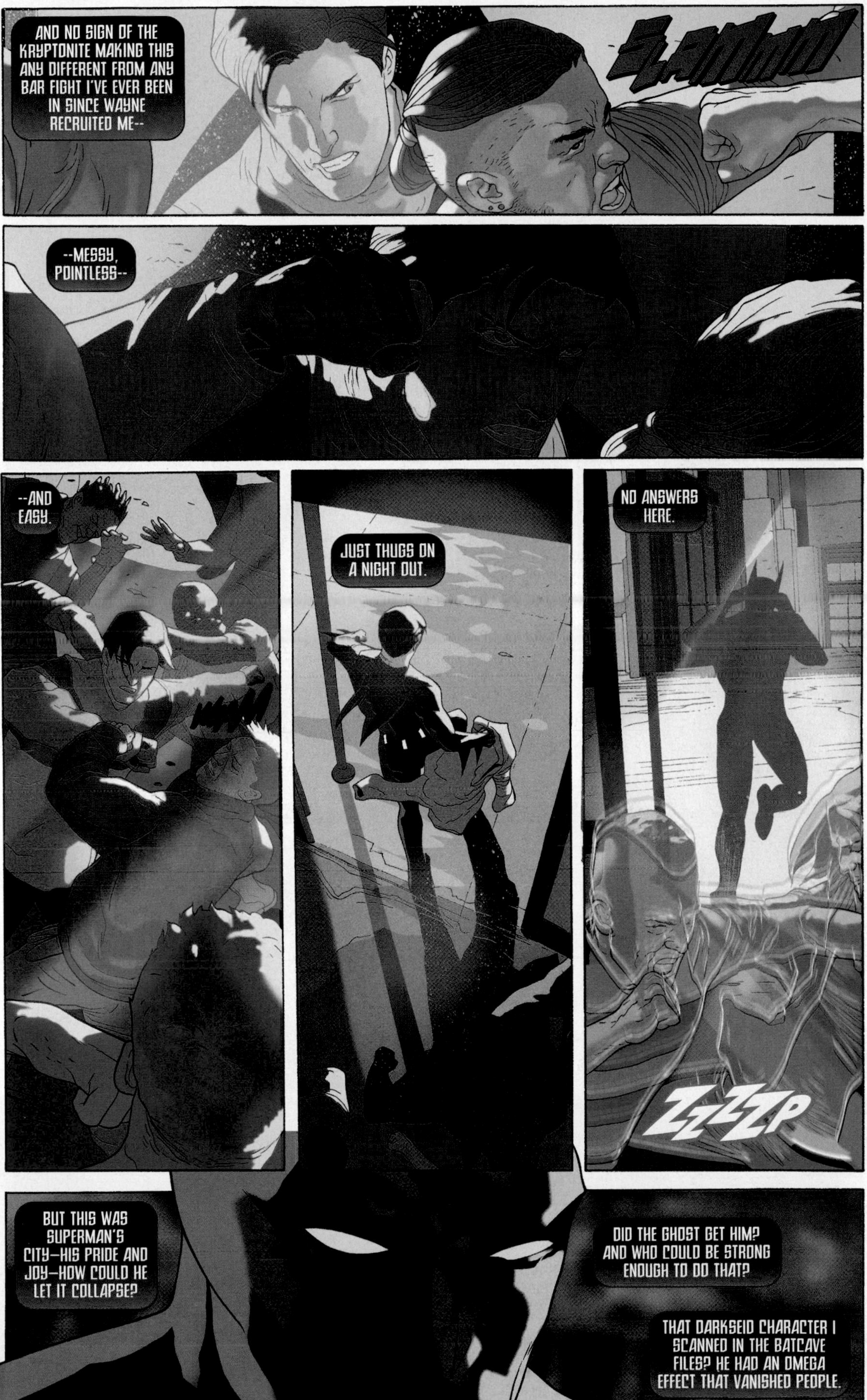
AND NO SIGN OF THE KRYPTONITE MAKING THIS ANY DIFFERENT FROM ANY BAR FIGHT I'VE EVER BEEN IN SINCE WAYNE RECRUITED ME--
--MESSY, POINTLESS--
--AND EASY.
JUST THUGS ON A NIGHT OUT.
NO ANSWERS HERE.
ZZZZP
BUT THIS WAS SUPERMAN'S CITY—HIS PRIDE AND JOY—HOW COULD HE LET IT COLLAPSE?
DID THE GHOST GET HIM? AND WHO COULD BE STRONG ENOUGH TO DO THAT?
THAT DARKSEID CHARACTER I SCANNED IN THE BATCAVE FILES? HE HAD AN OMEGA EFFECT THAT VANISHED PEOPLE.

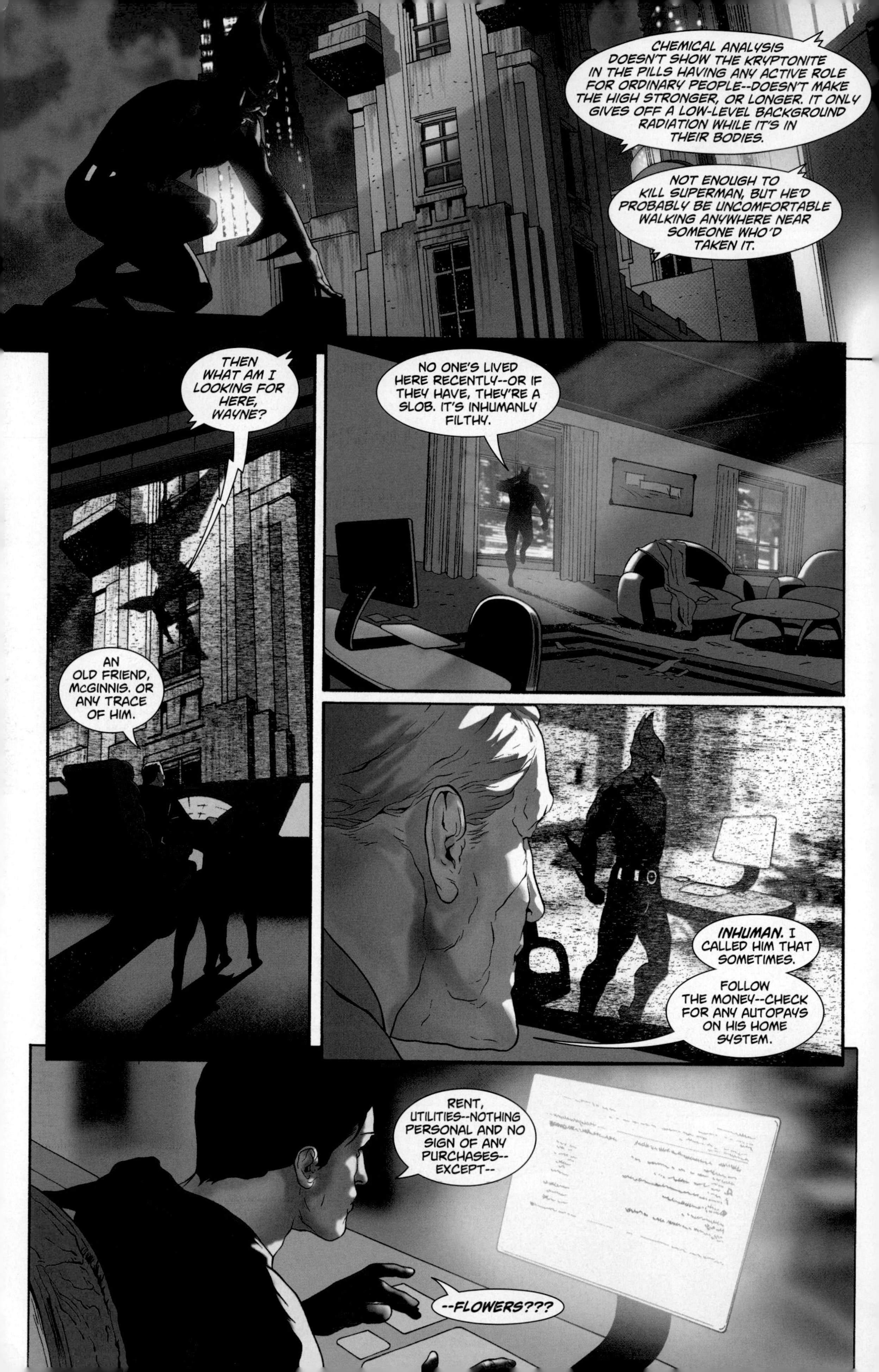
CHEMICAL ANALYSIS DOESN'T SHOW THE KRYPTONITE IN THE PILLS HAVING ANY ACTIVE ROLE FOR ORDINARY PEOPLE--DOESN'T MAKE THE HIGH STRONGER, OR LONGER. IT ONLY GIVES OFF A LOW-LEVEL BACKGROUND RADIATION WHILE IT'S IN THEIR BODIES.
NOT ENOUGH TO KILL SUPERMAN, BUT HE'D PROBABLY BE UNCOMFORTABLE WALKING ANYWHERE NEAR SOMEONE WHO'D TAKEN IT.
THEN WHAT AM I LOOKING FOR HERE, WAYNE?
AN OLD FRIEND, McGINNIS. OR ANY TRACE OF HIM.
NO ONE'S LIVED HERE RECENTLY--OR IF THEY HAVE, THEY'RE A SLOB. IT'S INHUMANLY FILTHY.
INHUMAN. I CALLED HIM THAT SOMETIMES.
FOLLOW THE MONEY--CHECK FOR ANY AUTOPAYS ON HIS HOME SYSTEM.
RENT, UTILITIES--NOTHING PERSONAL AND NO SIGN OF ANY PURCHASES--EXCEPT--
--FLOWERS???

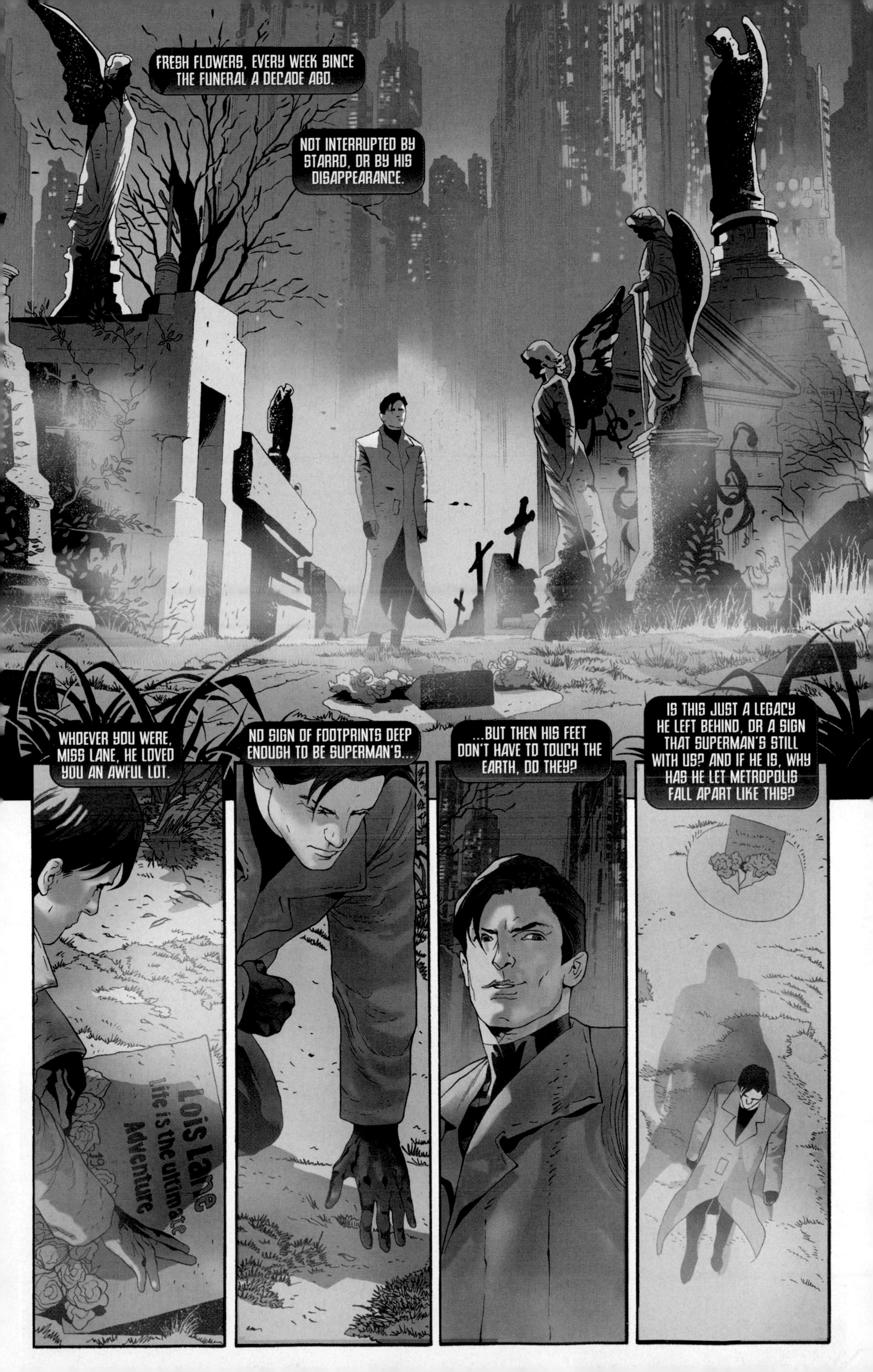
FRESH FLOWERS, EVERY WEEK SINCE THE FUNERAL A DECADE AGO.
NOT INTERRUPTED BY STARRO, OR BY HIS DISAPPEARANCE.
WHOEVER YOU WERE, MISS LANE, HE LOVED YOU AN AWFUL LOT.
Lois Lane
Life is the ultimate Adventure
NO SIGN OF FOOTPRINTS DEEP ENOUGH TO BE SUPERMAN'S...
...BUT THEN HIS FEET DON'T HAVE TO TOUCH THE EARTH, DO THEY?
IS THIS JUST A LEGACY HE LEFT BEHIND, OR A SIGN THAT SUPERMAN'S STILL WITH US? AND IF HE IS, WHY HAS HE LET METROPOLIS FALL APART LIKE THIS?

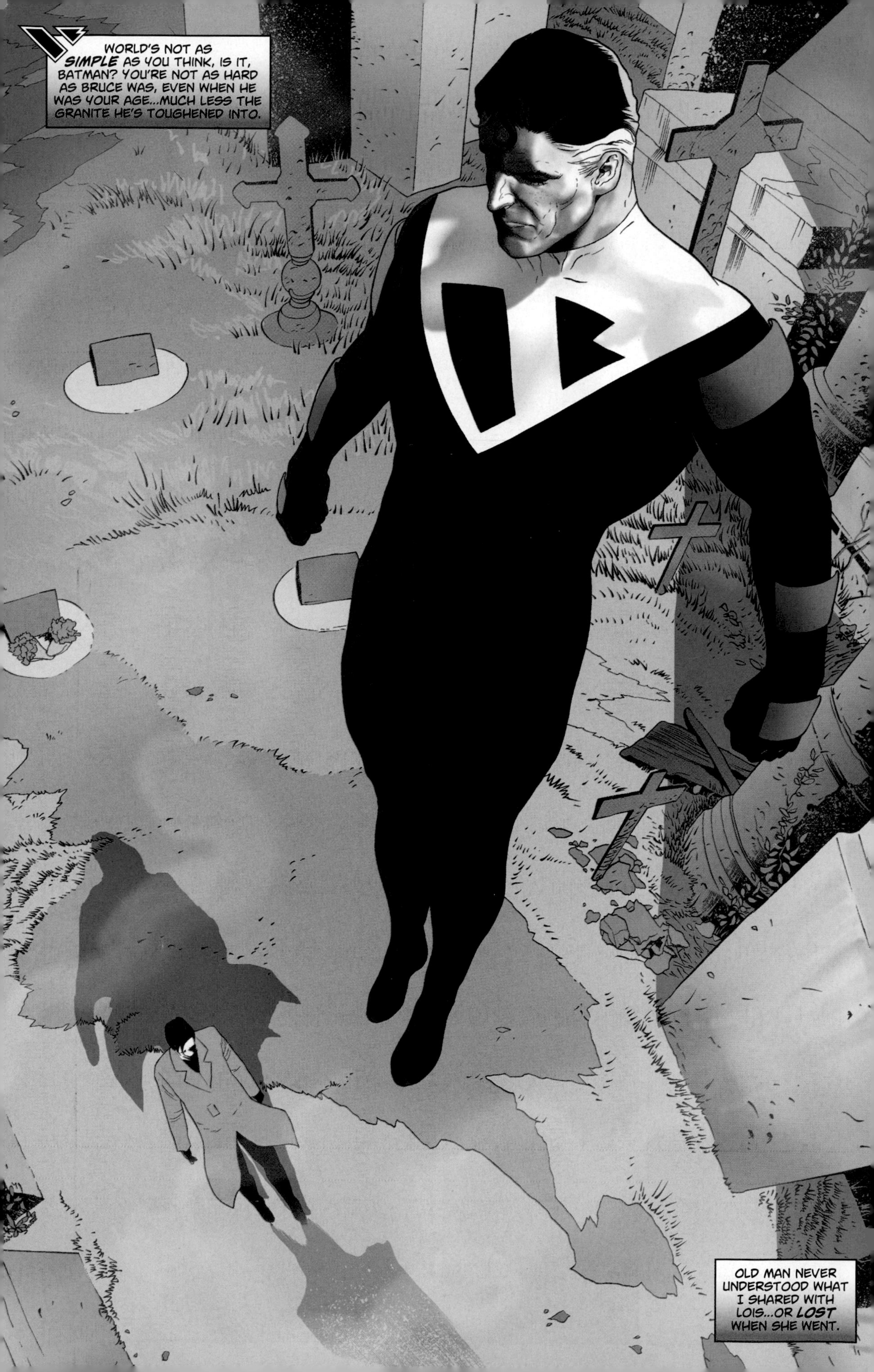
WORLD'S NOT AS *SIMPLE* AS YOU THINK, IS IT, BATMAN? YOU'RE NOT AS HARD AS BRUCE WAS, EVEN WHEN HE WAS YOUR AGE...MUCH LESS THE GRANITE HE'S TOUGHENED INTO.
OLD MAN NEVER UNDERSTOOD WHAT I SHARED WITH LOIS...OR *LOST* WHEN SHE WENT.

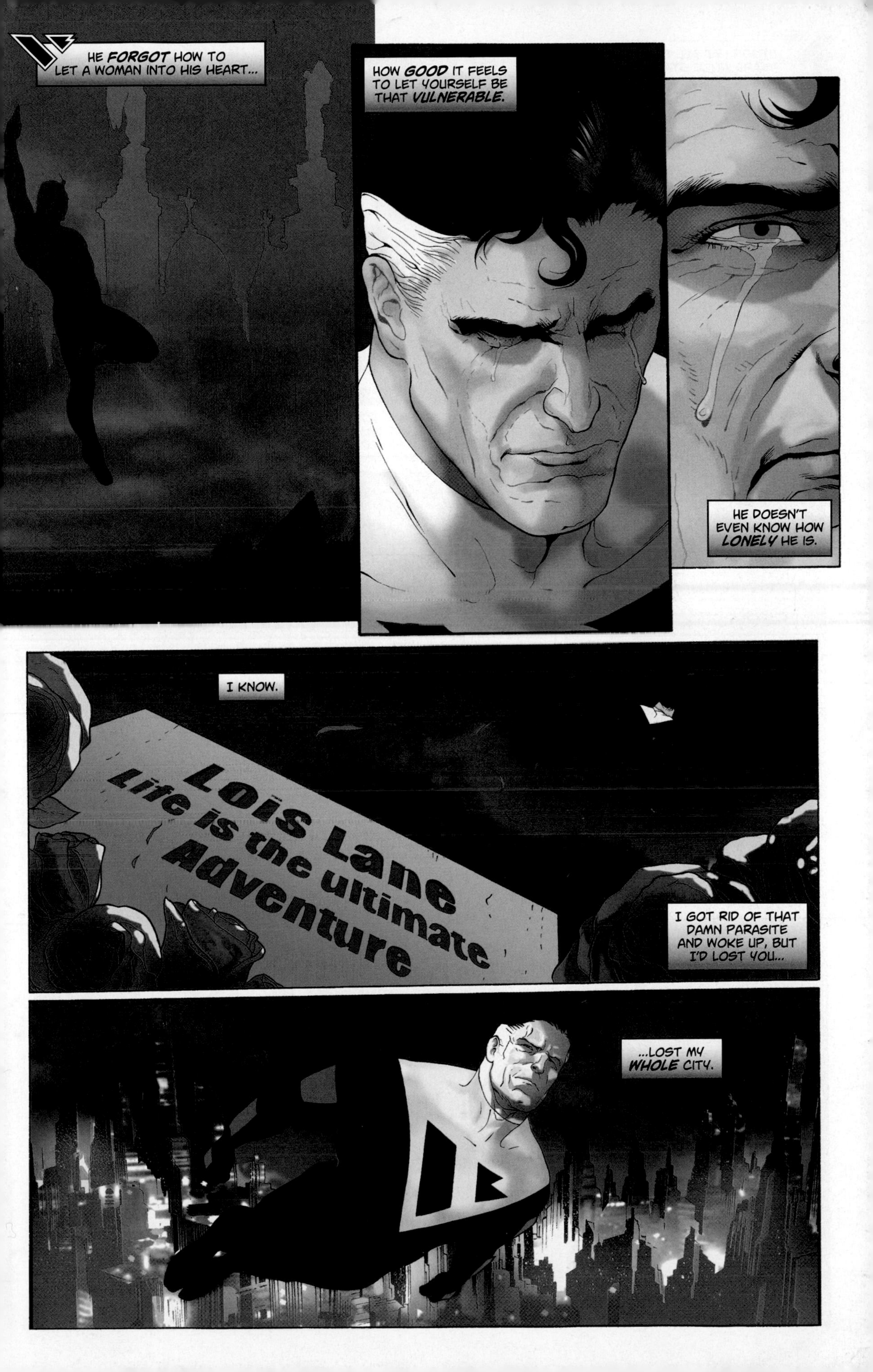
HE FORGOT HOW TO LET A WOMAN INTO HIS HEART...
HOW GOOD IT FEELS TO LET YOURSELF BE THAT VULNERABLE.
HE DOESN'T EVEN KNOW HOW LONELY HE IS.
I KNOW.
LOIS LANE
Life is the ultimate Adventure
I GOT RID OF THAT DAMN PARASITE AND WOKE UP, BUT I'D LOST YOU...
...LOST MY WHOLE CITY.

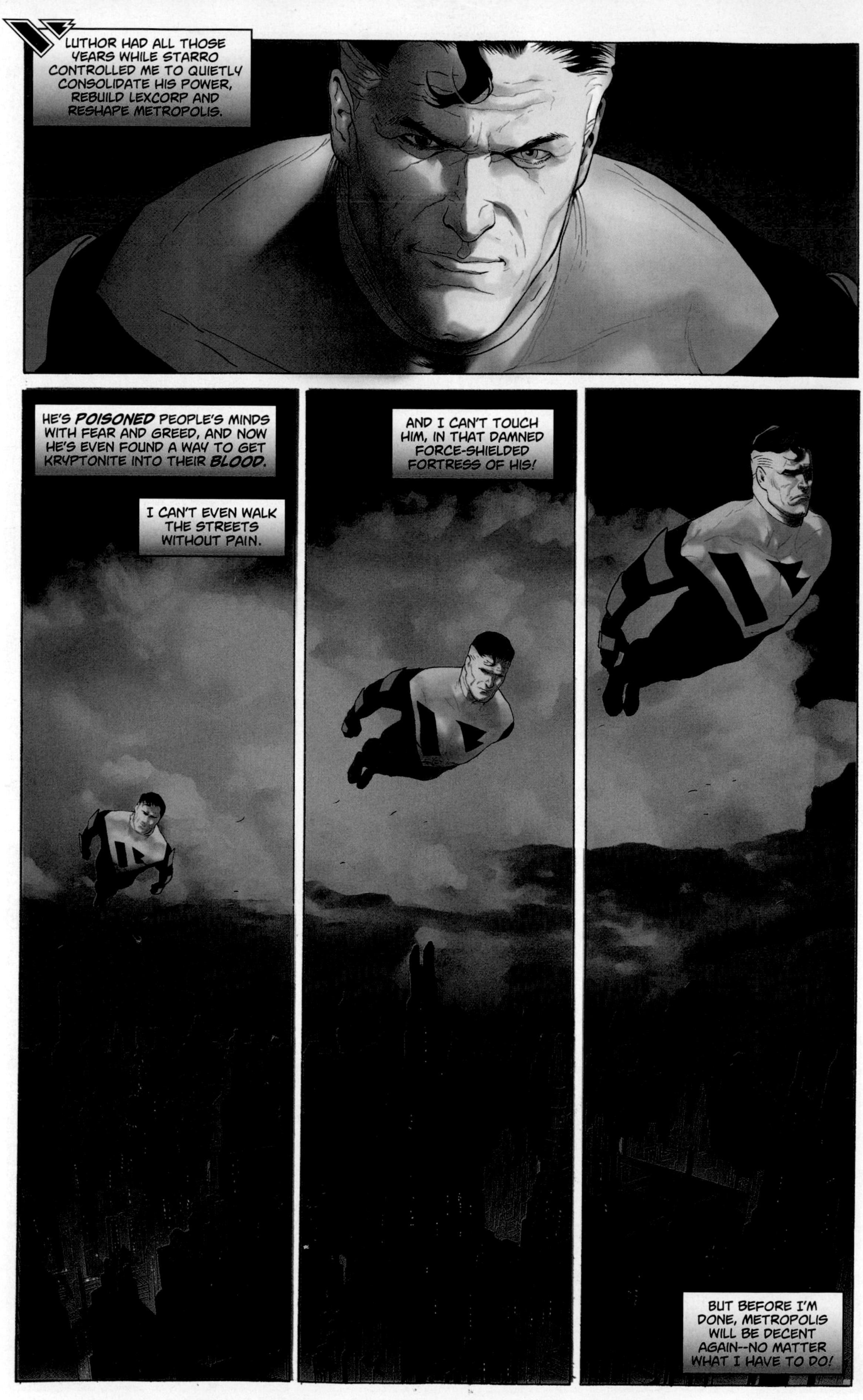
LUTHOR HAD ALL THOSE YEARS WHILE STARRO CONTROLLED ME TO QUIETLY CONSOLIDATE HIS POWER, REBUILD LEXCORP AND RESHAPE METROPOLIS.
HE'S POISONED PEOPLE'S MINDS WITH FEAR AND GREED, AND NOW HE'S EVEN FOUND A WAY TO GET KRYPTONITE INTO THEIR BLOOD.
I CAN'T EVEN WALK THE STREETS WITHOUT PAIN.
AND I CAN'T TOUCH HIM, IN THAT DAMNED FORCE-SHIELDED FORTRESS OF HIS!
BUT BEFORE I'M DONE, METROPOLIS WILL BE DECENT AGAIN--NO MATTER WHAT I HAVE TO DO!

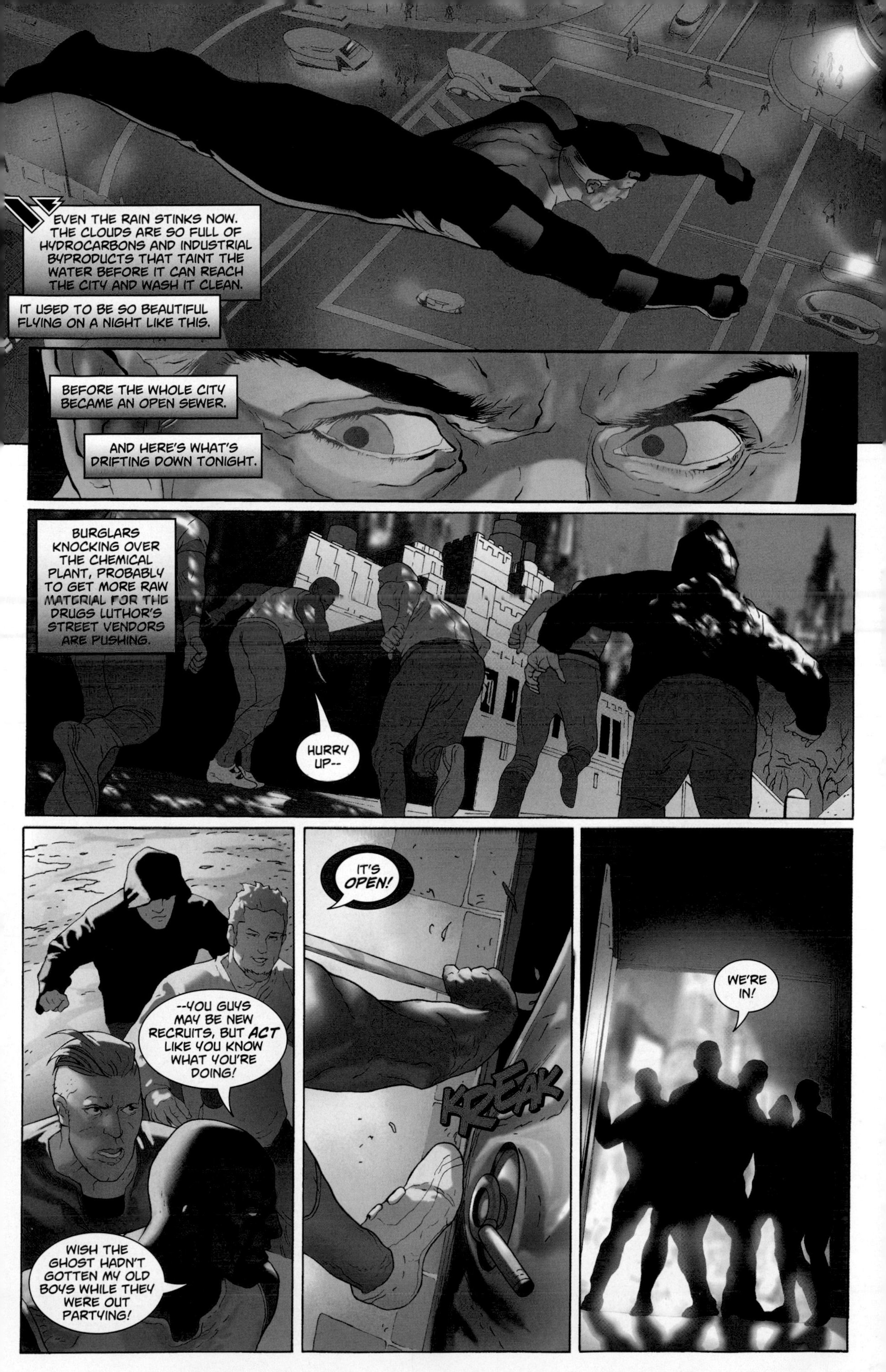

EVEN THE RAIN STINKS NOW. THE CLOUDS ARE SO FULL OF HYDROCARBONS AND INDUSTRIAL BYPRODUCTS THAT TAINT THE WATER BEFORE IT CAN REACH THE CITY AND WASH IT CLEAN.
IT USED TO BE SO BEAUTIFUL FLYING ON A NIGHT LIKE THIS.
BEFORE THE WHOLE CITY BECAME AN OPEN SEWER.
AND HERE'S WHAT'S DRIFTING DOWN TONIGHT.
BURGLARS KNOCKING OVER THE CHEMICAL PLANT, PROBABLY TO GET MORE RAW MATERIAL FOR THE DRUGS LUTHOR'S STREET VENDORS ARE PUSHING.
HURRY UP--
--YOU GUYS MAY BE NEW RECRUITS, BUT ACT LIKE YOU KNOW WHAT YOU'RE DOING!
WISH THE GHOST HADN'T GOTTEN MY OLD BOYS WHILE THEY WERE OUT PARTYING!
IT'S OPEN!
KREAK
WE'RE IN!

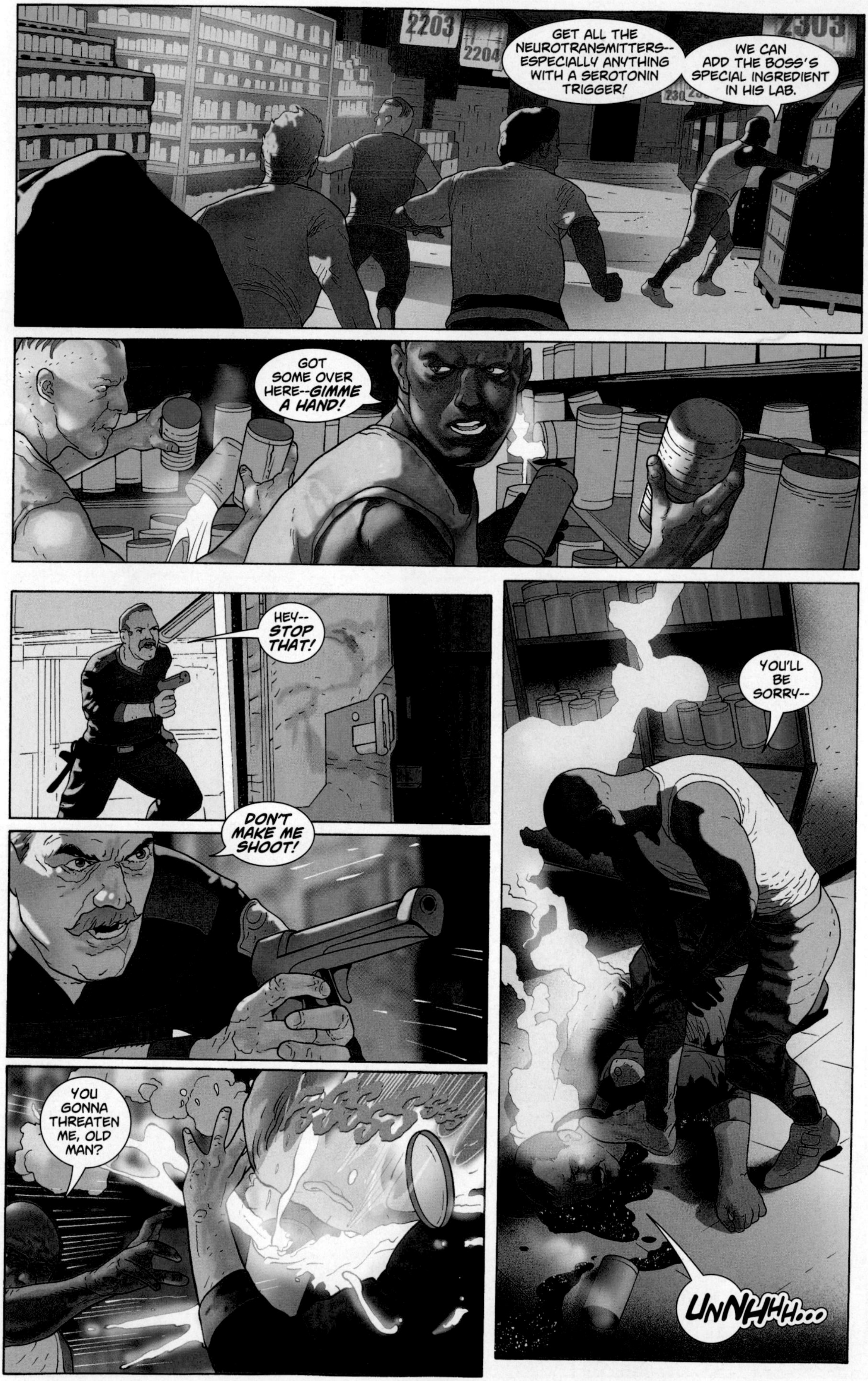

GET ALL THE NEUROTRANSMITTERS--ESPECIALLY ANYTHING WITH A SEROTONIN TRIGGER!
WE CAN ADD THE BOSS'S SPECIAL INGREDIENT IN HIS LAB.
GOT SOME OVER HERE--GIMME A HAND!
HEY--STOP THAT!
DON'T MAKE ME SHOOT!
YOU GONNA THREATEN ME, OLD MAN?
YOU'LL BE SORRY--
UNNHHH...

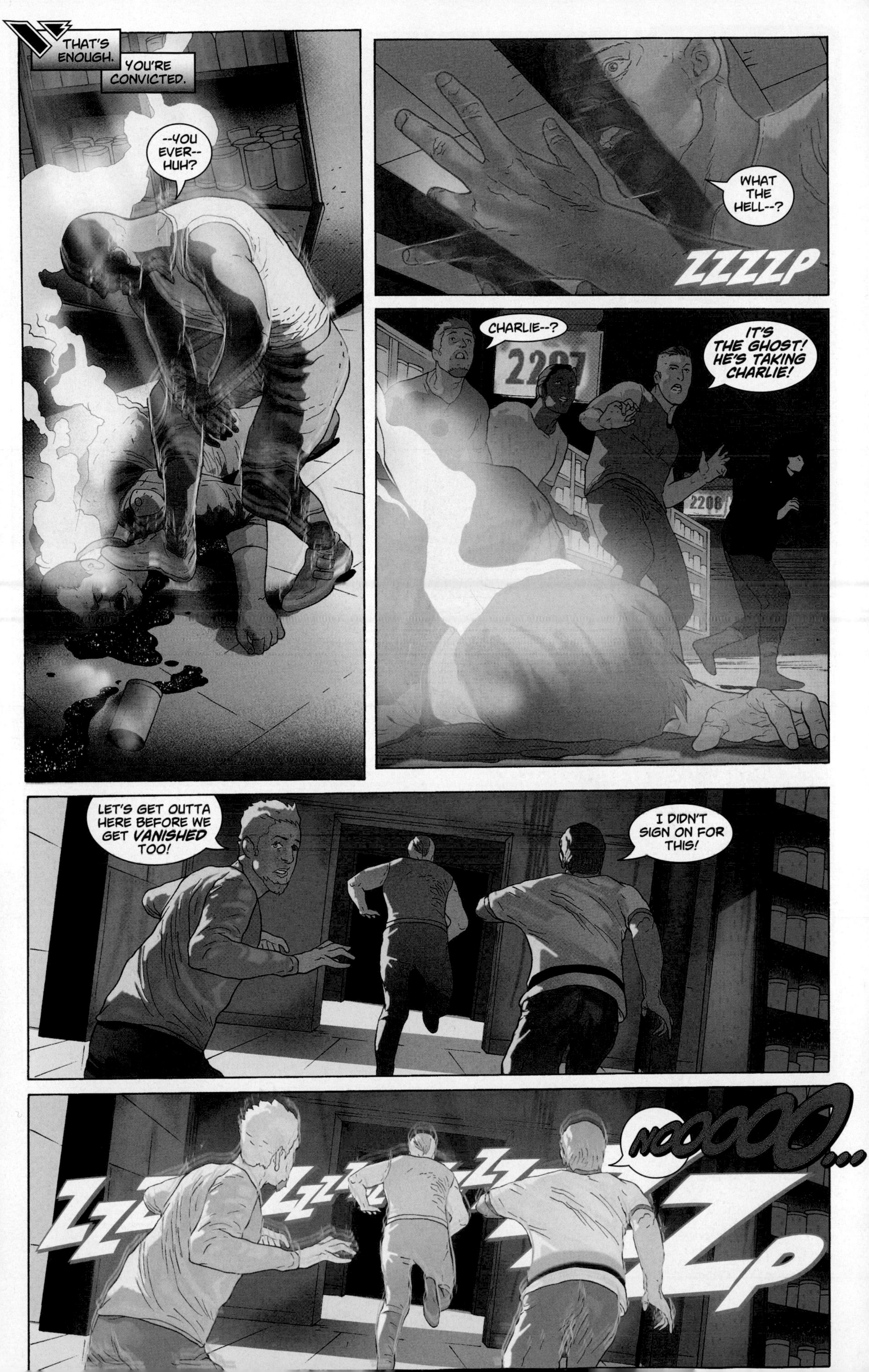
THAT'S ENOUGH.
YOU'RE CONVICTED.
--YOU EVER-- HUH?
WHAT THE HELL--?
ZZZZP
CHARLIE--?
2207
IT'S THE GHOST! HE'S TAKING CHARLIE!
2208
LET'S GET OUTTA HERE BEFORE WE GET VANISHED TOO!
I DIDN'T SIGN ON FOR THIS!
NOOOOO...
ZZZZZZZZZZP

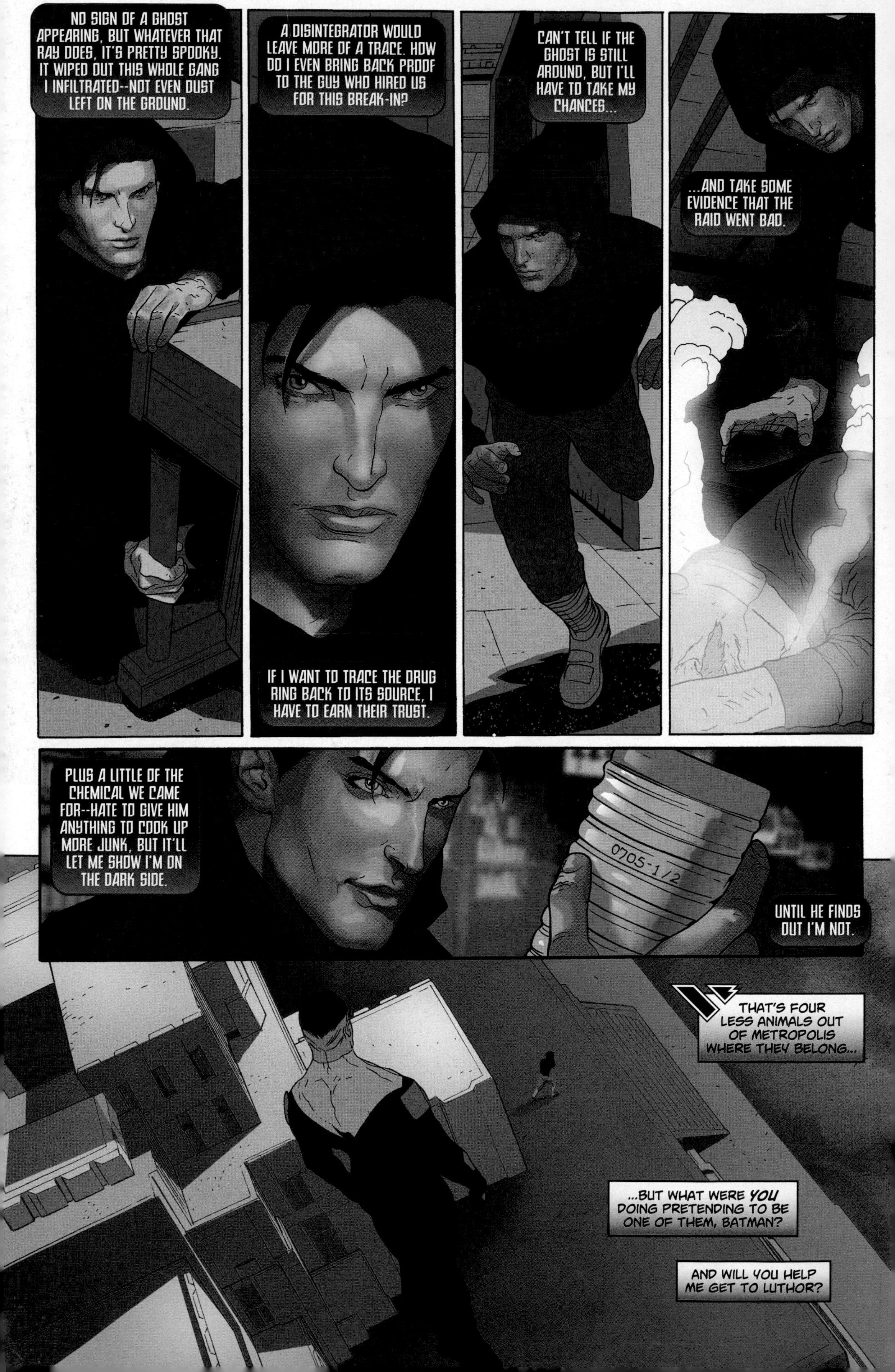

NO SIGN OF A GHOST APPEARING, BUT WHATEVER THAT RAY DOES, IT'S PRETTY SPOOKY. IT WIPED OUT THIS WHOLE GANG I INFILTRATED--NOT EVEN DUST LEFT ON THE GROUND.
A DISINTEGRATOR WOULD LEAVE MORE OF A TRACE. HOW DO I EVEN BRING BACK PROOF TO THE GUY WHO HIRED US FOR THIS BREAK-IN?
IF I WANT TO TRACE THE DRUG RING BACK TO ITS SOURCE, I HAVE TO EARN THEIR TRUST.
CAN'T TELL IF THE GHOST IS STILL AROUND, BUT I'LL HAVE TO TAKE MY CHANCES...
...AND TAKE SOME EVIDENCE THAT THE RAID WENT BAD.
PLUS A LITTLE OF THE CHEMICAL WE CAME FOR--HATE TO GIVE HIM ANYTHING TO COOK UP MORE JUNK, BUT IT'LL LET ME SHOW I'M ON THE DARK SIDE.
0705-1/2
UNTIL HE FINDS OUT I'M NOT.
THAT'S FOUR LESS ANIMALS OUT OF METROPOLIS WHERE THEY BELONG...
...BUT WHAT WERE YOU DOING PRETENDING TO BE ONE OF THEM, BATMAN?
AND WILL YOU HELP ME GET TO LUTHOR?

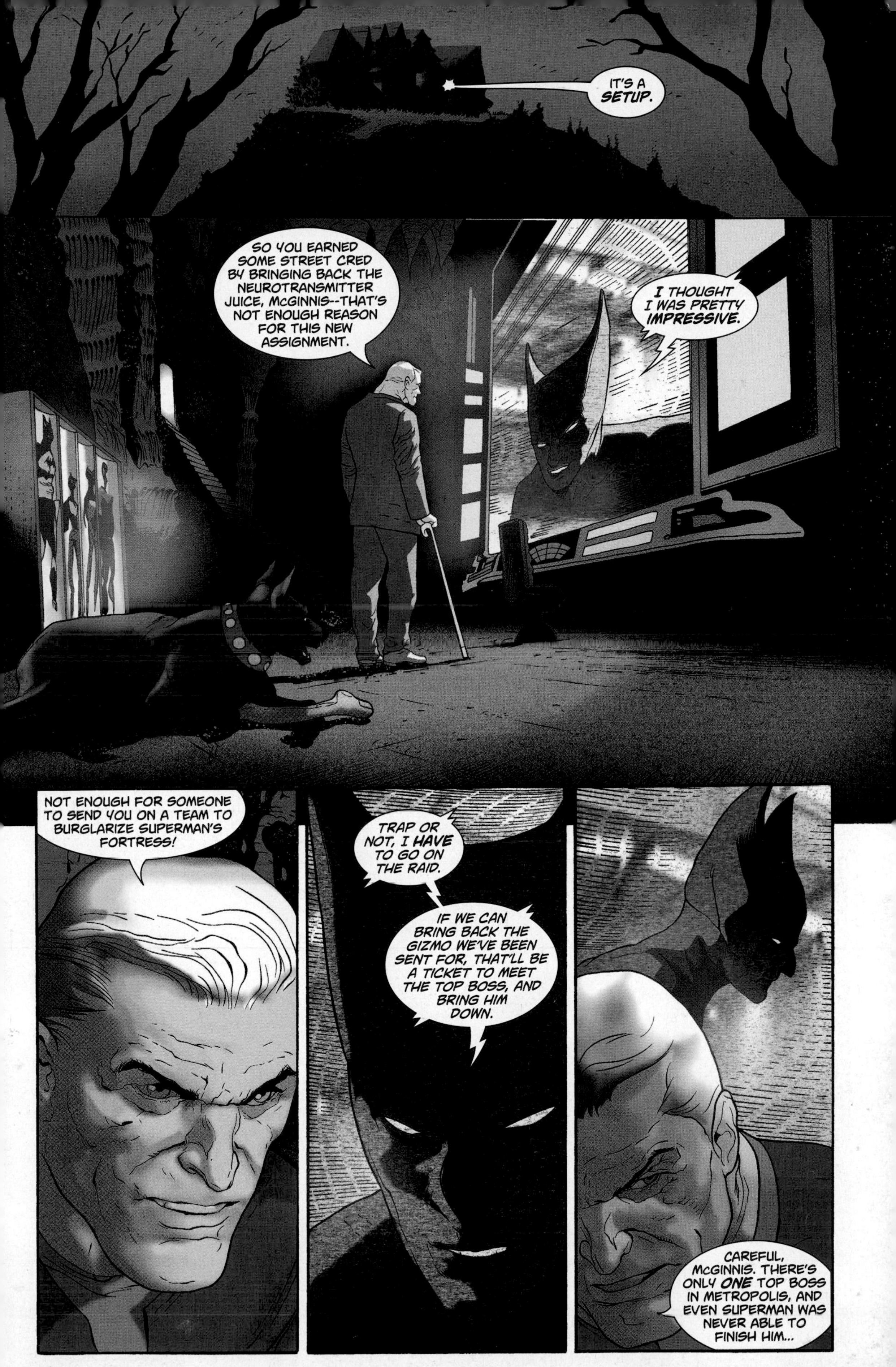
IT'S A SETUP.
SO YOU EARNED SOME STREET CRED BY BRINGING BACK THE NEUROTRANSMITTER JUICE, McGINNIS--THAT'S NOT ENOUGH REASON FOR THIS NEW ASSIGNMENT.
I THOUGHT I WAS PRETTY IMPRESSIVE.
NOT ENOUGH FOR SOMEONE TO SEND YOU ON A TEAM TO BURGLARIZE SUPERMAN'S FORTRESS!
TRAP OR NOT, I HAVE TO GO ON THE RAID.
IF WE CAN BRING BACK THE GIZMO WE'VE BEEN SENT FOR, THAT'LL BE A TICKET TO MEET THE TOP BOSS, AND BRING HIM DOWN.
CAREFUL, McGINNIS. THERE'S ONLY ONE TOP BOSS IN METROPOLIS, AND EVEN SUPERMAN WAS NEVER ABLE TO FINISH HIM...

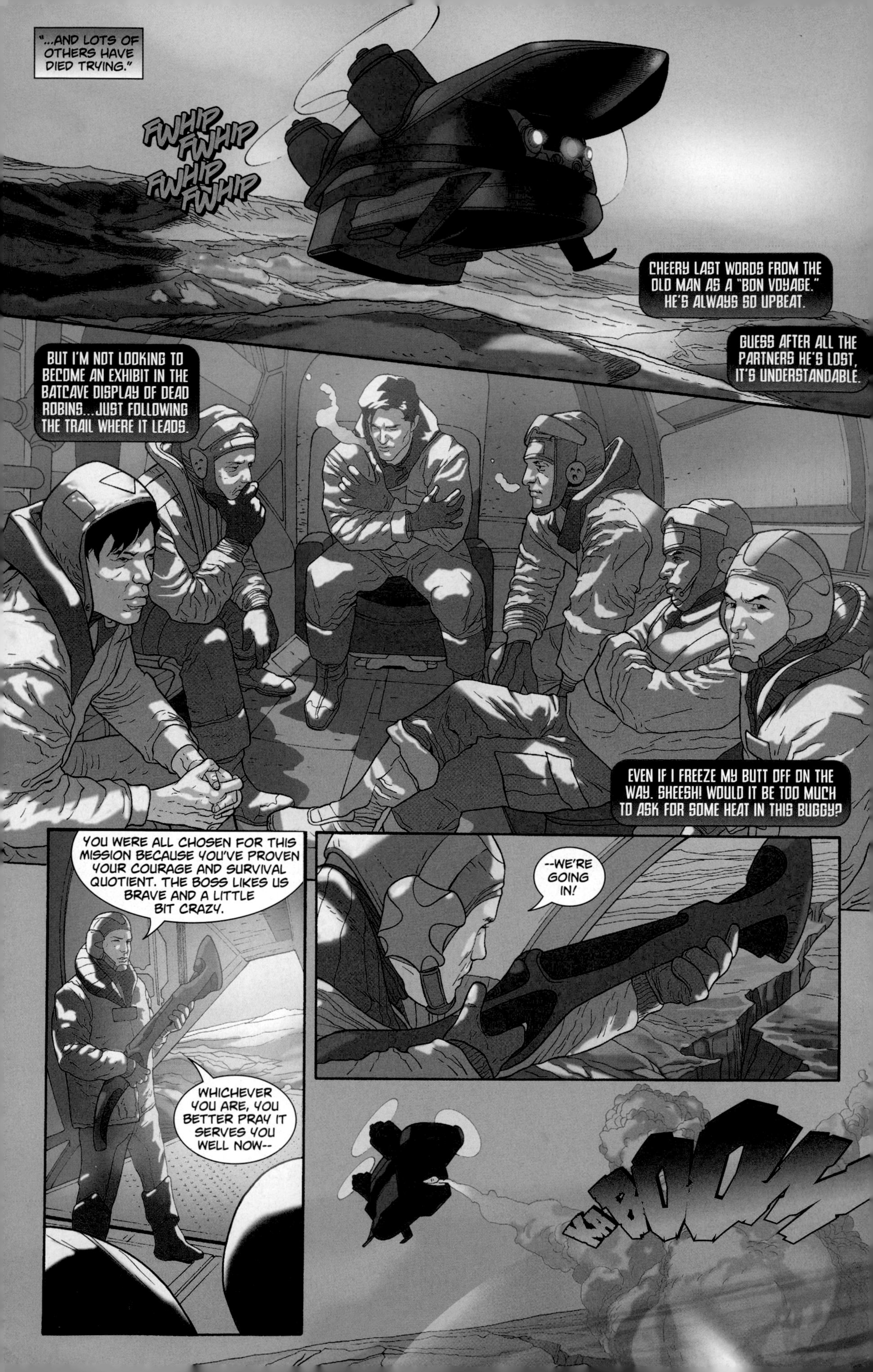
"...AND LOTS OF OTHERS HAVE DIED TRYING."
FWHIP FWHIP FWHIP FWHIP
CHEERY LAST WORDS FROM THE OLD MAN AS A "BON VOYAGE." HE'S ALWAYS SO UPBEAT.
GUESS AFTER ALL THE PARTNERS HE'S LOST, IT'S UNDERSTANDABLE.
BUT I'M NOT LOOKING TO BECOME AN EXHIBIT IN THE BATCAVE DISPLAY OF DEAD ROBINS...JUST FOLLOWING THE TRAIL WHERE IT LEADS.
EVEN IF I FREEZE MY BUTT OFF ON THE WAY. SHEESH! WOULD IT BE TOO MUCH TO ASK FOR SOME HEAT IN THIS BUGGY?
YOU WERE ALL CHOSEN FOR THIS MISSION BECAUSE YOU'VE PROVEN YOUR COURAGE AND SURVIVAL QUOTIENT. THE BOSS LIKES US BRAVE AND A LITTLE BIT CRAZY.
WHICHEVER YOU ARE, YOU BETTER PRAY IT SERVES YOU WELL NOW--
--WE'RE GOING IN!
KA-BOOM

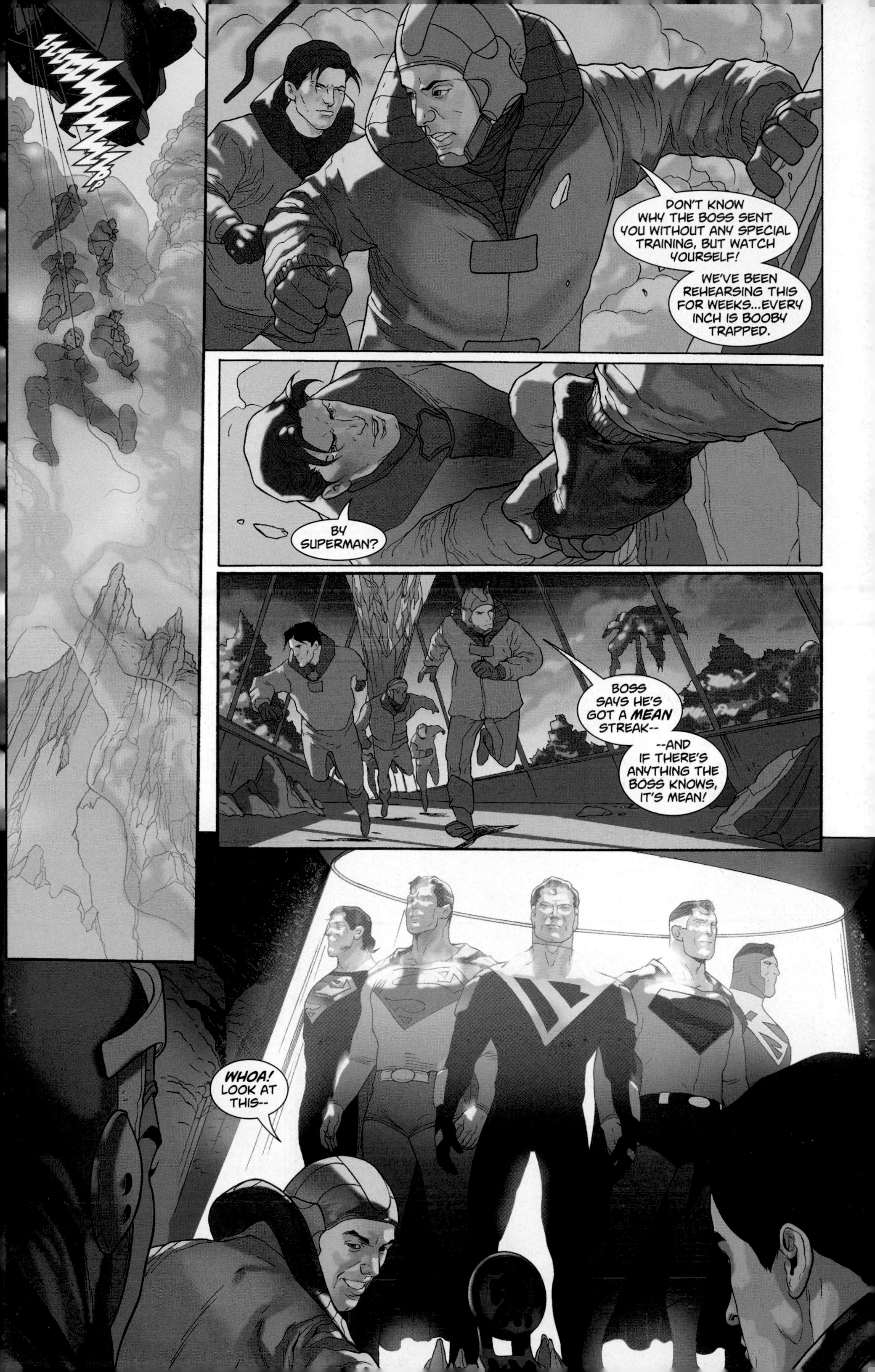

DON'T KNOW WHY THE BOSS SENT YOU WITHOUT ANY SPECIAL TRAINING, BUT WATCH YOURSELF!
WE'VE BEEN REHEARSING THIS FOR WEEKS...EVERY INCH IS BOOBY TRAPPED.
BY SUPERMAN?
BOSS SAYS HE'S GOT A MEAN STREAK--
--AND IF THERE'S ANYTHING THE BOSS KNOWS, IT'S MEAN!
WHOA! LOOK AT THIS--

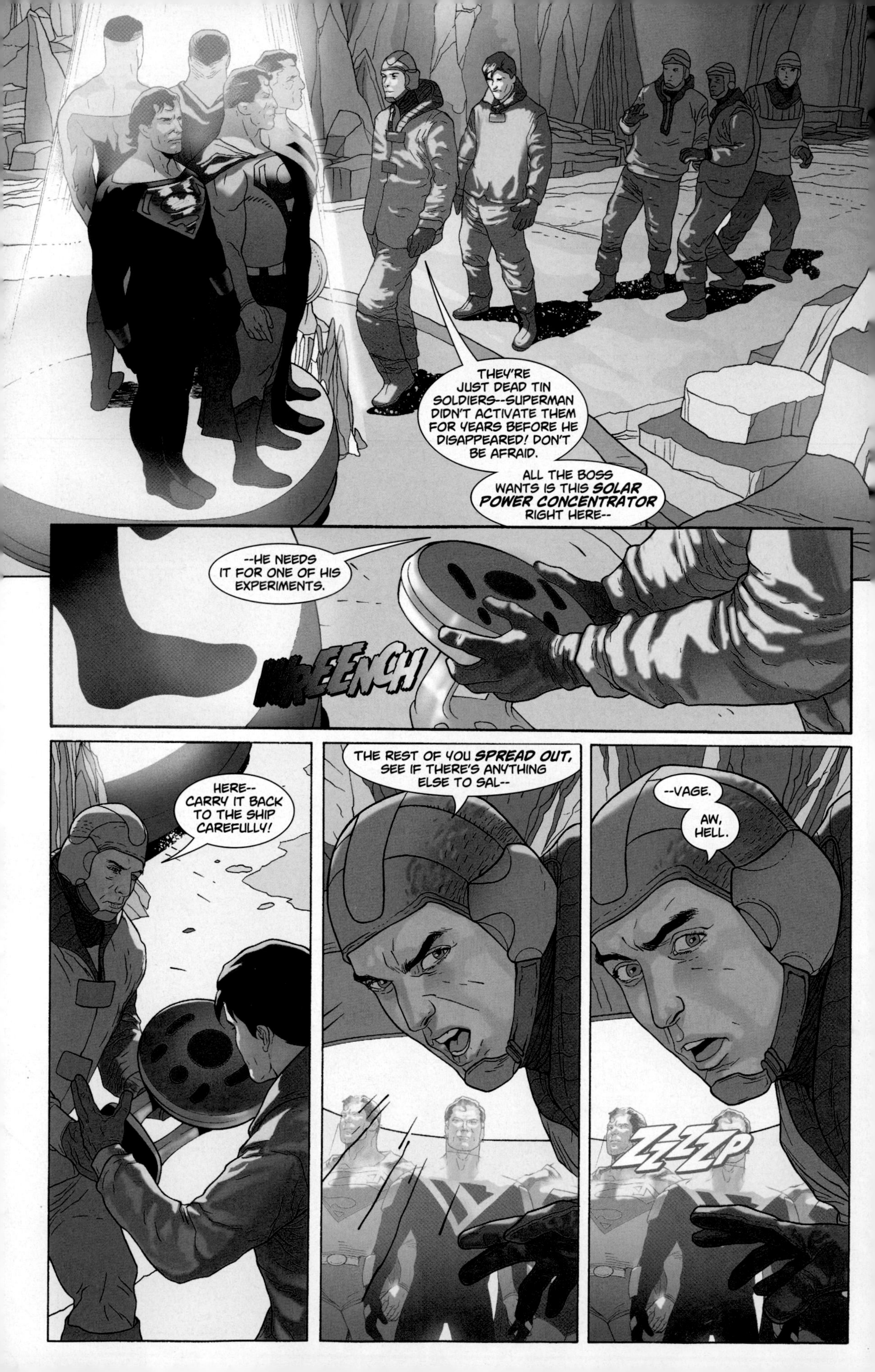
THEY'RE JUST DEAD TIN SOLDIERS--SUPERMAN DIDN'T ACTIVATE THEM FOR YEARS BEFORE HE DISAPPEARED! DON'T BE AFRAID.
ALL THE BOSS WANTS IS THIS SOLAR POWER CONCENTRATOR RIGHT HERE--
--HE NEEDS IT FOR ONE OF HIS EXPERIMENTS.
WREENCH
HERE-- CARRY IT BACK TO THE SHIP CAREFULLY!
THE REST OF YOU SPREAD OUT, SEE IF THERE'S ANYTHING ELSE TO SAL--
--VAGE.
AW, HELL.
ZZZZP

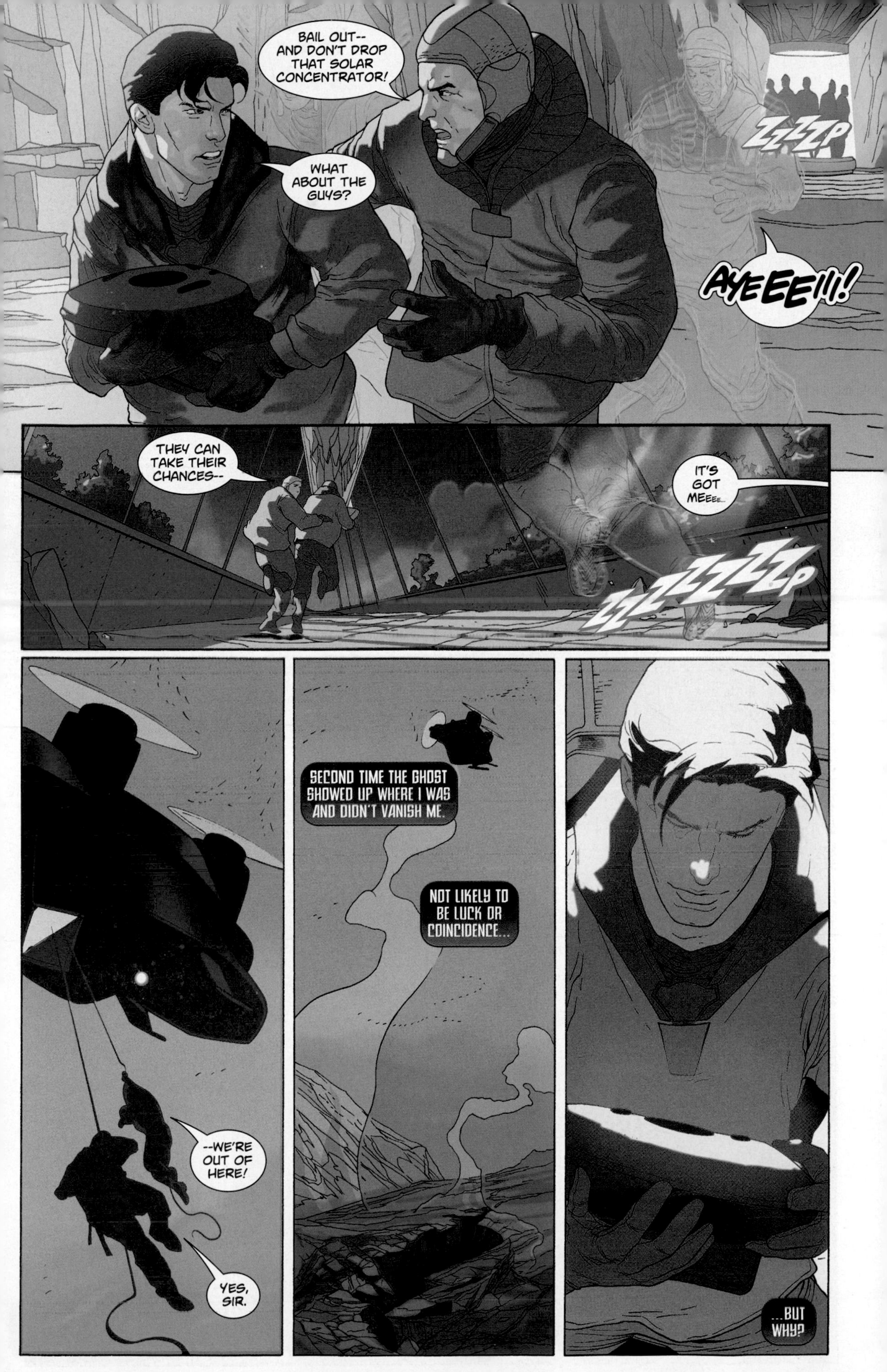
BAIL OUT-- AND DON'T DROP THAT SOLAR CONCENTRATOR!
WHAT ABOUT THE GUYS?
ZZZZP
AYEEEIII!
THEY CAN TAKE THEIR CHANCES--
IT'S GOT MEEEEE...
ZZZZZZZZP
--WE'RE OUT OF HERE!
YES, SIR.
SECOND TIME THE GHOST SHOWED UP WHERE I WAS AND DIDN'T VANISH ME.
NOT LIKELY TO BE LUCK OR COINCIDENCE...
...BUT WHY?

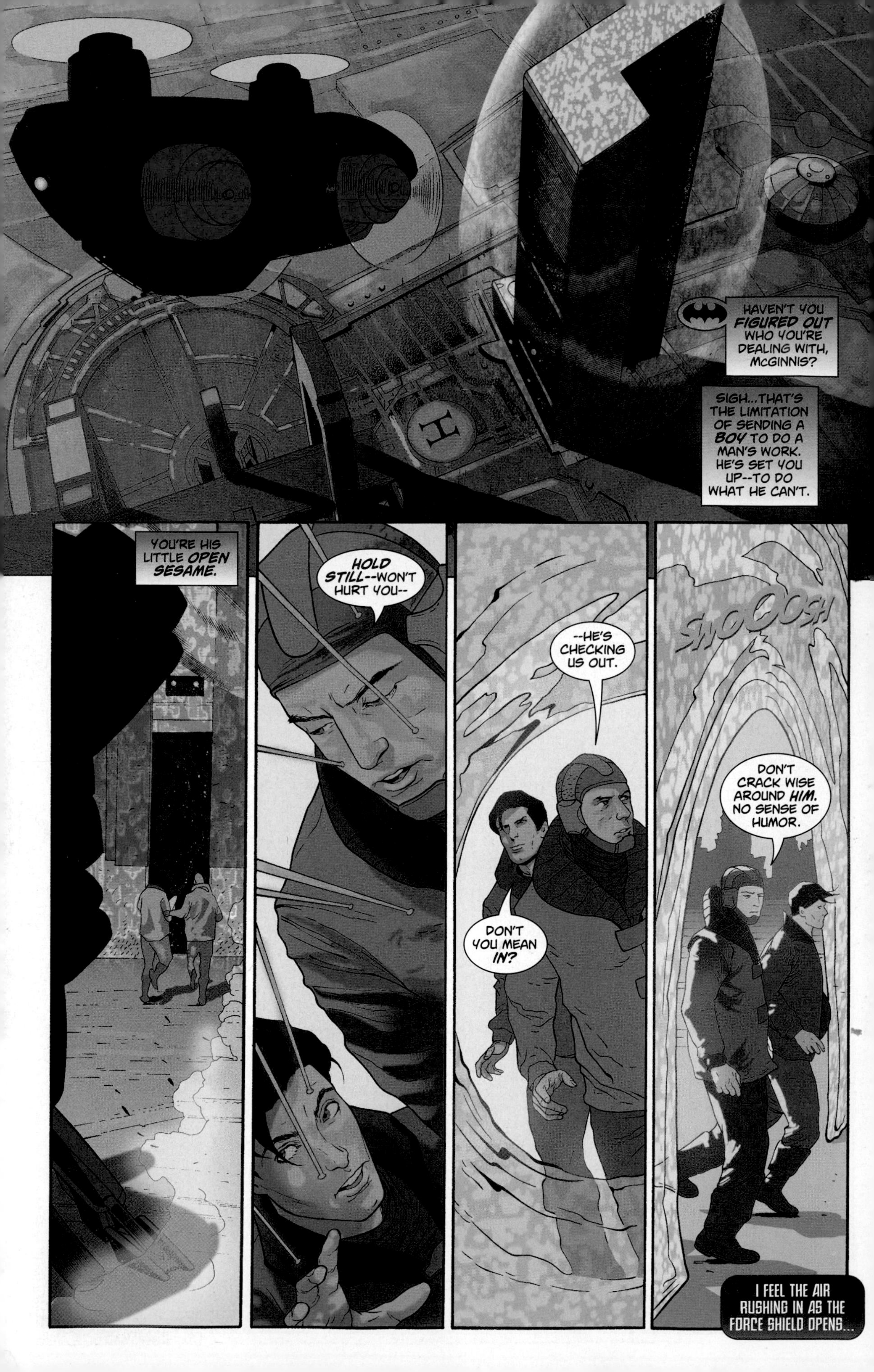

HAVEN'T YOU FIGURED OUT WHO YOU'RE DEALING WITH, McGINNIS?
SIGH...THAT'S THE LIMITATION OF SENDING A BOY TO DO A MAN'S WORK. HE'S SET YOU UP--TO DO WHAT HE CAN'T.
YOU'RE HIS LITTLE OPEN SESAME.
HOLD STILL--WON'T HURT YOU--
--HE'S CHECKING US OUT.
DON'T YOU MEAN IN?
SWOOOSH
DON'T CRACK WISE AROUND HIM. NO SENSE OF HUMOR.
I FEEL THE AIR RUSHING IN AS THE FORCE SHIELD OPENS...

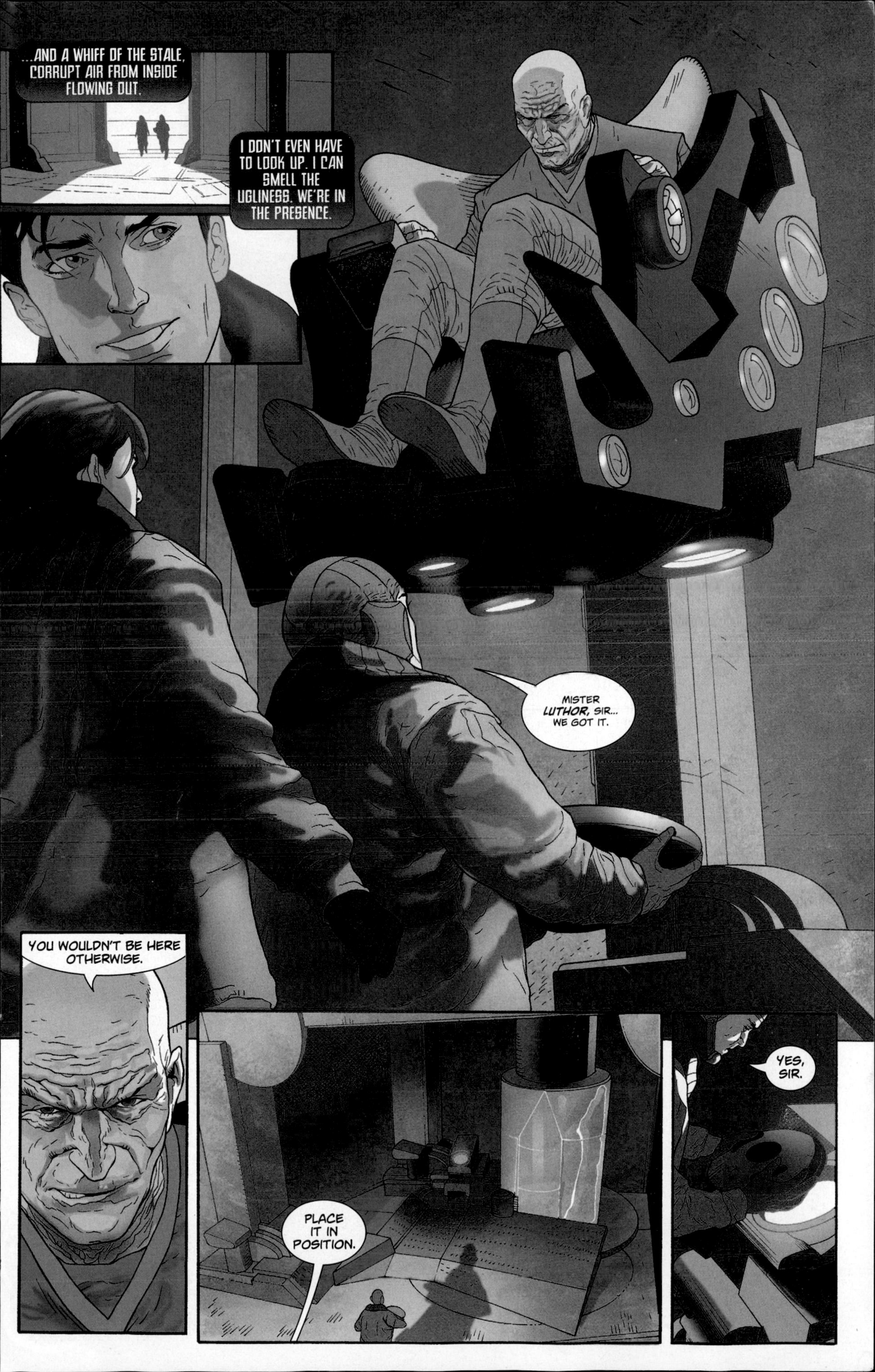
...AND A WHIFF OF THE STALE, CORRUPT AIR FROM INSIDE FLOWING OUT.
I DON'T EVEN HAVE TO LOOK UP. I CAN SMELL THE UGLINESS. WE'RE IN THE PRESENCE.
MISTER LUTHOR, SIR... WE GOT IT.
YOU WOULDN'T BE HERE OTHERWISE.
PLACE IT IN POSITION.
YES, SIR.

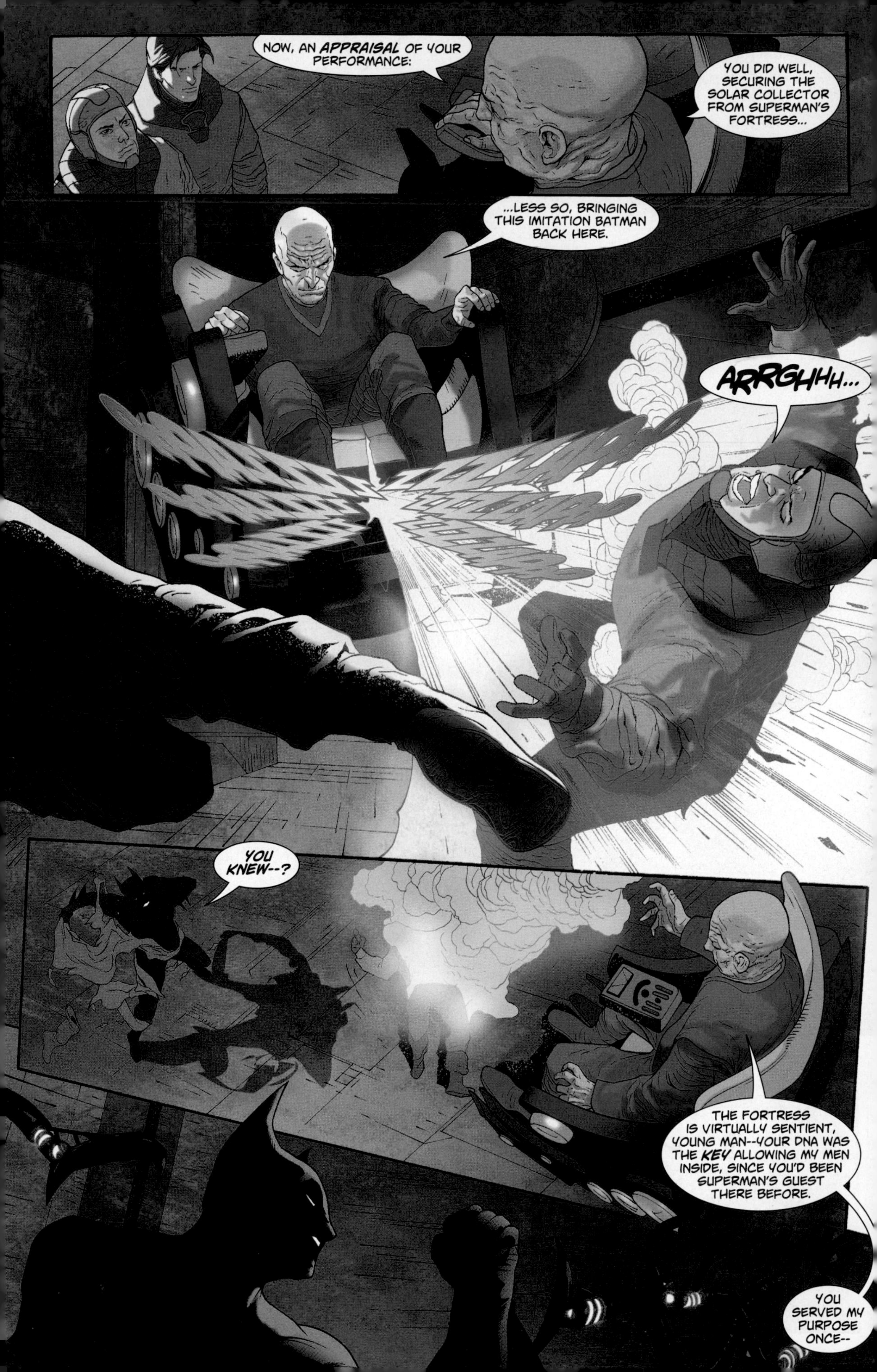
NOW, AN APPRAISAL OF YOUR PERFORMANCE:
YOU DID WELL, SECURING THE SOLAR COLLECTOR FROM SUPERMAN'S FORTRESS...
...LESS SO, BRINGING THIS IMITATION BATMAN BACK HERE.
ARRGHHH...
YOU KNEW--?
THE FORTRESS IS VIRTUALLY SENTIENT, YOUNG MAN--YOUR DNA WAS THE KEY ALLOWING MY MEN INSIDE, SINCE YOU'D BEEN SUPERMAN'S GUEST THERE BEFORE.
YOU SERVED MY PURPOSE ONCE--

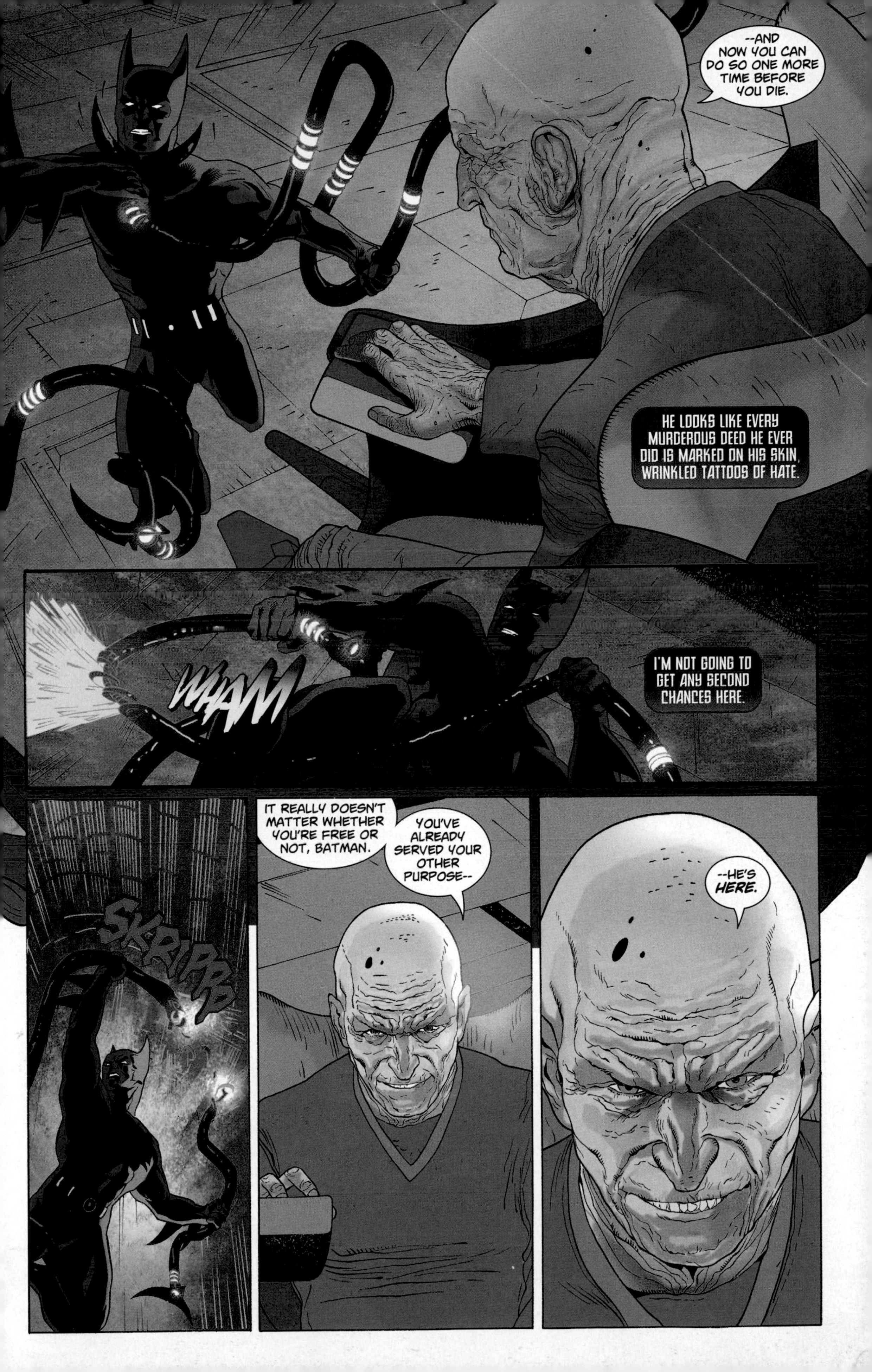
--AND NOW YOU CAN DO SO ONE MORE TIME BEFORE YOU DIE.
HE LOOKS LIKE EVERY MURDEROUS DEED HE EVER DID IS MARKED ON HIS SKIN, WRINKLED TATTOOS OF HATE.
WHAM
I'M NOT GOING TO GET ANY SECOND CHANCES HERE.
SKRIPPP
IT REALLY DOESN'T MATTER WHETHER YOU'RE FREE OR NOT, BATMAN.
YOU'VE ALREADY SERVED YOUR OTHER PURPOSE--
--HE'S HERE.

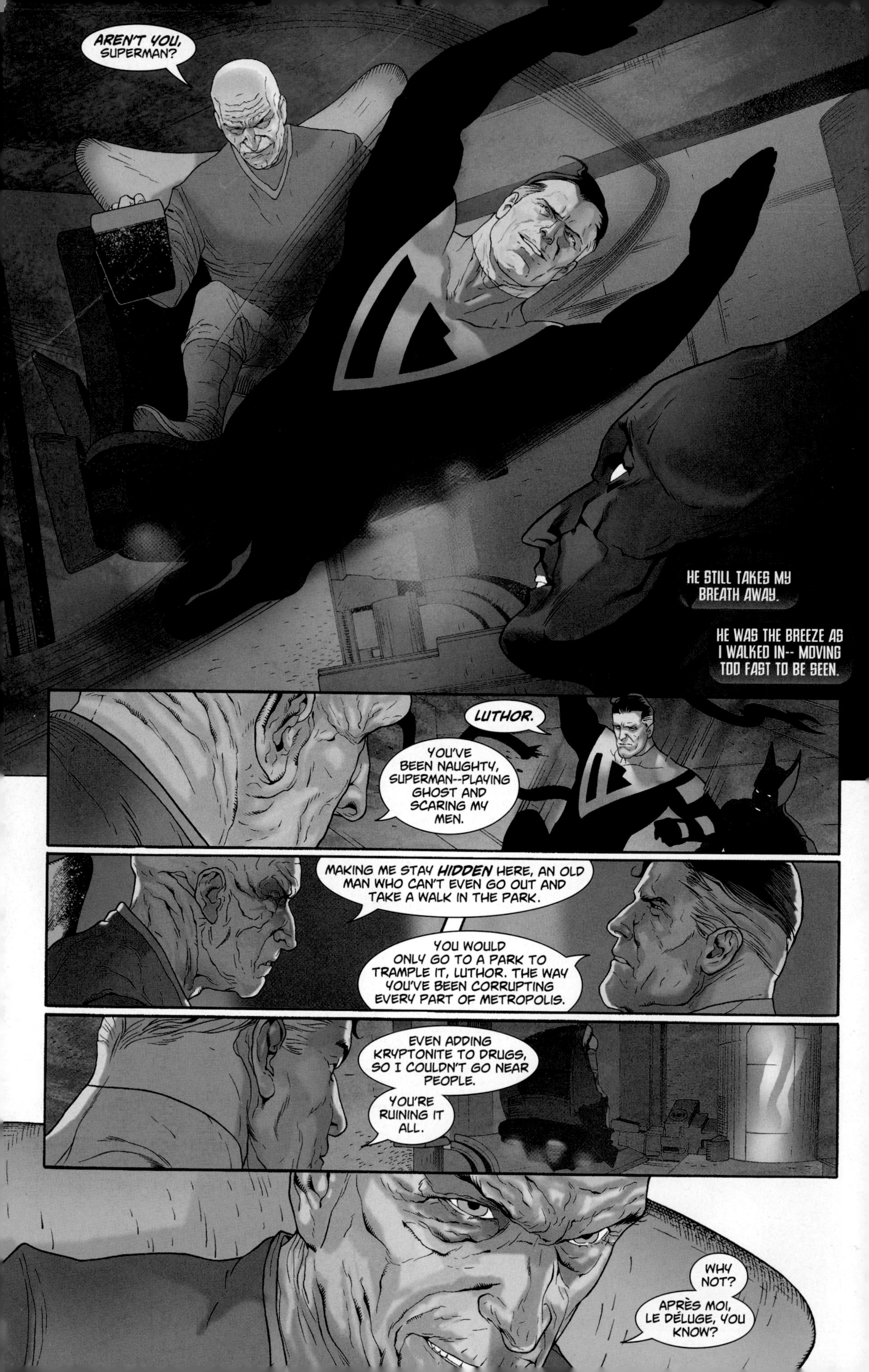
AREN'T YOU, SUPERMAN?
HE STILL TAKES MY BREATH AWAY.
HE WAS THE BREEZE AS I WALKED IN-- MOVING TOO FAST TO BE SEEN.
LUTHOR.
YOU'VE BEEN NAUGHTY, SUPERMAN--PLAYING GHOST AND SCARING MY MEN.
MAKING ME STAY HIDDEN HERE, AN OLD MAN WHO CAN'T EVEN GO OUT AND TAKE A WALK IN THE PARK.
YOU WOULD ONLY GO TO A PARK TO TRAMPLE IT, LUTHOR. THE WAY YOU'VE BEEN CORRUPTING EVERY PART OF METROPOLIS.
EVEN ADDING KRYPTONITE TO DRUGS, SO I COULDN'T GO NEAR PEOPLE.
YOU'RE RUINING IT ALL.
WHY NOT?
APRÈS MOI, LE DÉLUGE, YOU KNOW?

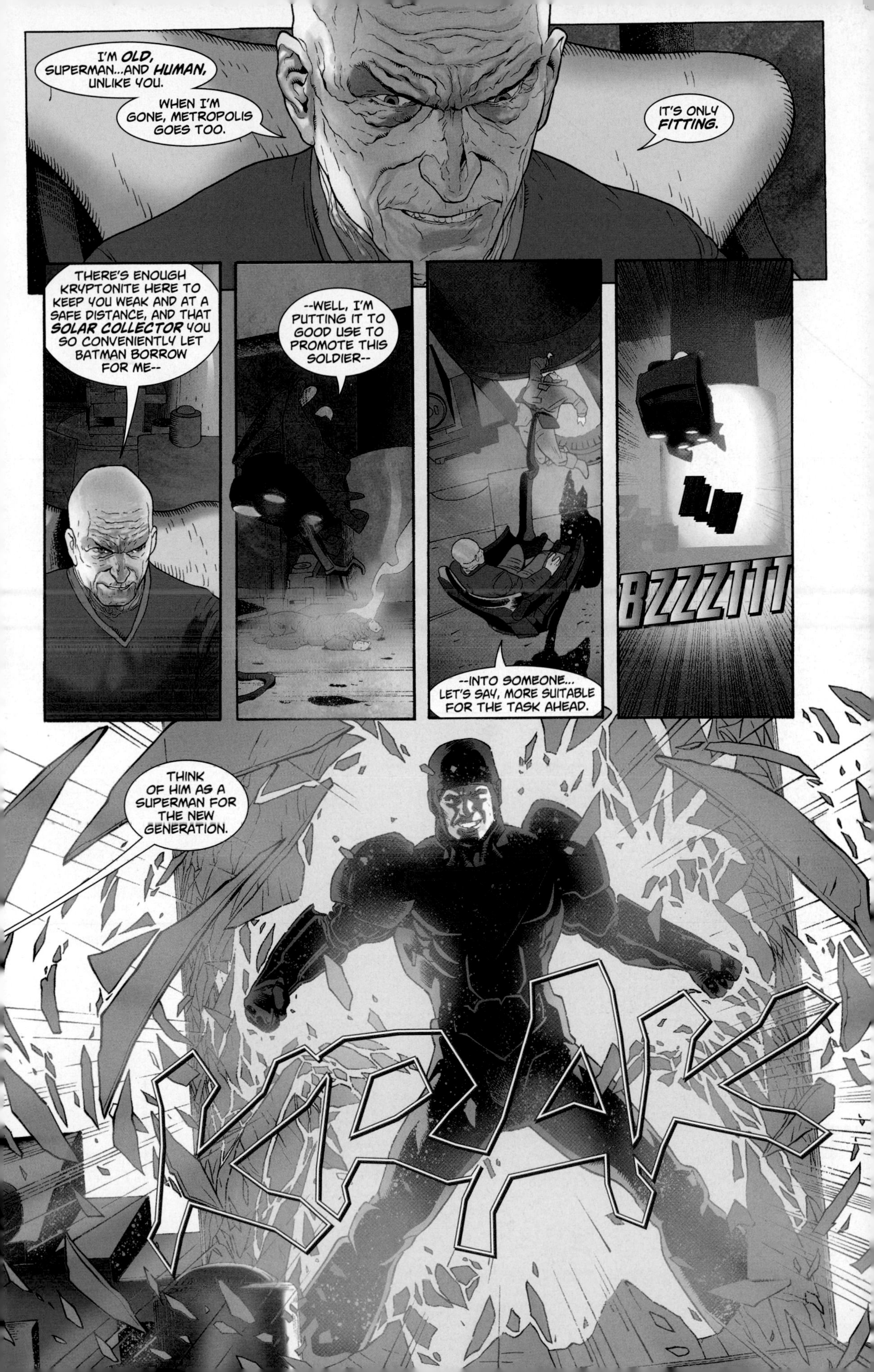
I'M OLD, SUPERMAN...AND HUMAN, UNLIKE YOU.
WHEN I'M GONE, METROPOLIS GOES TOO.
IT'S ONLY FITTING.
THERE'S ENOUGH KRYPTONITE HERE TO KEEP YOU WEAK AND AT A SAFE DISTANCE, AND THAT SOLAR COLLECTOR YOU SO CONVENIENTLY LET BATMAN BORROW FOR ME--
--WELL, I'M PUTTING IT TO GOOD USE TO PROMOTE THIS SOLDIER--
--INTO SOMEONE... LET'S SAY, MORE SUITABLE FOR THE TASK AHEAD.
BZZZTTT
THINK OF HIM AS A SUPERMAN FOR THE NEW GENERATION.

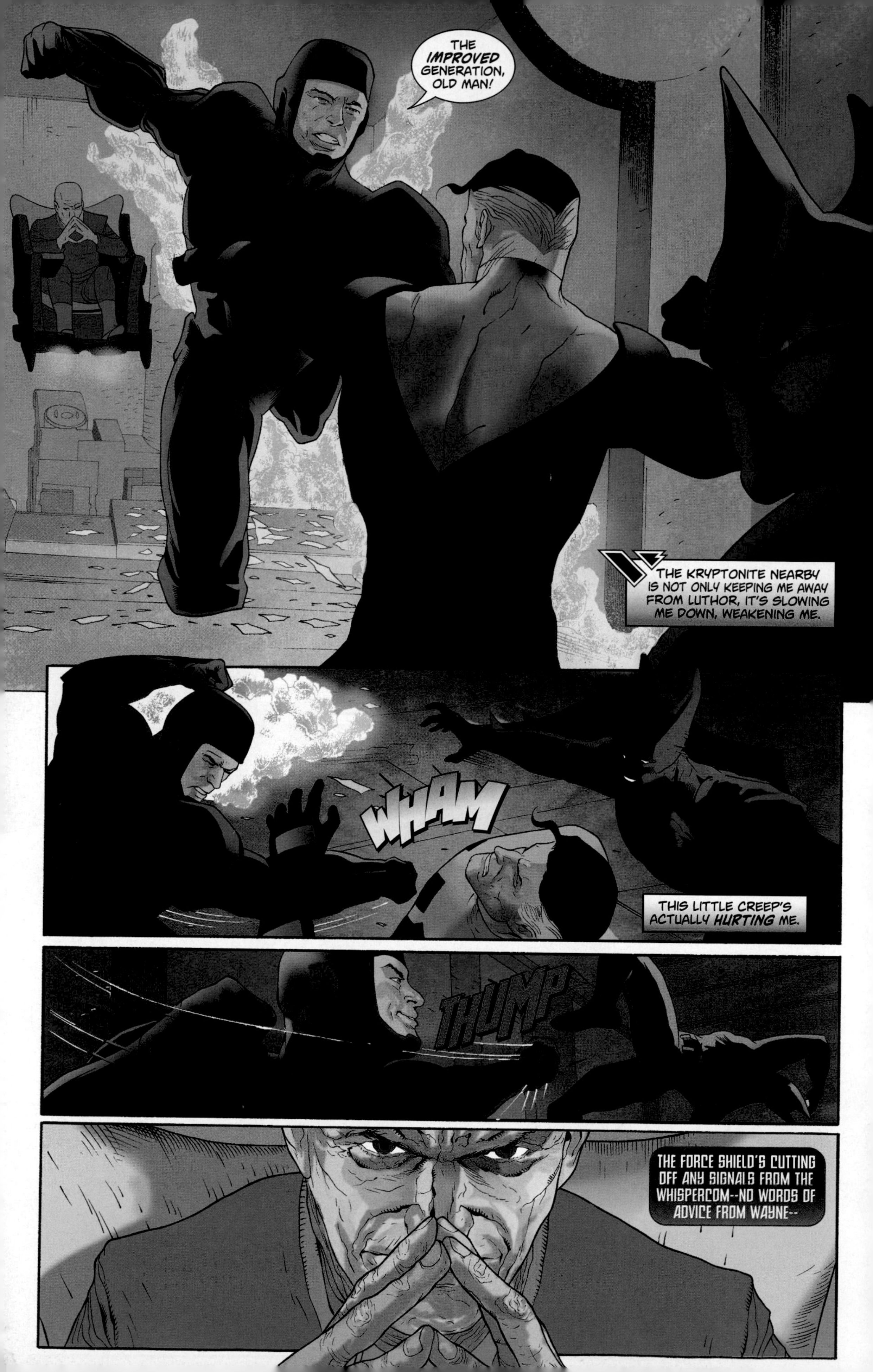
THE IMPROVED GENERATION, OLD MAN!
THE KRYPTONITE NEARBY IS NOT ONLY KEEPING ME AWAY FROM LUTHOR, IT'S SLOWING ME DOWN, WEAKENING ME.
WHAM
THIS LITTLE CREEP'S ACTUALLY HURTING ME.
THUMP
THE FORCE SHIELD'S CUTTING OFF ANY SIGNALS FROM THE WHISPERCOM--NO WORDS OF ADVICE FROM WAYNE--

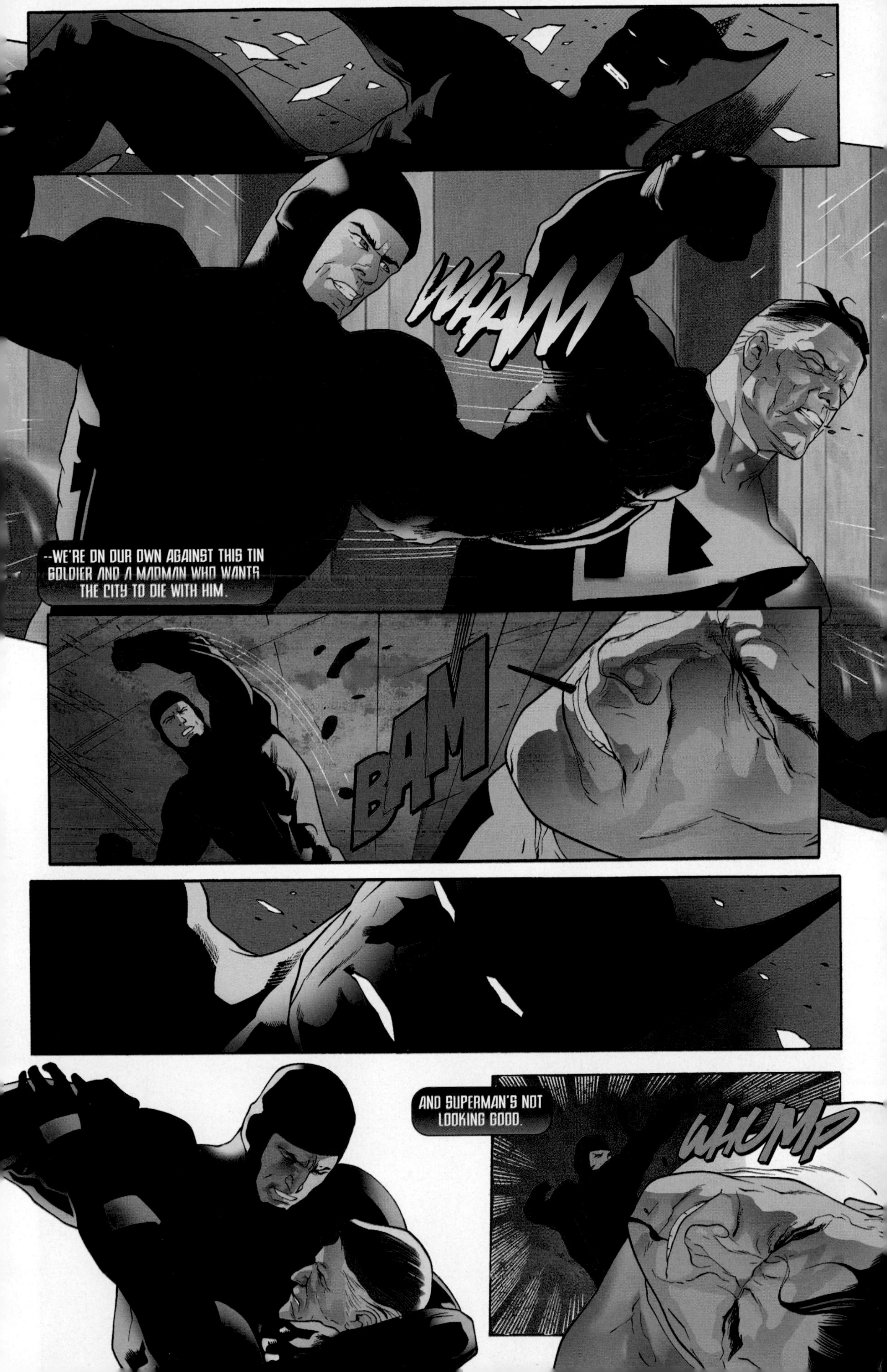
WHAM
--WE'RE ON OUR OWN AGAINST THIS TIN SOLDIER AND A MADMAN WHO WANTS THE CITY TO DIE WITH HIM.
BAM
AND SUPERMAN'S NOT LOOKING GOOD.
WHUMP

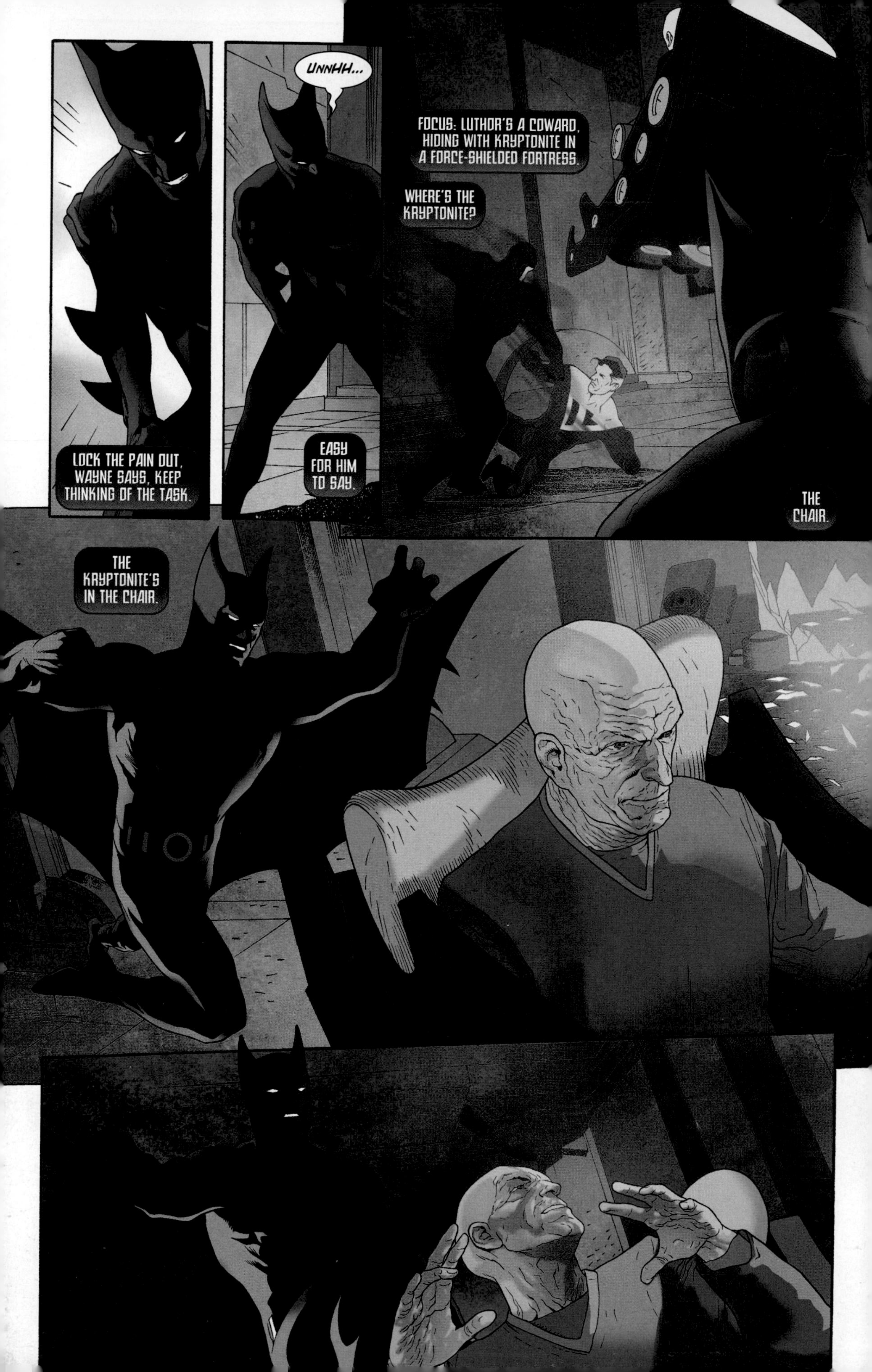
LOCK THE PAIN OUT, WAYNE SAYS, KEEP THINKING OF THE TASK.
UNNHH...
EASY FOR HIM TO SAY.
FOCUS: LUTHOR'S A COWARD, HIDING WITH KRYPTONITE IN A FORCE-SHIELDED FORTRESS.
WHERE'S THE KRYPTONITE?
THE CHAIR.
THE KRYPTONITE'S IN THE CHAIR.

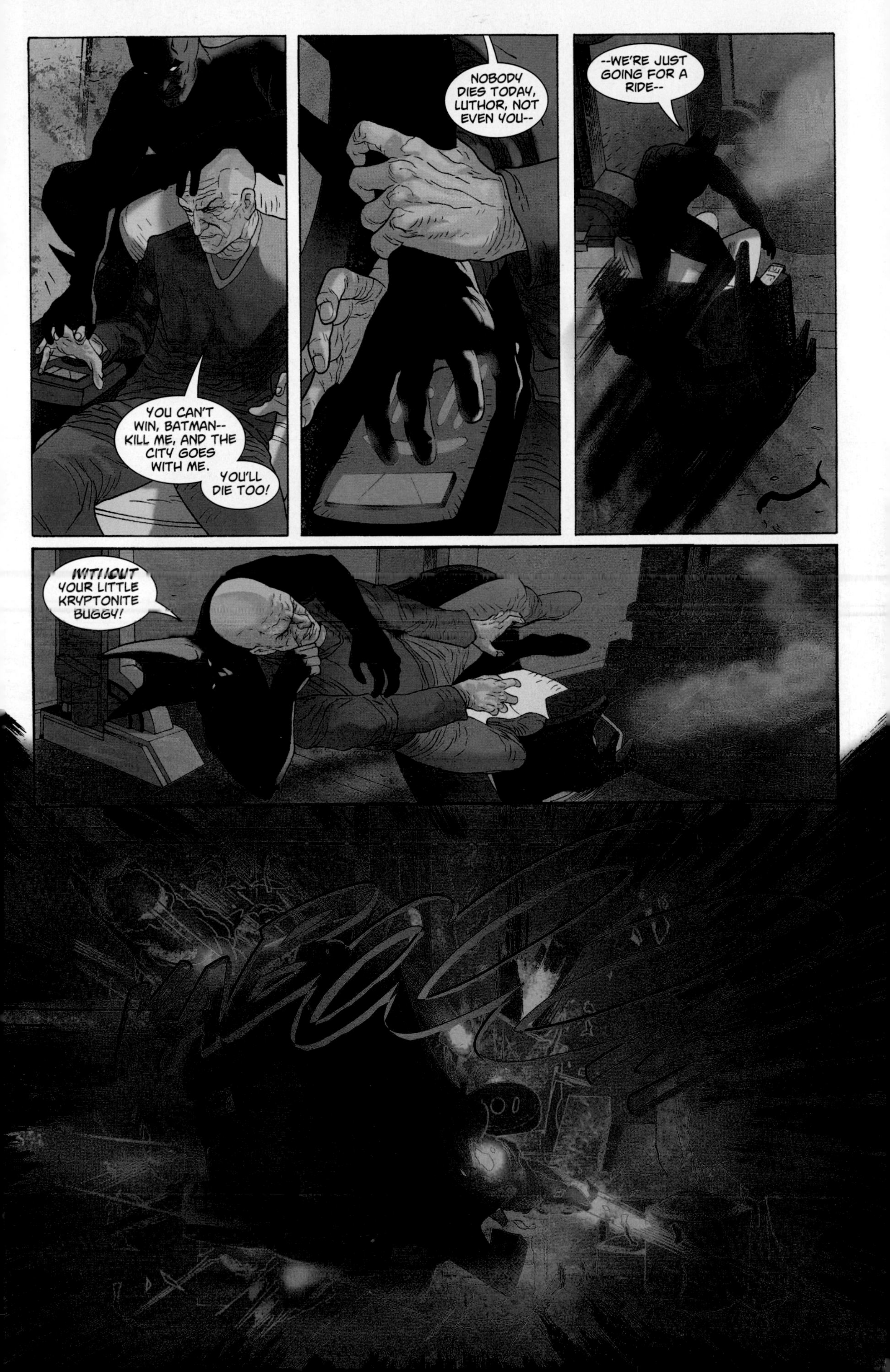
YOU CAN'T WIN, BATMAN-- KILL ME, AND THE CITY GOES WITH ME.
YOU'LL DIE TOO!
NOBODY DIES TODAY, LUTHOR, NOT EVEN YOU--
--WE'RE JUST GOING FOR A RIDE--
WITHOUT YOUR LITTLE KRYPTONITE BUGGY!

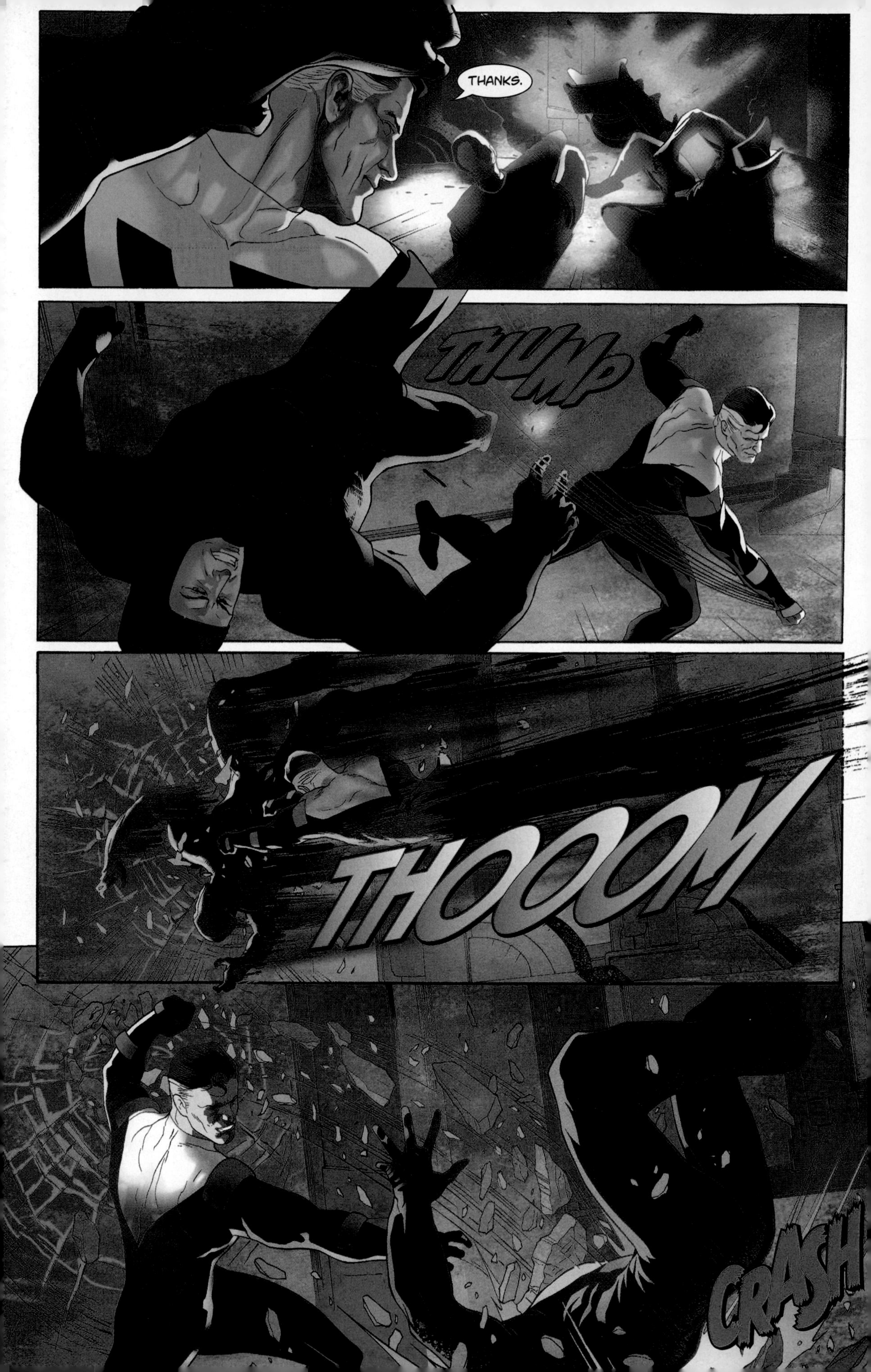
THANKS.
THUMP
THOOOM
CRASH

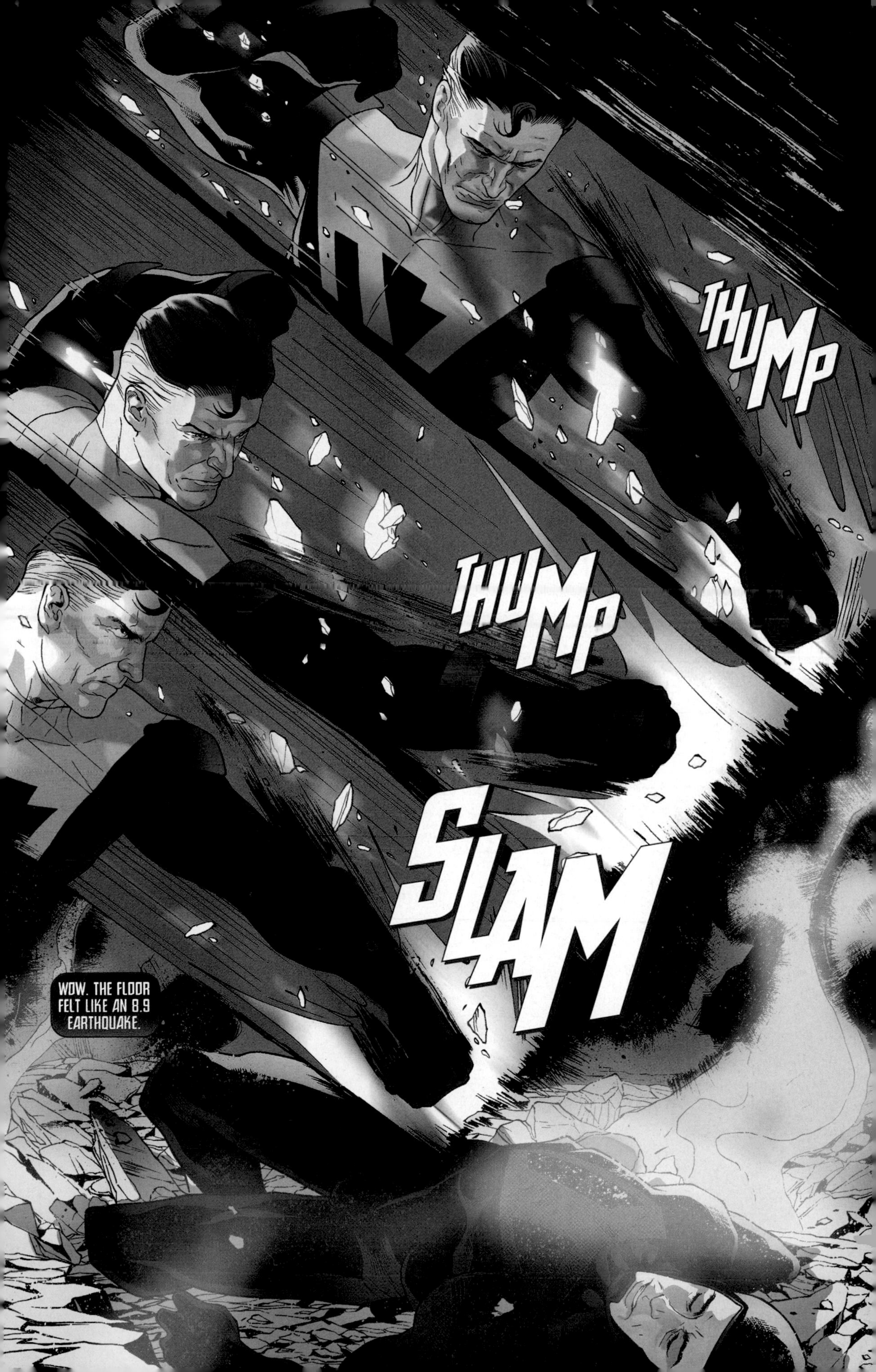
THUMP
THUMP
SLAM
WOW. THE FLOOR FELT LIKE AN 8.9 EARTHQUAKE.

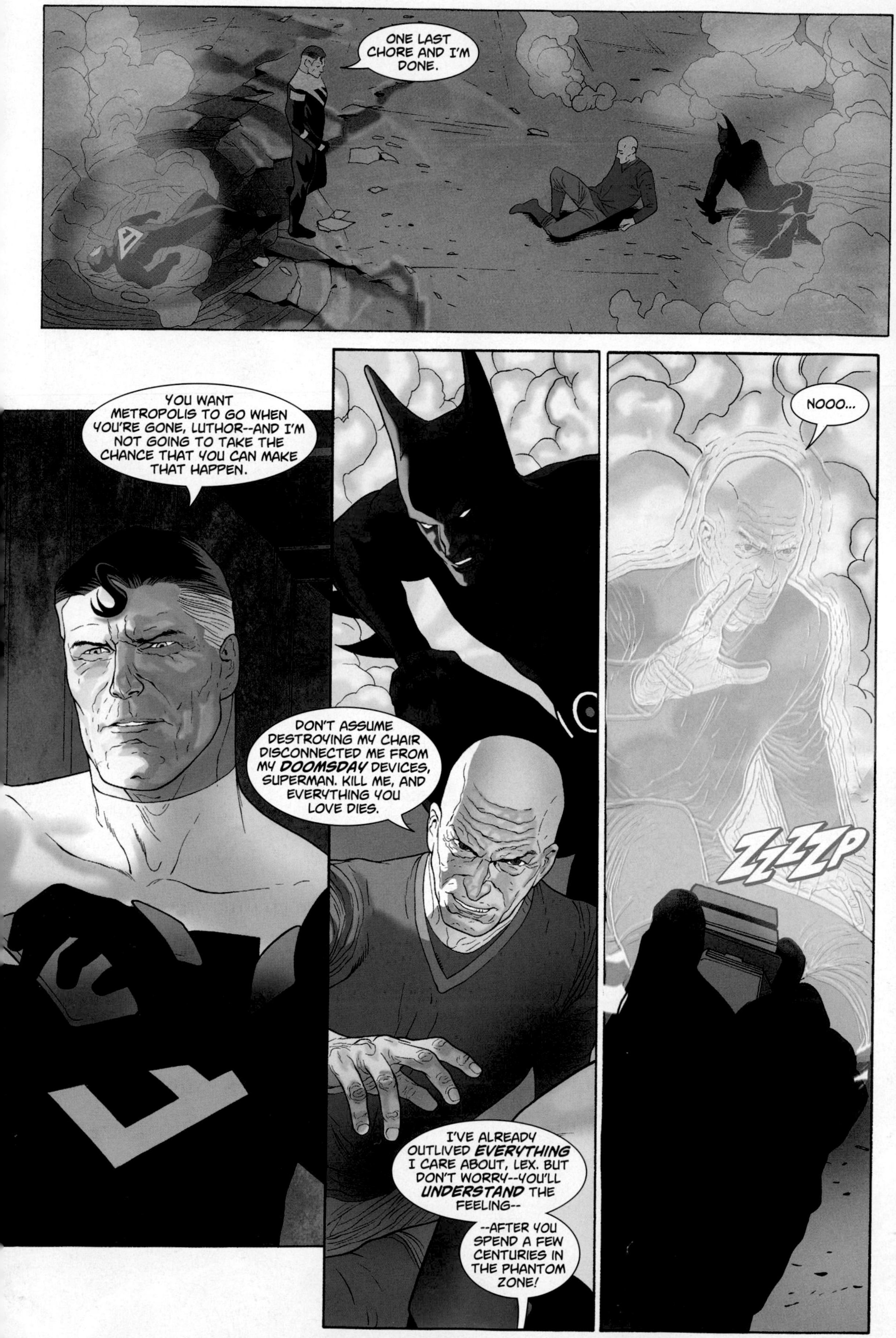
ONE LAST CHORE AND I'M DONE.
YOU WANT METROPOLIS TO GO WHEN YOU'RE GONE, LUTHOR--AND I'M NOT GOING TO TAKE THE CHANCE THAT YOU CAN MAKE THAT HAPPEN.
DON'T ASSUME DESTROYING MY CHAIR DISCONNECTED ME FROM MY DOOMSDAY DEVICES, SUPERMAN. KILL ME, AND EVERYTHING YOU LOVE DIES.
I'VE ALREADY OUTLIVED EVERYTHING I CARE ABOUT, LEX. BUT DON'T WORRY--YOU'LL UNDERSTAND THE FEELING--
--AFTER YOU SPEND A FEW CENTURIES IN THE PHANTOM ZONE!
NOOO...
ZZZZP

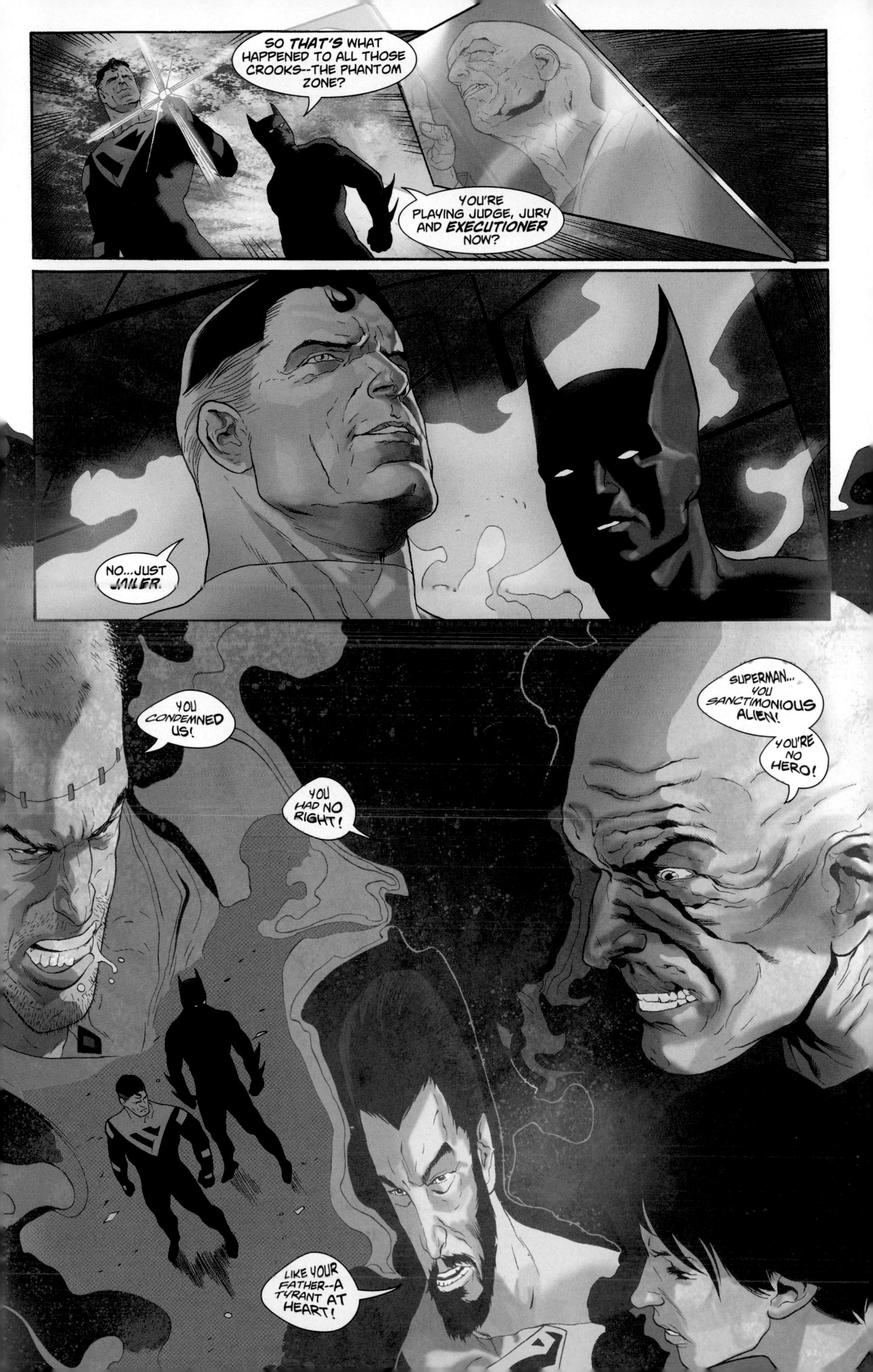
SO THAT'S WHAT HAPPENED TO ALL THOSE CROOKS--THE PHANTOM ZONE?
YOU'RE PLAYING JUDGE, JURY AND EXECUTIONER NOW?
NO...JUST JAILER.
YOU CONDEMNED US!
YOU HAD NO RIGHT!
SUPERMAN... YOU SANCTIMONIOUS ALIEN!
YOU'RE NO HERO!
LIKE YOUR FATHER--A TYRANT AT HEART!

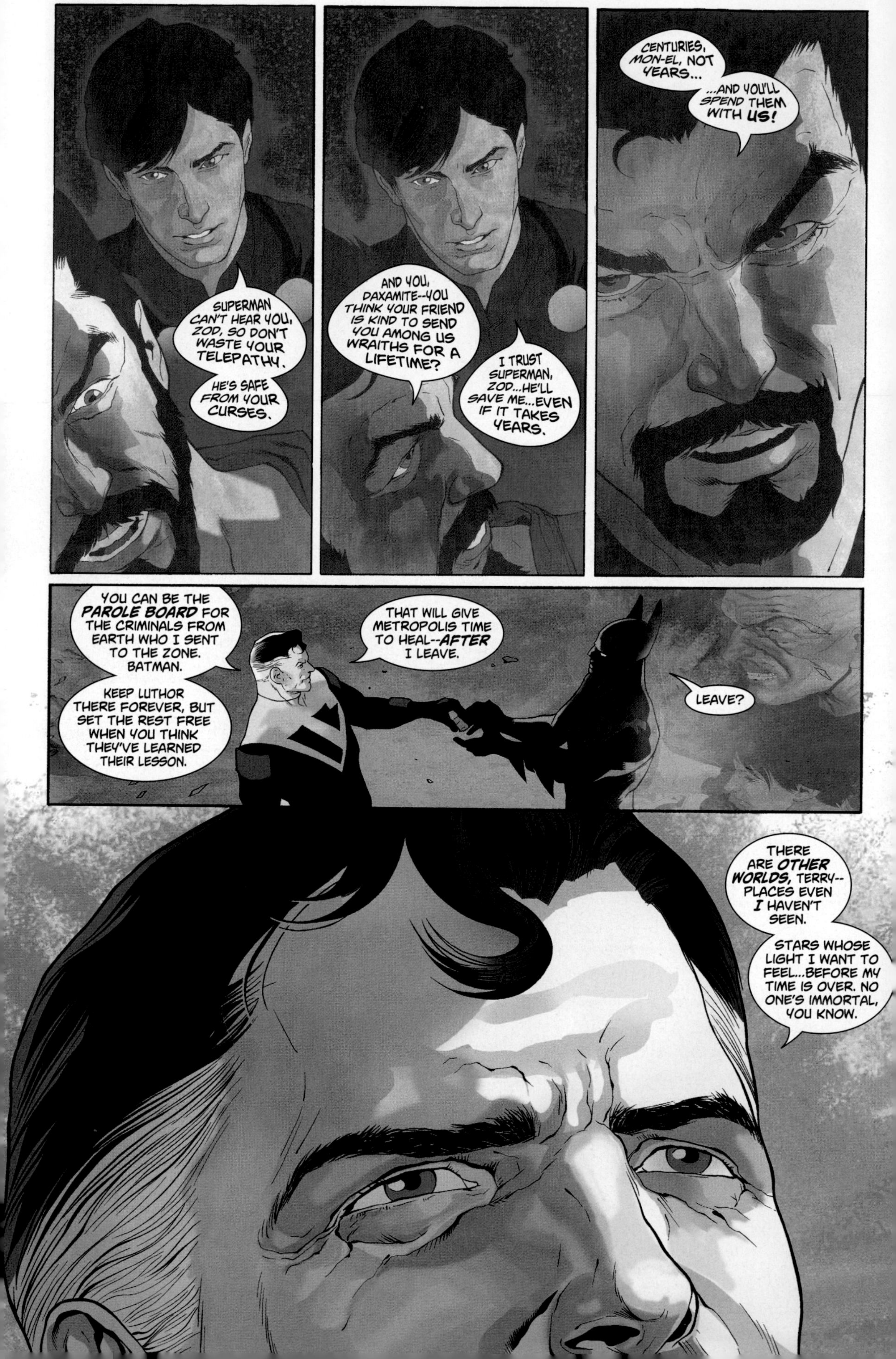
SUPERMAN CAN'T HEAR YOU, ZOD, SO DON'T WASTE YOUR TELEPATHY.
HE'S SAFE FROM YOUR CURSES.
AND YOU, DAXAMITE--YOU THINK YOUR FRIEND IS KIND TO SEND YOU AMONG US WRAITHS FOR A LIFETIME?
I TRUST SUPERMAN, ZOD...HE'LL SAVE ME...EVEN IF IT TAKES YEARS.
CENTURIES, MON-EL, NOT YEARS...
...AND YOU'LL SPEND THEM WITH US!
YOU CAN BE THE PAROLE BOARD FOR THE CRIMINALS FROM EARTH WHO I SENT TO THE ZONE. BATMAN.
KEEP LUTHOR THERE FOREVER, BUT SET THE REST FREE WHEN YOU THINK THEY'VE LEARNED THEIR LESSON.
THAT WILL GIVE METROPOLIS TIME TO HEAL--AFTER I LEAVE.
LEAVE?
THERE ARE OTHER WORLDS, TERRY--PLACES EVEN I HAVEN'T SEEN.
STARS WHOSE LIGHT I WANT TO FEEL...BEFORE MY TIME IS OVER. NO ONE'S IMMORTAL, YOU KNOW.

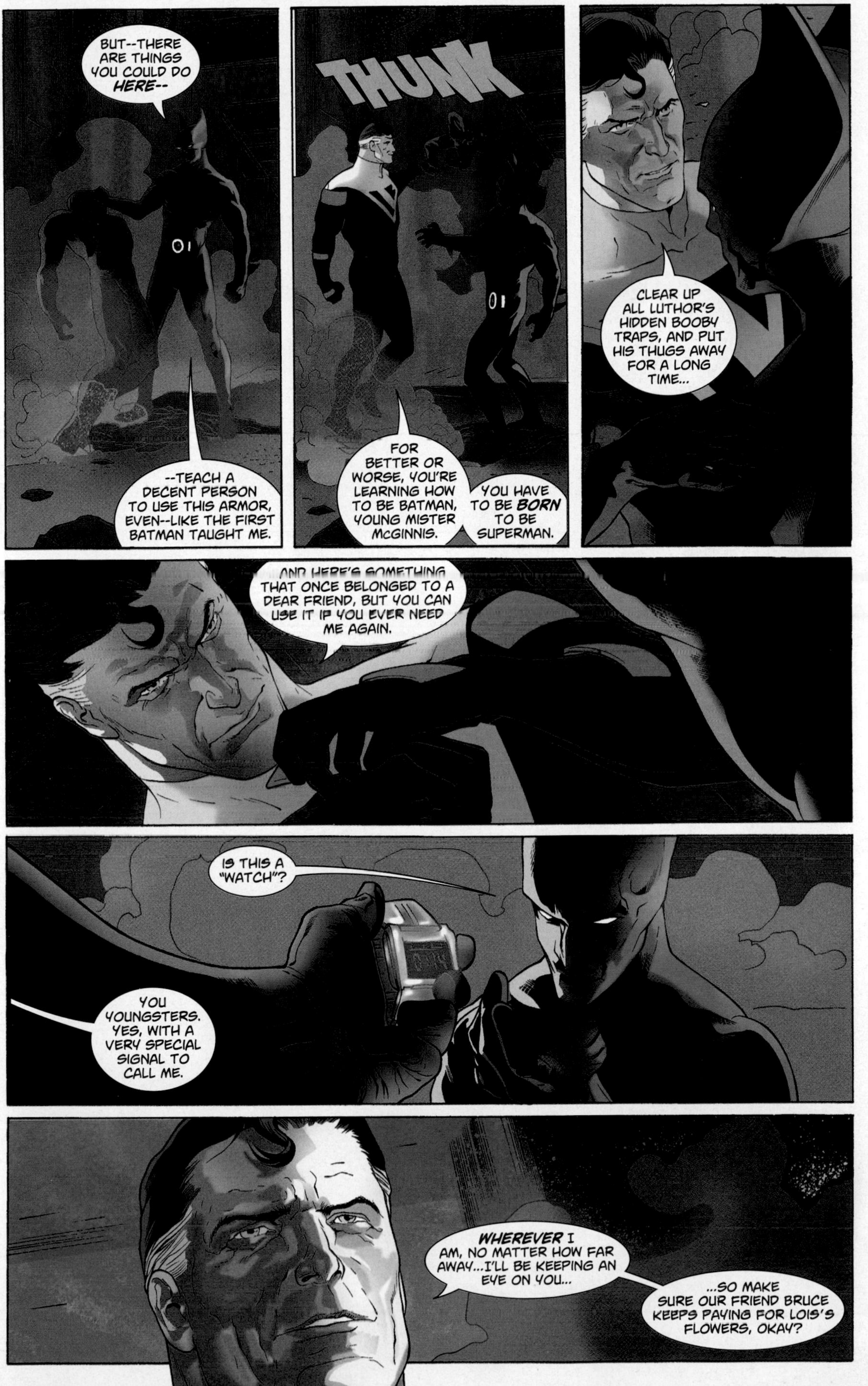
BUT--THERE ARE THINGS YOU COULD DO HERE--
--TEACH A DECENT PERSON TO USE THIS ARMOR, EVEN--LIKE THE FIRST BATMAN TAUGHT ME.
THUNK
FOR BETTER OR WORSE, YOU'RE LEARNING HOW TO BE BATMAN, YOUNG MISTER McGINNIS.
YOU HAVE TO BE BORN TO BE SUPERMAN.
CLEAR UP ALL LUTHOR'S HIDDEN BOOBY TRAPS, AND PUT HIS THUGS AWAY FOR A LONG TIME...
AND HERE'S SOMETHING THAT ONCE BELONGED TO A DEAR FRIEND, BUT YOU CAN USE IT IF YOU EVER NEED ME AGAIN.
IS THIS A "WATCH"?
YOU YOUNGSTERS. YES, WITH A VERY SPECIAL SIGNAL TO CALL ME.
WHEREVER I AM, NO MATTER HOW FAR AWAY...I'LL BE KEEPING AN EYE ON YOU...
...SO MAKE SURE OUR FRIEND BRUCE KEEPS PAYING FOR LOIS'S FLOWERS, OKAY?

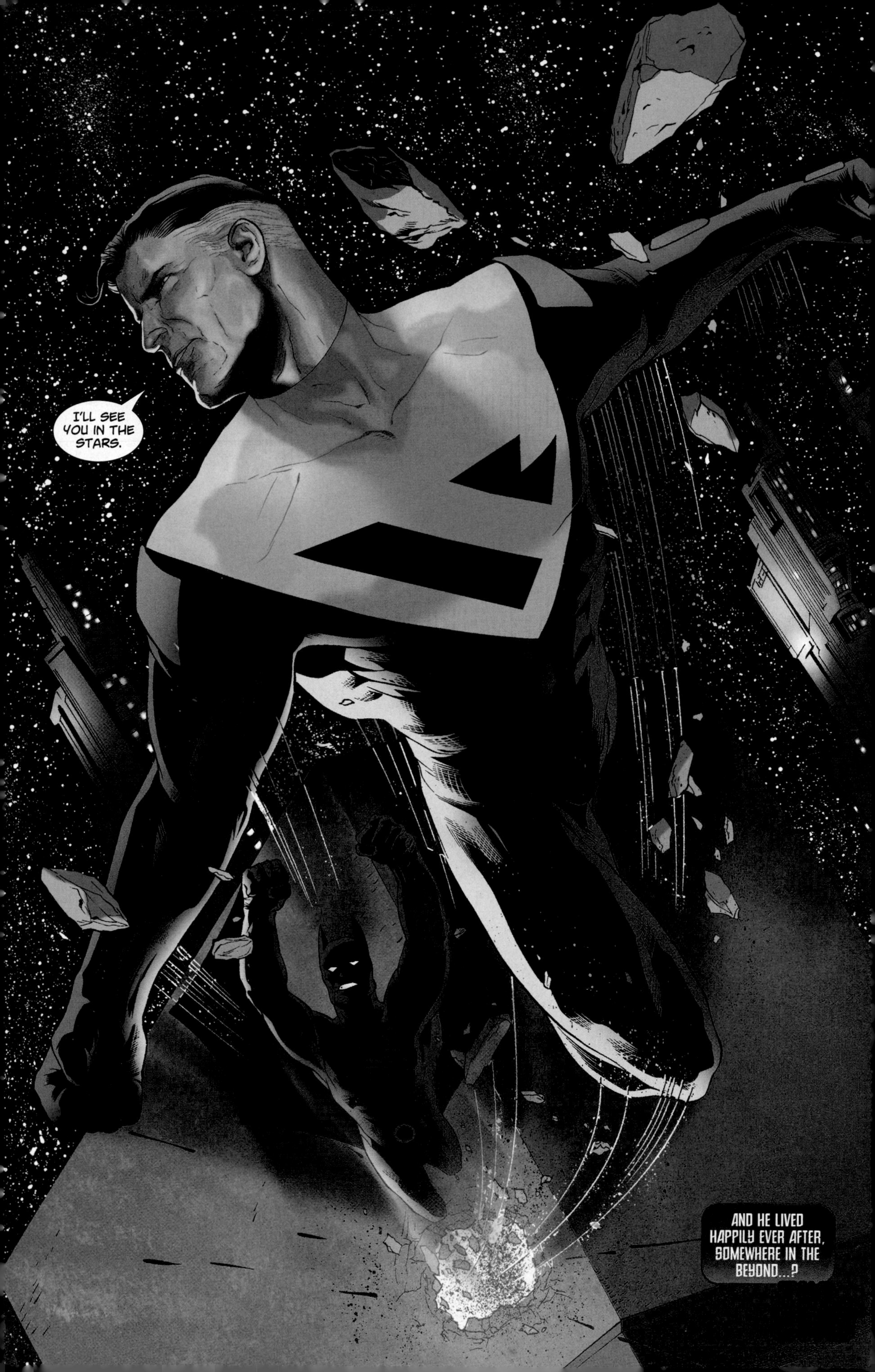
I'LL SEE YOU IN THE STARS.
AND HE LIVED HAPPILY EVER AFTER, SOMEWHERE IN THE BEYOND...?

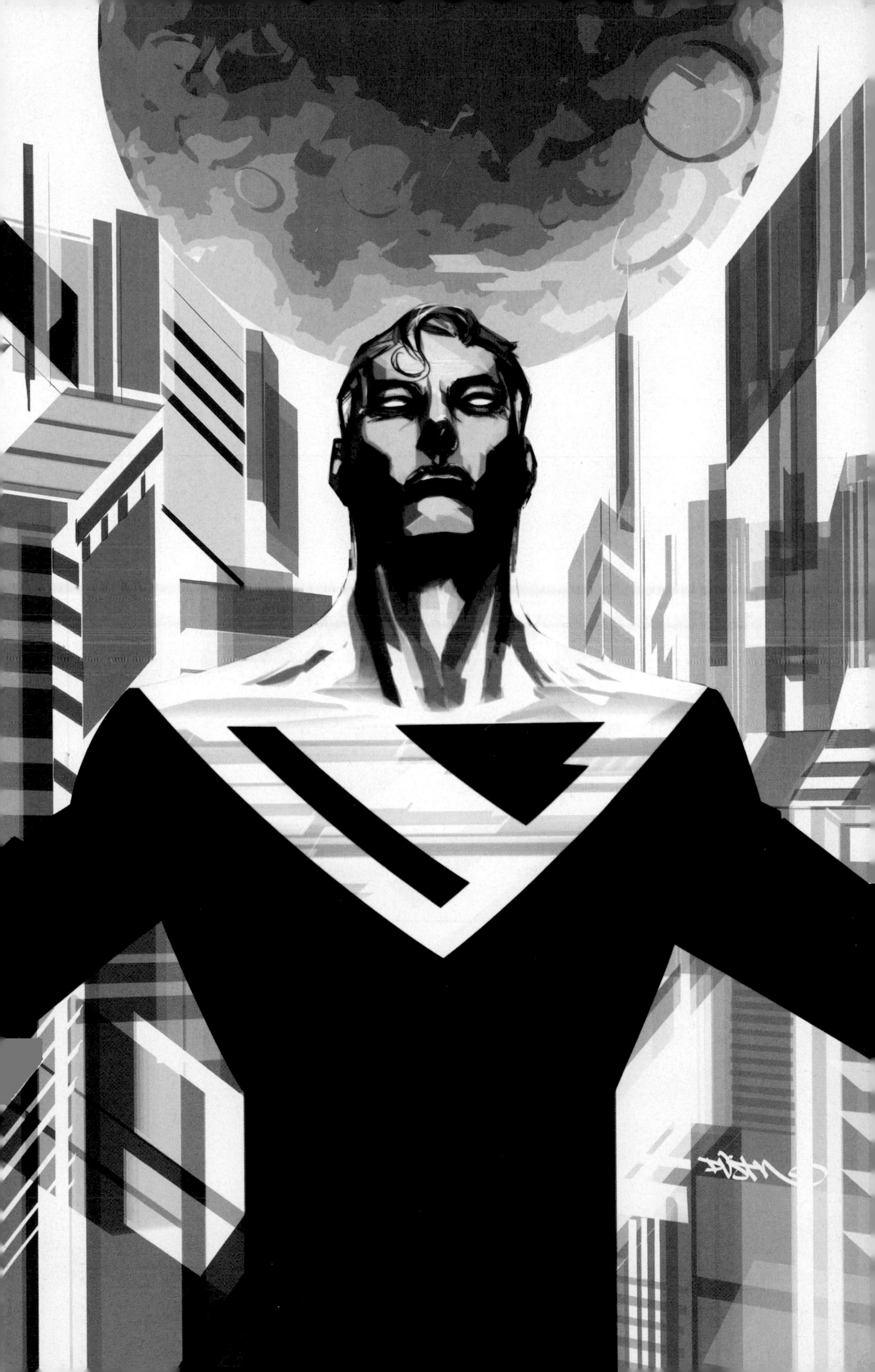

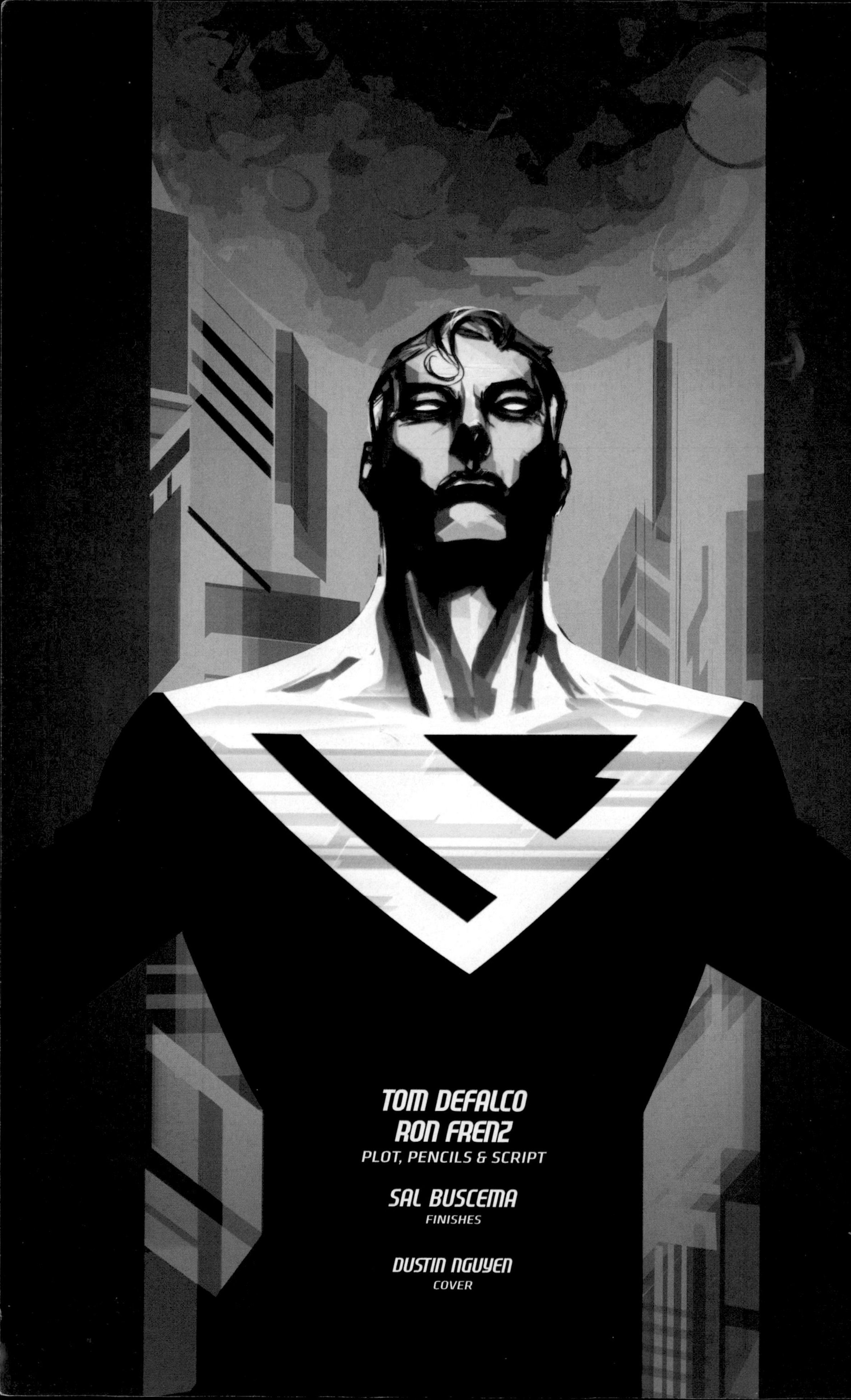
TOM DEFALCO
RON FRENZ
PLOT, PENCILS & SCRIPT
SAL BUSCEMA
FINISHES
DUSTIN NGUYEN
COVER

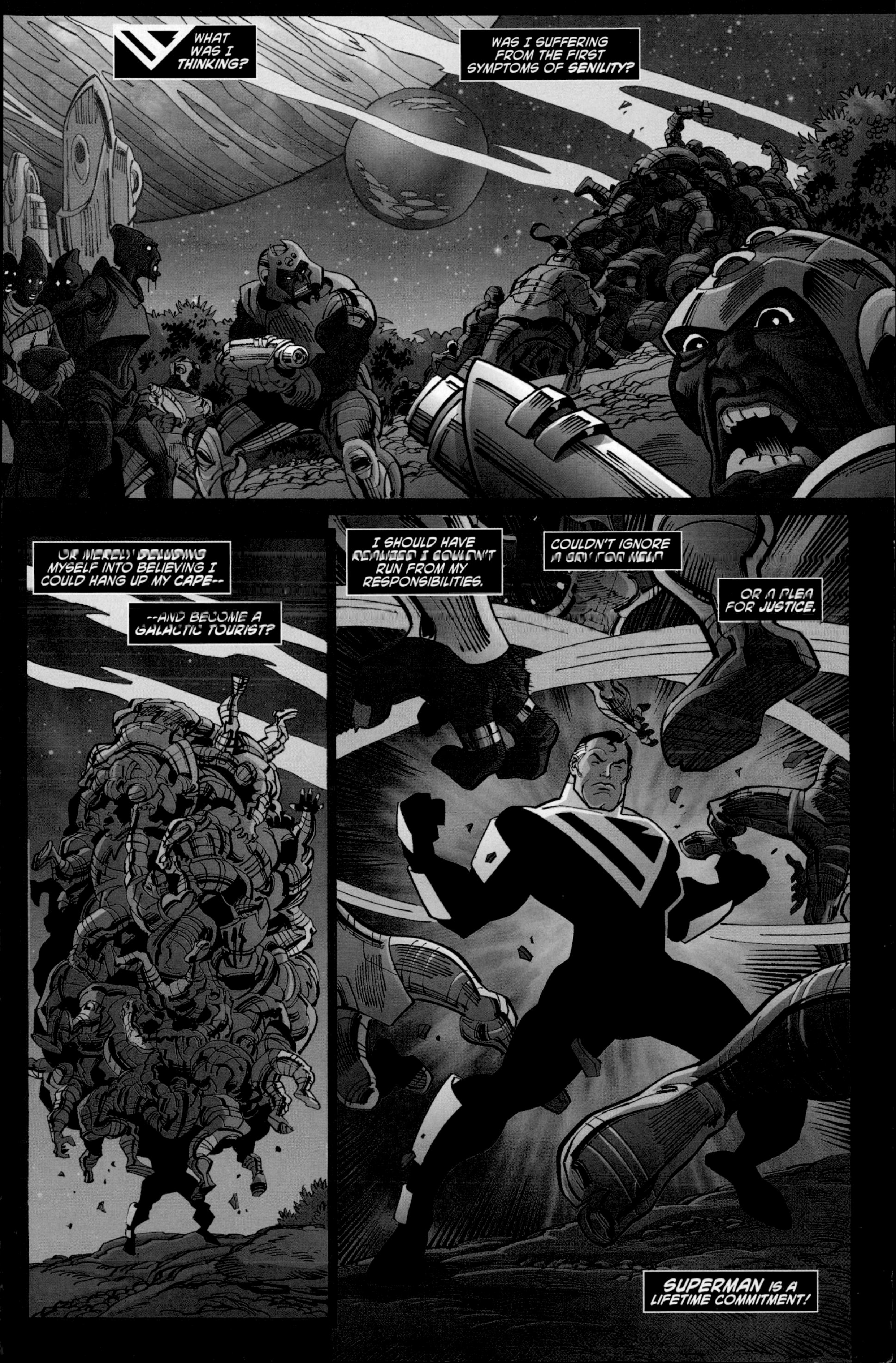
WHAT WAS I THINKING?
WAS I SUFFERING FROM THE FIRST SYMPTOMS OF SENILITY?
MYSELF INTO BELIEVING I COULD HANG UP MY CAPE--
--AND BECOME A GALACTIC TOURIST?
I SHOULD HAVE
RUN FROM MY RESPONSIBILITIES.
COULDN'T IGNORE
OR A PLEA FOR JUSTICE.
SUPERMAN IS A LIFETIME COMMITMENT!

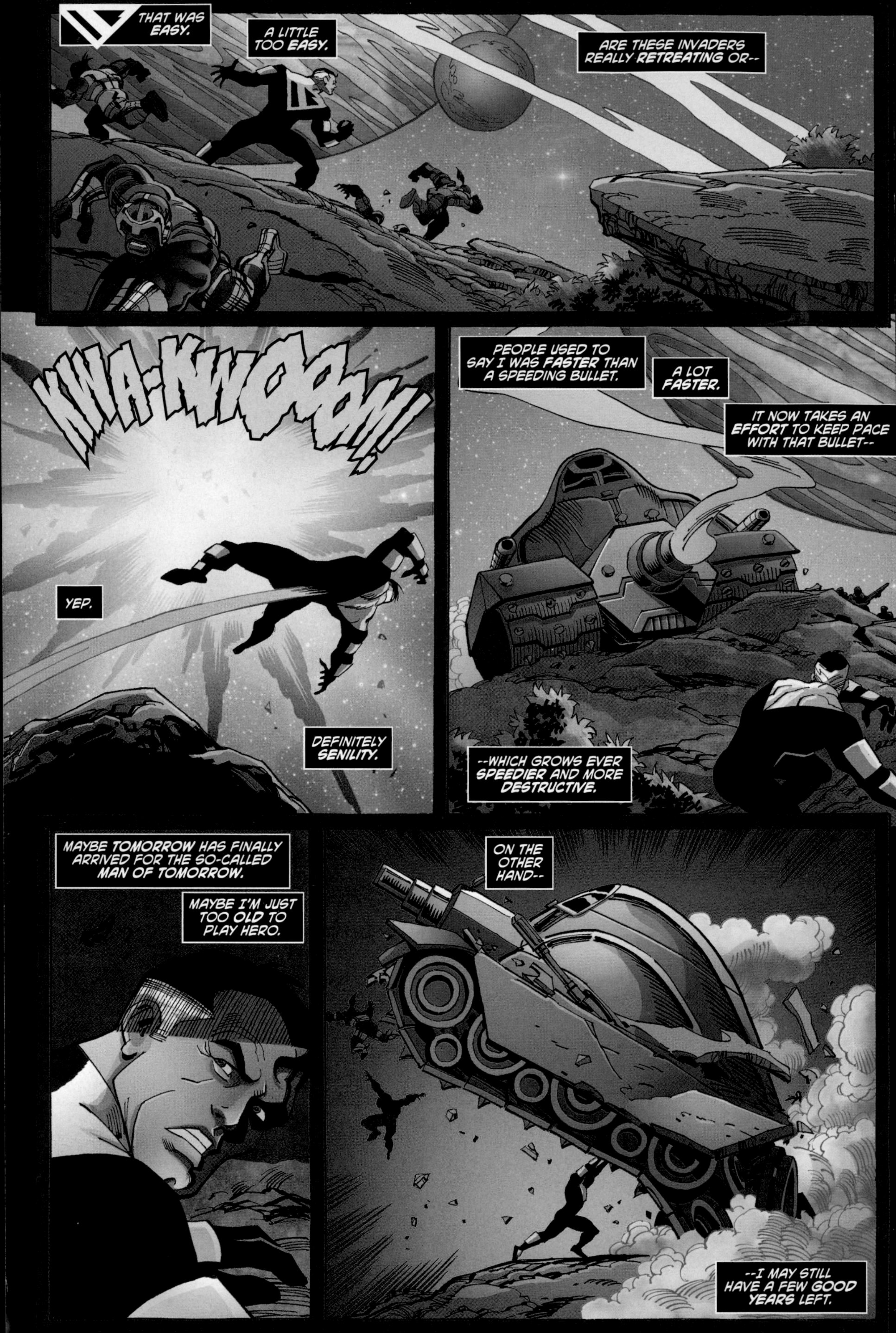
THAT WAS EASY.
A LITTLE TOO EASY.
ARE THESE INVADERS REALLY RETREATING OR--
KWA-KWOOOM!!
YEP.
DEFINITELY SENILITY.
PEOPLE USED TO SAY I WAS FASTER THAN A SPEEDING BULLET.
A LOT FASTER.
IT NOW TAKES AN EFFORT TO KEEP PACE WITH THAT BULLET--
--WHICH GROWS EVER SPEEDIER AND MORE DESTRUCTIVE.
MAYBE TOMORROW HAS FINALLY ARRIVED FOR THE SO-CALLED MAN OF TOMORROW.
MAYBE I'M JUST TOO OLD TO PLAY HERO.
ON THE OTHER HAND--
--I MAY STILL HAVE A FEW GOOD YEARS LEFT.

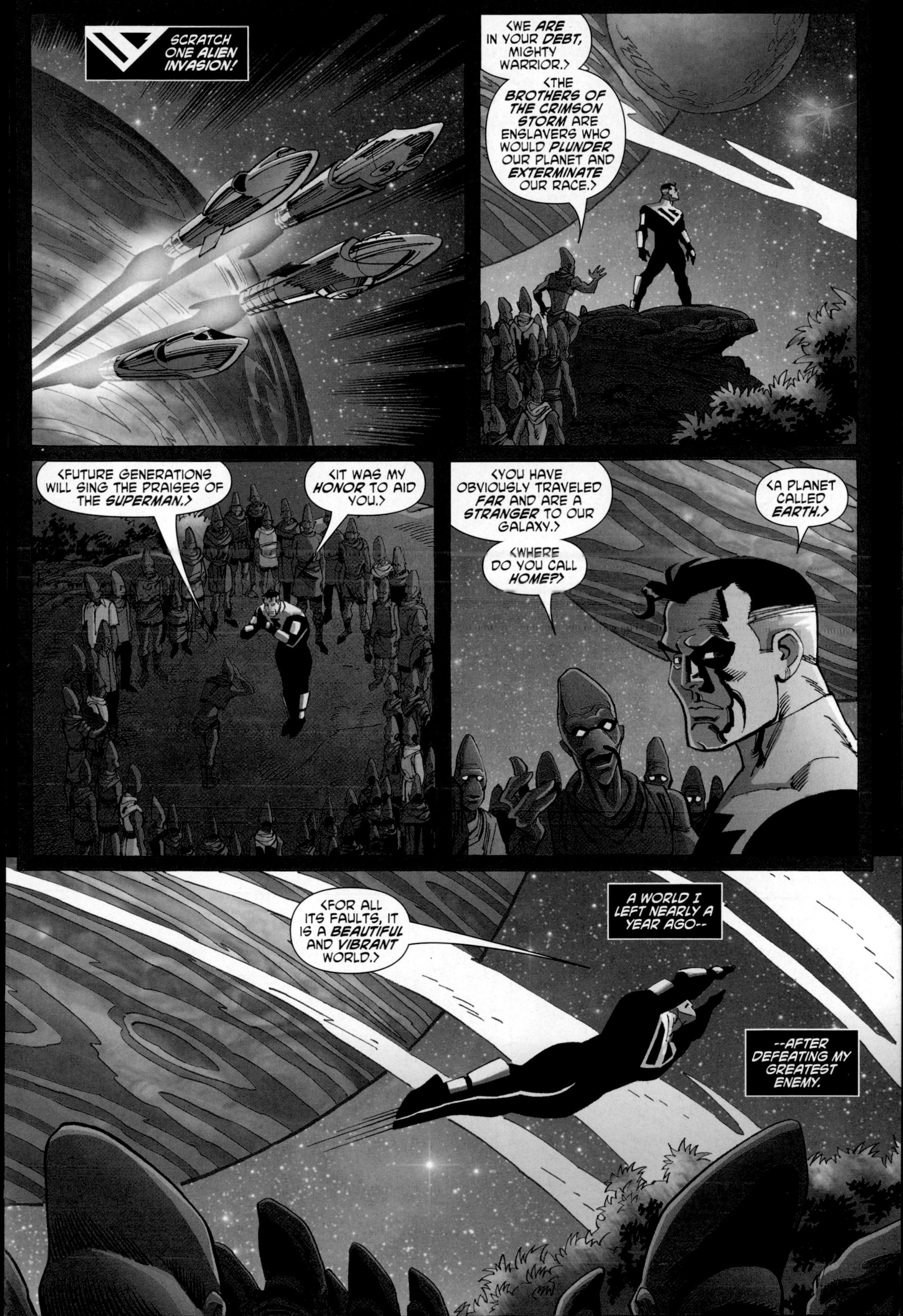
SCRATCH ONE ALIEN INVASION!
<WE ARE IN YOUR DEBT, MIGHTY WARRIOR.>
<THE BROTHERS OF THE CRIMSON STORM ARE ENSLAVERS WHO WOULD PLUNDER OUR PLANET AND EXTERMINATE OUR RACE.>
<FUTURE GENERATIONS WILL SING THE PRAISES OF THE SUPERMAN.>
<IT WAS MY HONOR TO AID YOU.>
<YOU HAVE OBVIOUSLY TRAVELED FAR AND ARE A STRANGER TO OUR GALAXY.>
<WHERE DO YOU CALL HOME?>
<A PLANET CALLED EARTH.>
<FOR ALL ITS FAULTS, IT IS A BEAUTIFUL AND VIBRANT WORLD.>
A WORLD I LEFT NEARLY A YEAR AGO--
--AFTER DEFEATING MY GREATEST ENEMY.

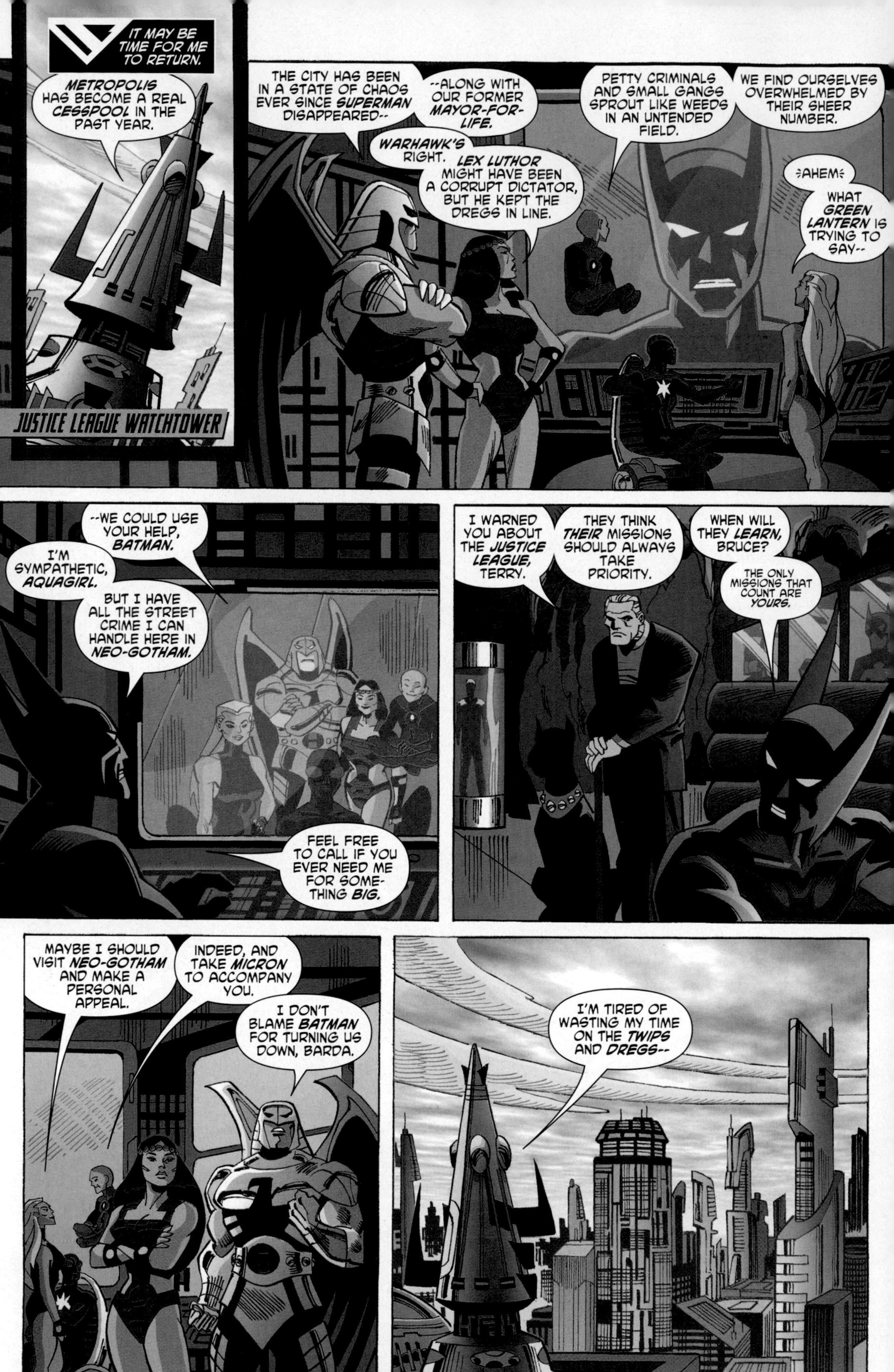
IT MAY BE TIME FOR ME TO RETURN.
METROPOLIS HAS BECOME A REAL CESSPOOL IN THE PAST YEAR.
JUSTICE LEAGUE WATCHTOWER
THE CITY HAS BEEN IN A STATE OF CHAOS EVER SINCE SUPERMAN DISAPPEARED--
--ALONG WITH OUR FORMER MAYOR-FOR-LIFE.
WARHAWK'S RIGHT.
LEX LUTHOR MIGHT HAVE BEEN A CORRUPT DICTATOR, BUT HE KEPT THE DREGS IN LINE.
PETTY CRIMINALS AND SMALL GANGS SPROUT LIKE WEEDS IN AN UNTENDED FIELD.
WE FIND OURSELVES OVERWHELMED BY THEIR SHEER NUMBER.
AHEM
WHAT GREEN LANTERN IS TRYING TO SAY--
--WE COULD USE YOUR HELP, BATMAN.
I'M SYMPATHETIC, AQUAGIRL.
BUT I HAVE ALL THE STREET CRIME I CAN HANDLE HERE IN NEO-GOTHAM.
FEEL FREE TO CALL IF YOU EVER NEED ME FOR SOME-THING BIG.
I WARNED YOU ABOUT THE JUSTICE LEAGUE, TERRY.
THEY THINK THEIR MISSIONS SHOULD ALWAYS TAKE PRIORITY.
WHEN WILL THEY LEARN, BRUCE?
THE ONLY MISSIONS THAT COUNT ARE YOURS.
MAYBE I SHOULD VISIT NEO-GOTHAM AND MAKE A PERSONAL APPEAL.
INDEED, AND TAKE MICRON TO ACCOMPANY YOU.
I DON'T BLAME BATMAN FOR TURNING US DOWN, BARDA.
I'M TIRED OF WASTING MY TIME ON THE TWIPS AND DREGS--

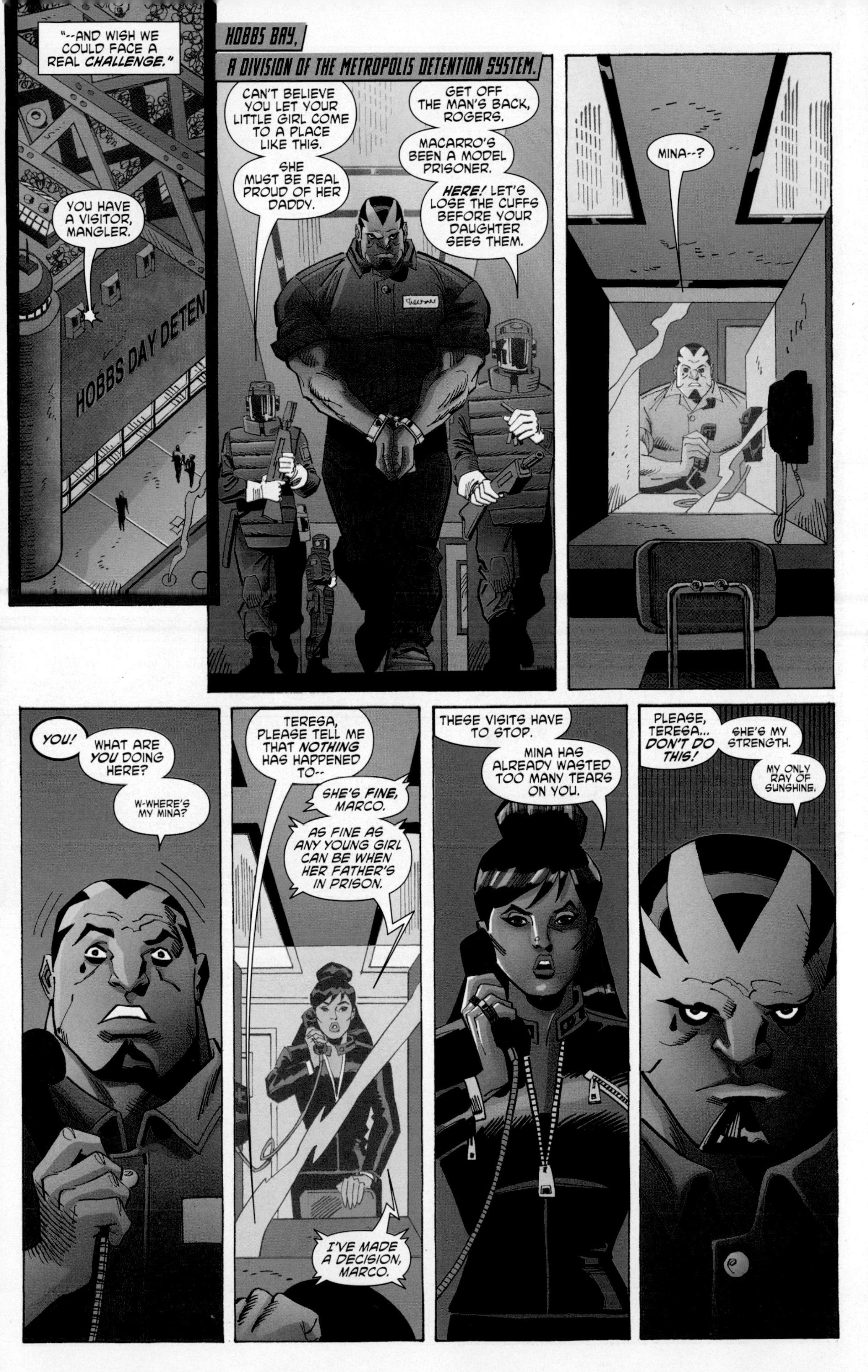
"--AND WISH WE COULD FACE A REAL CHALLENGE."
YOU HAVE A VISITOR, MANGLER.
HOBBS DAY DETEN
HOBBS BAY, A DIVISION OF THE METROPOLIS DETENTION SYSTEM.
CAN'T BELIEVE YOU LET YOUR LITTLE GIRL COME TO A PLACE LIKE THIS.
SHE MUST BE REAL PROUD OF HER DADDY.
GET OFF THE MAN'S BACK, ROGERS.
MACARRO'S BEEN A MODEL PRISONER.
HERE! LET'S LOSE THE CUFFS BEFORE YOUR DAUGHTER SEES THEM.
MINA--?
YOU!
WHAT ARE YOU DOING HERE?
W-WHERE'S MY MINA?
TERESA, PLEASE TELL ME THAT NOTHING HAS HAPPENED TO--
SHE'S FINE, MARCO.
AS FINE AS ANY YOUNG GIRL CAN BE WHEN HER FATHER'S IN PRISON.
I'VE MADE A DECISION, MARCO.
THESE VISITS HAVE TO STOP.
MINA HAS ALREADY WASTED TOO MANY TEARS ON YOU.
PLEASE, TERESA... DON'T DO THIS!
SHE'S MY STRENGTH.
MY ONLY RAY OF SUNSHINE.

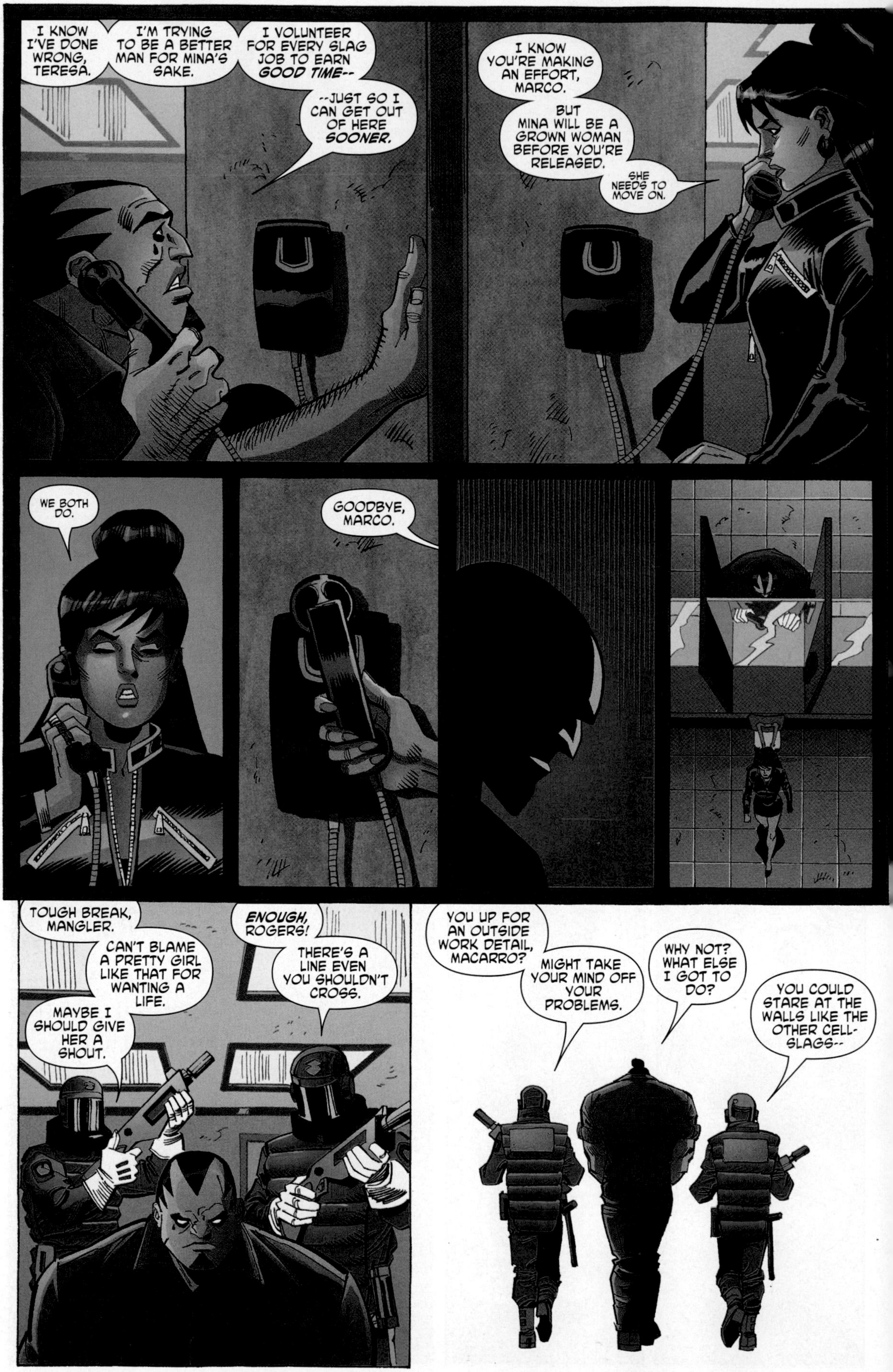
I KNOW I'VE DONE WRONG, TERESA.
I'M TRYING TO BE A BETTER MAN FOR MINA'S SAKE.
I VOLUNTEER FOR EVERY SLAG JOB TO EARN *GOOD TIME*--
--JUST SO I CAN GET OUT OF HERE *SOONER.*
I KNOW YOU'RE MAKING AN EFFORT, MARCO.
BUT MINA WILL BE A GROWN WOMAN BEFORE YOU'RE RELEASED.
SHE NEEDS TO MOVE ON.
WE BOTH DO.
GOODBYE, MARCO.
TOUGH BREAK, MANGLER.
CAN'T BLAME A PRETTY GIRL LIKE THAT FOR WANTING A LIFE.
MAYBE I SHOULD GIVE HER A SHOUT.
ENOUGH, ROGERS!
THERE'S A LINE EVEN YOU SHOULDN'T CROSS.
YOU UP FOR AN OUTSIDE WORK DETAIL, MACARRO?
MIGHT TAKE YOUR MIND OFF YOUR PROBLEMS.
WHY NOT? WHAT ELSE I GOT TO DO?
YOU COULD STARE AT THE WALLS LIKE THE OTHER CELL-SLAGS--

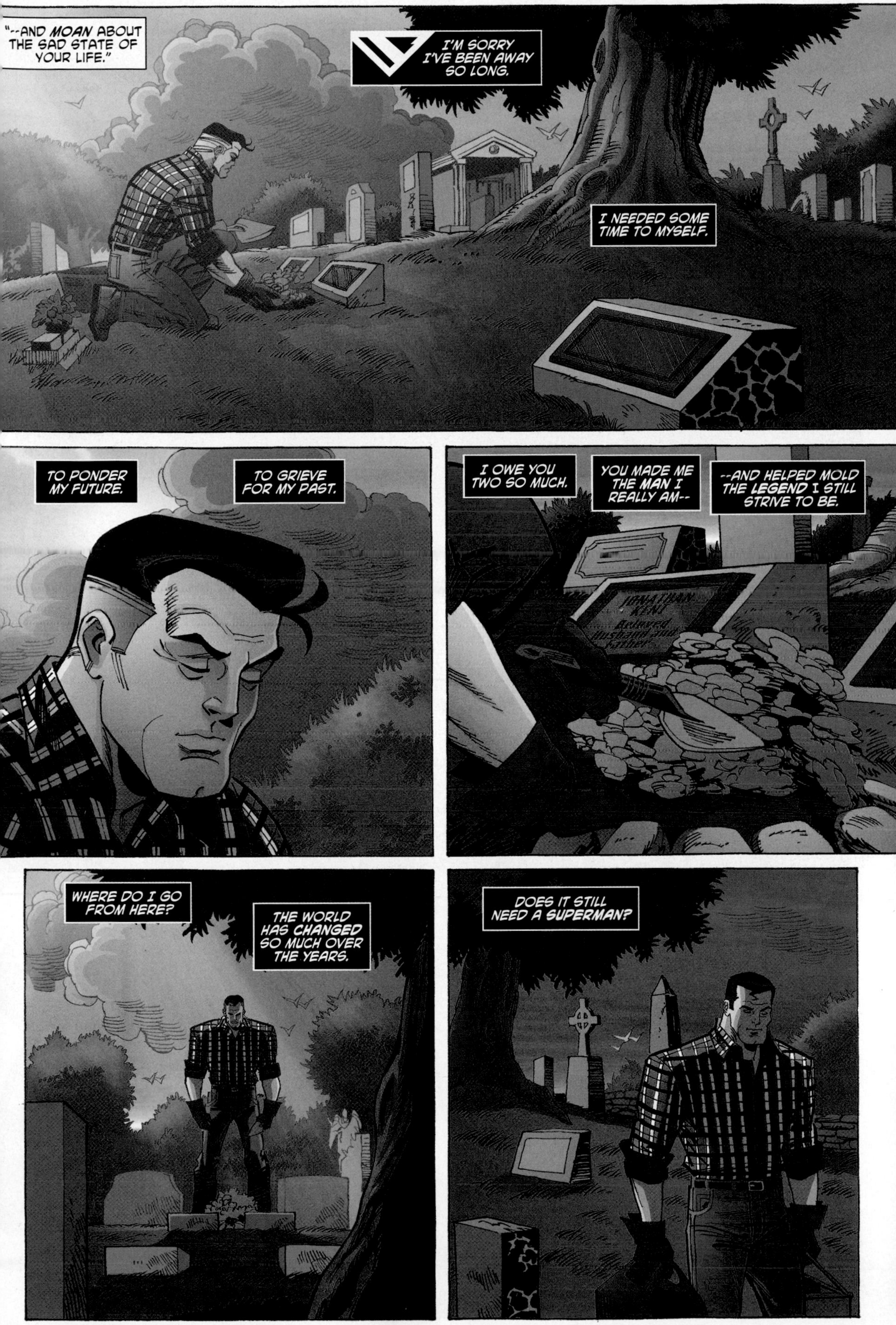
"--AND MOAN ABOUT THE SAD STATE OF YOUR LIFE."
I'M SORRY I'VE BEEN AWAY SO LONG.
I NEEDED SOME TIME TO MYSELF.
TO PONDER MY FUTURE.
TO GRIEVE FOR MY PAST.
I OWE YOU TWO SO MUCH.
YOU MADE ME THE MAN I REALLY AM--
--AND HELPED MOLD THE LEGEND I STILL STRIVE TO BE.
WHERE DO I GO FROM HERE?
THE WORLD HAS CHANGED SO MUCH OVER THE YEARS.
DOES IT STILL NEED A SUPERMAN?

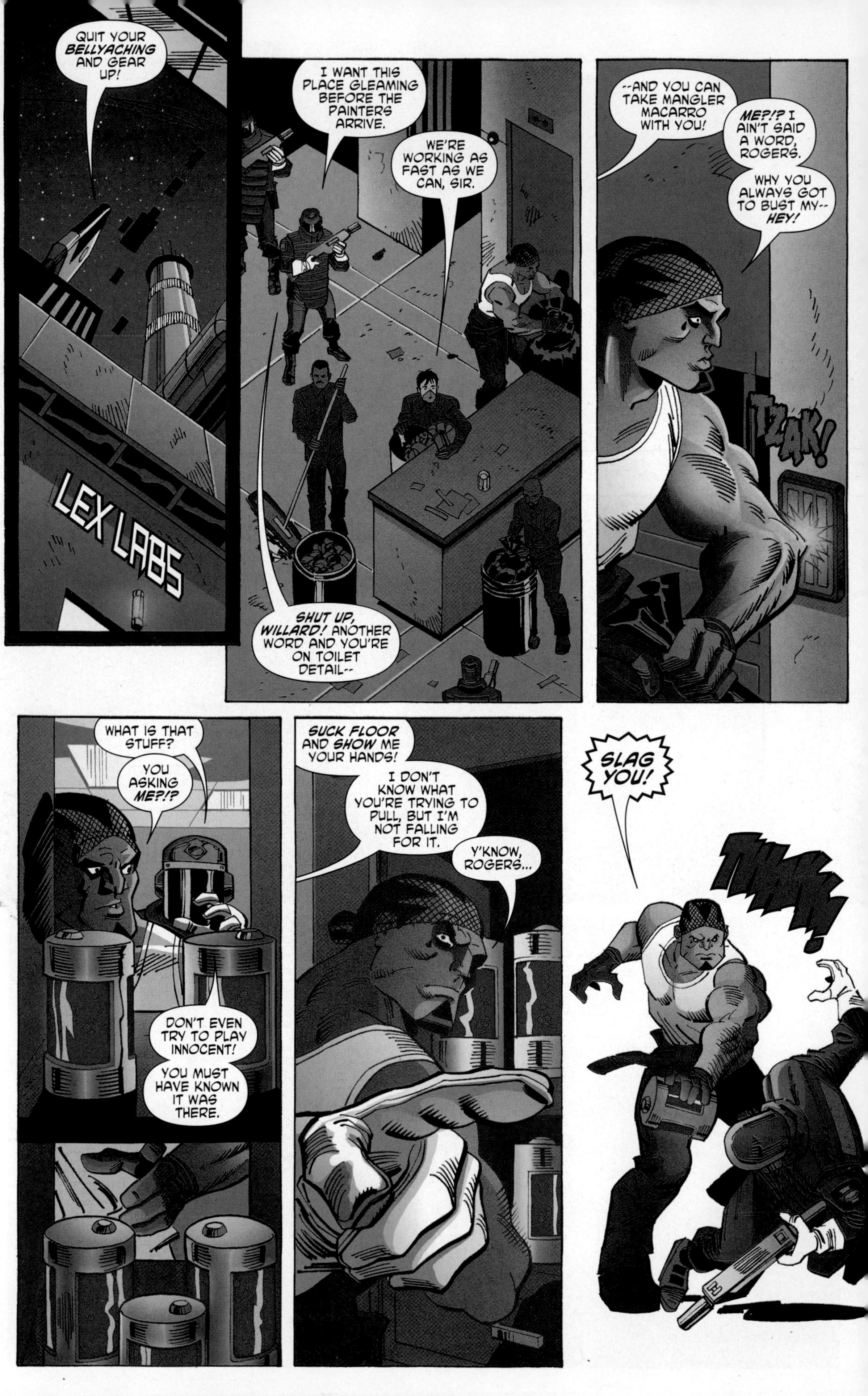
QUIT YOUR BELLYACHING AND GEAR UP!
LEX LABS
I WANT THIS PLACE GLEAMING BEFORE THE PAINTERS ARRIVE.
WE'RE WORKING AS FAST AS WE CAN, SIR.
SHUT UP, WILLARD! ANOTHER WORD AND YOU'RE ON TOILET DETAIL--
--AND YOU CAN TAKE MANGLER MACARRO WITH YOU!
ME?!? I AIN'T SAID A WORD, ROGERS.
WHY YOU ALWAYS GOT TO BUST MY-- HEY!
TZAK!
WHAT IS THAT STUFF?
YOU ASKING ME?!?
DON'T EVEN TRY TO PLAY INNOCENT!
YOU MUST HAVE KNOWN IT WAS THERE.
SUCK FLOOR AND SHOW ME YOUR HANDS!
I DON'T KNOW WHAT YOU'RE TRYING TO PULL, BUT I'M NOT FALLING FOR IT.
Y'KNOW, ROGERS...
SLAG YOU!

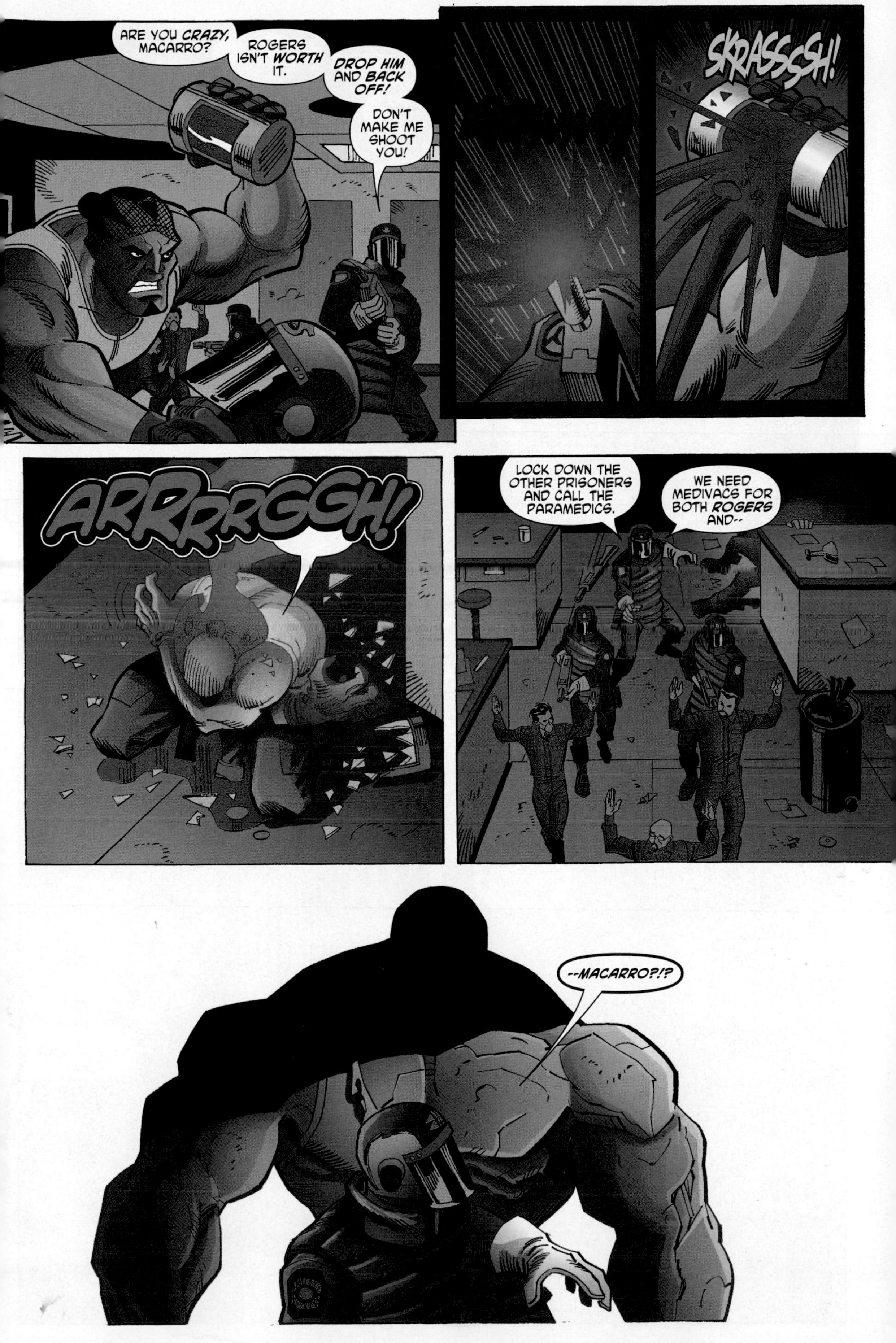
ARE YOU CRAZY, MACARRO?
ROGERS ISN'T WORTH IT.
DROP HIM AND BACK OFF!
DON'T MAKE ME SHOOT YOU!
SKRASSSSH!
ARRRRRGGH!
LOCK DOWN THE OTHER PRISONERS AND CALL THE PARAMEDICS.
WE NEED MEDIVACS FOR BOTH ROGERS AND--
--MACARRO?!?

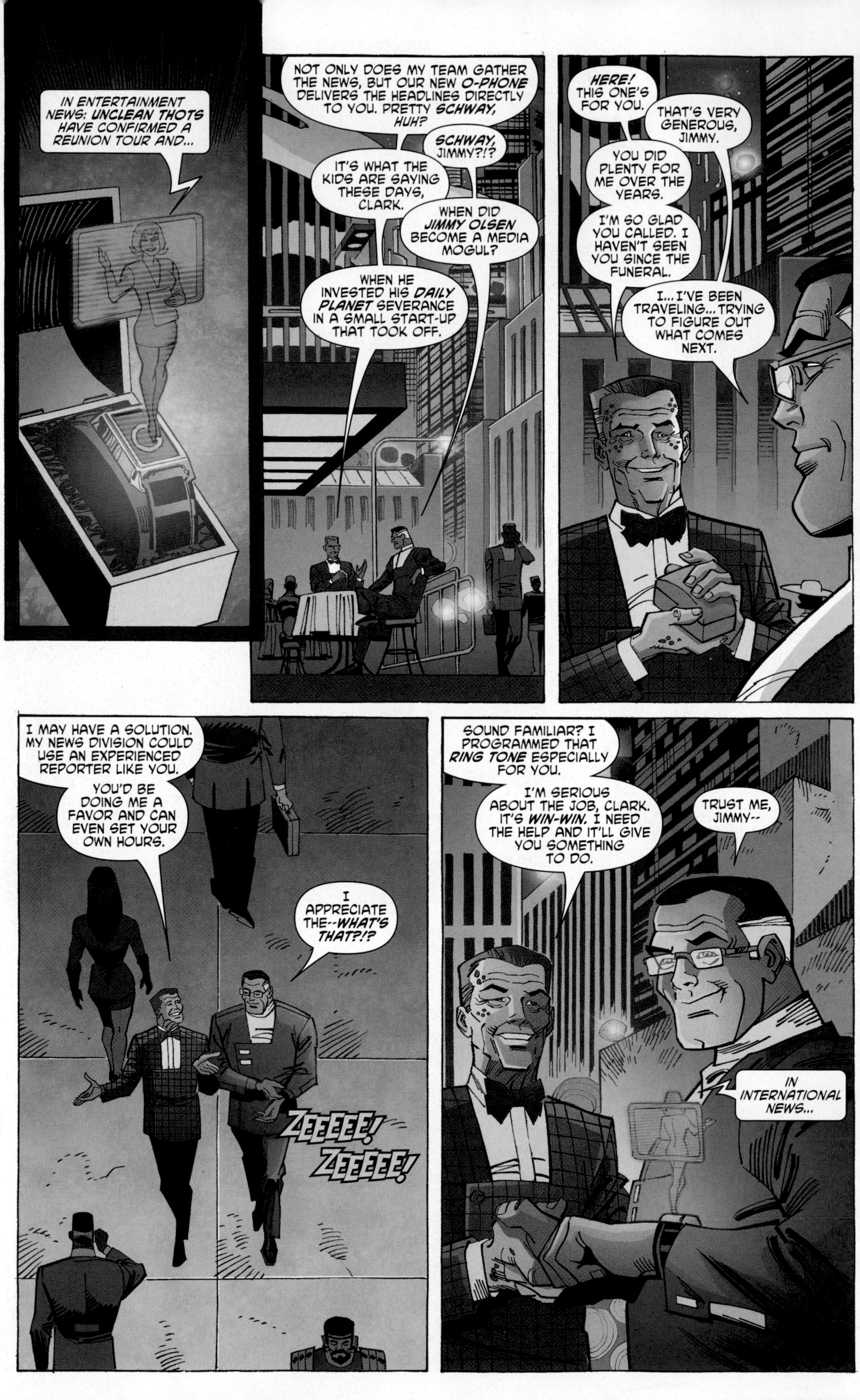
IN ENTERTAINMENT NEWS: UNCLEAN THOTS HAVE CONFIRMED A REUNION TOUR AND...
NOT ONLY DOES MY TEAM GATHER THE NEWS, BUT OUR NEW O-PHONE DELIVERS THE HEADLINES DIRECTLY TO YOU. PRETTY SCHWAY, HUH?
SCHWAY, JIMMY?!?
IT'S WHAT THE KIDS ARE SAYING THESE DAYS, CLARK.
WHEN DID JIMMY OLSEN BECOME A MEDIA MOGUL?
WHEN HE INVESTED HIS DAILY PLANET SEVERANCE IN A SMALL START-UP THAT TOOK OFF.
HERE! THIS ONE'S FOR YOU.
THAT'S VERY GENEROUS, JIMMY.
YOU DID PLENTY FOR ME OVER THE YEARS.
I'M SO GLAD YOU CALLED. I HAVEN'T SEEN YOU SINCE THE FUNERAL.
I...I'VE BEEN TRAVELING...TRYING TO FIGURE OUT WHAT COMES NEXT.
I MAY HAVE A SOLUTION. MY NEWS DIVISION COULD USE AN EXPERIENCED REPORTER LIKE YOU.
YOU'D BE DOING ME A FAVOR AND CAN EVEN SET YOUR OWN HOURS.
I APPRECIATE THE--WHAT'S THAT?!?
ZEEEEE! ZEEEEE!
SOUND FAMILIAR? I PROGRAMMED THAT RING TONE ESPECIALLY FOR YOU.
I'M SERIOUS ABOUT THE JOB, CLARK. IT'S WIN-WIN. I NEED THE HELP AND IT'LL GIVE YOU SOMETHING TO DO.
TRUST ME, JIMMY--
IN INTERNATIONAL NEWS...

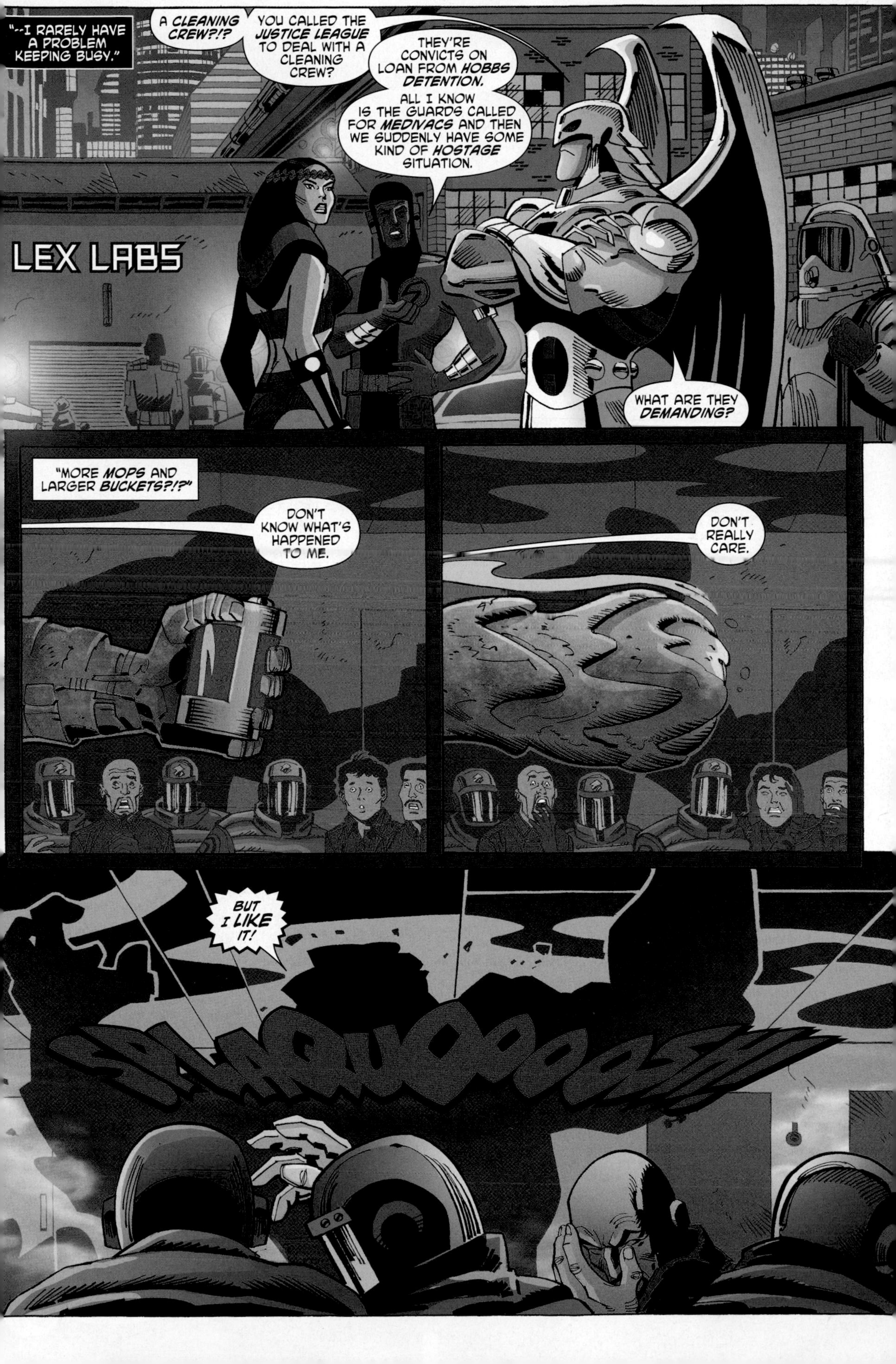
"--I RARELY HAVE A PROBLEM KEEPING BUSY."
A CLEANING CREW?!?
YOU CALLED THE JUSTICE LEAGUE TO DEAL WITH A CLEANING CREW?
THEY'RE CONVICTS ON LOAN FROM HOBBS DETENTION.
ALL I KNOW IS THE GUARDS CALLED FOR MEDIVACS AND THEN WE SUDDENLY HAVE SOME KIND OF HOSTAGE SITUATION.
LEX LABS
WHAT ARE THEY DEMANDING?
"MORE MOPS AND LARGER BUCKETS?!?"
DON'T KNOW WHAT'S HAPPENED TO ME.
DON'T REALLY CARE.
BUT I LIKE IT!
SPLAQUOOOOSH!!

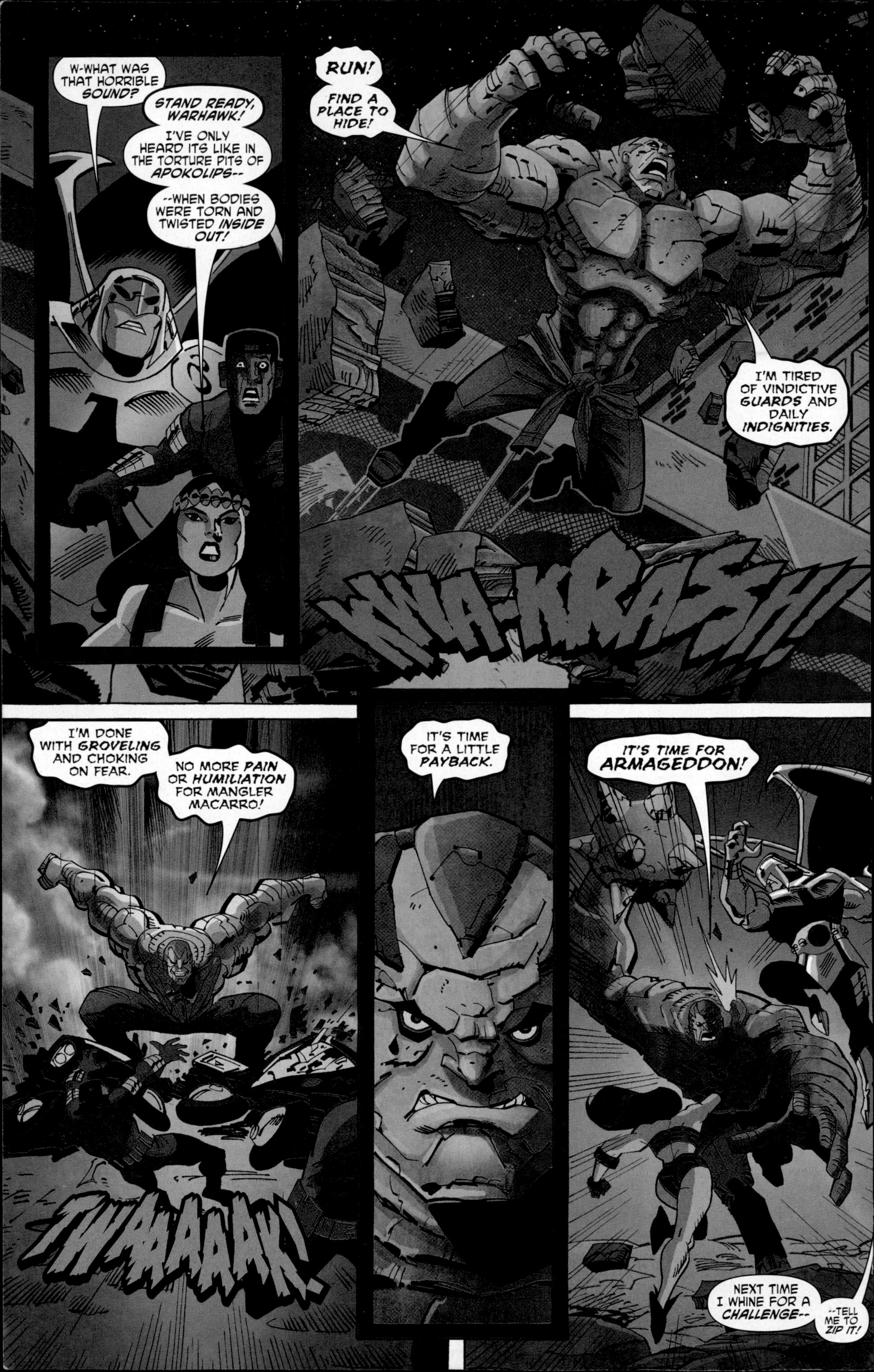
W-WHAT WAS THAT HORRIBLE SOUND?
STAND READY, WARHAWK!
I'VE ONLY HEARD ITS LIKE IN THE TORTURE PITS OF APOKOLIPS--
--WHEN BODIES WERE TORN AND TWISTED INSIDE OUT!
RUN!
FIND A PLACE TO HIDE!
I'M TIRED OF VINDICTIVE GUARDS AND DAILY INDIGNITIES.
KWA-KRASH!!
I'M DONE WITH GROVELING AND CHOKING ON FEAR.
NO MORE PAIN OR HUMILIATION FOR MANGLER MACARRO!
THWAAAAK!
IT'S TIME FOR A LITTLE PAYBACK.
IT'S TIME FOR ARMAGEDDON!
NEXT TIME I WHINE FOR A CHALLENGE--
--TELL ME TO ZIP IT!

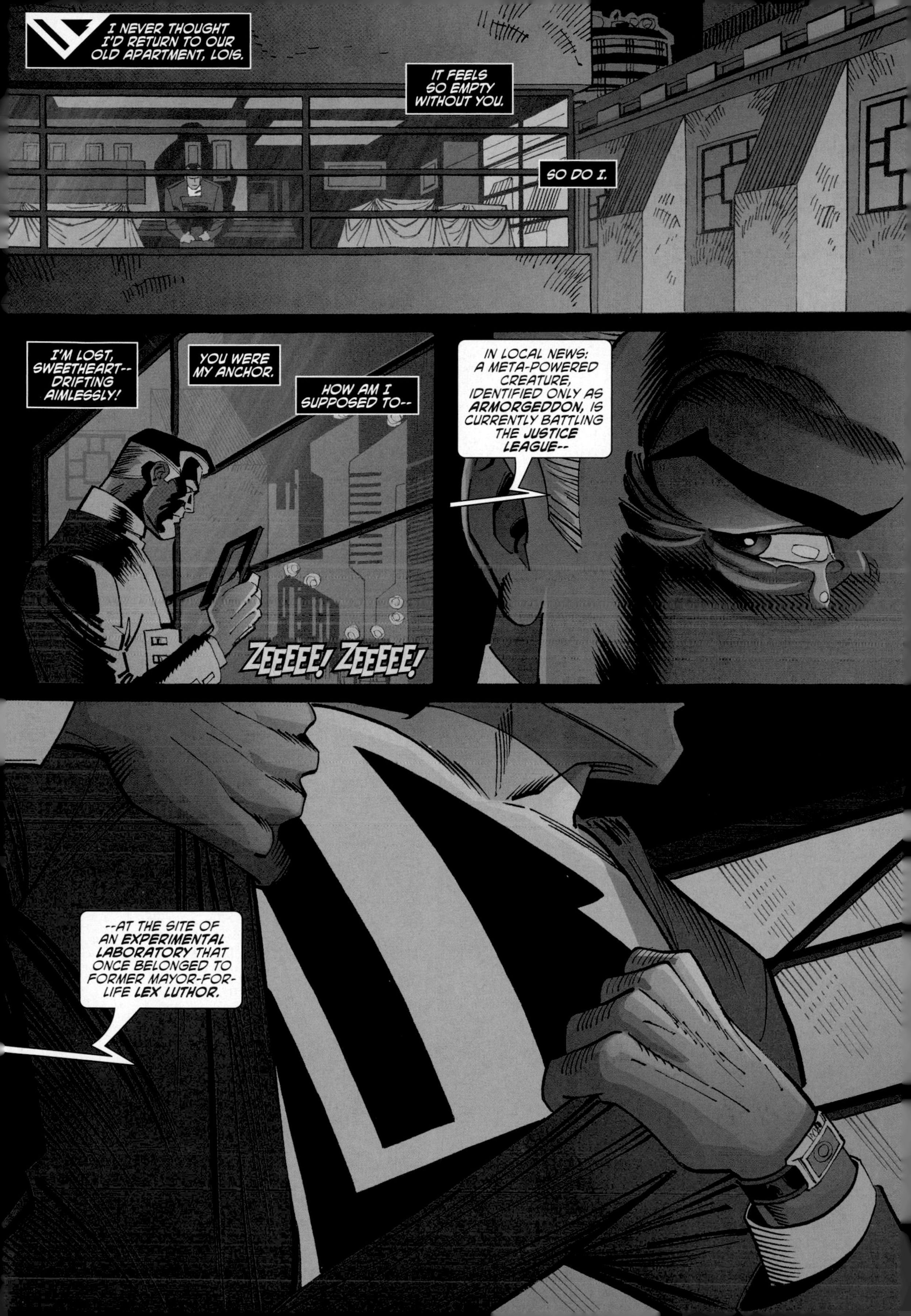
I NEVER THOUGHT I'D RETURN TO OUR OLD APARTMENT, LOIS.
IT FEELS SO EMPTY WITHOUT YOU.
SO DO I.
I'M LOST, SWEETHEART-- DRIFTING AIMLESSLY!
YOU WERE MY ANCHOR.
HOW AM I SUPPOSED TO--
IN LOCAL NEWS: A META-POWERED CREATURE, IDENTIFIED ONLY AS ARMORGEDDON, IS CURRENTLY BATTLING THE JUSTICE LEAGUE--
ZEEEEE! ZEEEEE!
--AT THE SITE OF AN EXPERIMENTAL LABORATORY THAT ONCE BELONGED TO FORMER MAYOR-FOR-LIFE LEX LUTHOR.

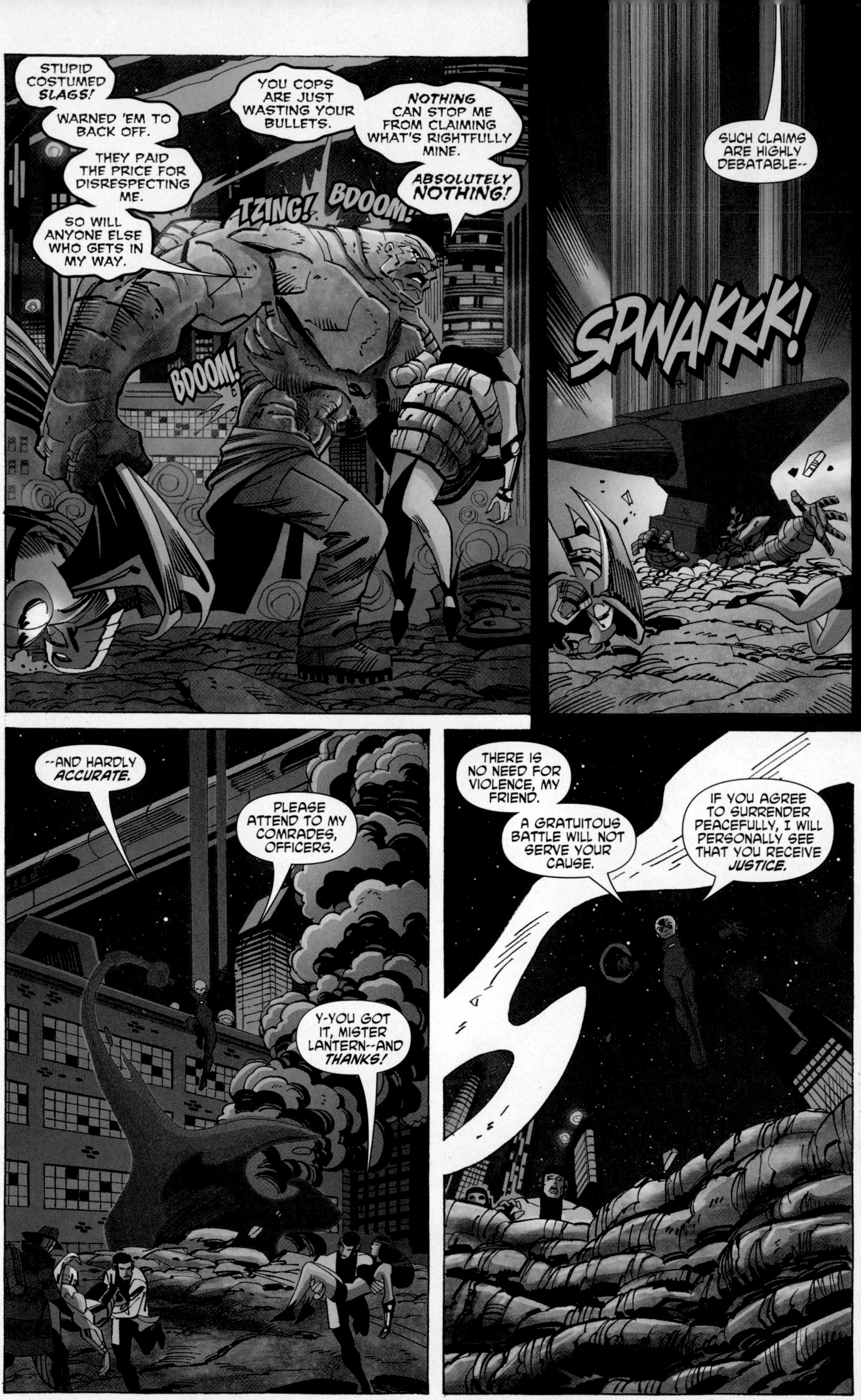
STUPID COSTUMED *SLAGS!*
WARNED 'EM TO BACK OFF.
THEY PAID THE PRICE FOR DISRESPECTING ME.
SO WILL ANYONE ELSE WHO GETS IN MY WAY.
YOU COPS ARE JUST WASTING YOUR BULLETS.
NOTHING CAN STOP ME FROM CLAIMING WHAT'S RIGHTFULLY MINE.
ABSOLUTELY **NOTHING!**
TZING!
BDOOM!
BDOOM!
SUCH CLAIMS ARE HIGHLY DEBATABLE--
SPWAKKK!
--AND HARDLY *ACCURATE.*
PLEASE ATTEND TO MY COMRADES, OFFICERS.
Y-YOU GOT IT, MISTER LANTERN--AND *THANKS!*
THERE IS NO NEED FOR VIOLENCE, MY FRIEND.
A GRATUITOUS BATTLE WILL NOT SERVE YOUR CAUSE.
IF YOU AGREE TO SURRENDER PEACEFULLY, I WILL PERSONALLY SEE THAT YOU RECEIVE *JUSTICE.*

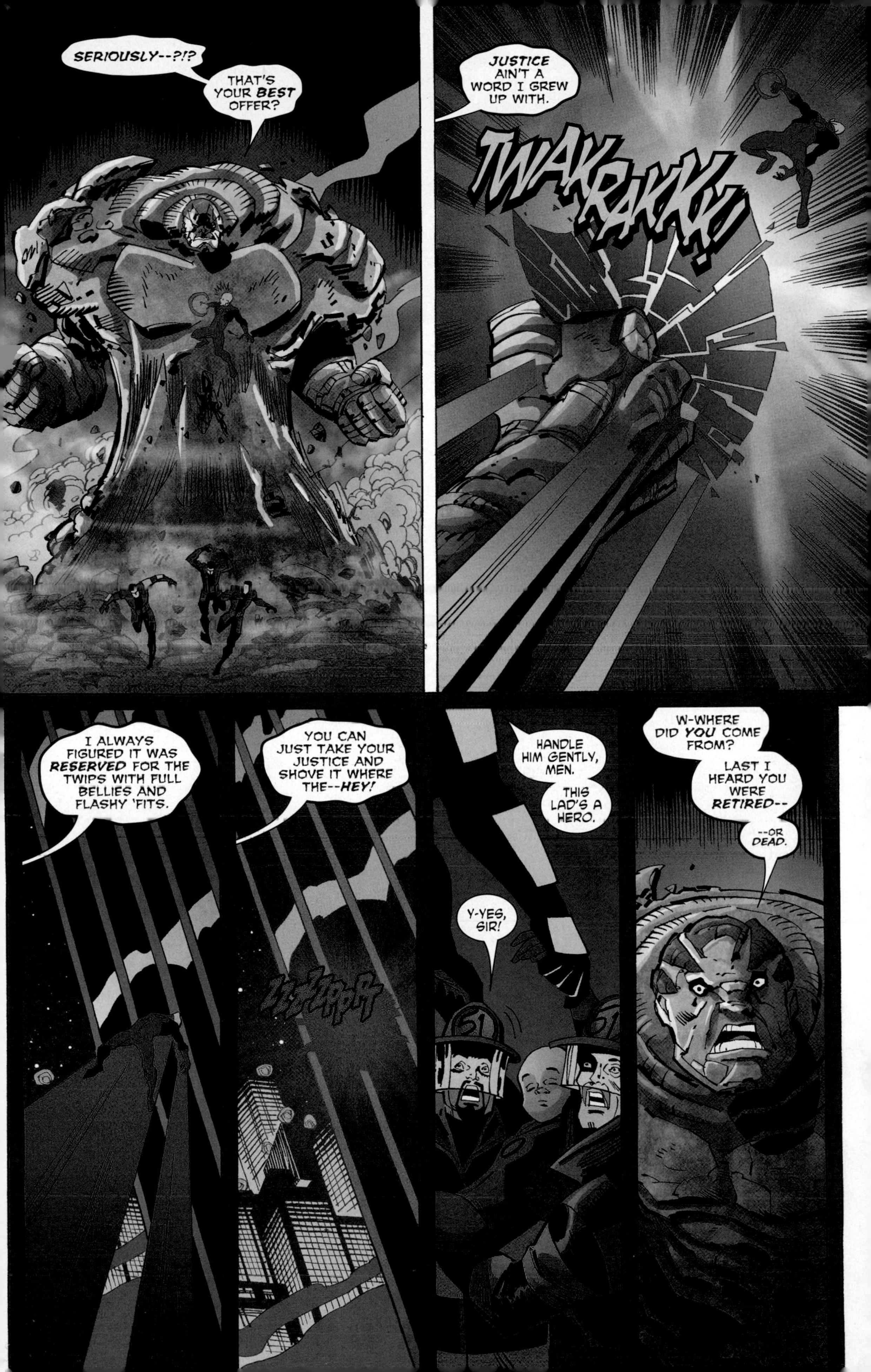
SERIOUSLY--?!?
THAT'S YOUR BEST OFFER?
JUSTICE AIN'T A WORD I GREW UP WITH.
TWAKRAKKK!
I ALWAYS FIGURED IT WAS RESERVED FOR THE TWIPS WITH FULL BELLIES AND FLASHY 'FITS.
YOU CAN JUST TAKE YOUR JUSTICE AND SHOVE IT WHERE THE--HEY!
HANDLE HIM GENTLY, MEN.
THIS LAD'S A HERO.
Y-YES, SIR!
W-WHERE DID YOU COME FROM?
LAST I HEARD YOU WERE RETIRED--
--OR DEAD.

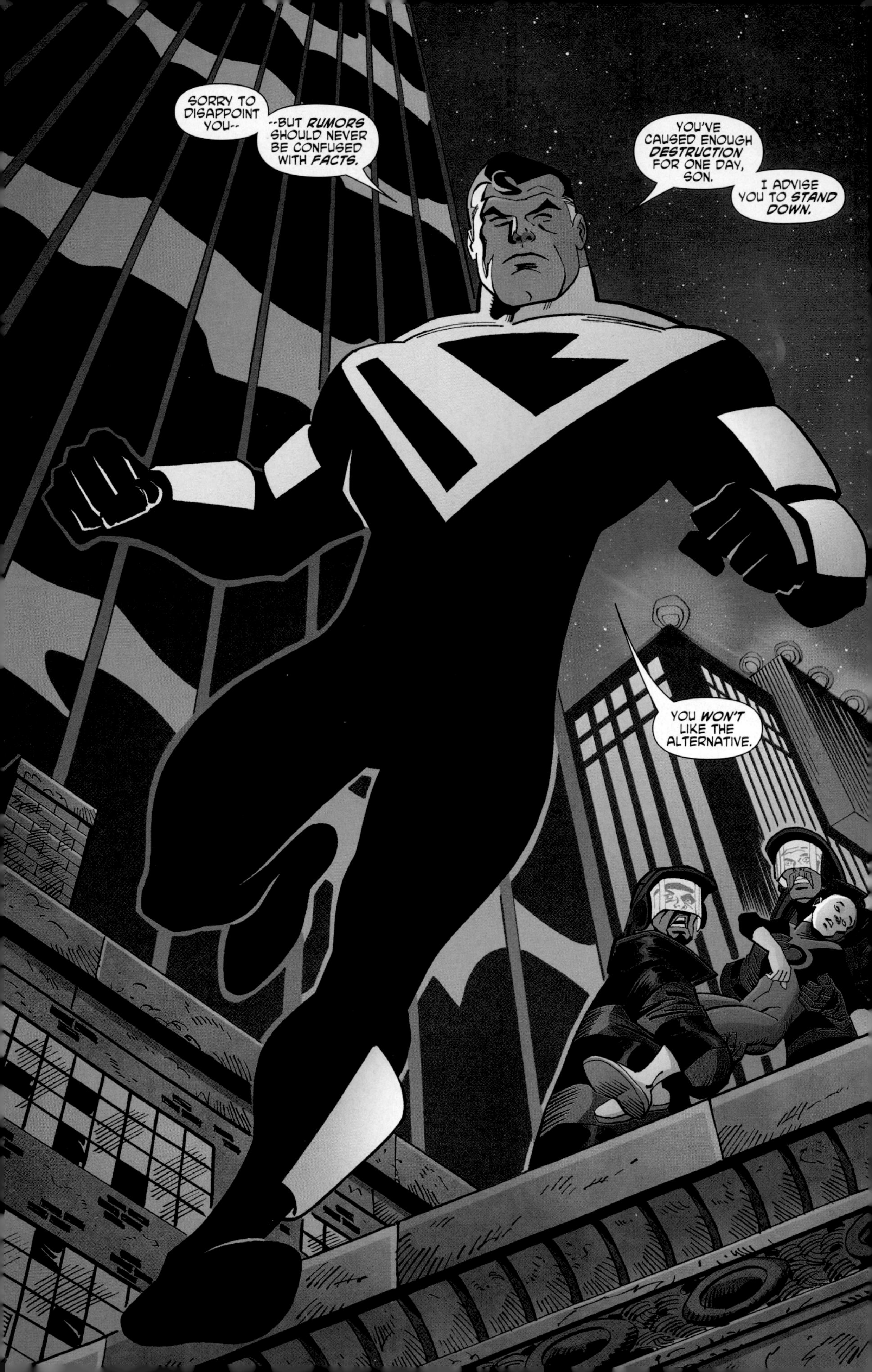
SORRY TO DISAPPOINT YOU--
--BUT RUMORS SHOULD NEVER BE CONFUSED WITH FACTS.
YOU'VE CAUSED ENOUGH DESTRUCTION FOR ONE DAY, SON.
I ADVISE YOU TO STAND DOWN.
YOU WON'T LIKE THE ALTERNATIVE.

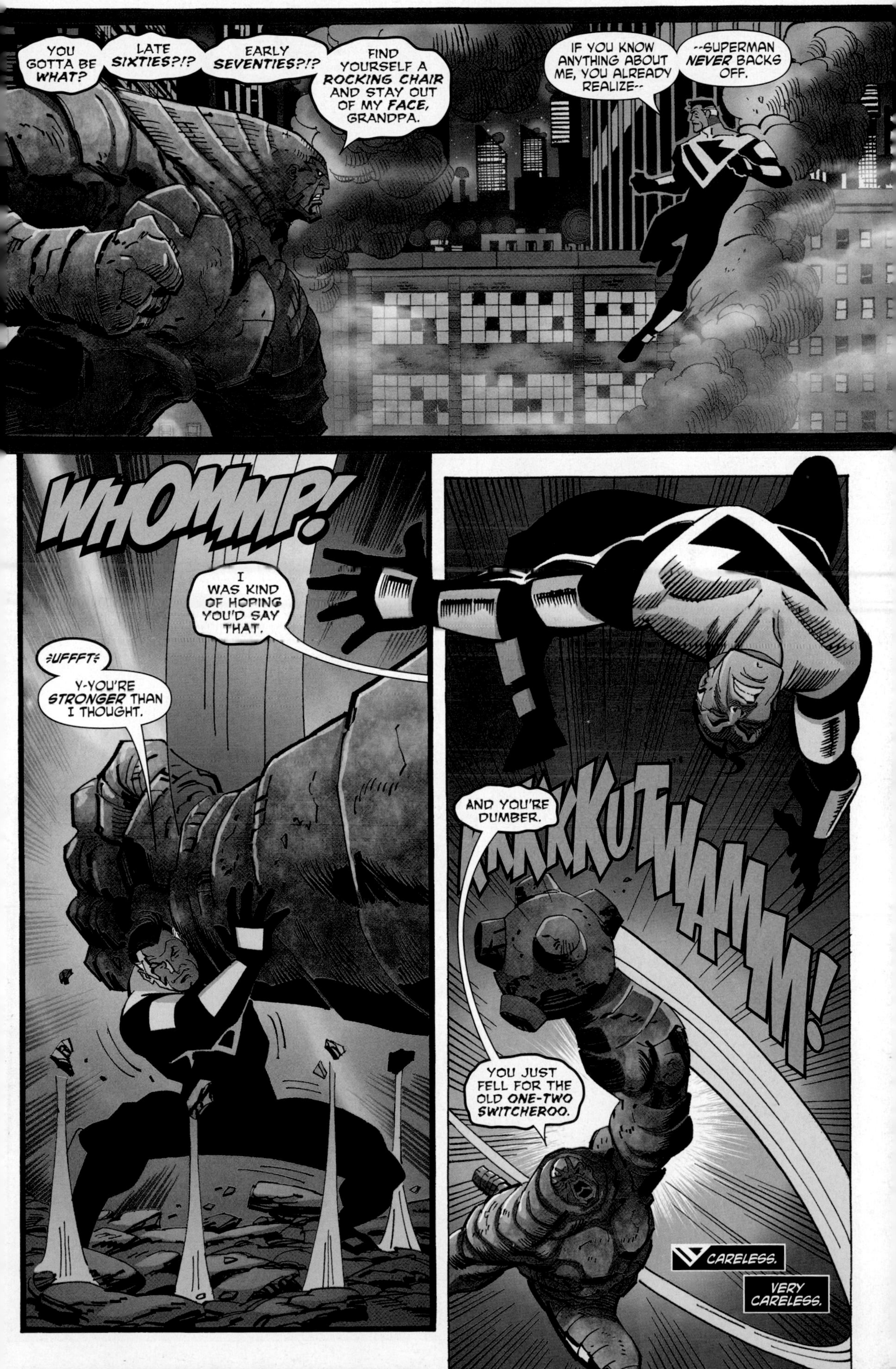
YOU GOTTA BE WHAT?
LATE SIXTIES?!?
EARLY SEVENTIES?!?
FIND YOURSELF A ROCKING CHAIR AND STAY OUT OF MY FACE, GRANDPA.
IF YOU KNOW ANYTHING ABOUT ME, YOU ALREADY REALIZE--
--SUPERMAN NEVER BACKS OFF.
WHOMMP!
I WAS KIND OF HOPING YOU'D SAY THAT.
UFFFT
Y-YOU'RE STRONGER THAN I THOUGHT.
AND YOU'RE DUMBER.
KUTWAMMM!
YOU JUST FELL FOR THE OLD ONE-TWO SWITCHEROO.
CARELESS.
VERY CARELESS.

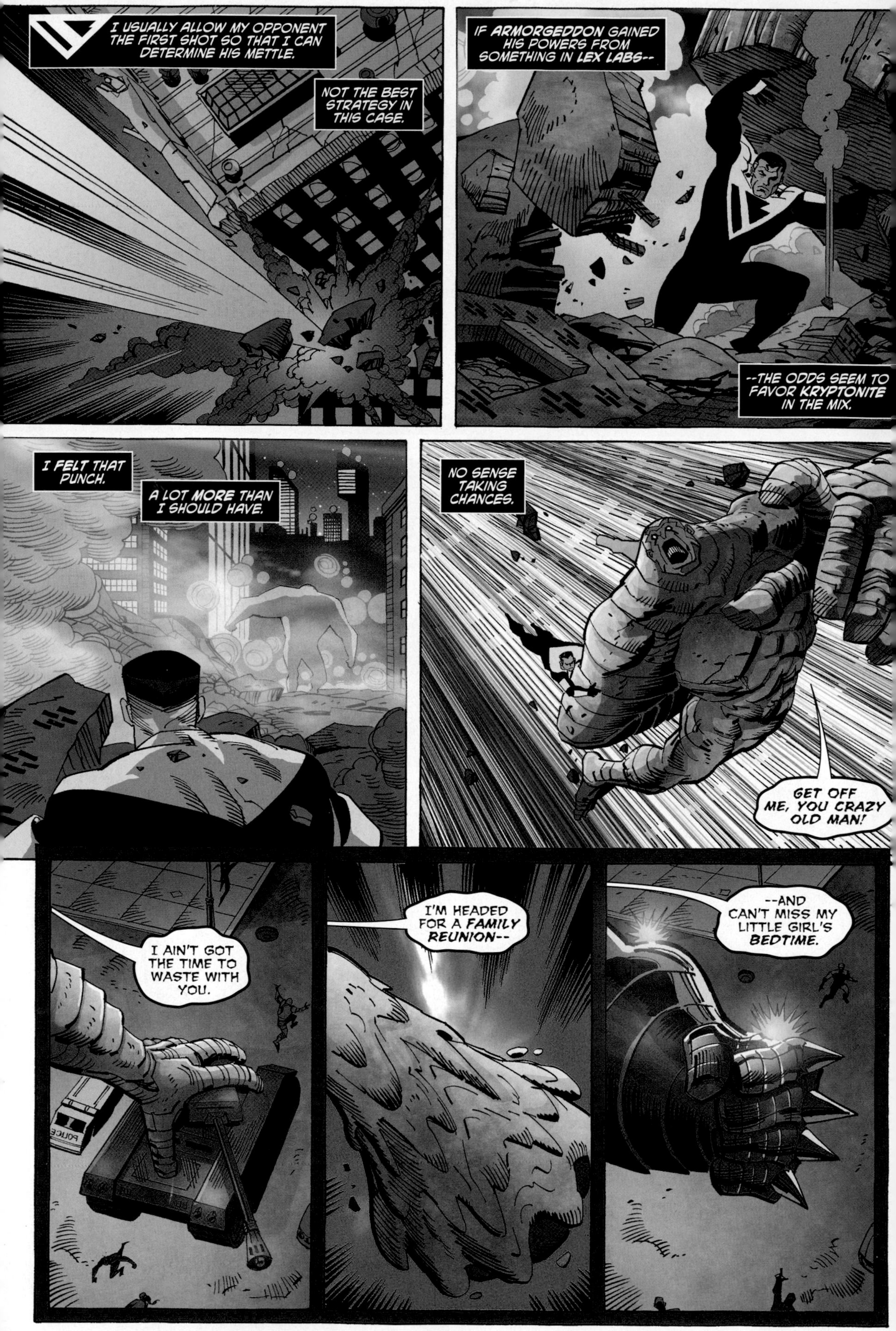
I USUALLY ALLOW MY OPPONENT THE FIRST SHOT SO THAT I CAN DETERMINE HIS METTLE.
NOT THE BEST STRATEGY IN THIS CASE.
IF ARMORGEDDON GAINED HIS POWERS FROM SOMETHING IN LEX LABS--
--THE ODDS SEEM TO FAVOR KRYPTONITE IN THE MIX.
I FELT THAT PUNCH.
A LOT MORE THAN I SHOULD HAVE.
NO SENSE TAKING CHANCES.
GET OFF ME, YOU CRAZY OLD MAN!
I AIN'T GOT THE TIME TO WASTE WITH YOU.
I'M HEADED FOR A FAMILY REUNION--
--AND CAN'T MISS MY LITTLE GIRL'S BEDTIME.
POLICE

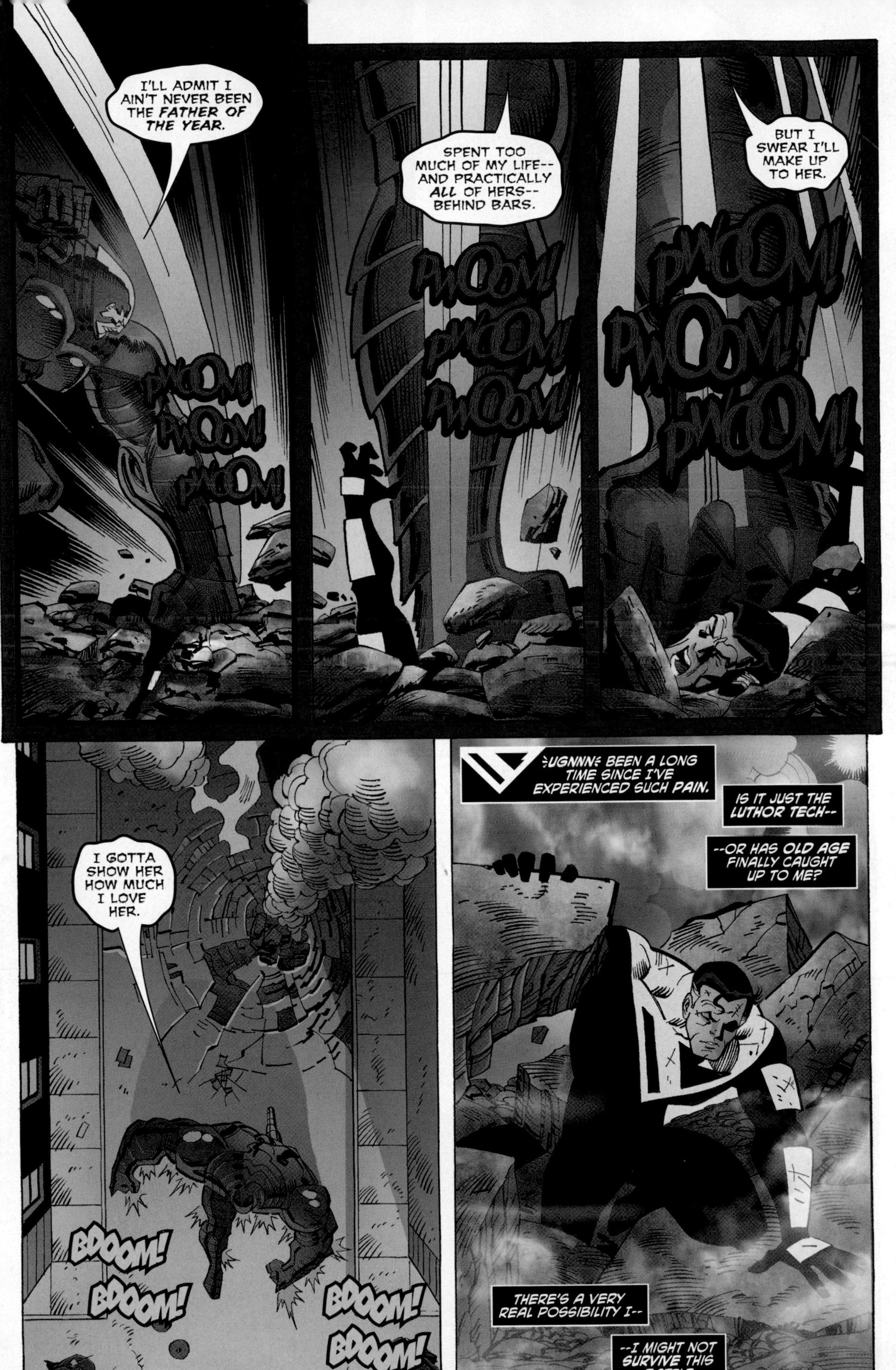
I'LL ADMIT I AIN'T NEVER BEEN THE FATHER OF THE YEAR.
PWOOM! PWOOM! PWOOM!
SPENT TOO MUCH OF MY LIFE-- AND PRACTICALLY ALL OF HERS-- BEHIND BARS.
PWOOM! PWOOM! PWOOM!
BUT I SWEAR I'LL MAKE UP TO HER.
PWOOM! PWOOM! PWOOM!
I GOTTA SHOW HER HOW MUCH I LOVE HER.
BDOOM! BDOOM!
BDOOM! BDOOM!
UGNNN BEEN A LONG TIME SINCE I'VE EXPERIENCED SUCH PAIN.
IS IT JUST THE LUTHOR TECH--
--OR HAS OLD AGE FINALLY CAUGHT UP TO ME?
THERE'S A VERY REAL POSSIBILITY I--
--I MIGHT NOT SURVIVE THIS BATTLE.

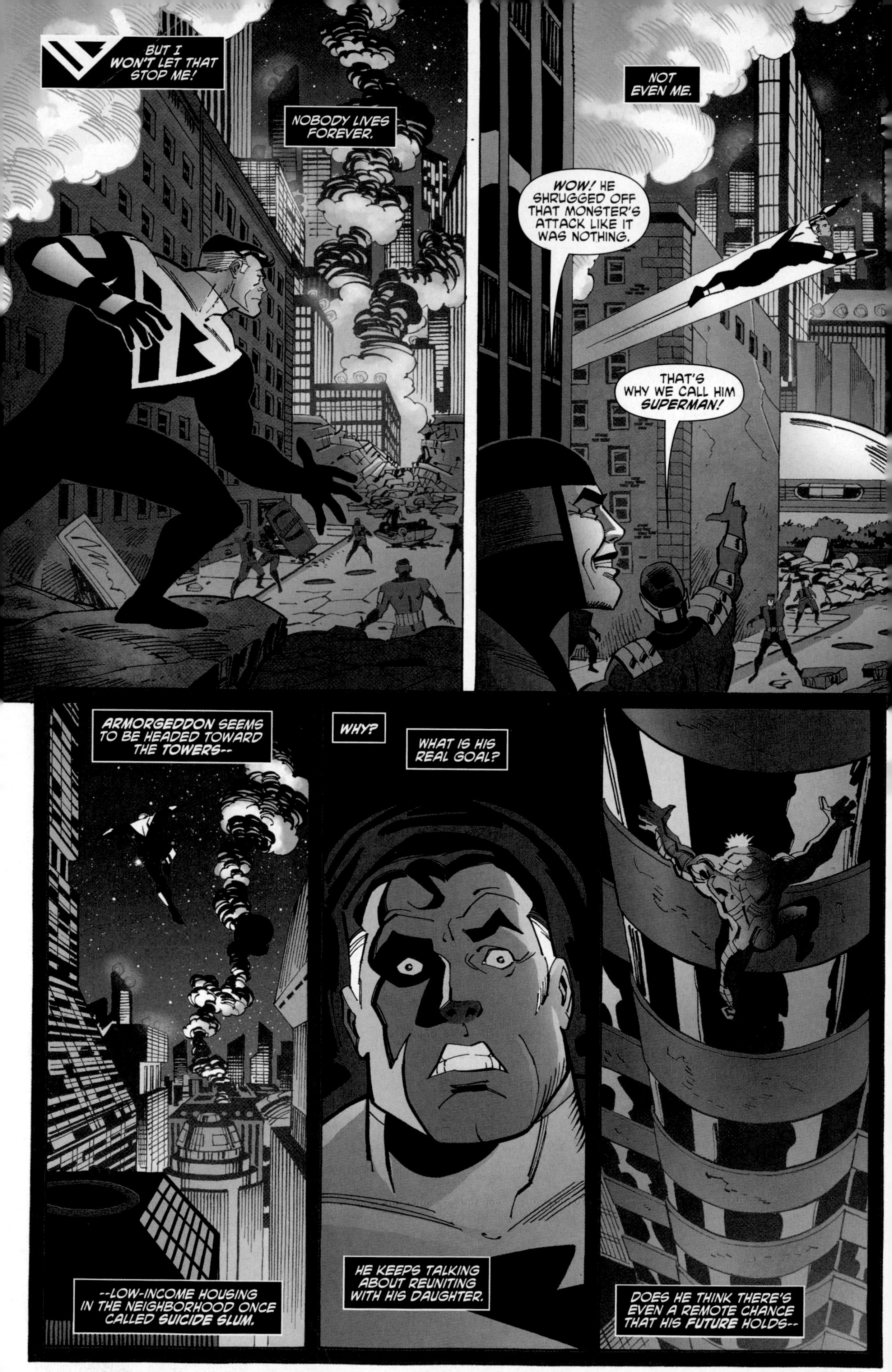
BUT I WON'T LET THAT STOP ME!
NOBODY LIVES FOREVER.
NOT EVEN ME.
WOW! HE SHRUGGED OFF THAT MONSTER'S ATTACK LIKE IT WAS NOTHING.
THAT'S WHY WE CALL HIM SUPERMAN!
ARMORGEDDON SEEMS TO BE HEADED TOWARD THE TOWERS--
--LOW-INCOME HOUSING IN THE NEIGHBORHOOD ONCE CALLED SUICIDE SLUM.
WHY?
WHAT IS HIS REAL GOAL?
HE KEEPS TALKING ABOUT REUNITING WITH HIS DAUGHTER.
DOES HE THINK THERE'S EVEN A REMOTE CHANCE THAT HIS FUTURE HOLDS--

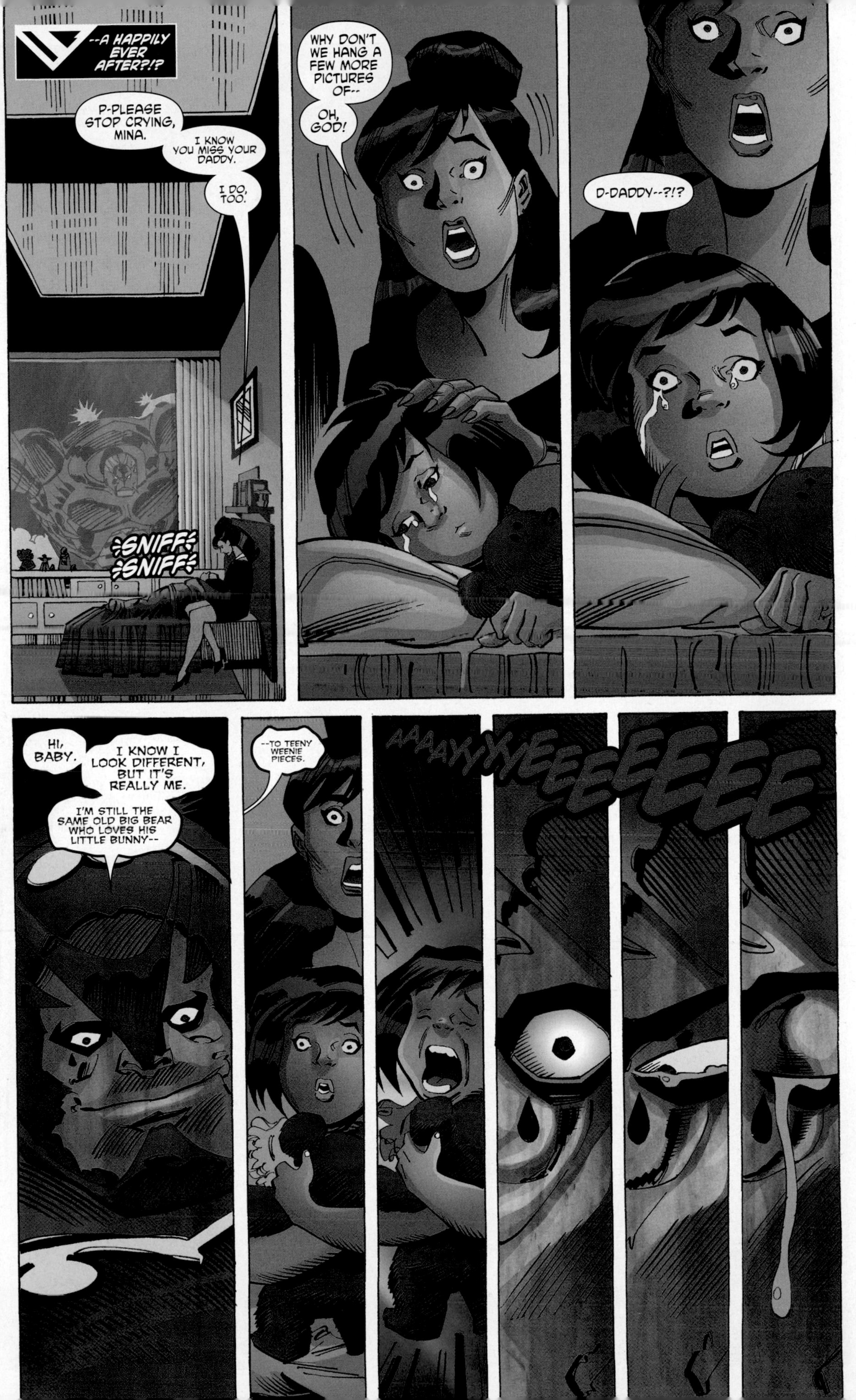
--A HAPPILY EVER AFTER?!?
P-PLEASE STOP CRYING, MINA.
I KNOW YOU MISS YOUR DADDY.
I DO, TOO.
SNIFF SNIFF
WHY DON'T WE HANG A FEW MORE PICTURES OF--
OH, GOD!
D-DADDY--?!?
HI, BABY.
I KNOW I LOOK DIFFERENT, BUT IT'S REALLY ME.
I'M STILL THE SAME OLD BIG BEAR WHO LOVES HIS LITTLE BUNNY--
--TO TEENY WEENIE PIECES.
AAAAYYYEEEEEEEEE

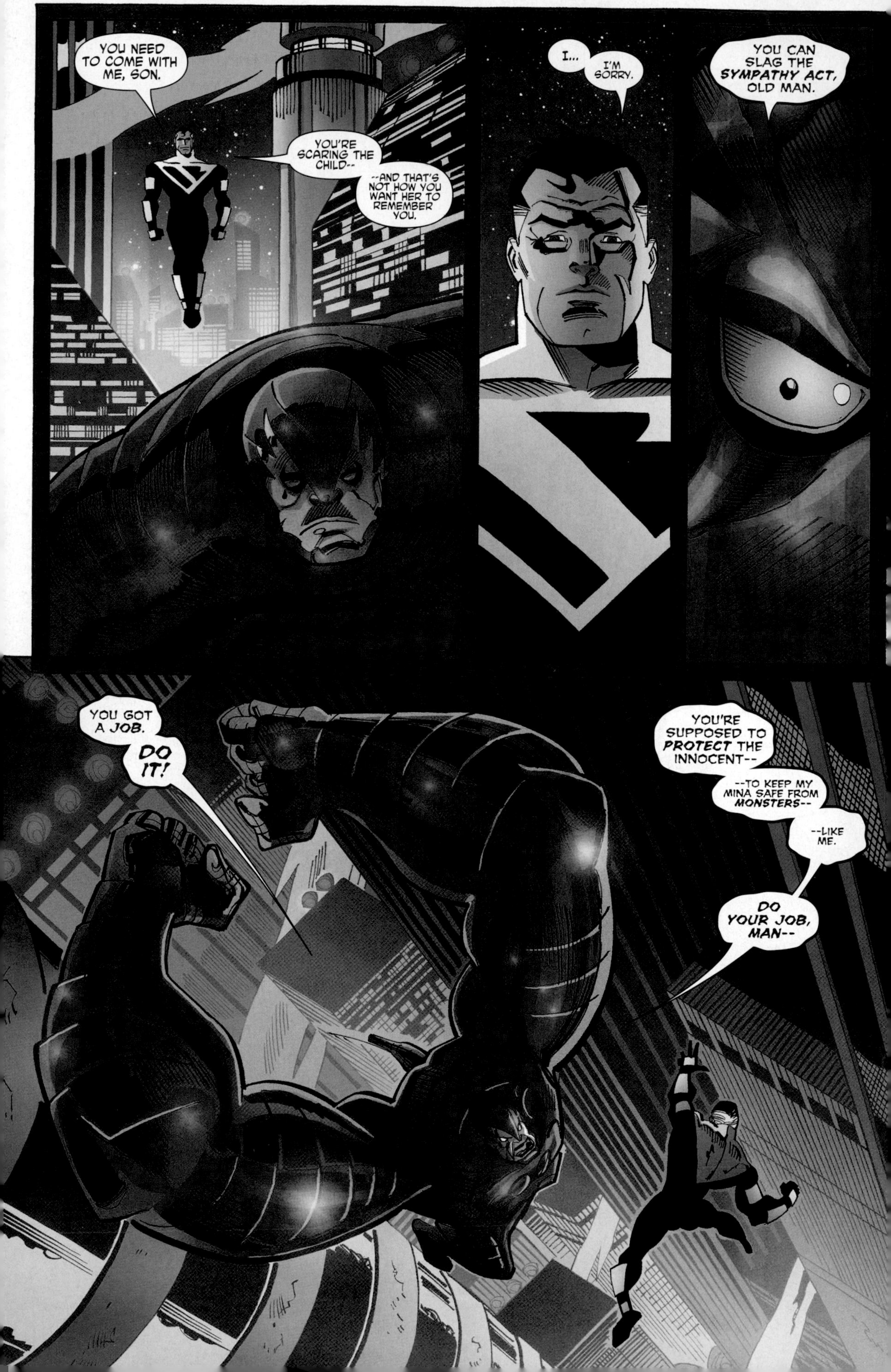

YOU NEED TO COME WITH ME, SON.
YOU'RE SCARING THE CHILD--
--AND THAT'S NOT HOW YOU WANT HER TO REMEMBER YOU.
I...
I'M SORRY.
YOU CAN SLAG THE SYMPATHY ACT, OLD MAN.
YOU GOT A JOB.
DO IT!
YOU'RE SUPPOSED TO PROTECT THE INNOCENT--
--TO KEEP MY MINA SAFE FROM MONSTERS--
--LIKE ME.
DO YOUR JOB, MAN--

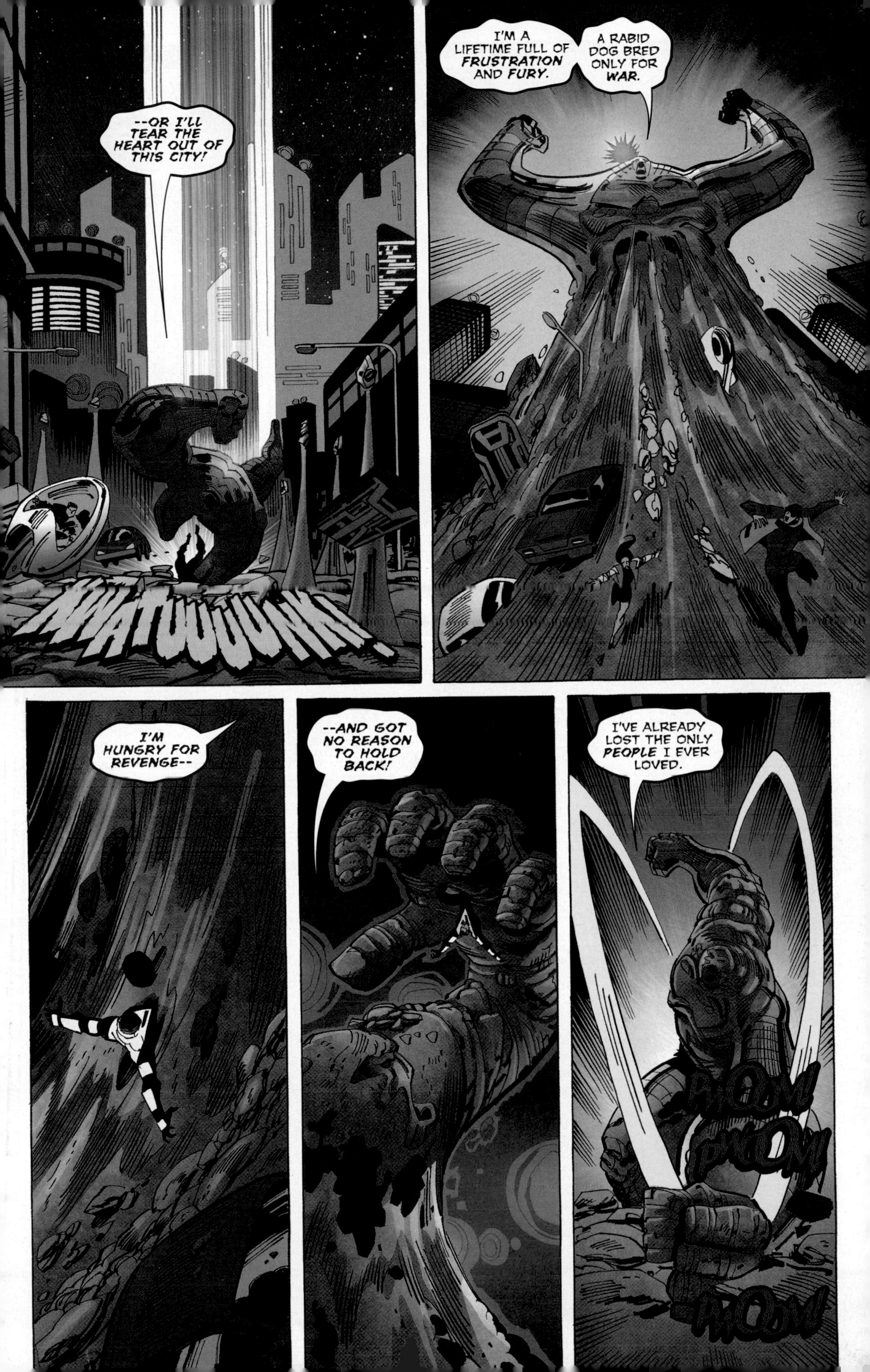
--OR I'LL TEAR THE HEART OUT OF THIS CITY!
WHATOOOOOM!
I'M A LIFETIME FULL OF FRUSTRATION AND FURY.
A RABID DOG BRED ONLY FOR WAR.
I'M HUNGRY FOR REVENGE--
--AND GOT NO REASON TO HOLD BACK!
I'VE ALREADY LOST THE ONLY PEOPLE I EVER LOVED.
PHOOM
PHOOM
PHOOM

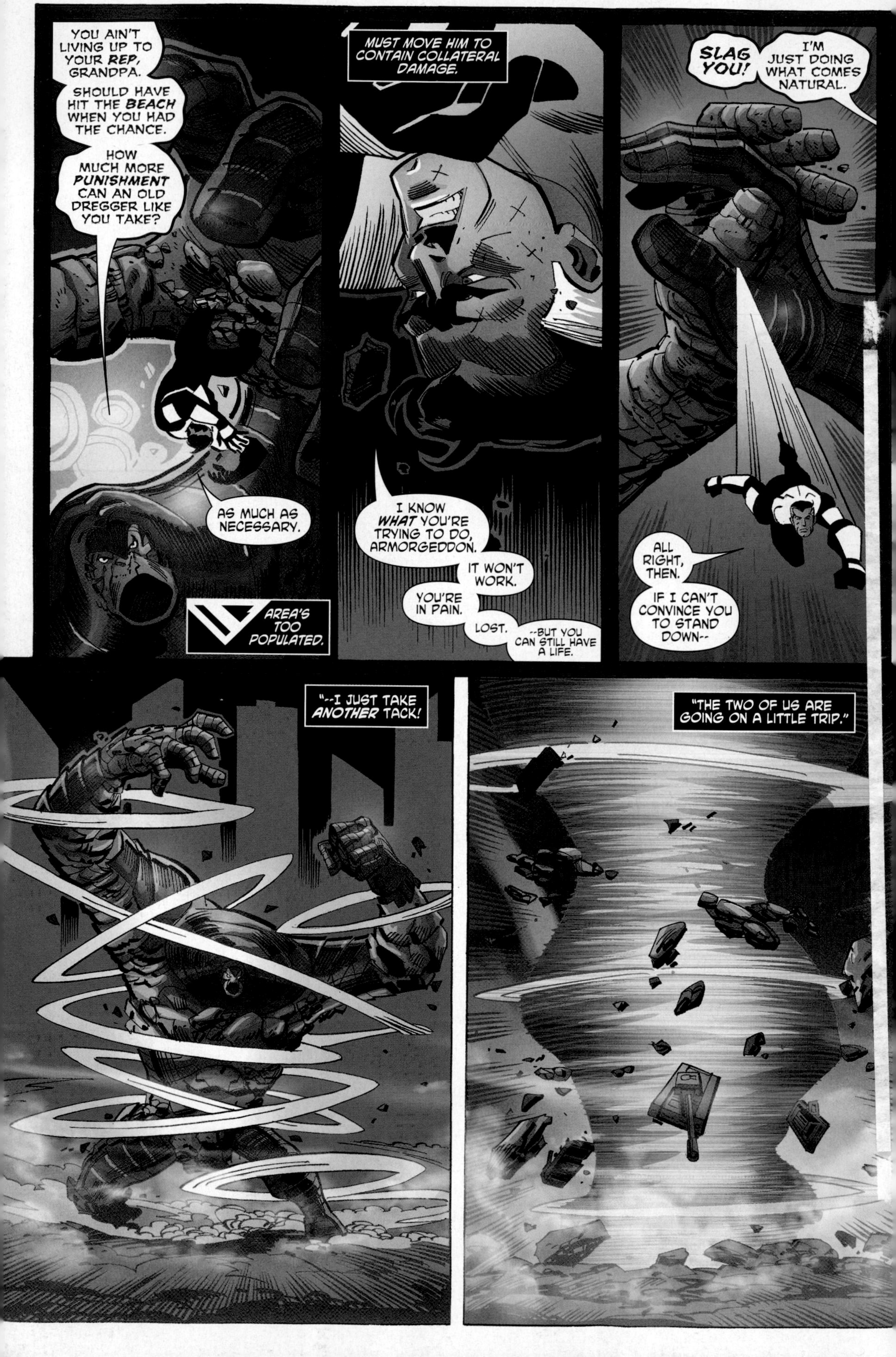
YOU AIN'T LIVING UP TO YOUR REP, GRANDPA.
SHOULD HAVE HIT THE BEACH WHEN YOU HAD THE CHANCE.
HOW MUCH MORE PUNISHMENT CAN AN OLD DREGGER LIKE YOU TAKE?
AS MUCH AS NECESSARY.
AREA'S TOO POPULATED.
MUST MOVE HIM TO CONTAIN COLLATERAL DAMAGE.
I KNOW WHAT YOU'RE TRYING TO DO, ARMORGEDDON.
IT WON'T WORK.
YOU'RE IN PAIN.
LOST.
--BUT YOU CAN STILL HAVE A LIFE.
SLAG YOU!
I'M JUST DOING WHAT COMES NATURAL.
ALL RIGHT, THEN.
IF I CAN'T CONVINCE YOU TO STAND DOWN--
"--I JUST TAKE ANOTHER TACK!
"THE TWO OF US ARE GOING ON A LITTLE TRIP."

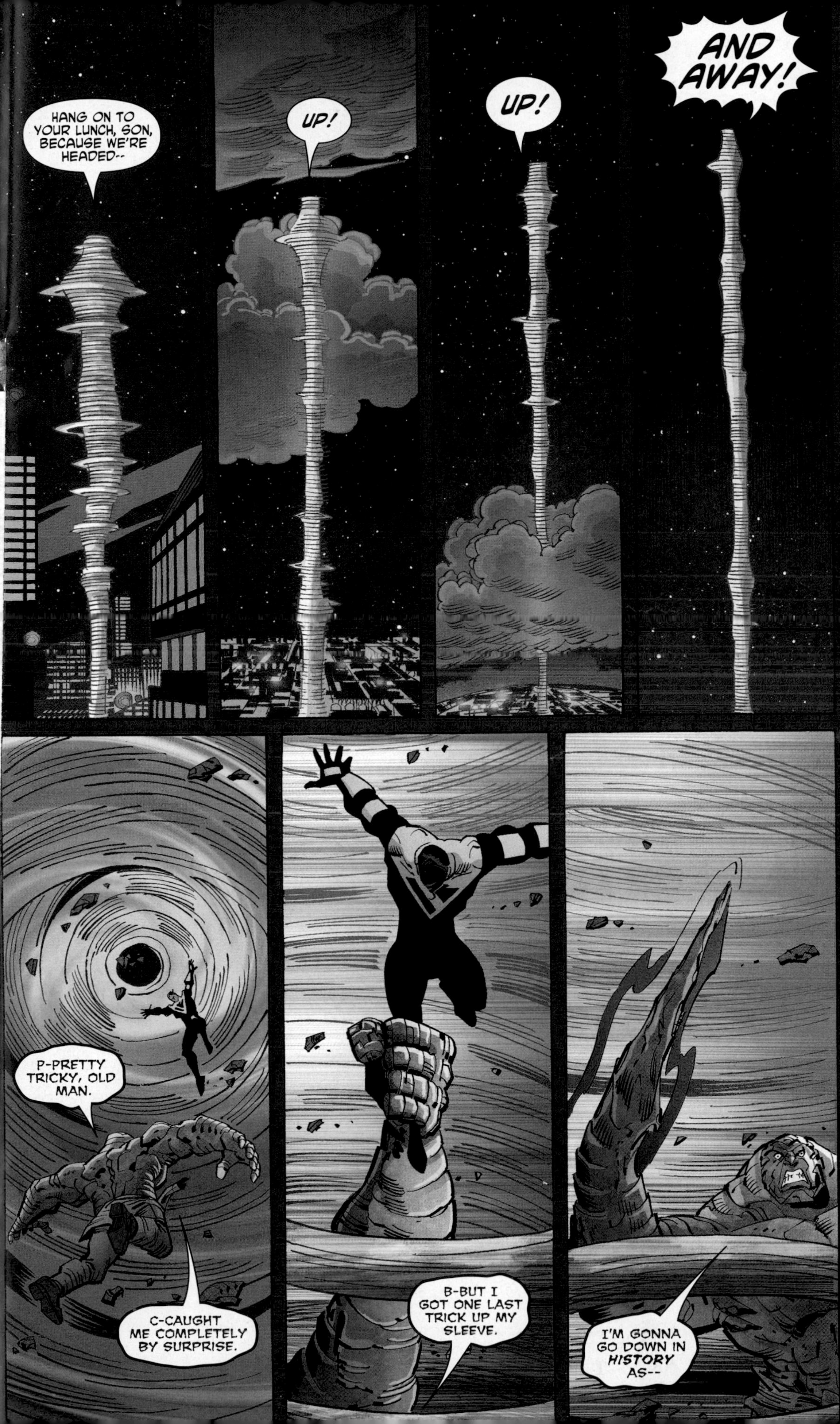
HANG ON TO YOUR LUNCH, SON, BECAUSE WE'RE HEADED--
UP!
UP!
AND AWAY!
P-PRETTY TRICKY, OLD MAN.
C-CAUGHT ME COMPLETELY BY SURPRISE.
B-BUT I GOT ONE LAST TRICK UP MY SLEEVE.
I'M GONNA GO DOWN IN HISTORY AS--

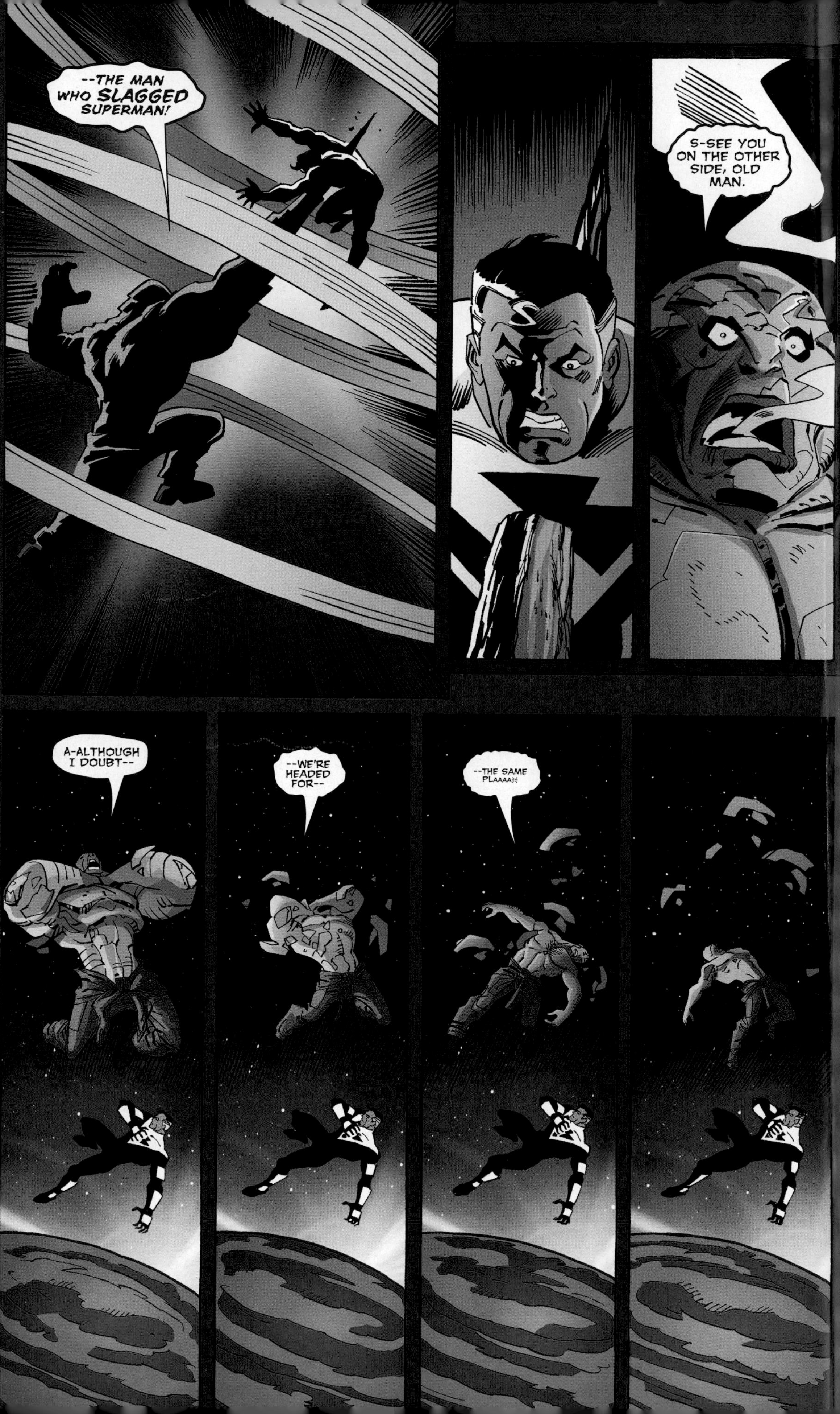
--THE MAN WHO SLAGGED SUPERMAN!
S-SEE YOU ON THE OTHER SIDE, OLD MAN.
A-ALTHOUGH I DOUBT--
--WE'RE HEADED FOR--
--THE SAME PLAAAA--

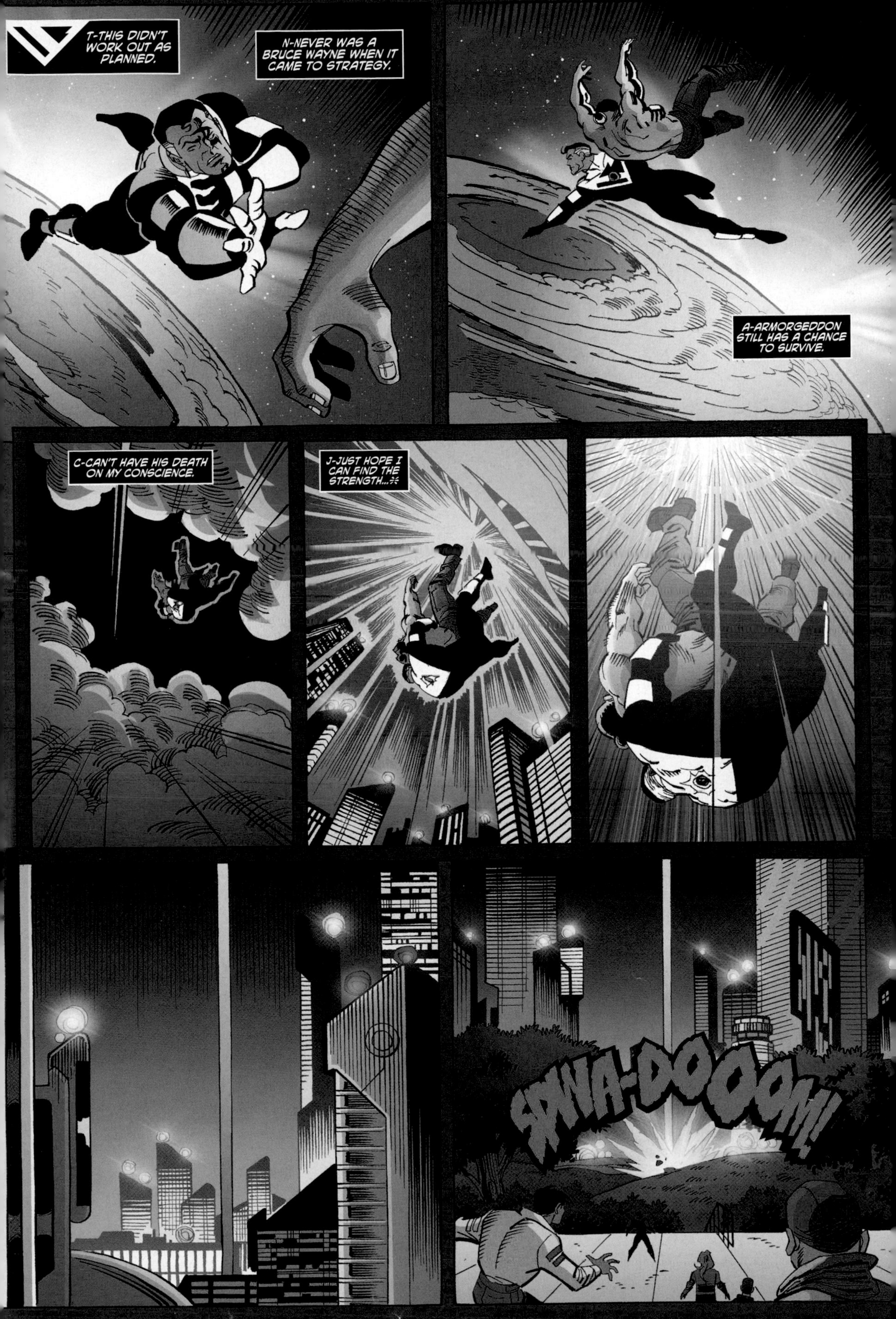
T-THIS DIDN'T WORK OUT AS PLANNED.
N-NEVER WAS A BRUCE WAYNE WHEN IT CAME TO STRATEGY.
A-ARMORGEDDON STILL HAS A CHANCE TO SURVIVE.
C-CAN'T HAVE HIS DEATH ON MY CONSCIENCE.
J-JUST HOPE I CAN FIND THE STRENGTH...
SPWA-DOOOM!

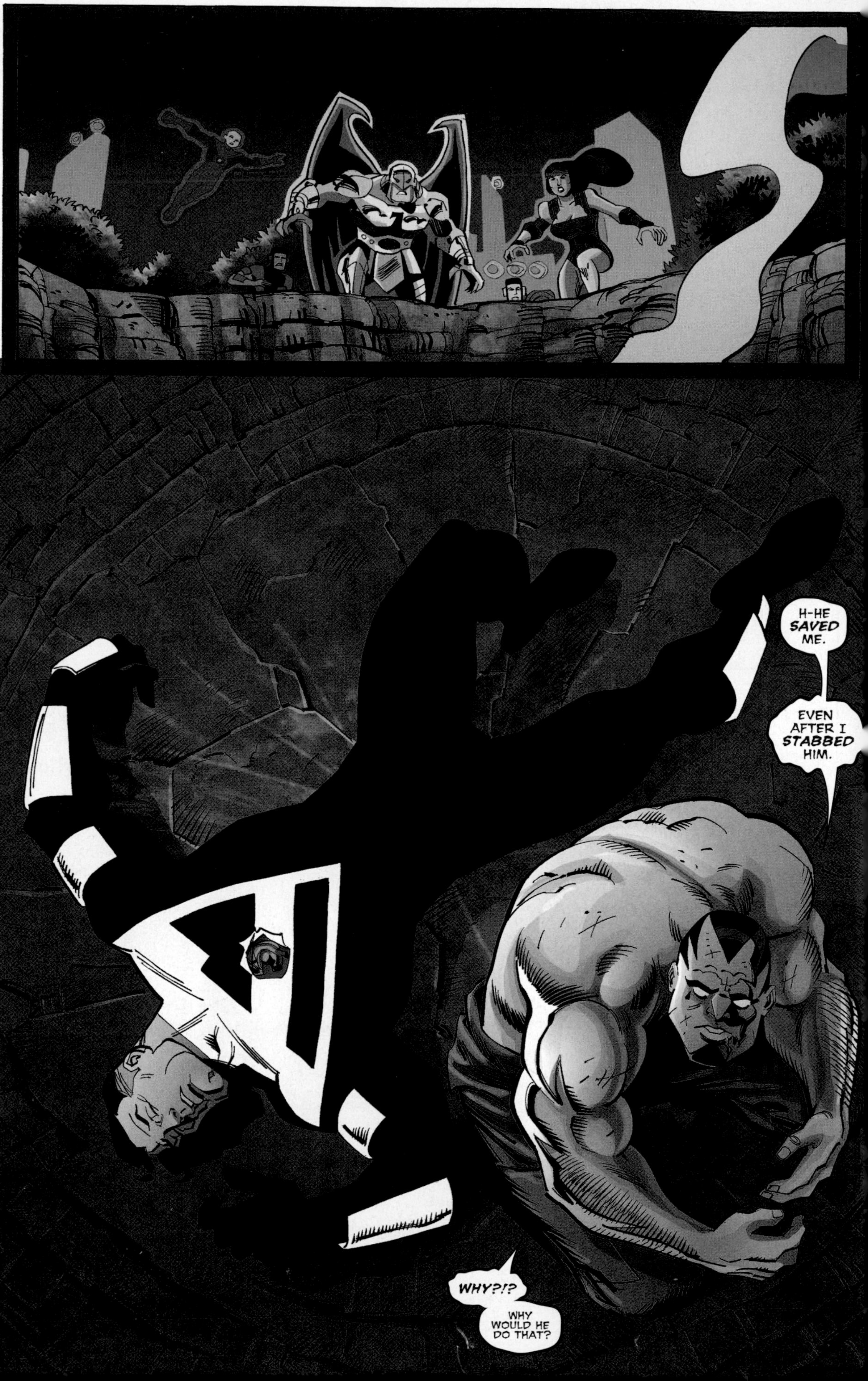
H-HE SAVED ME.
EVEN AFTER I STABBED HIM.
WHY?!?
WHY WOULD HE DO THAT?

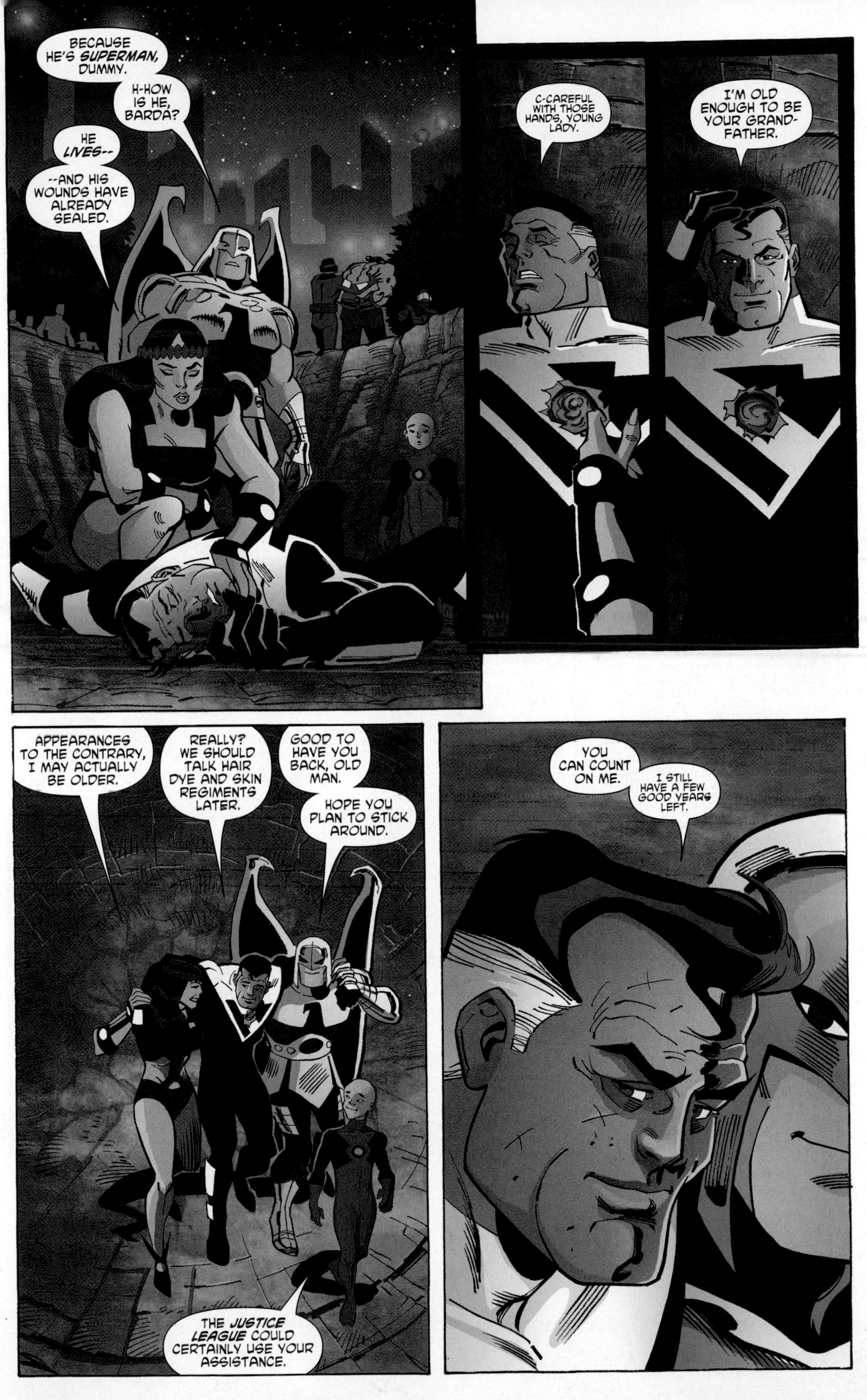
BECAUSE HE'S *SUPERMAN,* DUMMY.
H-HOW IS HE, BARDA?
HE *LIVES--*
--AND HIS WOUNDS HAVE ALREADY SEALED.
C-CAREFUL WITH THOSE HANDS, YOUNG LADY.
I'M OLD ENOUGH TO BE YOUR GRAND-FATHER.
APPEARANCES TO THE CONTRARY, I MAY ACTUALLY BE OLDER.
REALLY? WE SHOULD TALK HAIR DYE AND SKIN REGIMENTS LATER.
GOOD TO HAVE YOU BACK, OLD MAN.
HOPE YOU PLAN TO STICK AROUND.
THE *JUSTICE LEAGUE* COULD CERTAINLY USE YOUR ASSISTANCE.
YOU CAN COUNT ON ME.
I STILL HAVE A FEW GOOD YEARS LEFT.

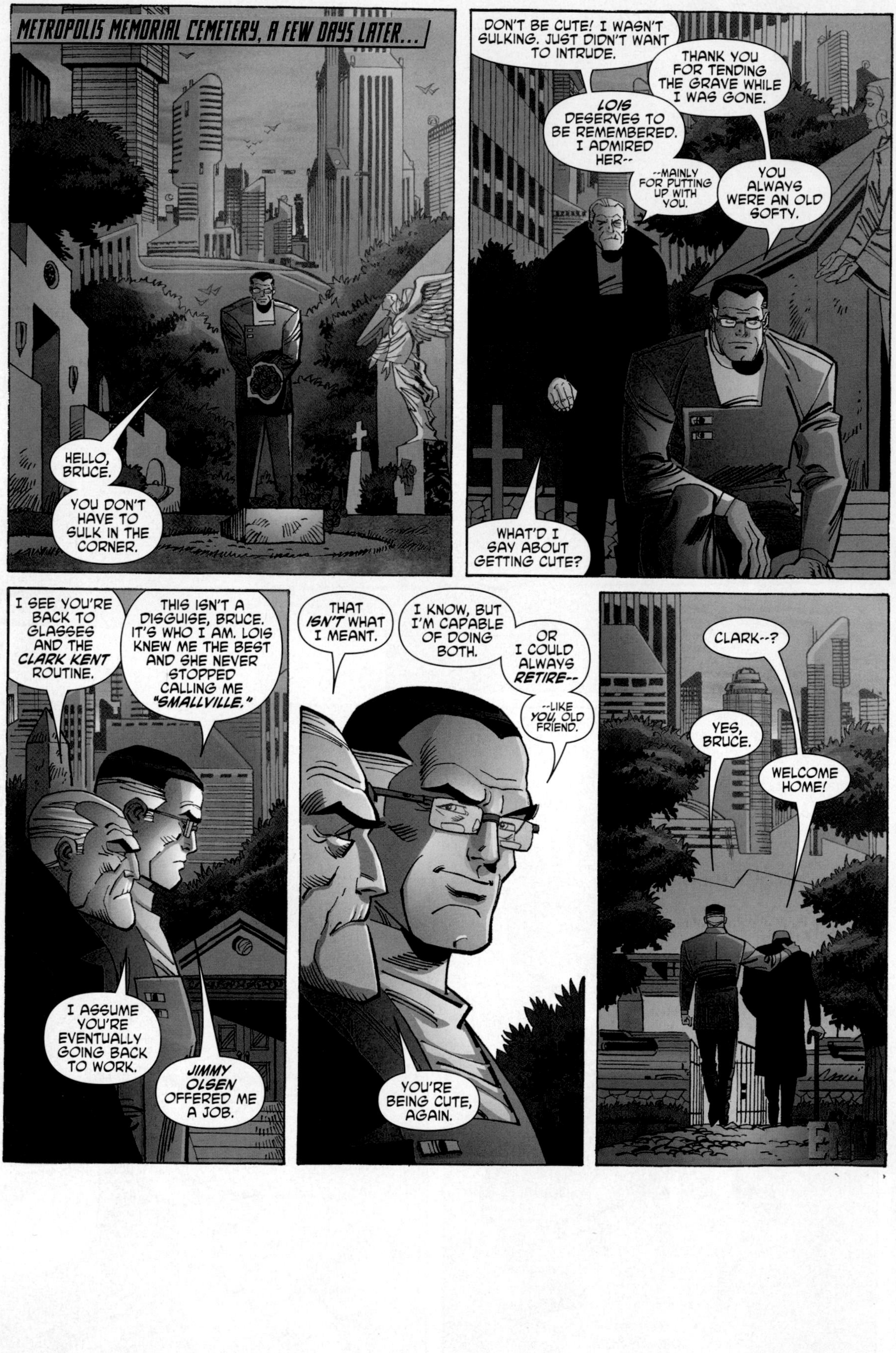
METROPOLIS MEMORIAL CEMETERY, A FEW DAYS LATER...
HELLO, BRUCE.
YOU DON'T HAVE TO SULK IN THE CORNER.
DON'T BE CUTE! I WASN'T SULKING. JUST DIDN'T WANT TO INTRUDE.
LOIS DESERVES TO BE REMEMBERED. I ADMIRED HER--
--MAINLY FOR PUTTING UP WITH YOU.
THANK YOU FOR TENDING THE GRAVE WHILE I WAS GONE.
YOU ALWAYS WERE AN OLD SOFTY.
WHAT'D I SAY ABOUT GETTING CUTE?
I SEE YOU'RE BACK TO GLASSES AND THE CLARK KENT ROUTINE.
THIS ISN'T A DISGUISE, BRUCE. IT'S WHO I AM. LOIS KNEW ME THE BEST AND SHE NEVER STOPPED CALLING ME "SMALLVILLE."
I ASSUME YOU'RE EVENTUALLY GOING BACK TO WORK.
JIMMY OLSEN OFFERED ME A JOB.
THAT ISN'T WHAT I MEANT.
I KNOW, BUT I'M CAPABLE OF DOING BOTH.
OR I COULD ALWAYS RETIRE--
--LIKE YOU, OLD FRIEND.
YOU'RE BEING CUTE, AGAIN.
CLARK--?
YES, BRUCE.
WELCOME HOME!

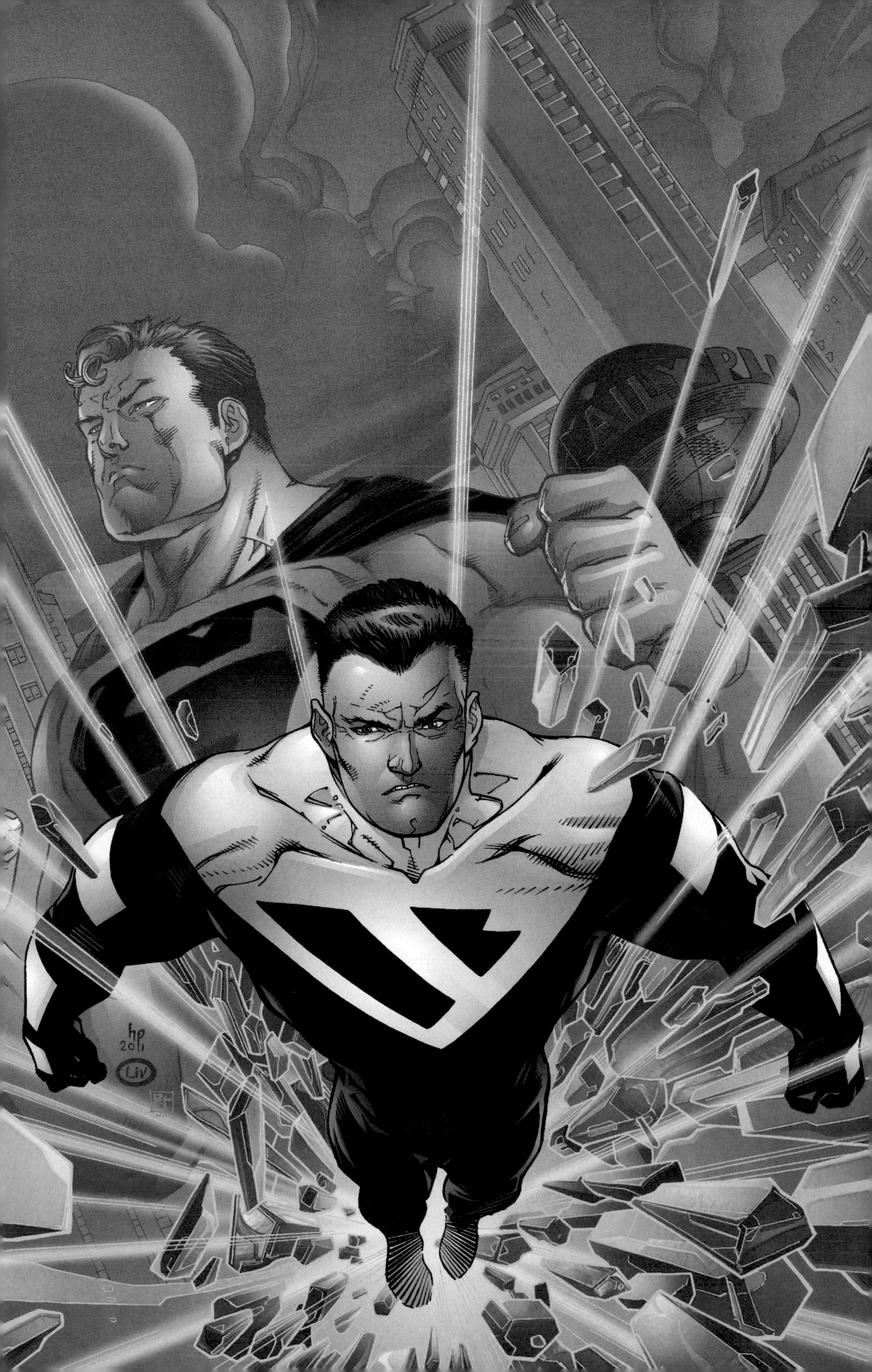
hp
2011
Liv

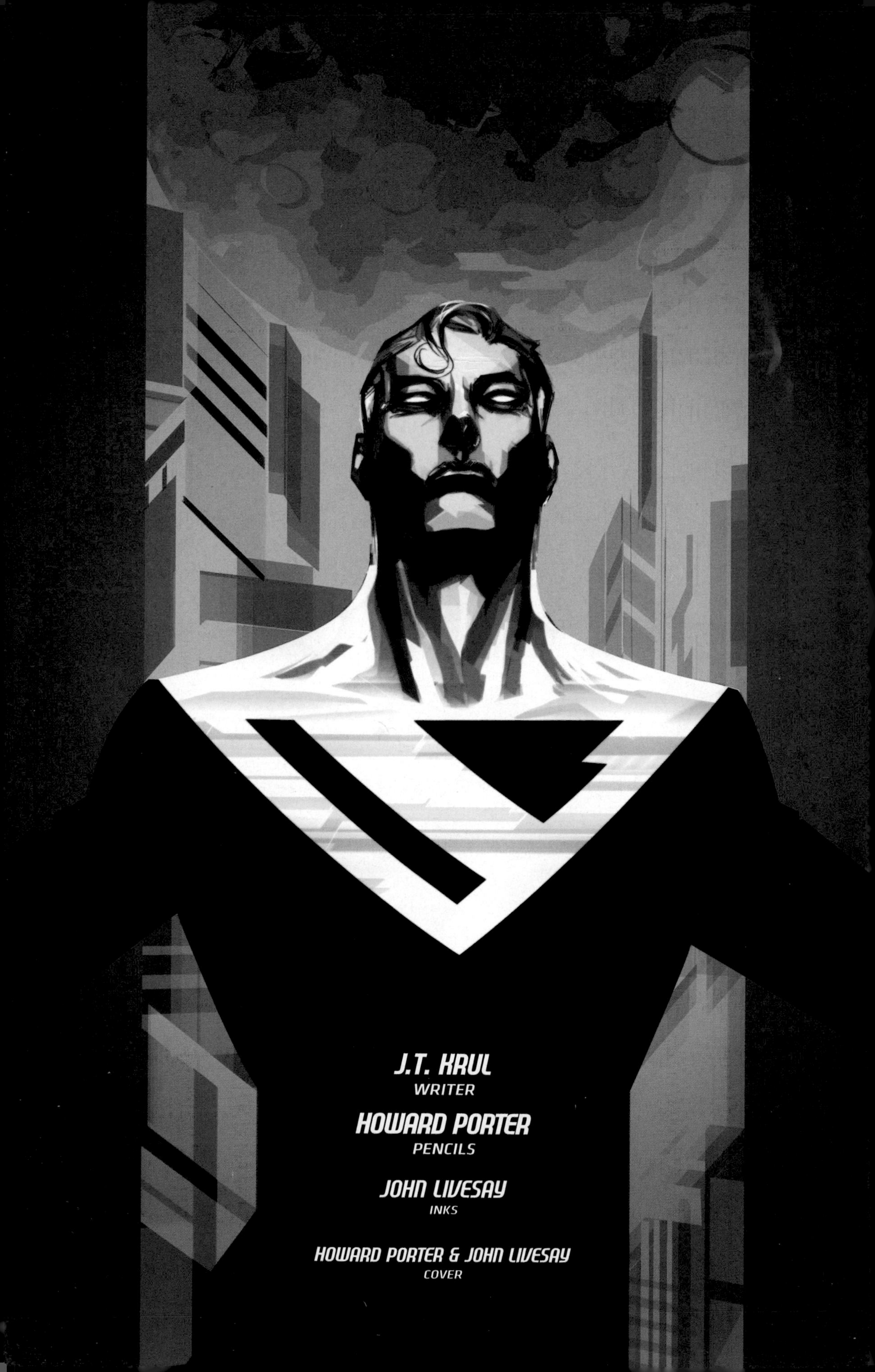
J.T. KRUL
WRITER
HOWARD PORTER
PENCILS
JOHN LIVESAY
INKS
HOWARD PORTER & JOHN LIVESAY
COVER

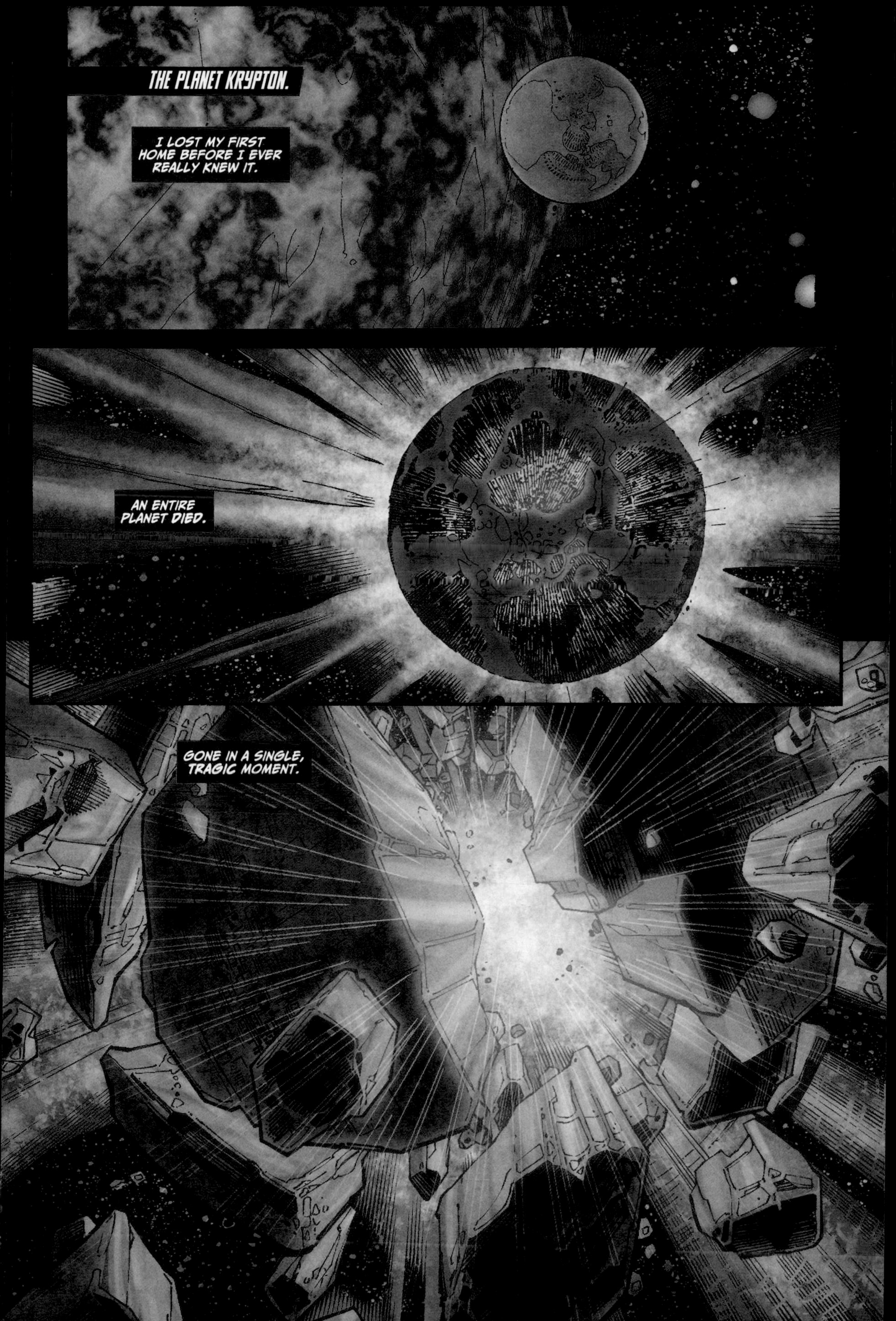
THE PLANET KRYPTON.
I LOST MY FIRST HOME BEFORE I EVER REALLY KNEW IT.
AN ENTIRE PLANET DIED.
GONE IN A SINGLE, TRAGIC MOMENT.

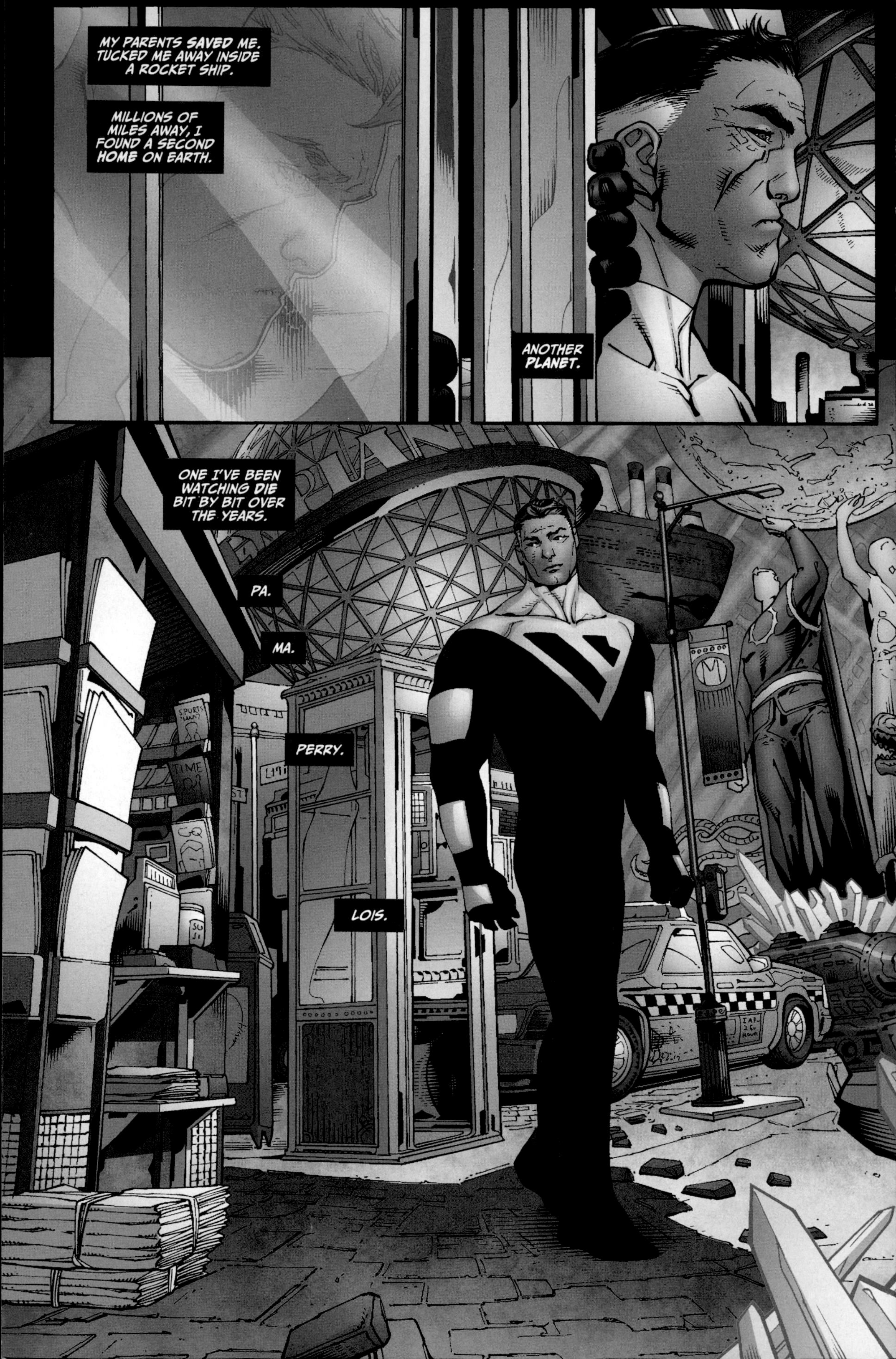
MY PARENTS SAVED ME. TUCKED ME AWAY INSIDE A ROCKET SHIP.
MILLIONS OF MILES AWAY, I FOUND A SECOND HOME ON EARTH.
ANOTHER PLANET.
ONE I'VE BEEN WATCHING DIE BIT BY BIT OVER THE YEARS.
PA.
MA.
PERRY.
LOIS.

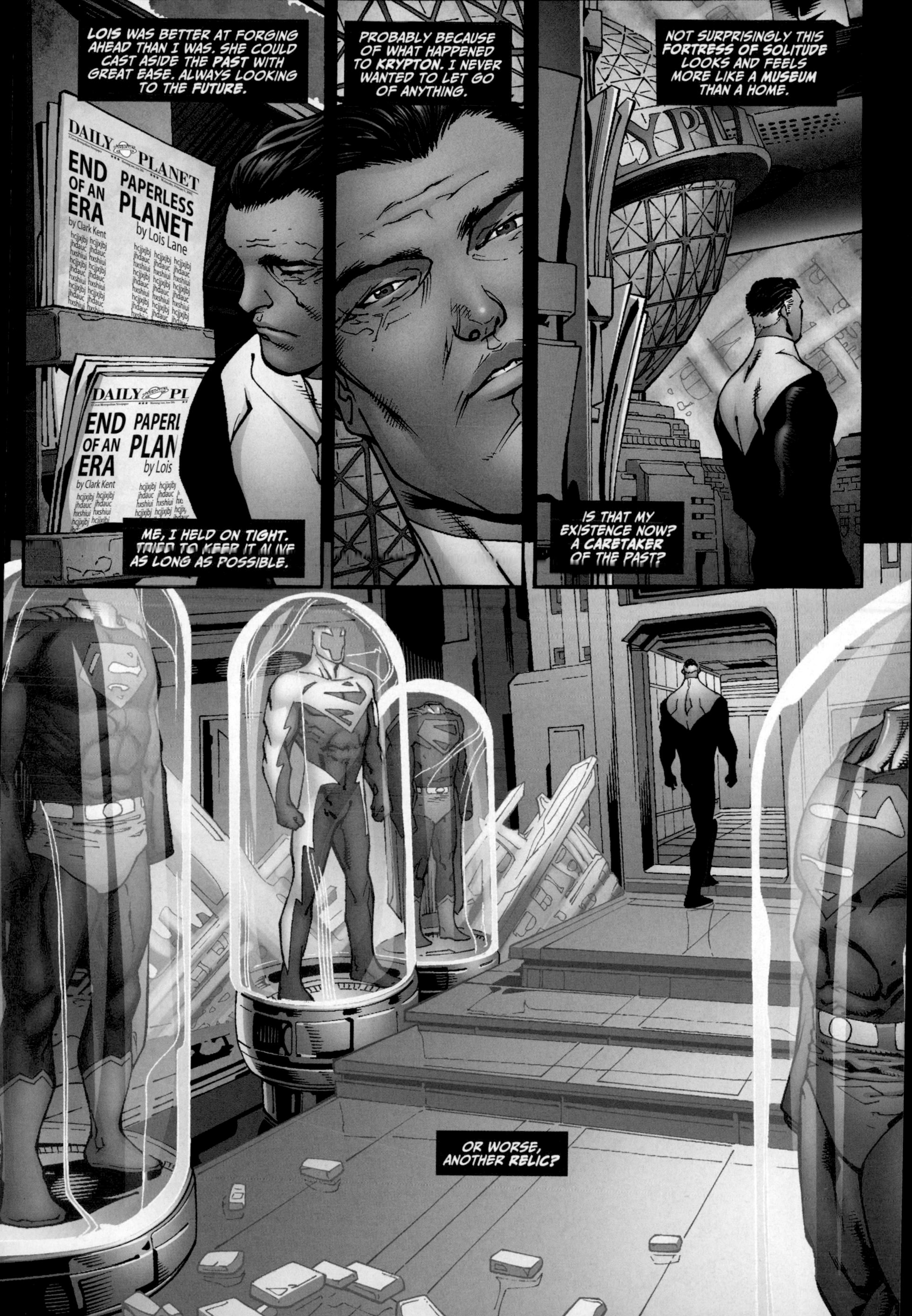
LOIS WAS BETTER AT FORGING AHEAD THAN I WAS. SHE COULD CAST ASIDE THE PAST WITH GREAT EASE. ALWAYS LOOKING TO THE FUTURE.
DAILY PLANET
END OF AN ERA
by Clark Kent
PAPERLESS PLANET
by Lois Lane
ME, I HELD ON TIGHT. TRIED TO KEEP IT ALIVE AS LONG AS POSSIBLE.
PROBABLY BECAUSE OF WHAT HAPPENED TO KRYPTON. I NEVER WANTED TO LET GO OF ANYTHING.
NOT SURPRISINGLY THIS FORTRESS OF SOLITUDE LOOKS AND FEELS MORE LIKE A MUSEUM THAN A HOME.
IS THAT MY EXISTENCE NOW? A CARETAKER OF THE PAST?
OR WORSE, ANOTHER RELIC?

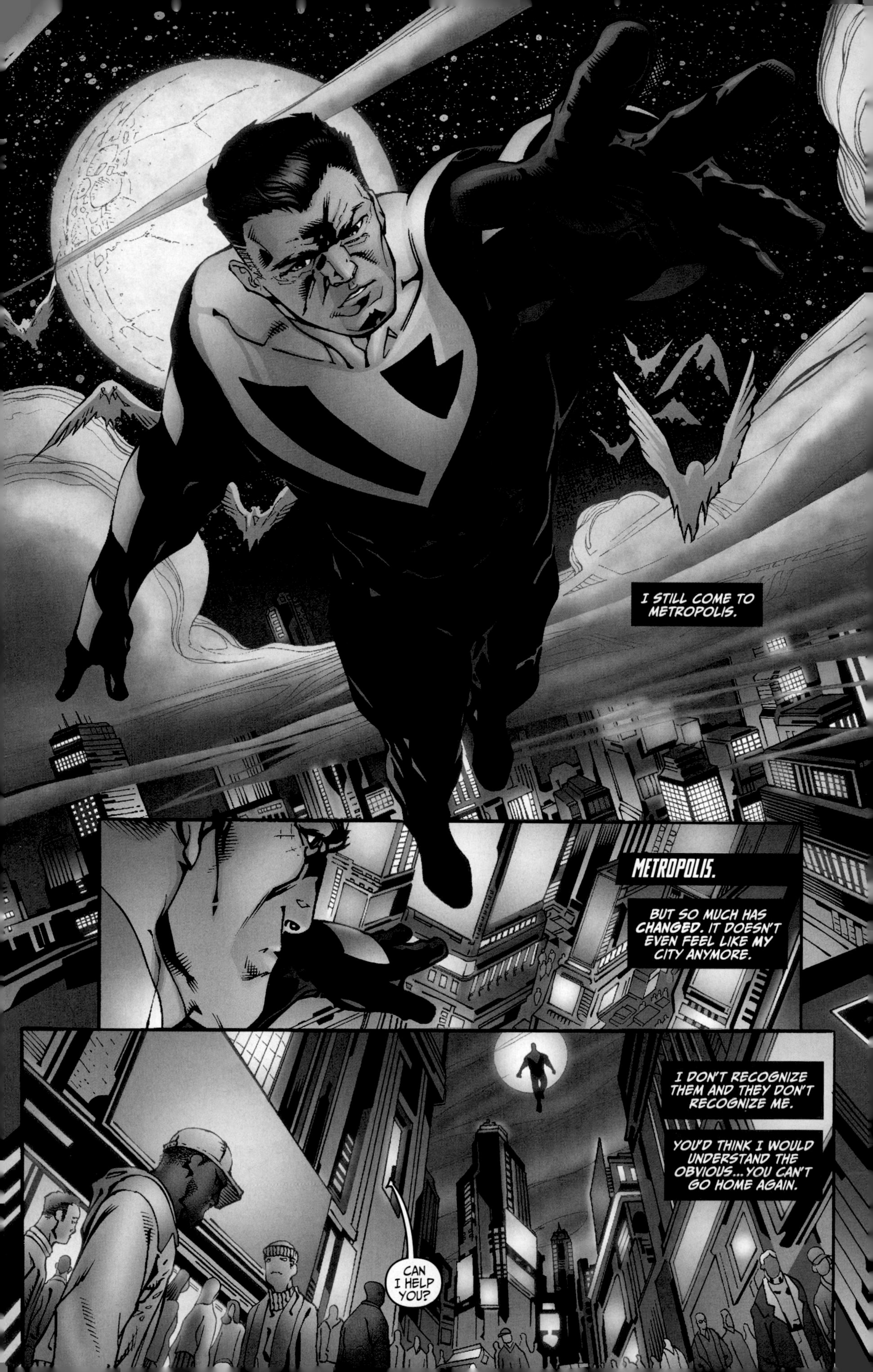
I STILL COME TO METROPOLIS.
METROPOLIS.
BUT SO MUCH HAS CHANGED. IT DOESN'T EVEN FEEL LIKE MY CITY ANYMORE.
I DON'T RECOGNIZE THEM AND THEY DON'T RECOGNIZE ME.
YOU'D THINK I WOULD UNDERSTAND THE OBVIOUS... YOU CAN'T GO HOME AGAIN.
CAN I HELP YOU?

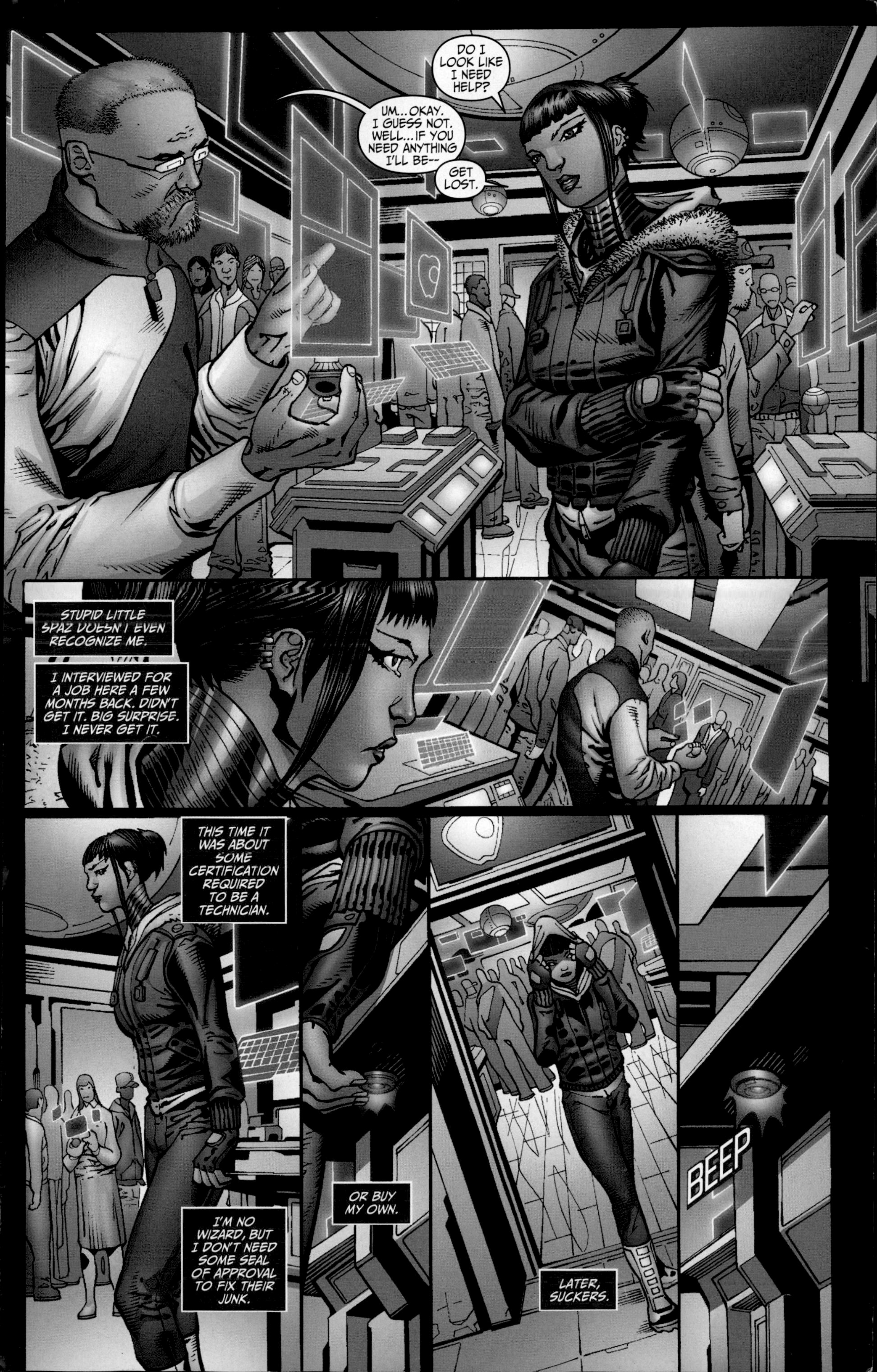
DO I LOOK LIKE I NEED HELP?
UM...OKAY. I GUESS NOT. WELL...IF YOU NEED ANYTHING I'LL BE--
GET LOST.
STUPID LITTLE SPAZ DOESN'T EVEN RECOGNIZE ME.
I INTERVIEWED FOR A JOB HERE A FEW MONTHS BACK. DIDN'T GET IT. BIG SURPRISE. I NEVER GET IT.
THIS TIME IT WAS ABOUT SOME CERTIFICATION REQUIRED TO BE A TECHNICIAN.
I'M NO WIZARD, BUT I DON'T NEED SOME SEAL OF APPROVAL TO FIX THEIR JUNK.
OR BUY MY OWN.
LATER, SUCKERS.
BEEP

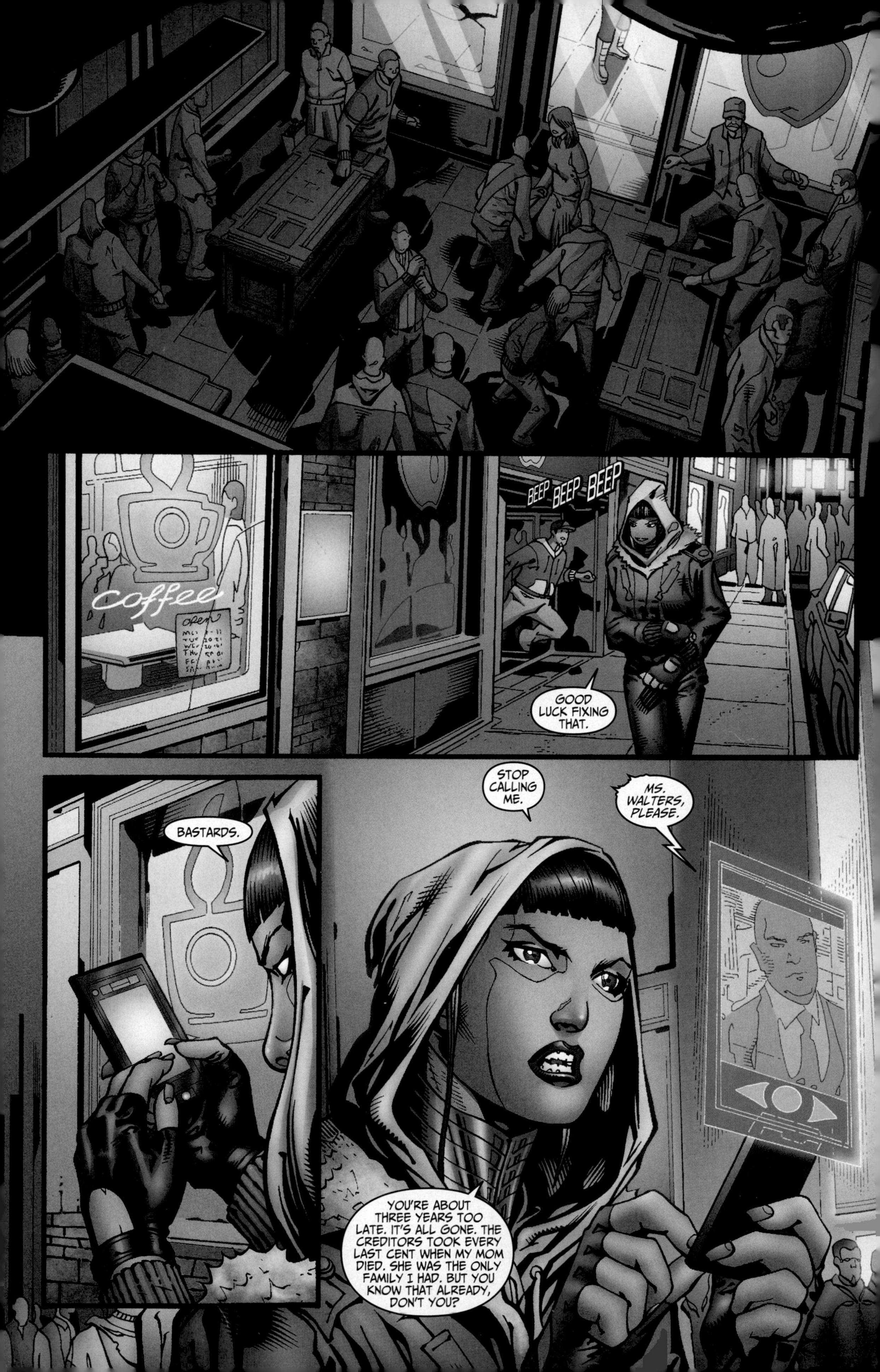
BEEP BEEP BEEP
coffee
GOOD LUCK FIXING THAT.
BASTARDS.
STOP CALLING ME.
MS. WALTERS, PLEASE.
YOU'RE ABOUT THREE YEARS TOO LATE. IT'S ALL GONE. THE CREDITORS TOOK EVERY LAST CENT WHEN MY MOM DIED. SHE WAS THE ONLY FAMILY I HAD. BUT YOU KNOW THAT ALREADY, DON'T YOU?

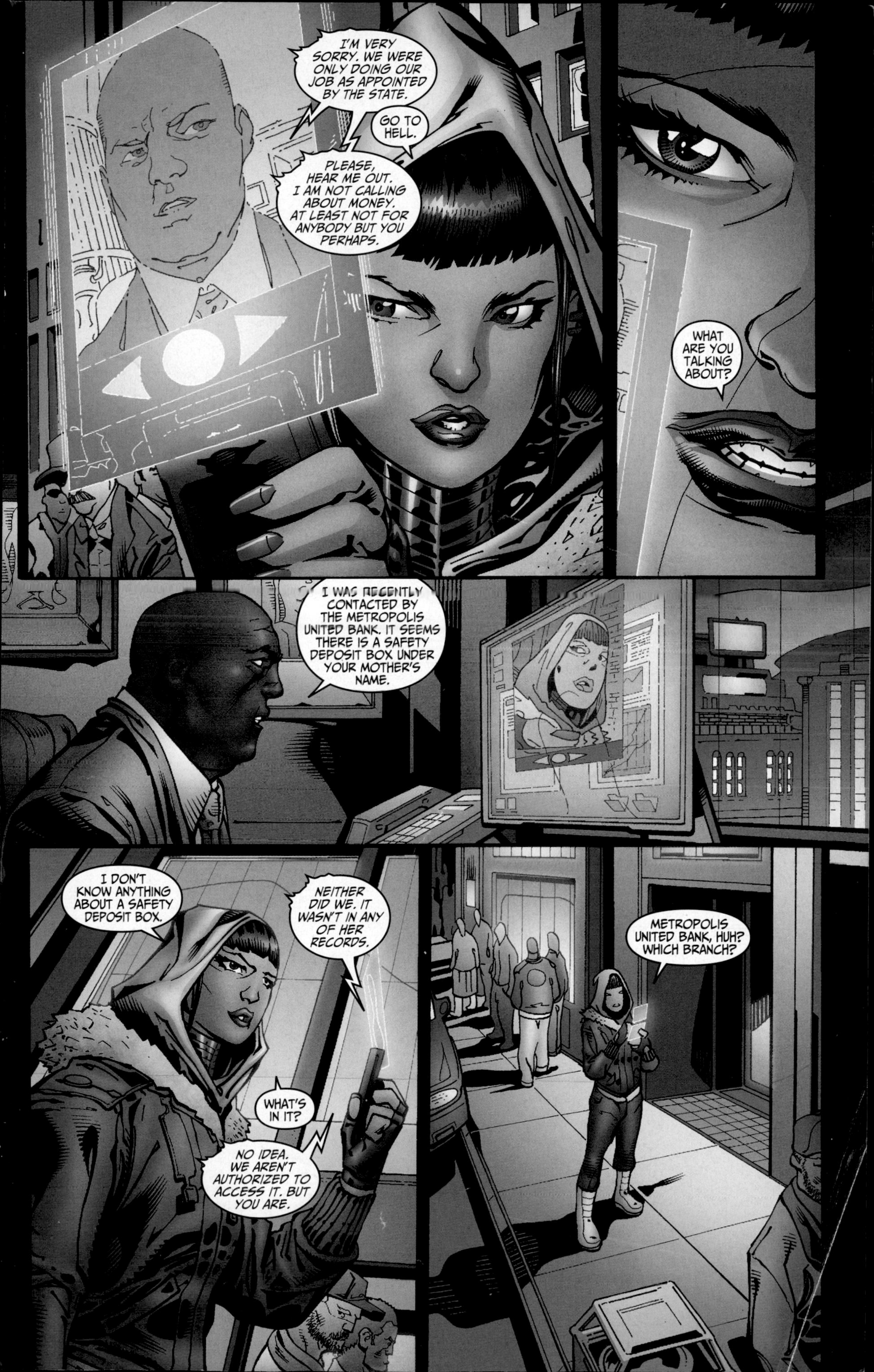
I'M VERY SORRY. WE WERE ONLY DOING OUR JOB AS APPOINTED BY THE STATE.
GO TO HELL.
PLEASE, HEAR ME OUT. I AM NOT CALLING ABOUT MONEY. AT LEAST NOT FOR ANYBODY BUT YOU PERHAPS.
WHAT ARE YOU TALKING ABOUT?
I WAS RECENTLY CONTACTED BY THE METROPOLIS UNITED BANK. IT SEEMS THERE IS A SAFETY DEPOSIT BOX UNDER YOUR MOTHER'S NAME.
I DON'T KNOW ANYTHING ABOUT A SAFETY DEPOSIT BOX.
NEITHER DID WE. IT WASN'T IN ANY OF HER RECORDS.
WHAT'S IN IT?
NO IDEA. WE AREN'T AUTHORIZED TO ACCESS IT. BUT YOU ARE.
METROPOLIS UNITED BANK, HUH? WHICH BRANCH?

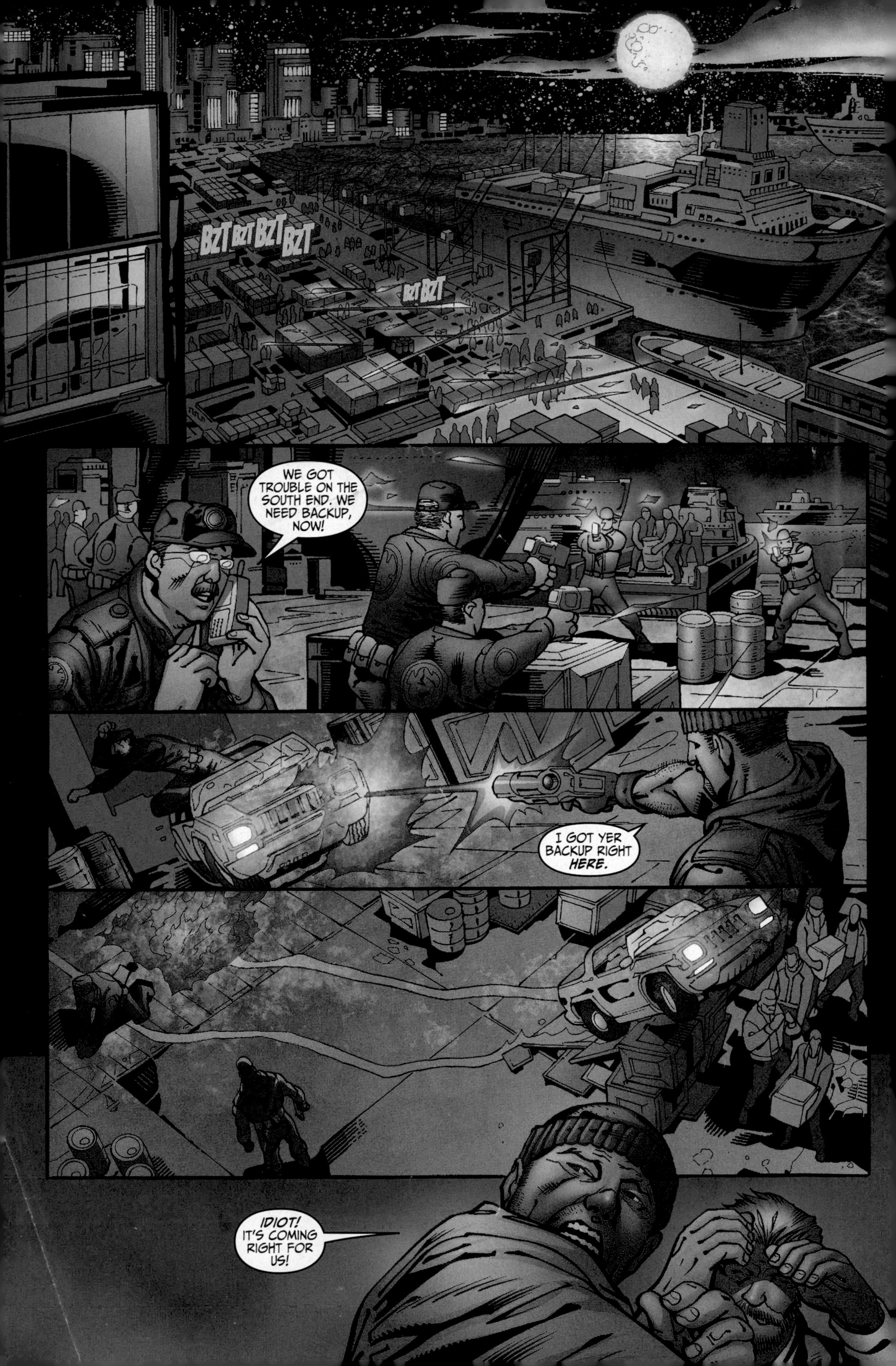
BZT BZT BZT BZT
BZT BZT
WE GOT TROUBLE ON THE SOUTH END. WE NEED BACKUP, NOW!
I GOT YER BACKUP RIGHT *HERE.*
IDIOT! IT'S COMING RIGHT FOR US!

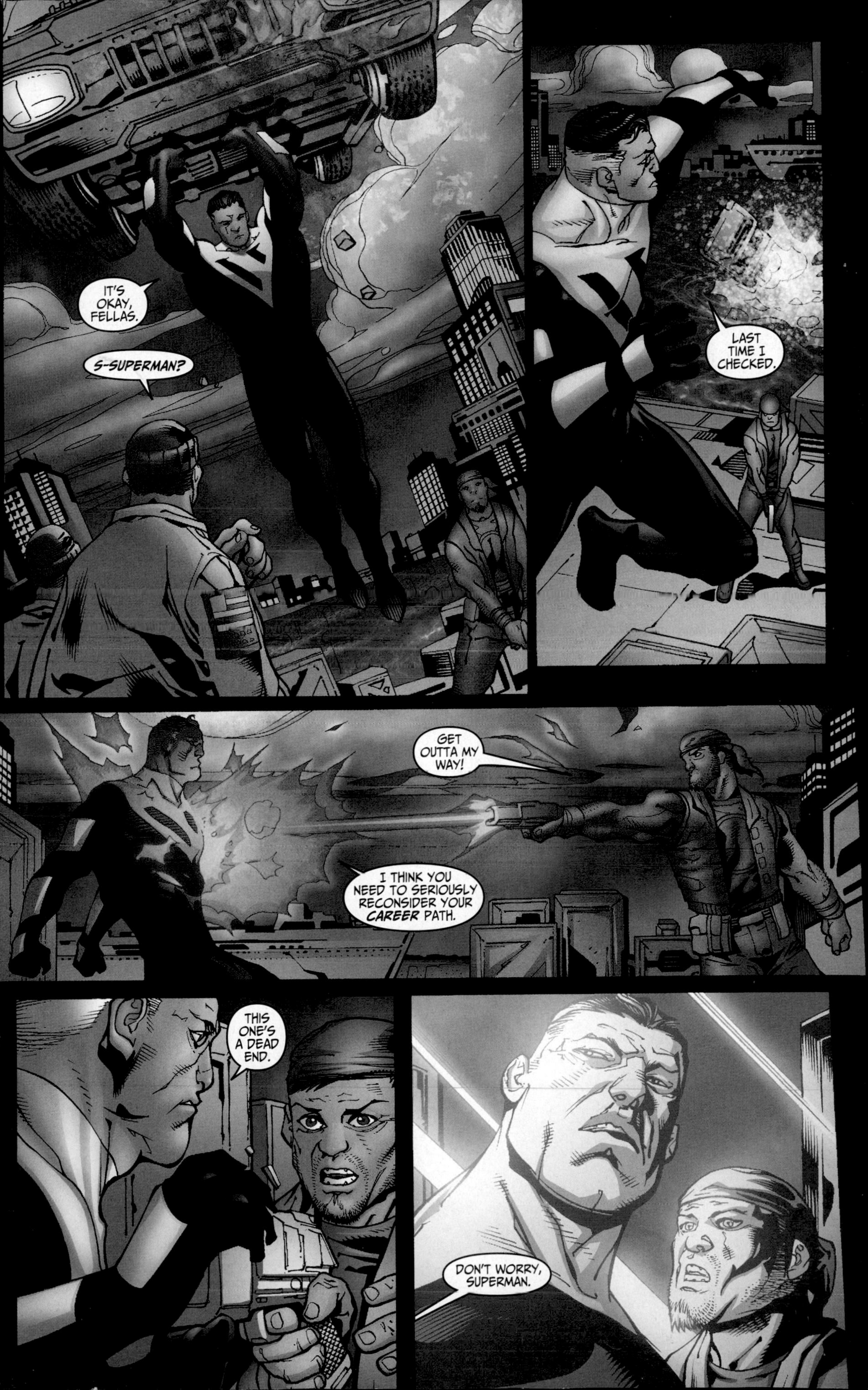
IT'S OKAY, FELLAS.
S-SUPERMAN?
LAST TIME I CHECKED.
GET OUTTA MY WAY!
I THINK YOU NEED TO SERIOUSLY RECONSIDER YOUR CAREER PATH.
THIS ONE'S A DEAD END.
DON'T WORRY, SUPERMAN.

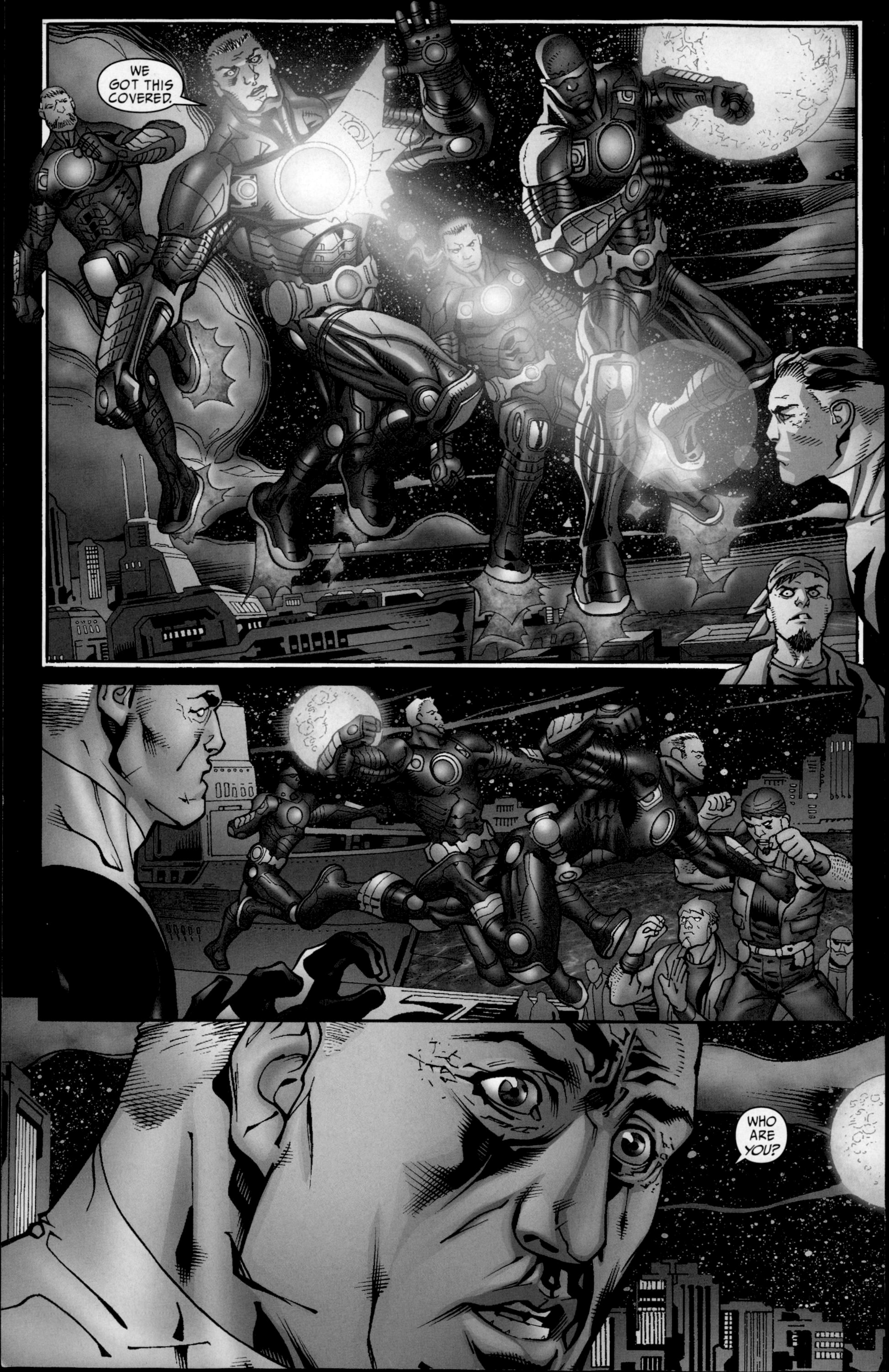
WE GOT THIS COVERED.
WHO ARE YOU?

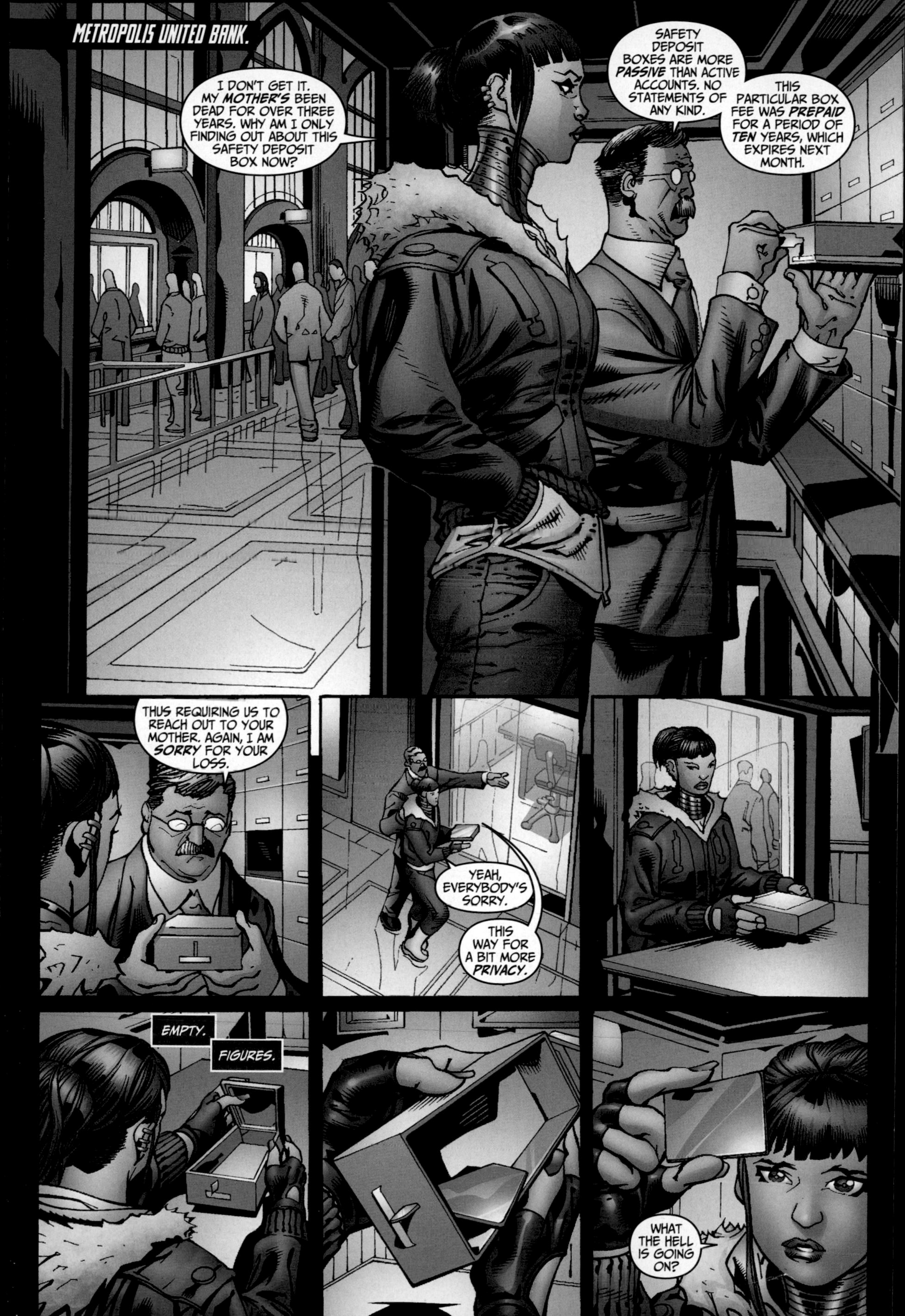
METROPOLIS UNITED BANK.
I DON'T GET IT. MY MOTHER'S BEEN DEAD FOR OVER THREE YEARS. WHY AM I ONLY FINDING OUT ABOUT THIS SAFETY DEPOSIT BOX NOW?
SAFETY DEPOSIT BOXES ARE MORE PASSIVE THAN ACTIVE ACCOUNTS. NO STATEMENTS OF ANY KIND.
THIS PARTICULAR BOX FEE WAS PREPAID FOR A PERIOD OF TEN YEARS, WHICH EXPIRES NEXT MONTH.
THUS REQUIRING US TO REACH OUT TO YOUR MOTHER. AGAIN, I AM SORRY FOR YOUR LOSS.
YEAH, EVERYBODY'S SORRY.
THIS WAY FOR A BIT MORE PRIVACY.
EMPTY.
FIGURES.
WHAT THE HELL IS GOING ON?

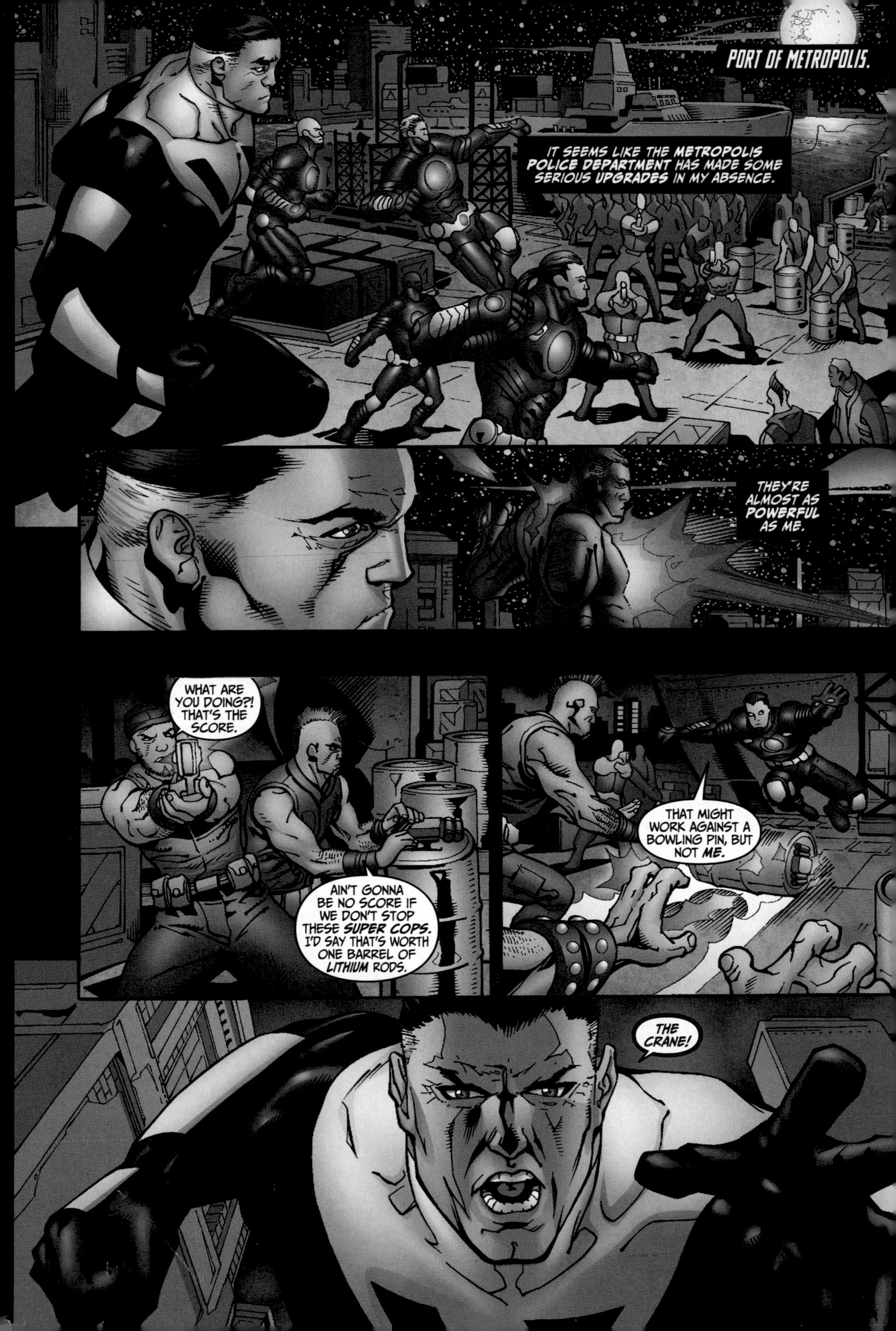
PORT OF METROPOLIS.
IT SEEMS LIKE THE METROPOLIS POLICE DEPARTMENT HAS MADE SOME SERIOUS UPGRADES IN MY ABSENCE.
THEY'RE ALMOST AS POWERFUL AS ME.
WHAT ARE YOU DOING?! THAT'S THE SCORE.
AIN'T GONNA BE NO SCORE IF WE DON'T STOP THESE SUPER COPS. I'D SAY THAT'S WORTH ONE BARREL OF LITHIUM RODS.
THAT MIGHT WORK AGAINST A BOWLING PIN, BUT NOT ME.
THE CRANE!

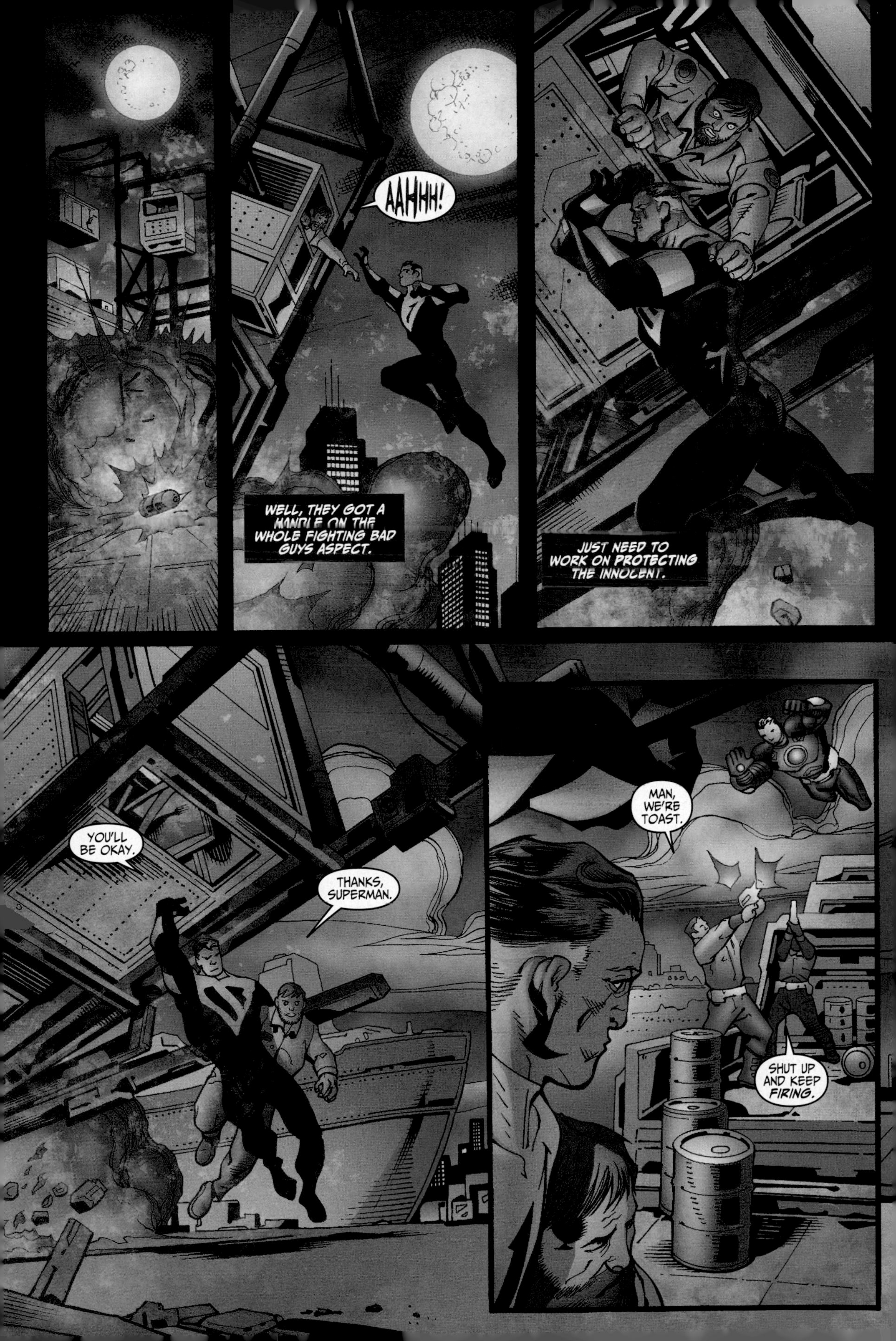
AAHHH!
WELL, THEY GOT A HANDLE ON THE WHOLE FIGHTING BAD GUYS ASPECT.
JUST NEED TO WORK ON PROTECTING THE INNOCENT.
YOU'LL BE OKAY.
THANKS, SUPERMAN.
MAN, WE'RE TOAST.
SHUT UP AND KEEP FIRING.

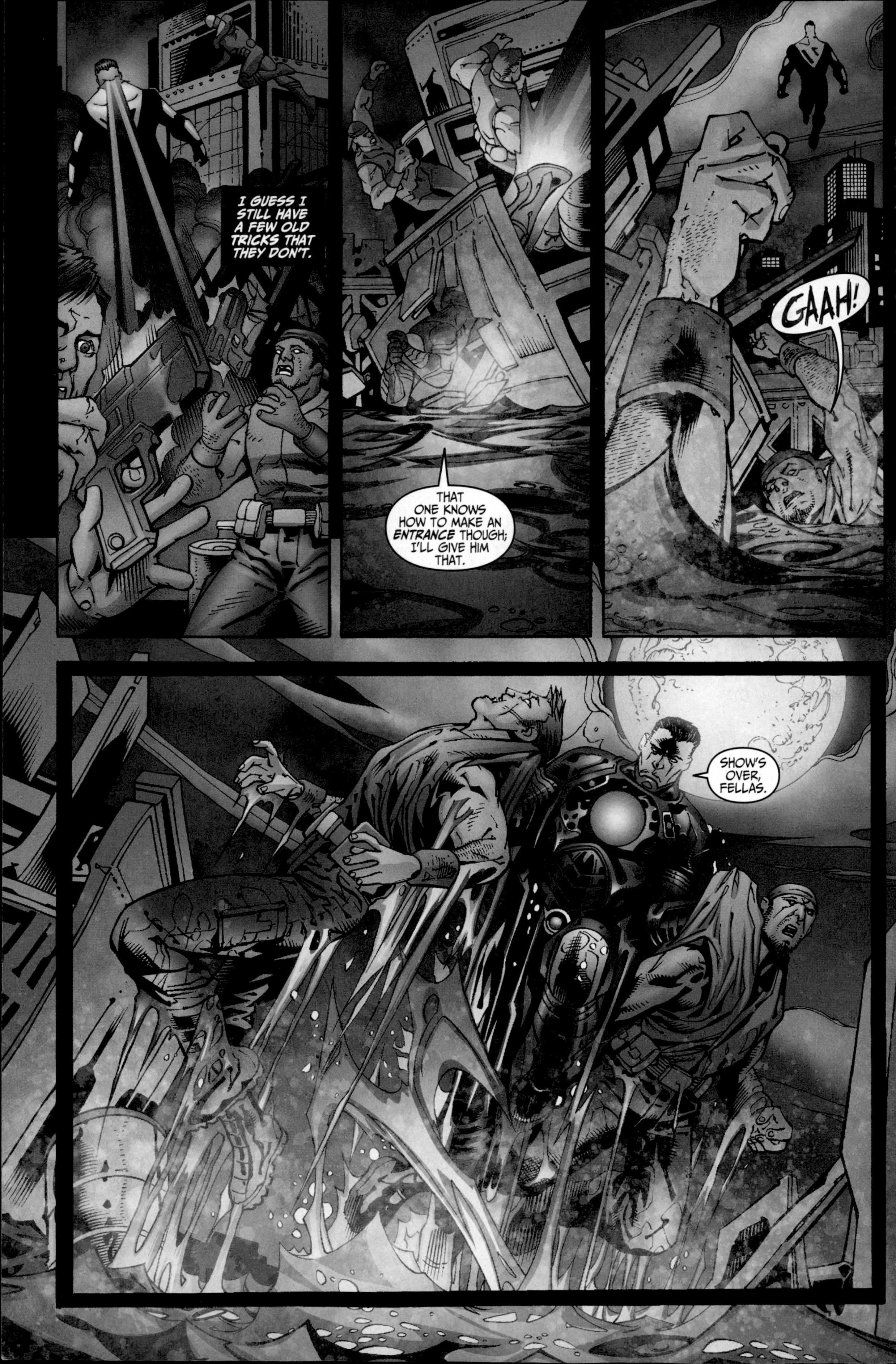
I GUESS I STILL HAVE A FEW OLD TRICKS THAT THEY DON'T.
THAT ONE KNOWS HOW TO MAKE AN ENTRANCE THOUGH; I'LL GIVE HIM THAT.
GAAH!
SHOW'S OVER, FELLAS.

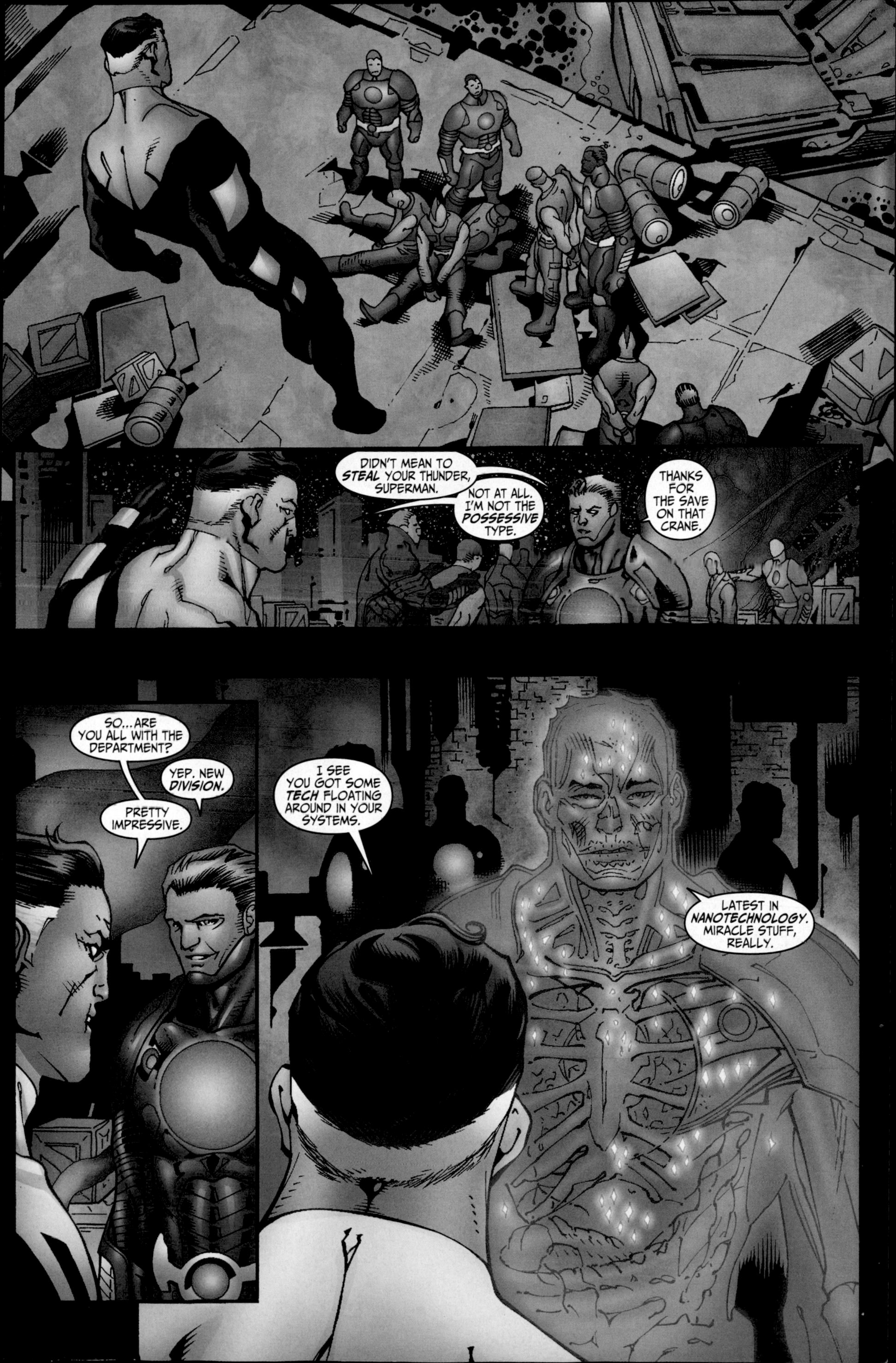

DIDN'T MEAN TO STEAL YOUR THUNDER, SUPERMAN.
NOT AT ALL. I'M NOT THE POSSESSIVE TYPE.
THANKS FOR THE SAVE ON THAT CRANE.
SO...ARE YOU ALL WITH THE DEPARTMENT?
YEP. NEW DIVISION.
PRETTY IMPRESSIVE.
I SEE YOU GOT SOME TECH FLOATING AROUND IN YOUR SYSTEMS.
LATEST IN NANOTECHNOLOGY. MIRACLE STUFF, REALLY.

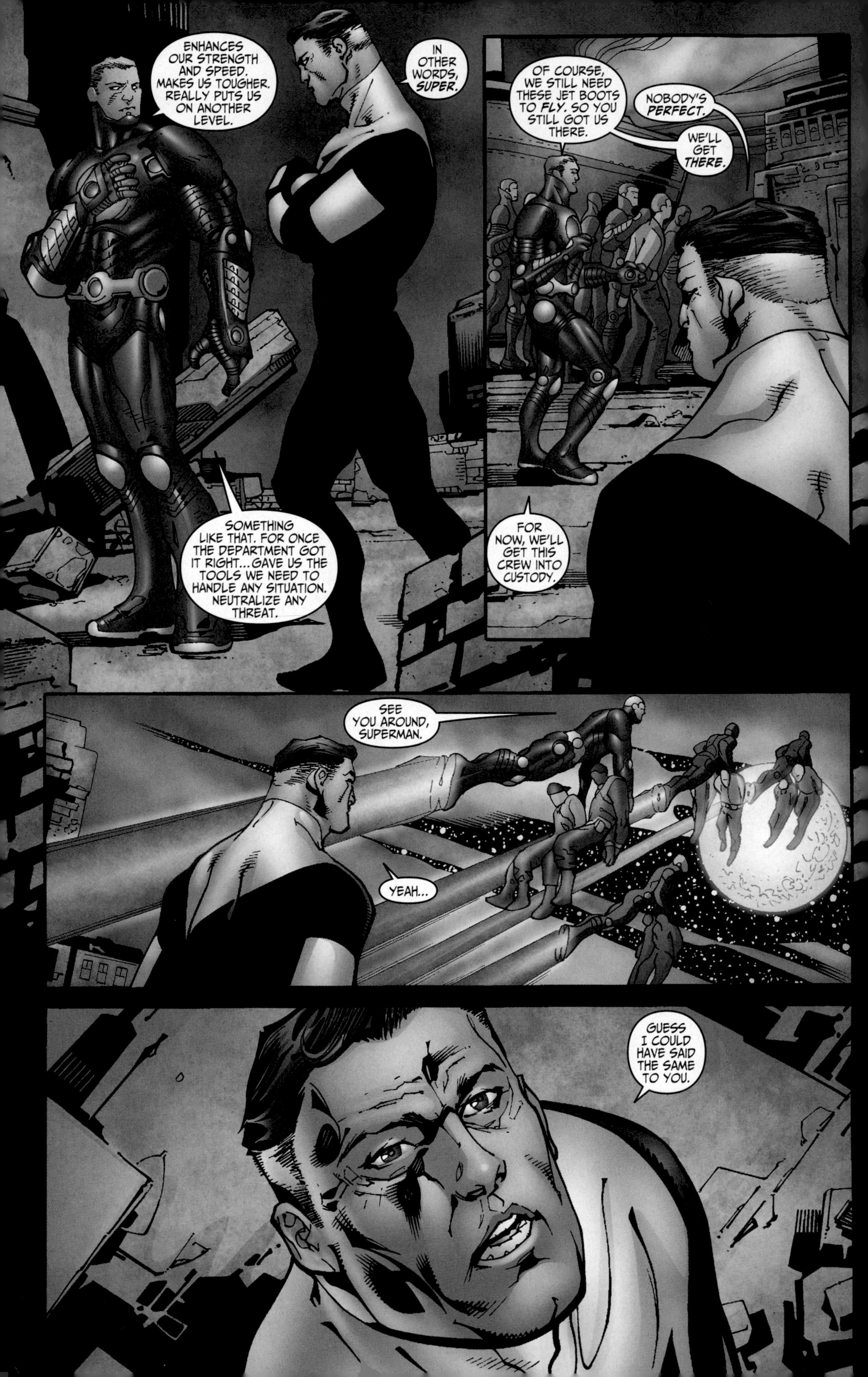
ENHANCES OUR STRENGTH AND SPEED. MAKES US TOUGHER. REALLY PUTS US ON ANOTHER LEVEL.
IN OTHER WORDS, SUPER.
SOMETHING LIKE THAT. FOR ONCE THE DEPARTMENT GOT IT RIGHT...GAVE US THE TOOLS WE NEED TO HANDLE ANY SITUATION. NEUTRALIZE ANY THREAT.
OF COURSE, WE STILL NEED THESE JET BOOTS TO FLY. SO YOU STILL GOT US THERE.
NOBODY'S PERFECT.
WE'LL GET THERE.
FOR NOW, WE'LL GET THIS CREW INTO CUSTODY.
SEE YOU AROUND, SUPERMAN.
YEAH...
GUESS I COULD HAVE SAID THE SAME TO YOU.

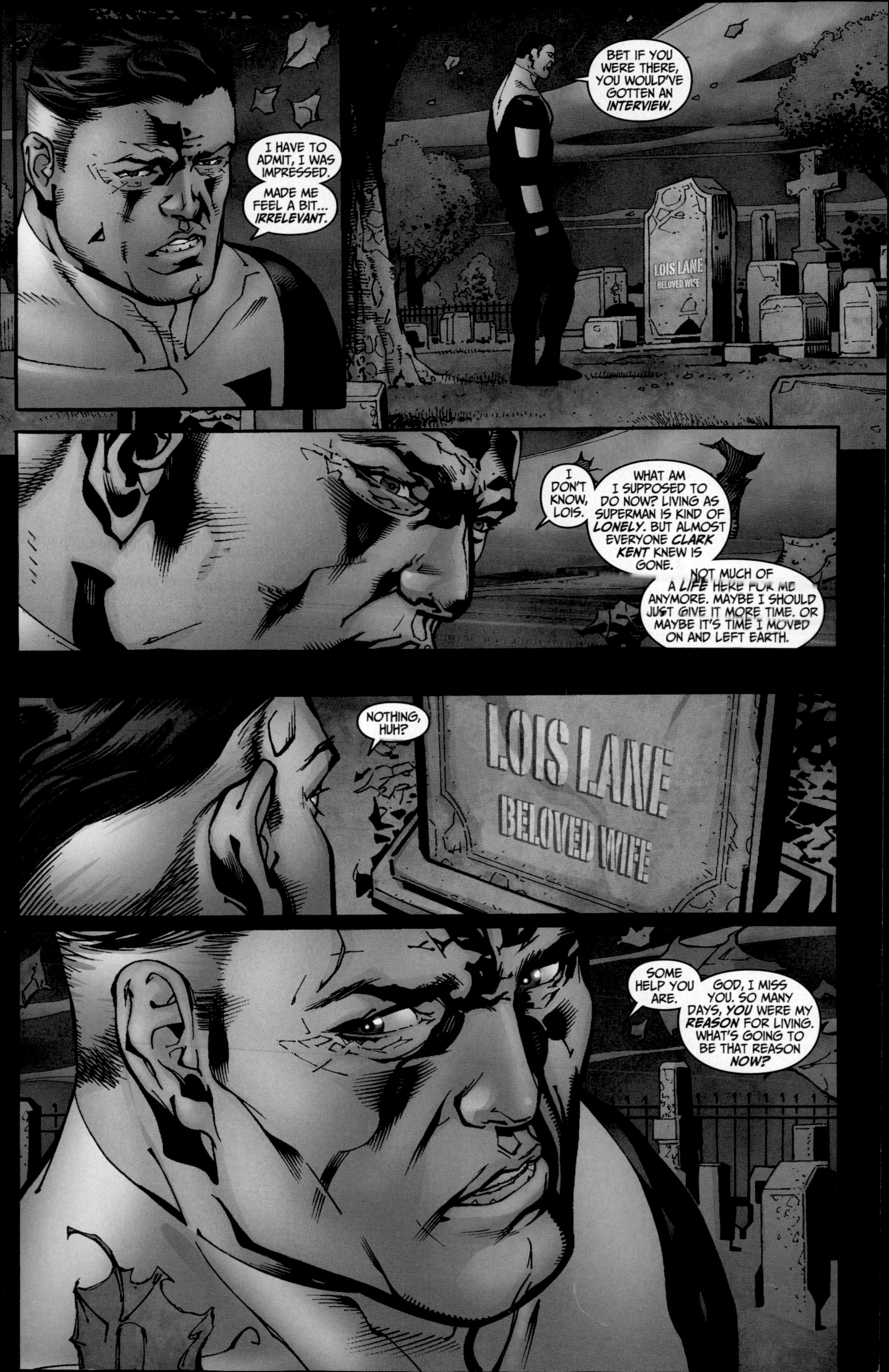
I HAVE TO ADMIT, I WAS IMPRESSED.
MADE ME FEEL A BIT... IRRELEVANT.
BET IF YOU WERE THERE, YOU WOULD'VE GOTTEN AN INTERVIEW.
LOIS LANE
BELOVED WIFE
I DON'T KNOW, LOIS.
WHAT AM I SUPPOSED TO DO NOW? LIVING AS SUPERMAN IS KIND OF LONELY. BUT ALMOST EVERYONE CLARK KENT KNEW IS GONE.
NOT MUCH OF A LIFE HERE FOR ME ANYMORE. MAYBE I SHOULD JUST GIVE IT MORE TIME. OR MAYBE IT'S TIME I MOVED ON AND LEFT EARTH.
NOTHING, HUH?
LOIS LANE
BELOVED WIFE
SOME HELP YOU ARE.
GOD, I MISS YOU. SO MANY DAYS, YOU WERE MY REASON FOR LIVING. WHAT'S GOING TO BE THAT REASON NOW?

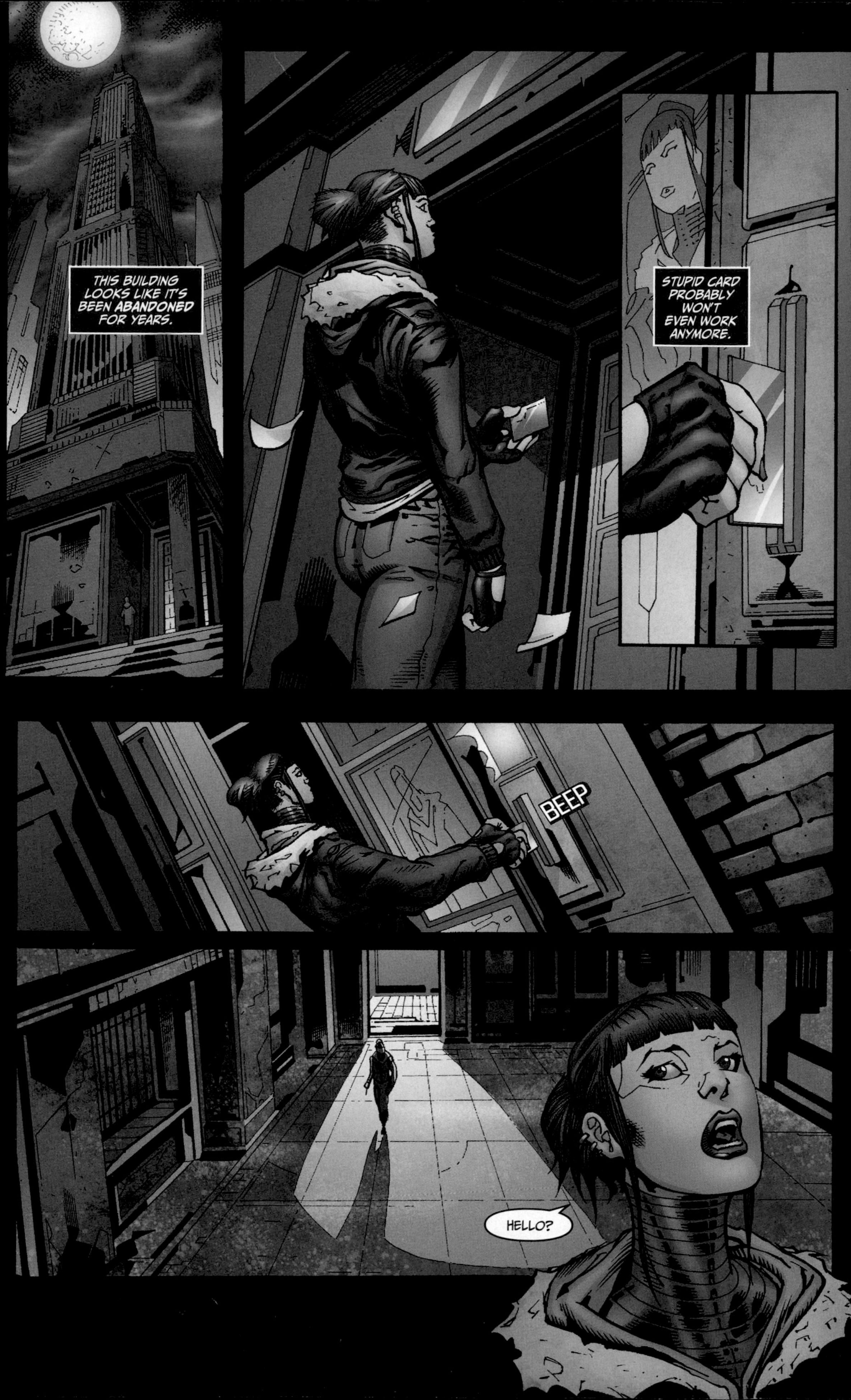
THIS BUILDING LOOKS LIKE IT'S BEEN ABANDONED FOR YEARS.
STUPID CARD PROBABLY WON'T EVEN WORK ANYMORE.
BEEP
HELLO?

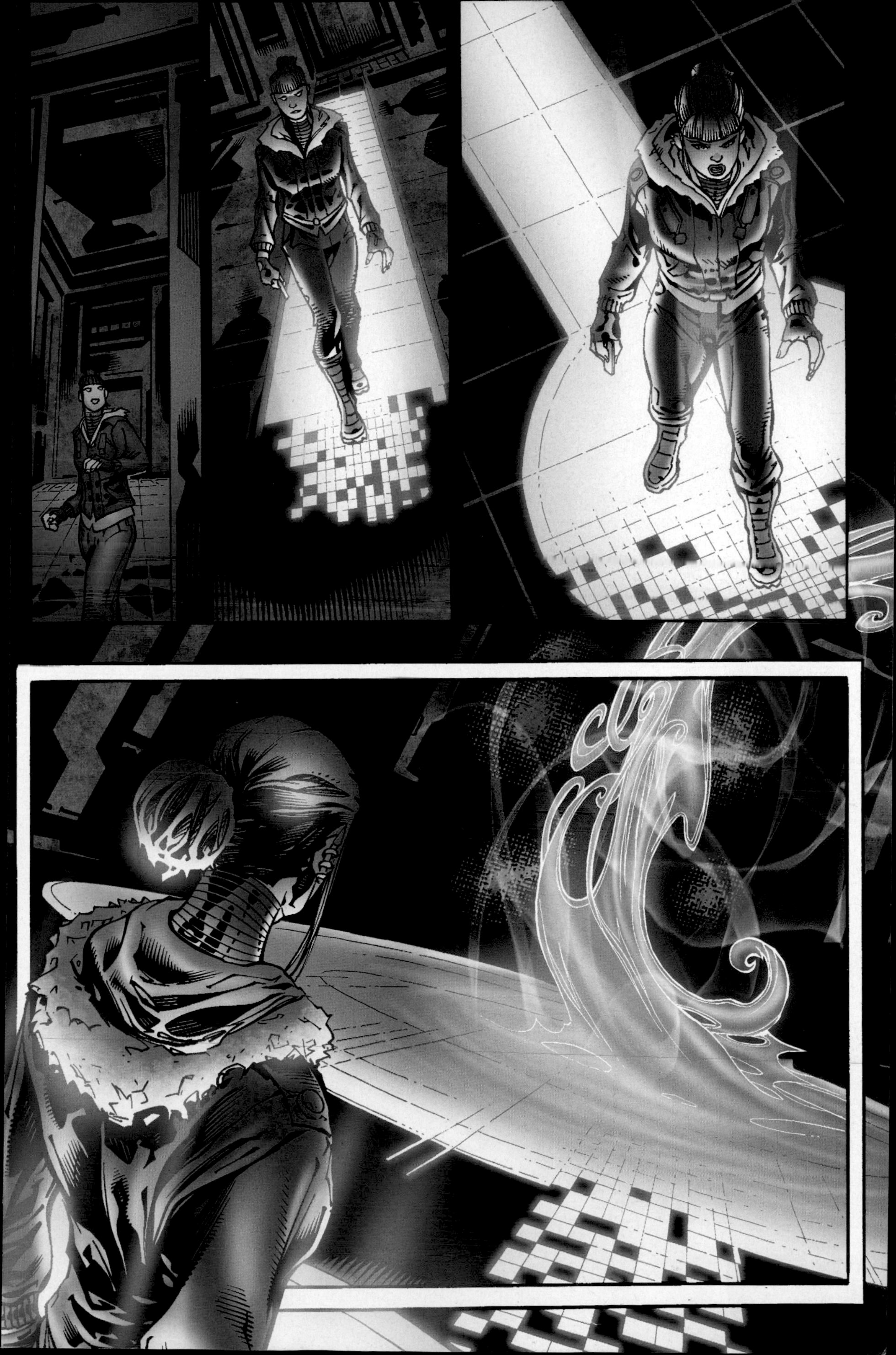

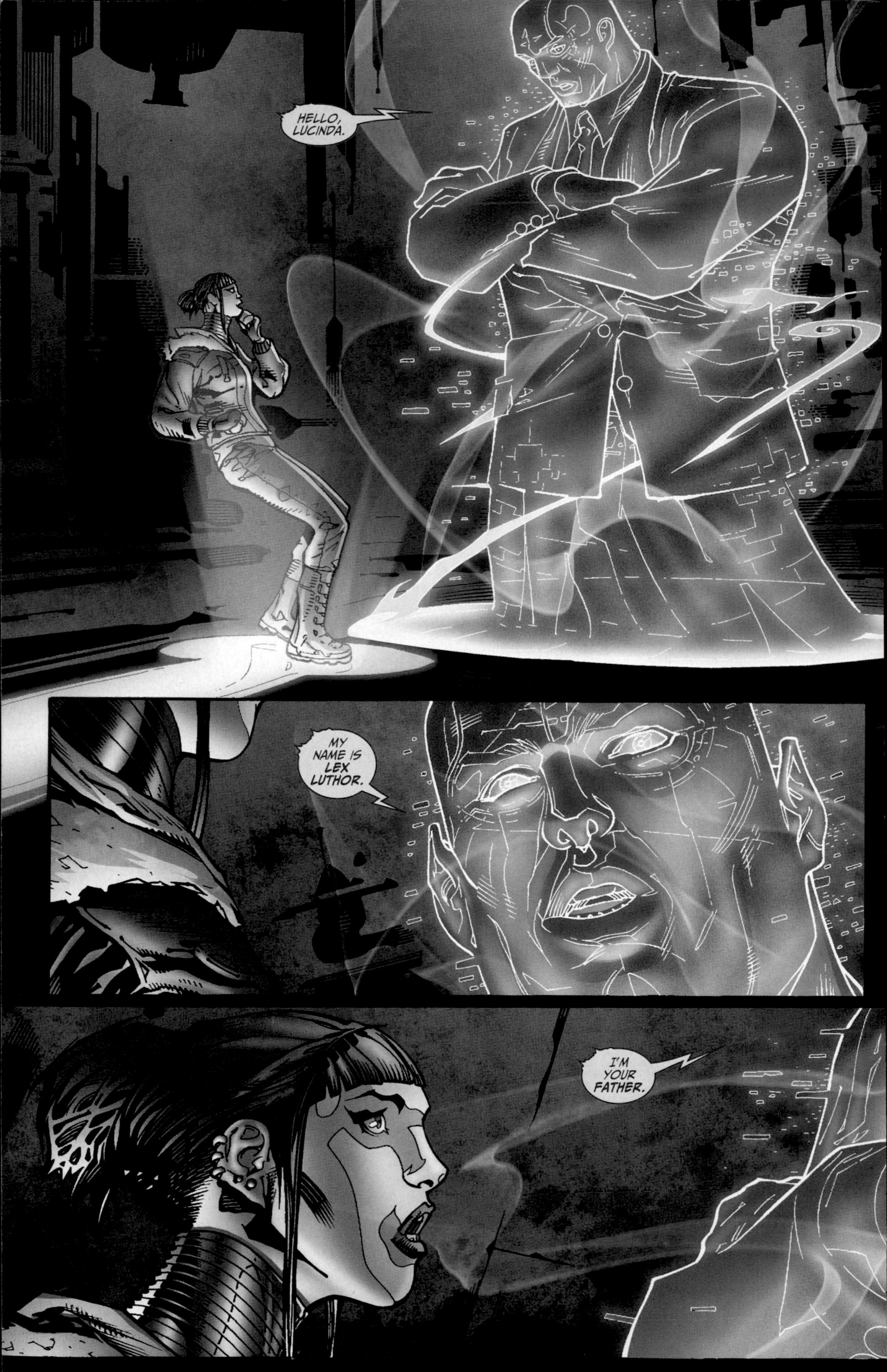
HELLO, LUCINDA.
MY NAME IS LEX LUTHOR.
I'M YOUR FATHER.

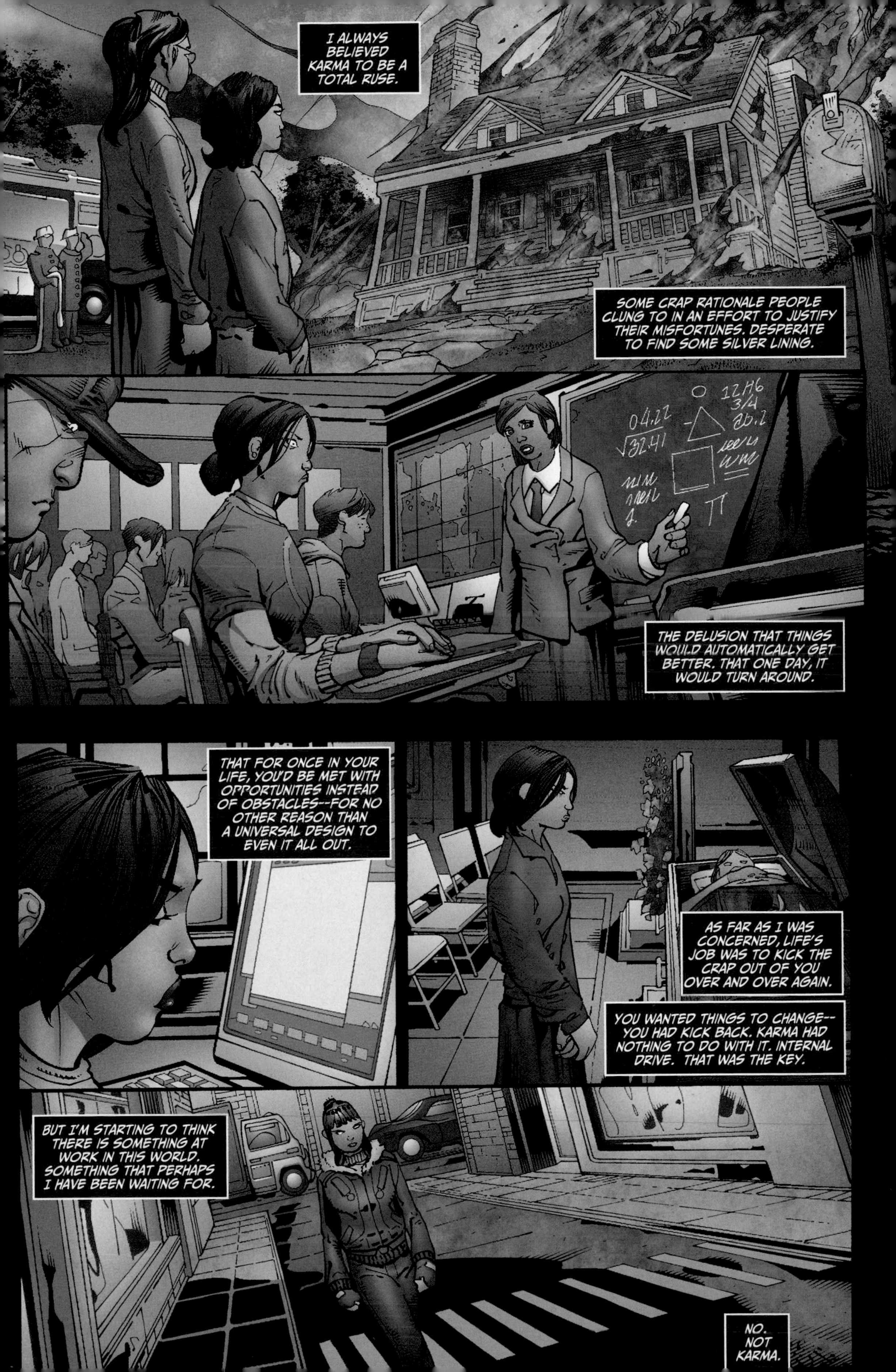
I ALWAYS BELIEVED KARMA TO BE A TOTAL RUSE.
SOME CRAP RATIONALE PEOPLE CLUNG TO IN AN EFFORT TO JUSTIFY THEIR MISFORTUNES. DESPERATE TO FIND SOME SILVER LINING.
THE DELUSION THAT THINGS WOULD AUTOMATICALLY GET BETTER. THAT ONE DAY, IT WOULD TURN AROUND.
THAT FOR ONCE IN YOUR LIFE, YOU'D BE MET WITH OPPORTUNITIES INSTEAD OF OBSTACLES--FOR NO OTHER REASON THAN A UNIVERSAL DESIGN TO EVEN IT ALL OUT.
AS FAR AS I WAS CONCERNED, LIFE'S JOB WAS TO KICK THE CRAP OUT OF YOU OVER AND OVER AGAIN.
YOU WANTED THINGS TO CHANGE--YOU HAD KICK BACK. KARMA HAD NOTHING TO DO WITH IT. INTERNAL DRIVE. THAT WAS THE KEY.
BUT I'M STARTING TO THINK THERE IS SOMETHING AT WORK IN THIS WORLD. SOMETHING THAT PERHAPS I HAVE BEEN WAITING FOR.
NO. NOT KARMA.

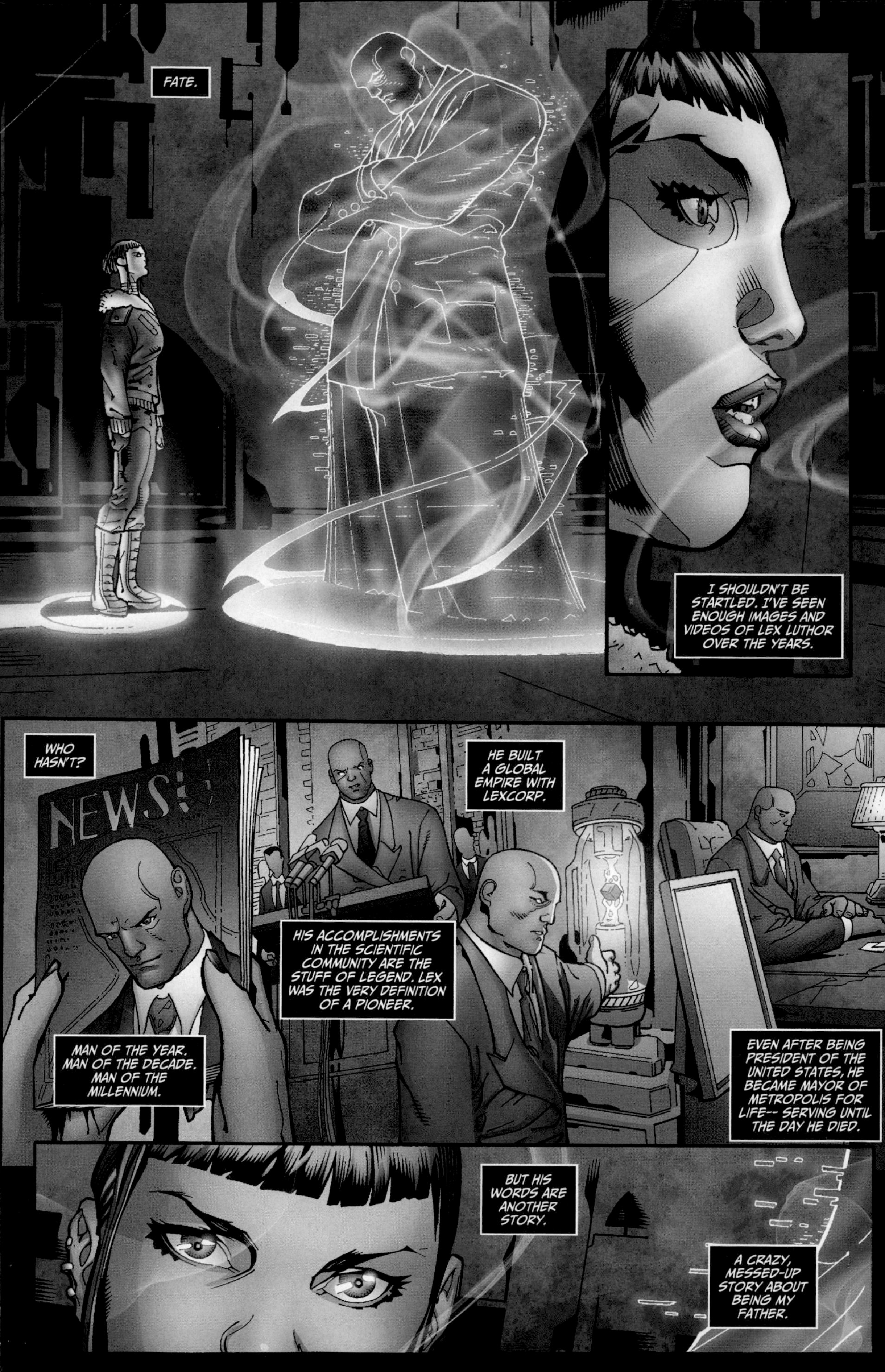
FATE.
I SHOULDN'T BE STARTLED. I'VE SEEN ENOUGH IMAGES AND VIDEOS OF LEX LUTHOR OVER THE YEARS.
WHO HASN'T?
NEWS
HE BUILT A GLOBAL EMPIRE WITH LEXCORP.
HIS ACCOMPLISHMENTS IN THE SCIENTIFIC COMMUNITY ARE THE STUFF OF LEGEND. LEX WAS THE VERY DEFINITION OF A PIONEER.
MAN OF THE YEAR. MAN OF THE DECADE. MAN OF THE MILLENNIUM.
EVEN AFTER BEING PRESIDENT OF THE UNITED STATES, HE BECAME MAYOR OF METROPOLIS FOR LIFE-- SERVING UNTIL THE DAY HE DIED.
BUT HIS WORDS ARE ANOTHER STORY.
A CRAZY, MESSED-UP STORY ABOUT BEING MY FATHER.

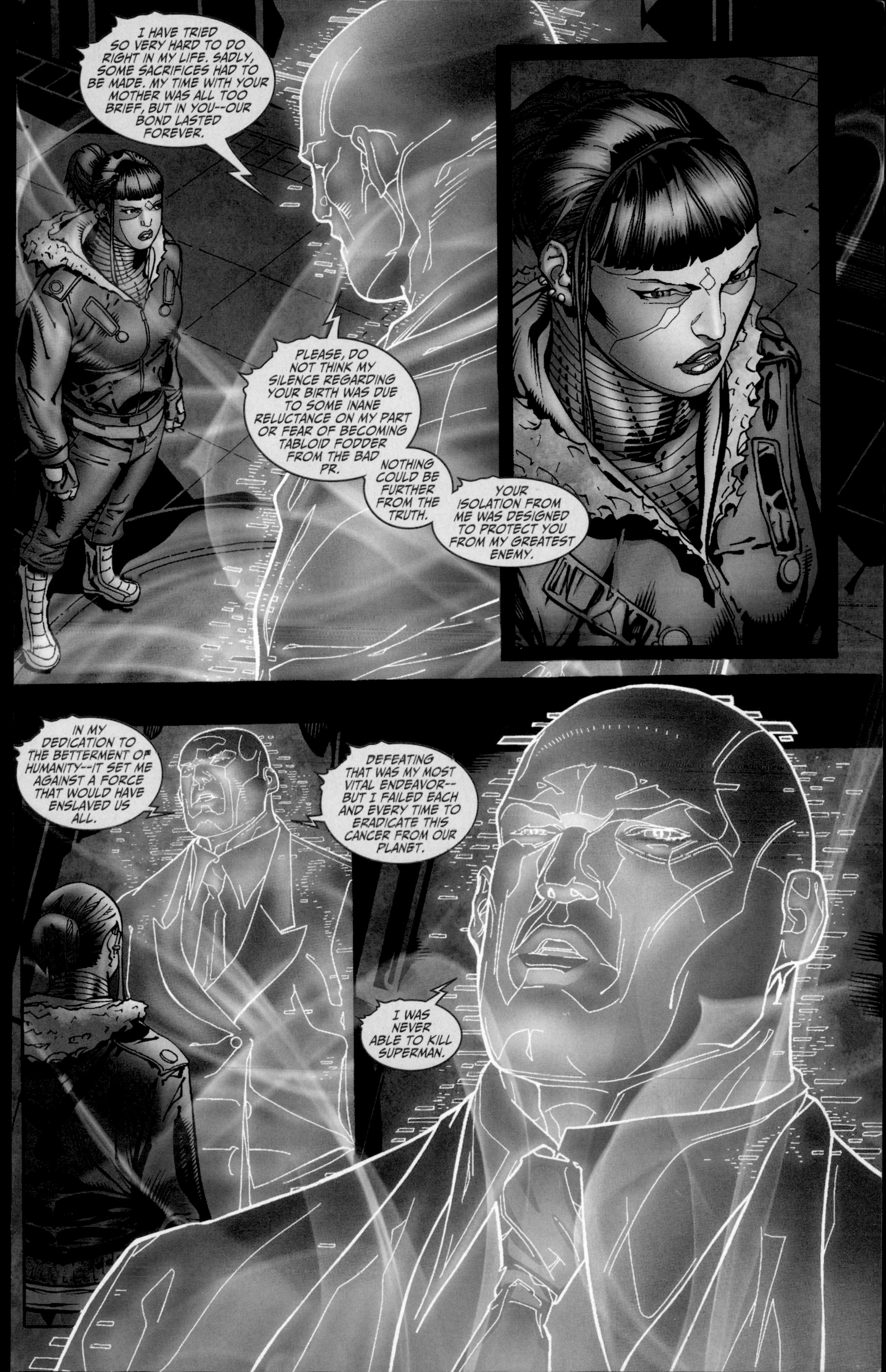
I HAVE TRIED SO VERY HARD TO DO RIGHT IN MY LIFE. SADLY, SOME SACRIFICES HAD TO BE MADE. MY TIME WITH YOUR MOTHER WAS ALL TOO BRIEF, BUT IN YOU--OUR BOND LASTED FOREVER.
PLEASE, DO NOT THINK MY SILENCE REGARDING YOUR BIRTH WAS DUE TO SOME INANE RELUCTANCE ON MY PART OR FEAR OF BECOMING TABLOID FODDER FROM THE BAD PR.
NOTHING COULD BE FURTHER FROM THE TRUTH.
YOUR ISOLATION FROM ME WAS DESIGNED TO PROTECT YOU FROM MY GREATEST ENEMY.
IN MY DEDICATION TO THE BETTERMENT OF HUMANITY--IT SET ME AGAINST A FORCE THAT WOULD HAVE ENSLAVED US ALL.
DEFEATING THAT WAS MY MOST VITAL ENDEAVOR--BUT I FAILED EACH AND EVERY TIME TO ERADICATE THIS CANCER FROM OUR PLANET.
I WAS NEVER ABLE TO KILL SUPERMAN.

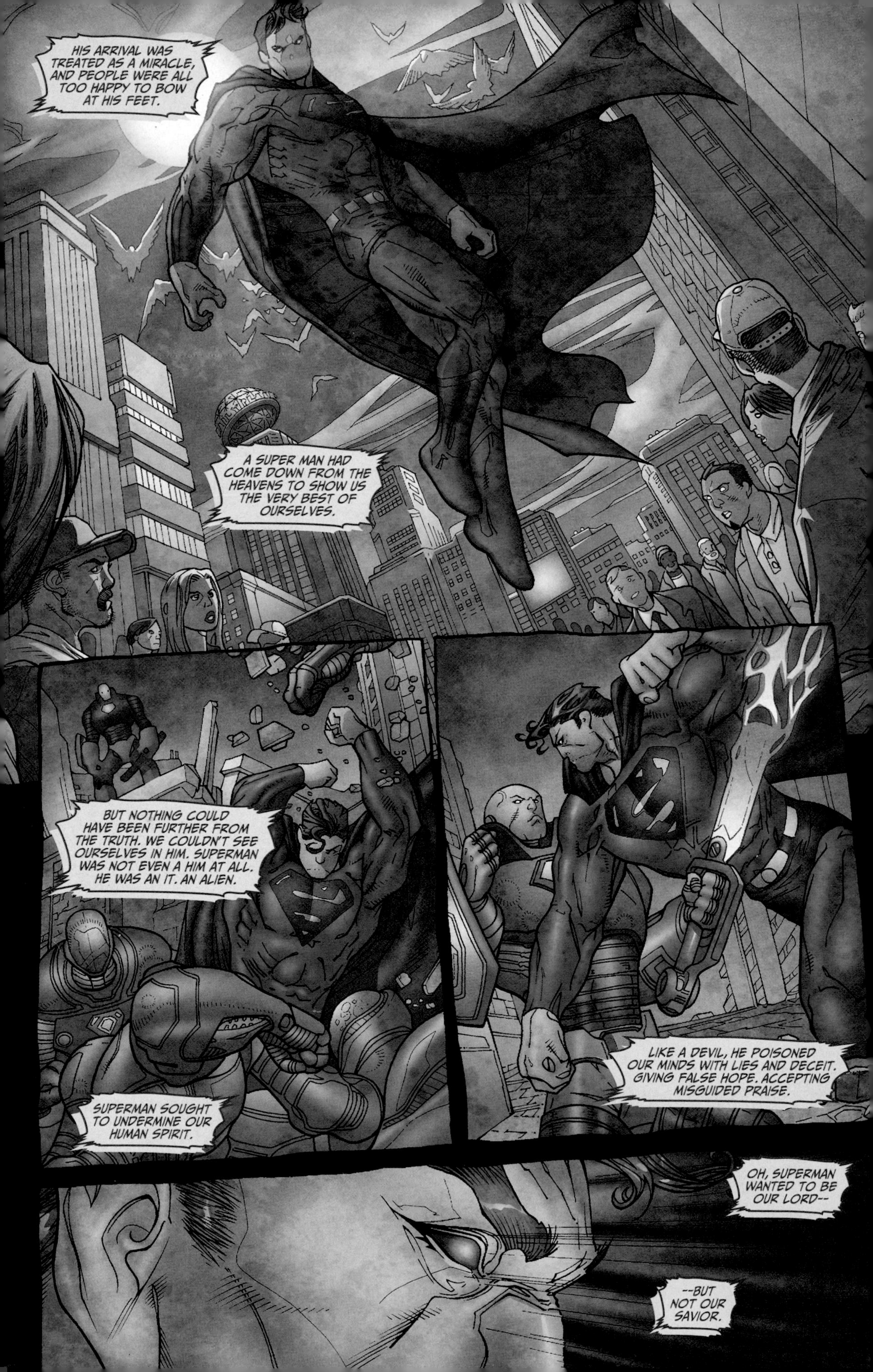
HIS ARRIVAL WAS TREATED AS A MIRACLE, AND PEOPLE WERE ALL TOO HAPPY TO BOW AT HIS FEET.
A SUPER MAN HAD COME DOWN FROM THE HEAVENS TO SHOW US THE VERY BEST OF OURSELVES.
BUT NOTHING COULD HAVE BEEN FURTHER FROM THE TRUTH. WE COULDN'T SEE OURSELVES IN HIM. SUPERMAN WAS NOT EVEN A HIM AT ALL. HE WAS AN IT. AN ALIEN.
SUPERMAN SOUGHT TO UNDERMINE OUR HUMAN SPIRIT.
LIKE A DEVIL, HE POISONED OUR MINDS WITH LIES AND DECEIT. GIVING FALSE HOPE. ACCEPTING MISGUIDED PRAISE.
OH, SUPERMAN WANTED TO BE OUR LORD--
--BUT NOT OUR SAVIOR.

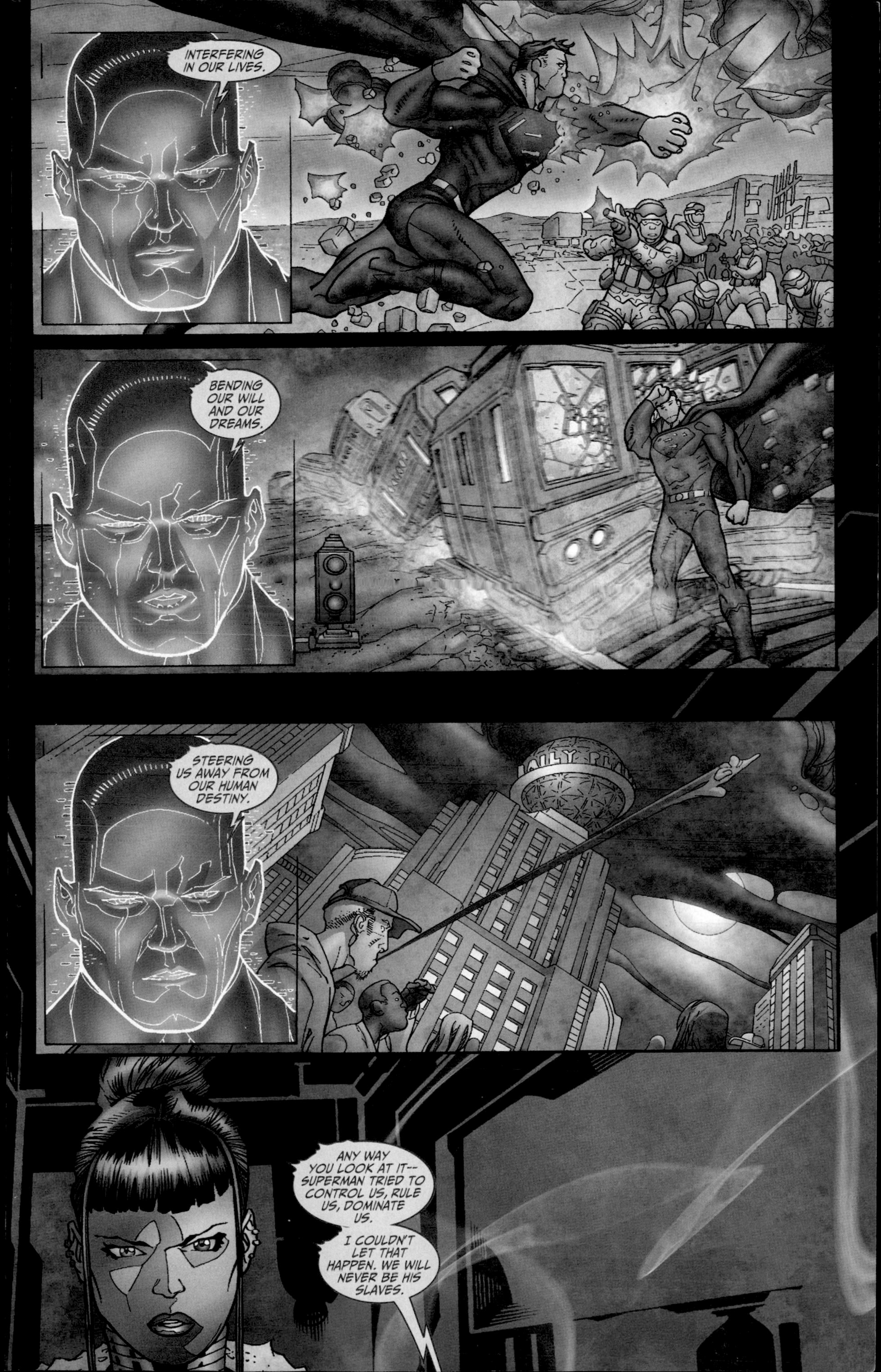
INTERFERING IN OUR LIVES.
BENDING OUR WILL AND OUR DREAMS.
STEERING US AWAY FROM OUR HUMAN DESTINY.
ANY WAY YOU LOOK AT IT-- SUPERMAN TRIED TO CONTROL US, RULE US, DOMINATE US.
I COULDN'T LET THAT HAPPEN. WE WILL NEVER BE HIS SLAVES.

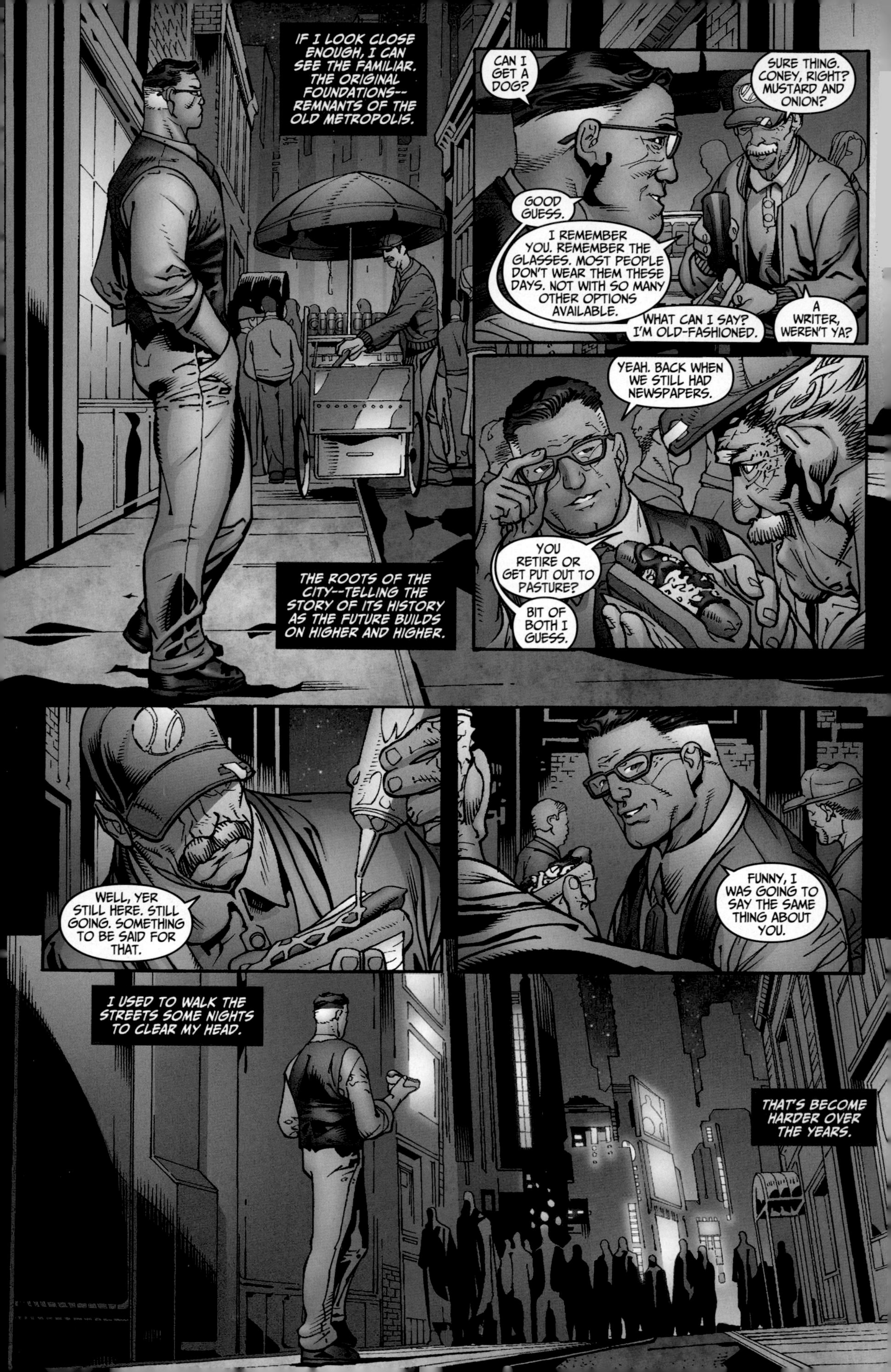
IF I LOOK CLOSE ENOUGH, I CAN SEE THE FAMILIAR. THE ORIGINAL FOUNDATIONS-- REMNANTS OF THE OLD METROPOLIS.
CAN I GET A DOG?
SURE THING. CONEY, RIGHT? MUSTARD AND ONION?
GOOD GUESS.
I REMEMBER YOU. REMEMBER THE GLASSES. MOST PEOPLE DON'T WEAR THEM THESE DAYS. NOT WITH SO MANY OTHER OPTIONS AVAILABLE.
WHAT CAN I SAY? I'M OLD-FASHIONED.
A WRITER, WEREN'T YA?
YEAH. BACK WHEN WE STILL HAD NEWSPAPERS.
YOU RETIRE OR GET PUT OUT TO PASTURE?
BIT OF BOTH I GUESS.
THE ROOTS OF THE CITY--TELLING THE STORY OF ITS HISTORY AS THE FUTURE BUILDS ON HIGHER AND HIGHER.
WELL, YER STILL HERE. STILL GOING. SOMETHING TO BE SAID FOR THAT.
FUNNY, I WAS GOING TO SAY THE SAME THING ABOUT YOU.
I USED TO WALK THE STREETS SOME NIGHTS TO CLEAR MY HEAD.
THAT'S BECOME HARDER OVER THE YEARS.

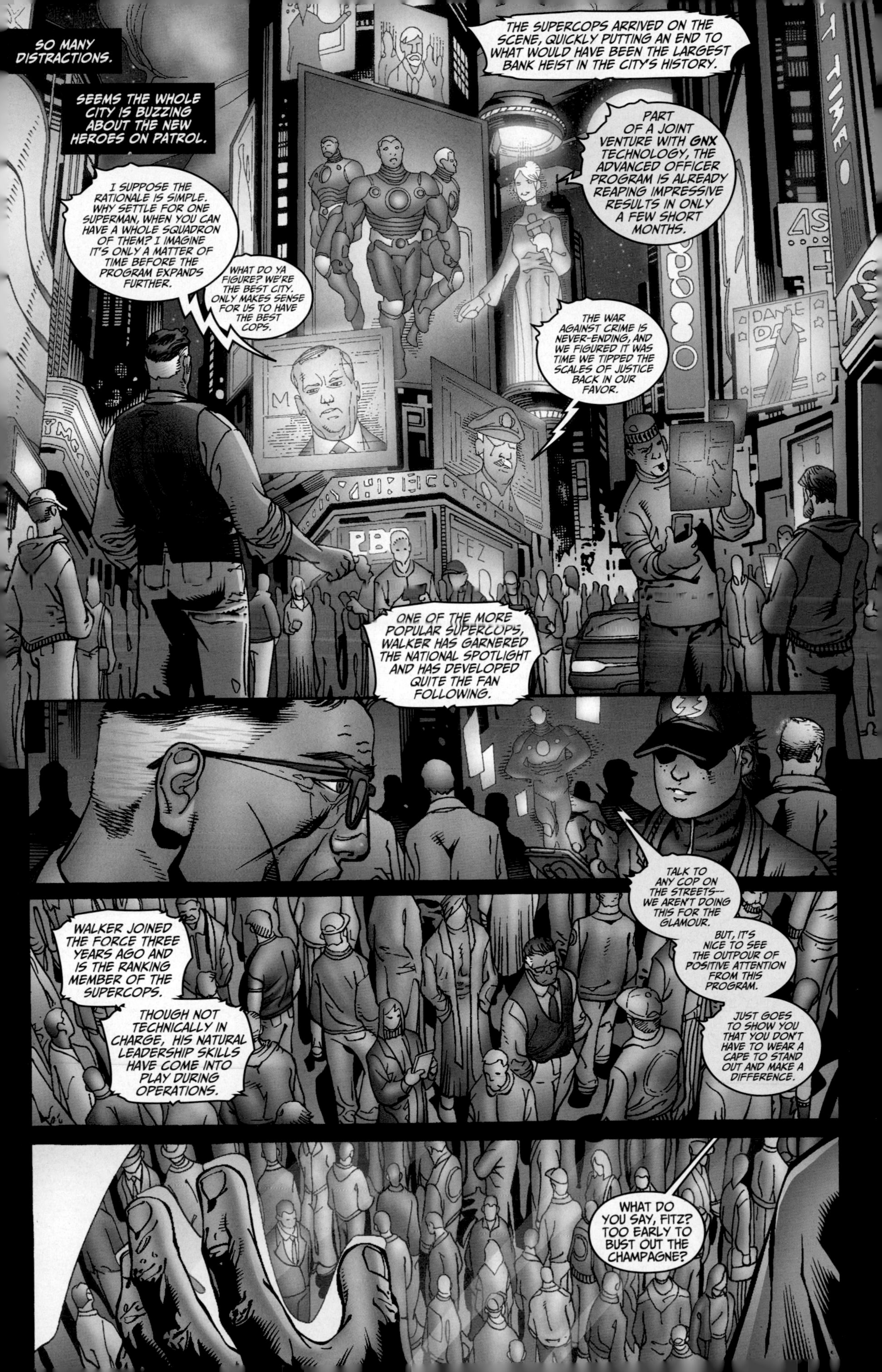
SO MANY DISTRACTIONS.
SEEMS THE WHOLE CITY IS BUZZING ABOUT THE NEW HEROES ON PATROL.
THE SUPERCOPS ARRIVED ON THE SCENE, QUICKLY PUTTING AN END TO WHAT WOULD HAVE BEEN THE LARGEST BANK HEIST IN THE CITY'S HISTORY.
PART OF A JOINT VENTURE WITH GNX TECHNOLOGY, THE ADVANCED OFFICER PROGRAM IS ALREADY REAPING IMPRESSIVE RESULTS IN ONLY A FEW SHORT MONTHS.
I SUPPOSE THE RATIONALE IS SIMPLE. WHY SETTLE FOR ONE SUPERMAN, WHEN YOU CAN HAVE A WHOLE SQUADRON OF THEM? I IMAGINE IT'S ONLY A MATTER OF TIME BEFORE THE PROGRAM EXPANDS FURTHER.
WHAT DO YA FIGURE? WE'RE THE BEST CITY. ONLY MAKES SENSE FOR US TO HAVE THE BEST COPS.
THE WAR AGAINST CRIME IS NEVER-ENDING, AND WE FIGURED IT WAS TIME WE TIPPED THE SCALES OF JUSTICE BACK IN OUR FAVOR.
ONE OF THE MORE POPULAR SUPERCOPS, WALKER HAS GARNERED THE NATIONAL SPOTLIGHT AND HAS DEVELOPED QUITE THE FAN FOLLOWING.
TALK TO ANY COP ON THE STREETS-- WE AREN'T DOING THIS FOR THE GLAMOUR.
BUT, IT'S NICE TO SEE THE OUTPOUR OF POSITIVE ATTENTION FROM THIS PROGRAM.
JUST GOES TO SHOW YOU THAT YOU DON'T HAVE TO WEAR A CAPE TO STAND OUT AND MAKE A DIFFERENCE.
WALKER JOINED THE FORCE THREE YEARS AGO AND IS THE RANKING MEMBER OF THE SUPERCOPS.
THOUGH NOT TECHNICALLY IN CHARGE, HIS NATURAL LEADERSHIP SKILLS HAVE COME INTO PLAY DURING OPERATIONS.
WHAT DO YOU SAY, FITZ? TOO EARLY TO BUST OUT THE CHAMPAGNE?

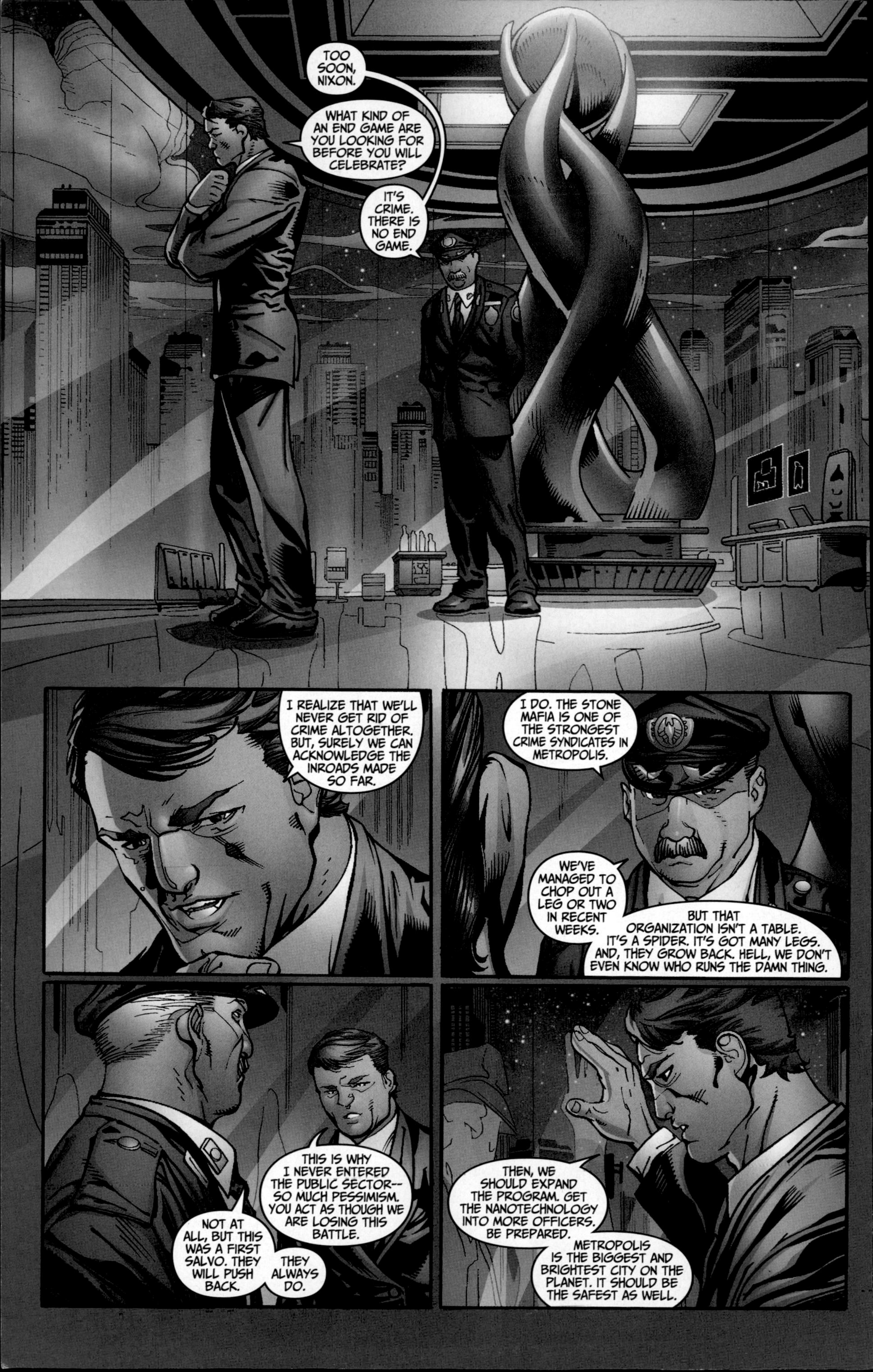
TOO SOON, NIXON.
WHAT KIND OF AN END GAME ARE YOU LOOKING FOR BEFORE YOU WILL CELEBRATE?
IT'S CRIME. THERE IS NO END GAME.
I REALIZE THAT WE'LL NEVER GET RID OF CRIME ALTOGETHER. BUT, SURELY WE CAN ACKNOWLEDGE THE INROADS MADE SO FAR.
I DO. THE STONE MAFIA IS ONE OF THE STRONGEST CRIME SYNDICATES IN METROPOLIS.
WE'VE MANAGED TO CHOP OUT A LEG OR TWO IN RECENT WEEKS.
BUT THAT ORGANIZATION ISN'T A TABLE. IT'S A SPIDER. IT'S GOT MANY LEGS. AND, THEY GROW BACK. HELL, WE DON'T EVEN KNOW WHO RUNS THE DAMN THING.
THIS IS WHY I NEVER ENTERED THE PUBLIC SECTOR--SO MUCH PESSIMISM. YOU ACT AS THOUGH WE ARE LOSING THIS BATTLE.
NOT AT ALL, BUT THIS WAS A FIRST SALVO. THEY WILL PUSH BACK.
THEY ALWAYS DO.
THEN, WE SHOULD EXPAND THE PROGRAM. GET THE NANOTECHNOLOGY INTO MORE OFFICERS. BE PREPARED.
METROPOLIS IS THE BIGGEST AND BRIGHTEST CITY ON THE PLANET. IT SHOULD BE THE SAFEST AS WELL.

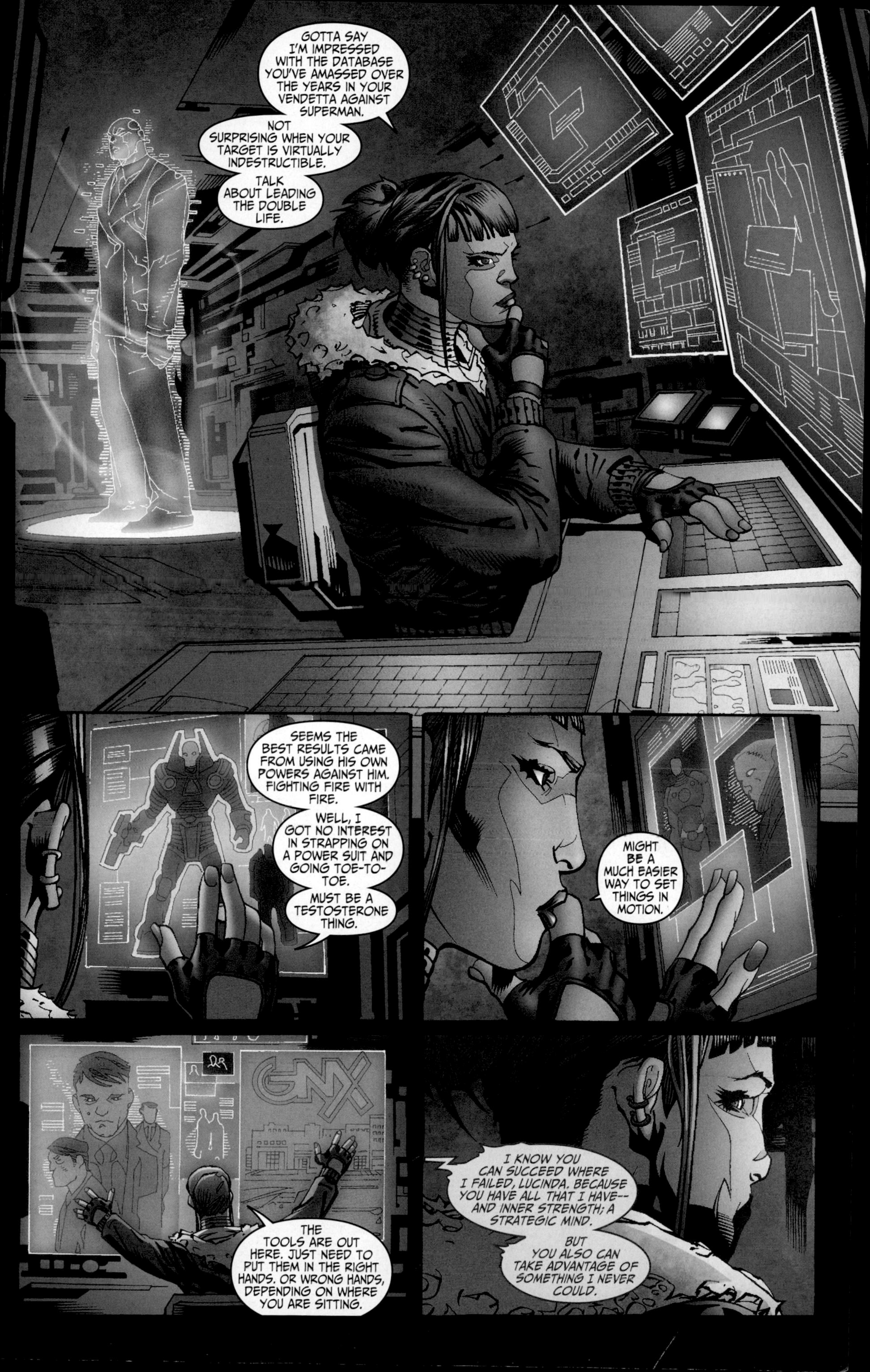
GOTTA SAY I'M IMPRESSED WITH THE DATABASE YOU'VE AMASSED OVER THE YEARS IN YOUR VENDETTA AGAINST SUPERMAN.
NOT SURPRISING WHEN YOUR TARGET IS VIRTUALLY INDESTRUCTIBLE.
TALK ABOUT LEADING THE DOUBLE LIFE.
SEEMS THE BEST RESULTS CAME FROM USING HIS OWN POWERS AGAINST HIM. FIGHTING FIRE WITH FIRE.
WELL, I GOT NO INTEREST IN STRAPPING ON A POWER SUIT AND GOING TOE-TO-TOE.
MUST BE A TESTOSTERONE THING.
MIGHT BE A MUCH EASIER WAY TO SET THINGS IN MOTION.
GNX
THE TOOLS ARE OUT HERE. JUST NEED TO PUT THEM IN THE RIGHT HANDS. OR WRONG HANDS, DEPENDING ON WHERE YOU ARE SITTING.
I KNOW YOU CAN SUCCEED WHERE I FAILED, LUCINDA. BECAUSE YOU HAVE ALL THAT I HAVE-- AND INNER STRENGTH; A STRATEGIC MIND.
BUT YOU ALSO CAN TAKE ADVANTAGE OF SOMETHING I NEVER COULD.

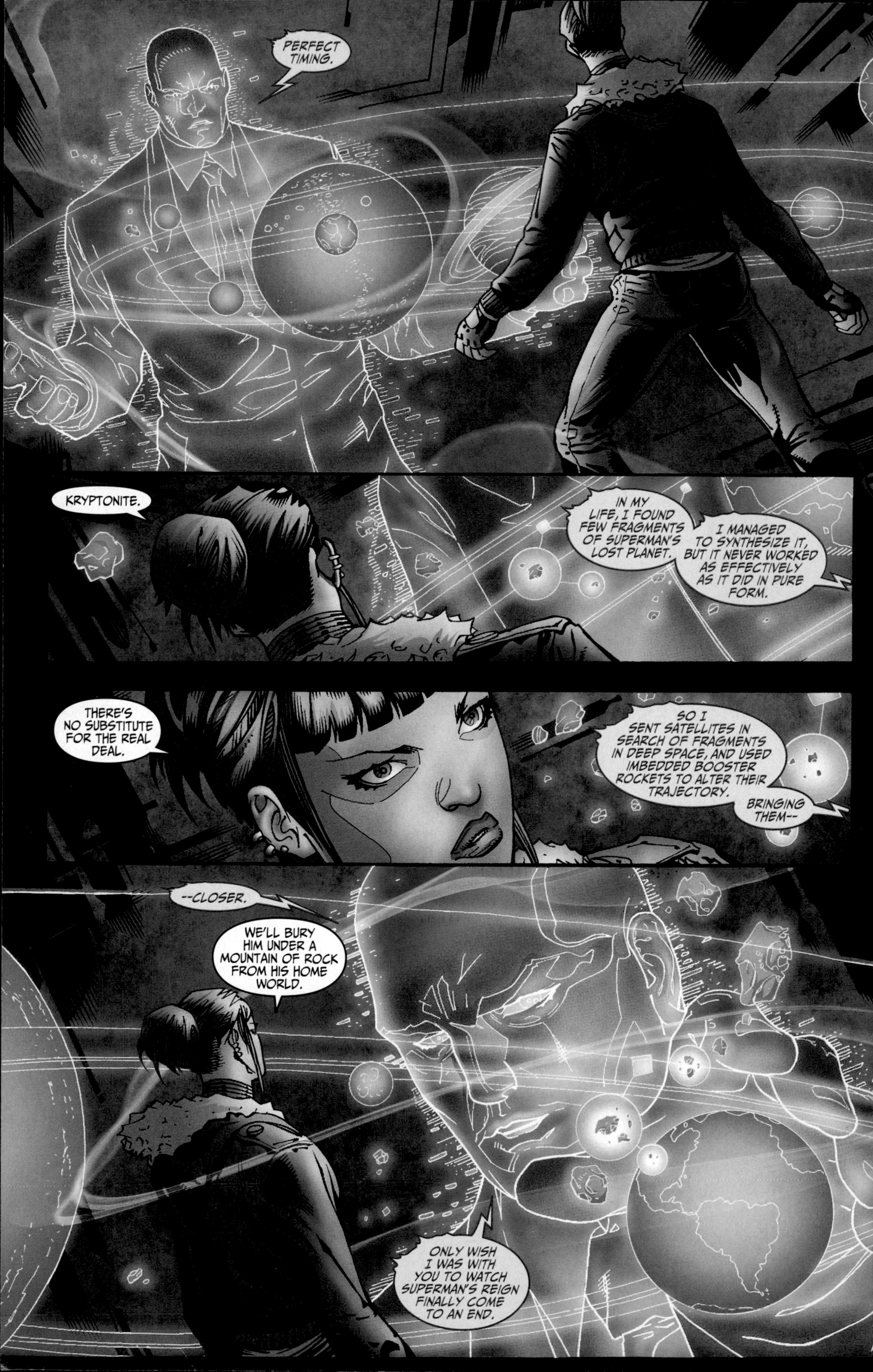
PERFECT TIMING.
KRYPTONITE.
IN MY LIFE, I FOUND FEW FRAGMENTS OF SUPERMAN'S LOST PLANET.
I MANAGED TO SYNTHESIZE IT, BUT IT NEVER WORKED AS EFFECTIVELY AS IT DID IN PURE FORM.
THERE'S NO SUBSTITUTE FOR THE REAL DEAL.
SO I SENT SATELLITES IN SEARCH OF FRAGMENTS IN DEEP SPACE, AND USED IMBEDDED BOOSTER ROCKETS TO ALTER THEIR TRAJECTORY.
BRINGING THEM--
--CLOSER.
WE'LL BURY HIM UNDER A MOUNTAIN OF ROCK FROM HIS HOME WORLD.
ONLY WISH I WAS WITH YOU TO WATCH SUPERMAN'S REIGN FINALLY COME TO AN END.

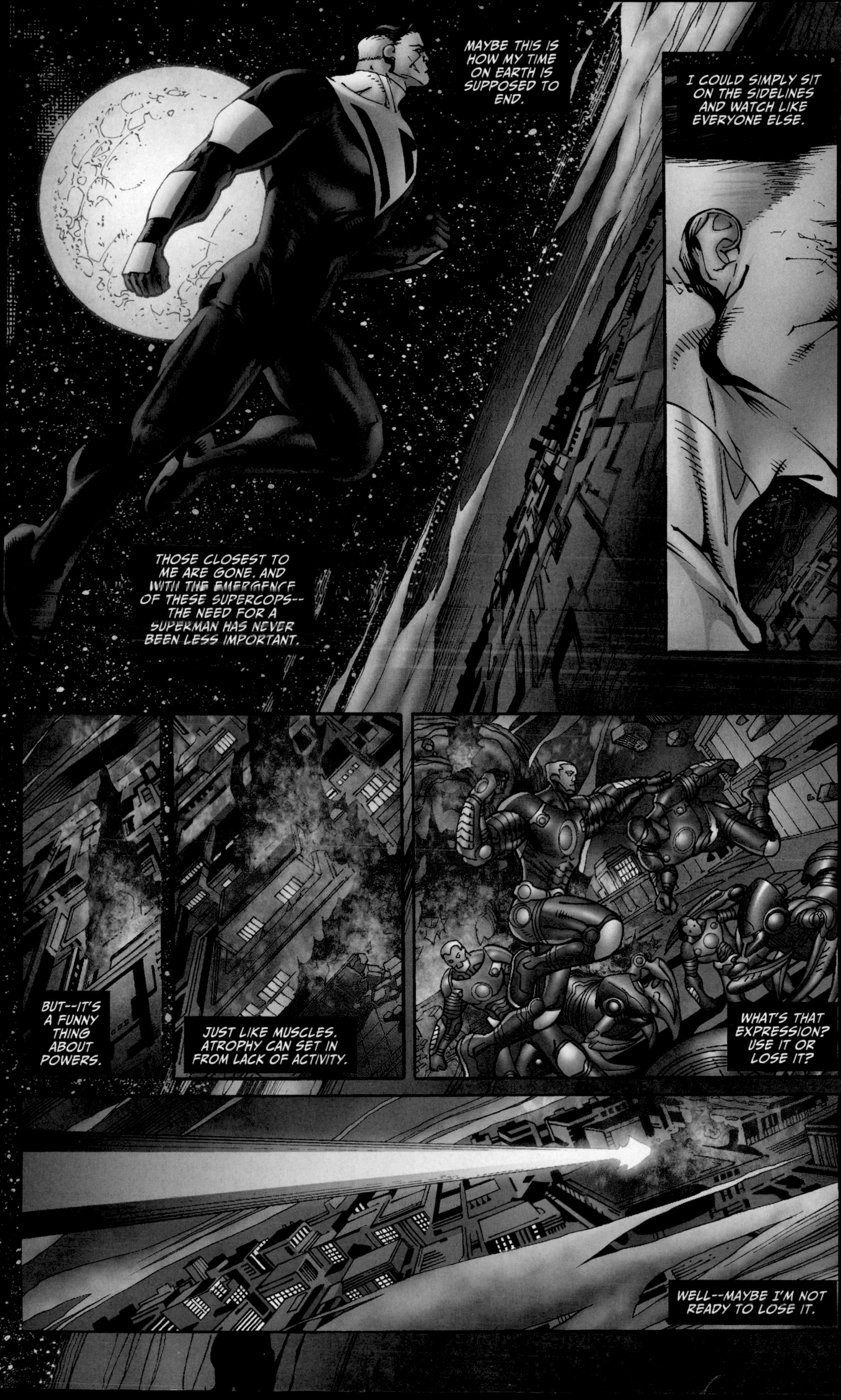
MAYBE THIS IS HOW MY TIME ON EARTH IS SUPPOSED TO END.
I COULD SIMPLY SIT ON THE SIDELINES AND WATCH LIKE EVERYONE ELSE.
THOSE CLOSEST TO ME ARE GONE. AND WITH THE EMERGENCE OF THESE SUPERCOPS-- THE NEED FOR A SUPERMAN HAS NEVER BEEN LESS IMPORTANT.
BUT--IT'S A FUNNY THING ABOUT POWERS.
JUST LIKE MUSCLES. ATROPHY CAN SET IN FROM LACK OF ACTIVITY.
WHAT'S THAT EXPRESSION? USE IT OR LOSE IT?
WELL--MAYBE I'M NOT READY TO LOSE IT.

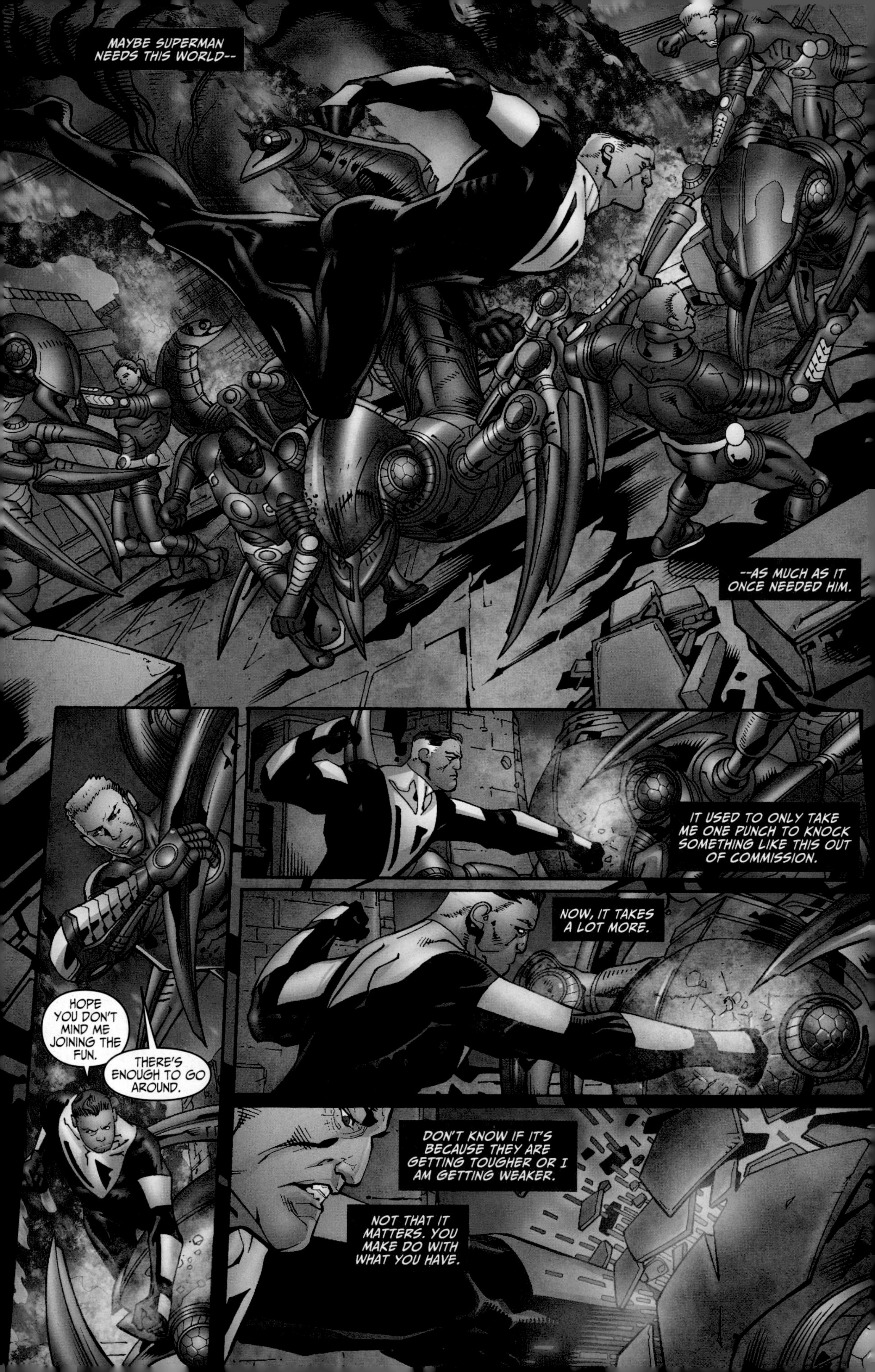
MAYBE SUPERMAN NEEDS THIS WORLD--
--AS MUCH AS IT ONCE NEEDED HIM.
IT USED TO ONLY TAKE ME ONE PUNCH TO KNOCK SOMETHING LIKE THIS OUT OF COMMISSION.
NOW, IT TAKES A LOT MORE.
HOPE YOU DON'T MIND ME JOINING THE FUN.
THERE'S ENOUGH TO GO AROUND.
DON'T KNOW IF IT'S BECAUSE THEY ARE GETTING TOUGHER OR I AM GETTING WEAKER.
NOT THAT IT MATTERS. YOU MAKE DO WITH WHAT YOU HAVE.

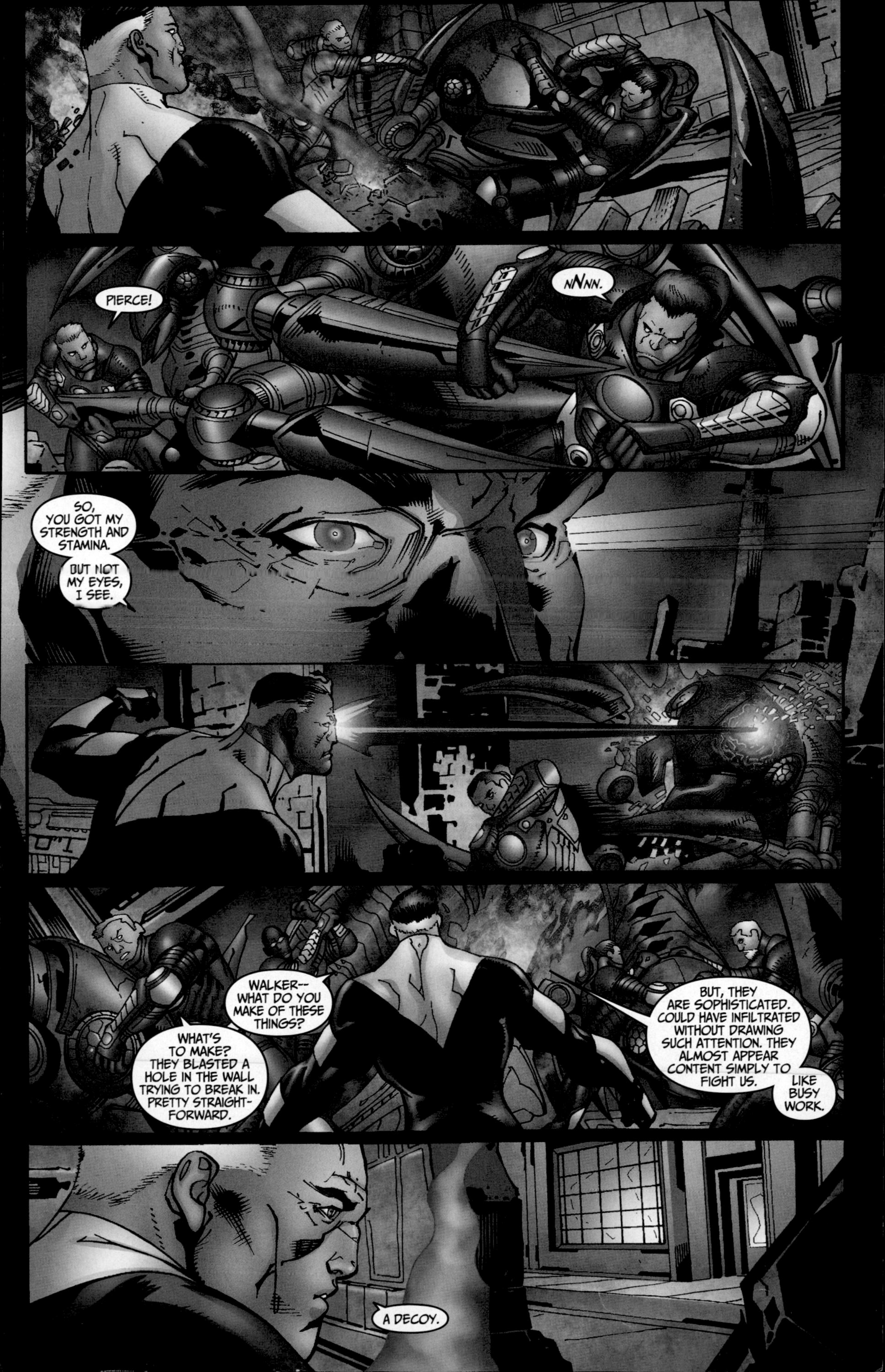
PIERCE!
NNNN.
SO, YOU GOT MY STRENGTH AND STAMINA.
BUT NOT MY EYES, I SEE.
WALKER-- WHAT DO YOU MAKE OF THESE THINGS?
WHAT'S TO MAKE? THEY BLASTED A HOLE IN THE WALL TRYING TO BREAK IN. PRETTY STRAIGHT-FORWARD.
BUT, THEY ARE SOPHISTICATED. COULD HAVE INFILTRATED WITHOUT DRAWING SUCH ATTENTION. THEY ALMOST APPEAR CONTENT SIMPLY TO FIGHT US.
LIKE BUSY WORK.
A DECOY.

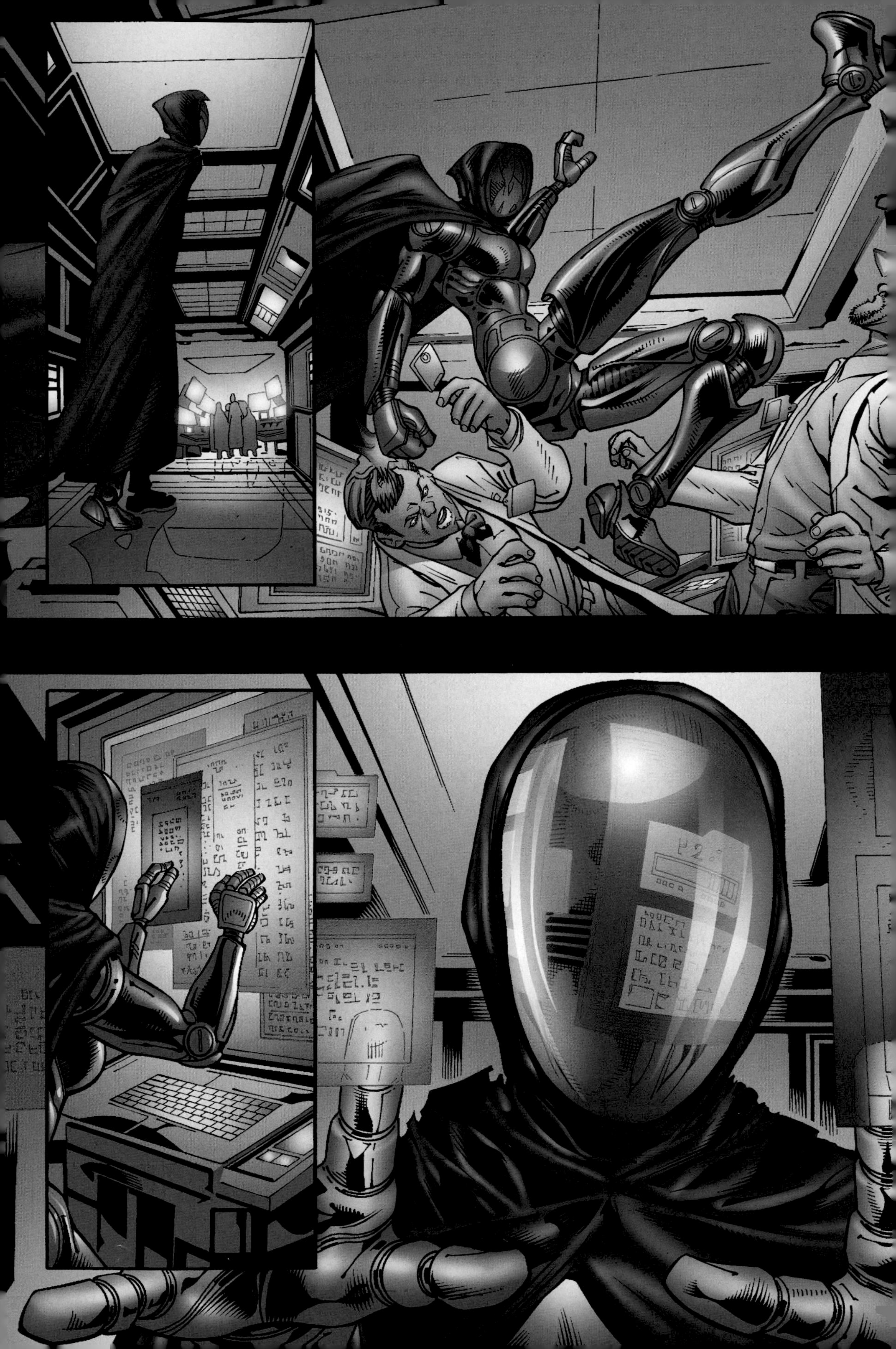

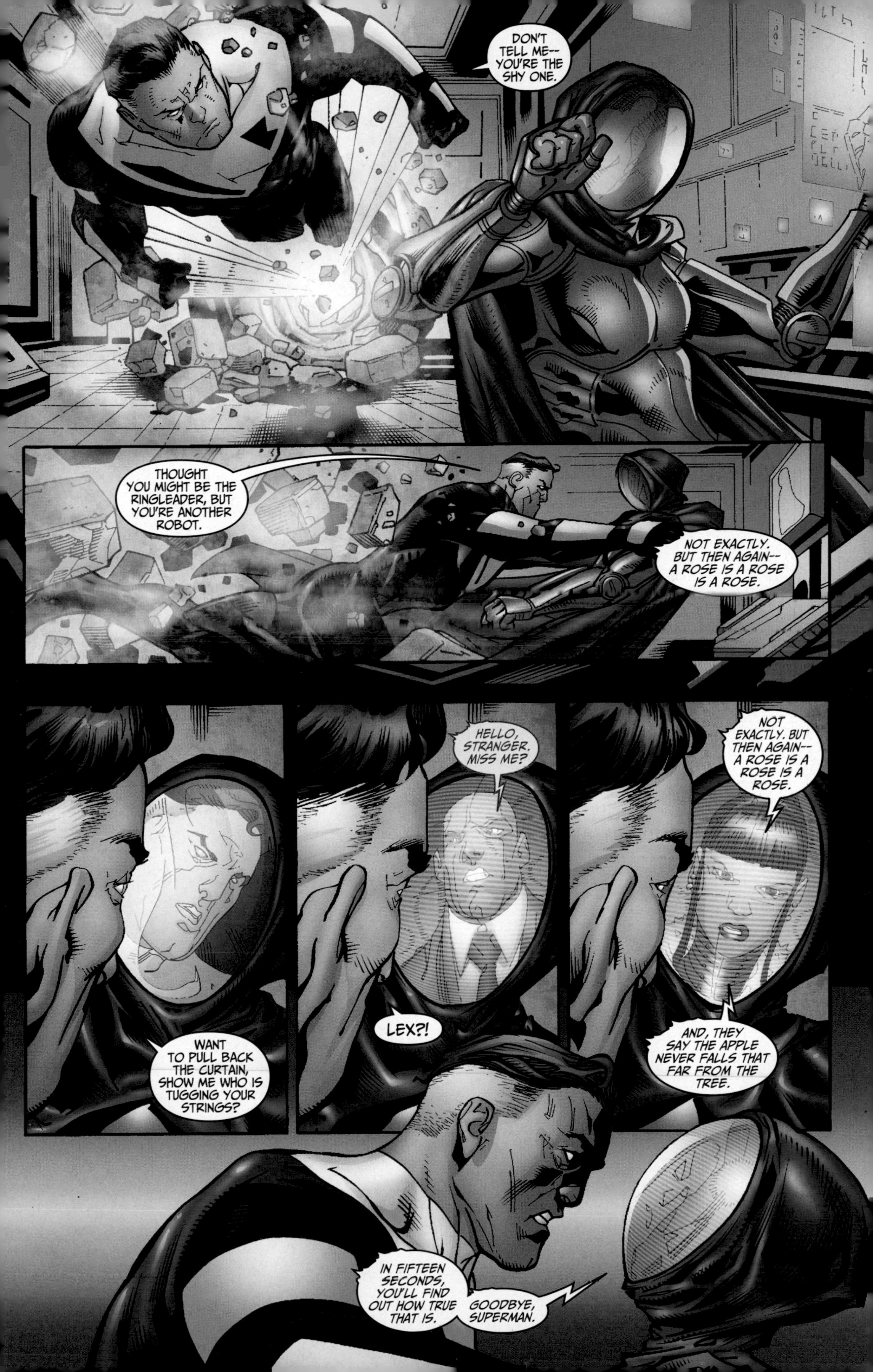
DON'T TELL ME-- YOU'RE THE SHY ONE.
THOUGHT YOU MIGHT BE THE RINGLEADER, BUT YOU'RE ANOTHER ROBOT.
NOT EXACTLY. BUT THEN AGAIN-- A ROSE IS A ROSE IS A ROSE.
WANT TO PULL BACK THE CURTAIN, SHOW ME WHO IS TUGGING YOUR STRINGS?
HELLO, STRANGER. MISS ME?
LEX?!
NOT EXACTLY. BUT THEN AGAIN-- A ROSE IS A ROSE IS A ROSE.
AND, THEY SAY THE APPLE NEVER FALLS THAT FAR FROM THE TREE.
IN FIFTEEN SECONDS, YOU'LL FIND OUT HOW TRUE THAT IS.
GOODBYE, SUPERMAN.

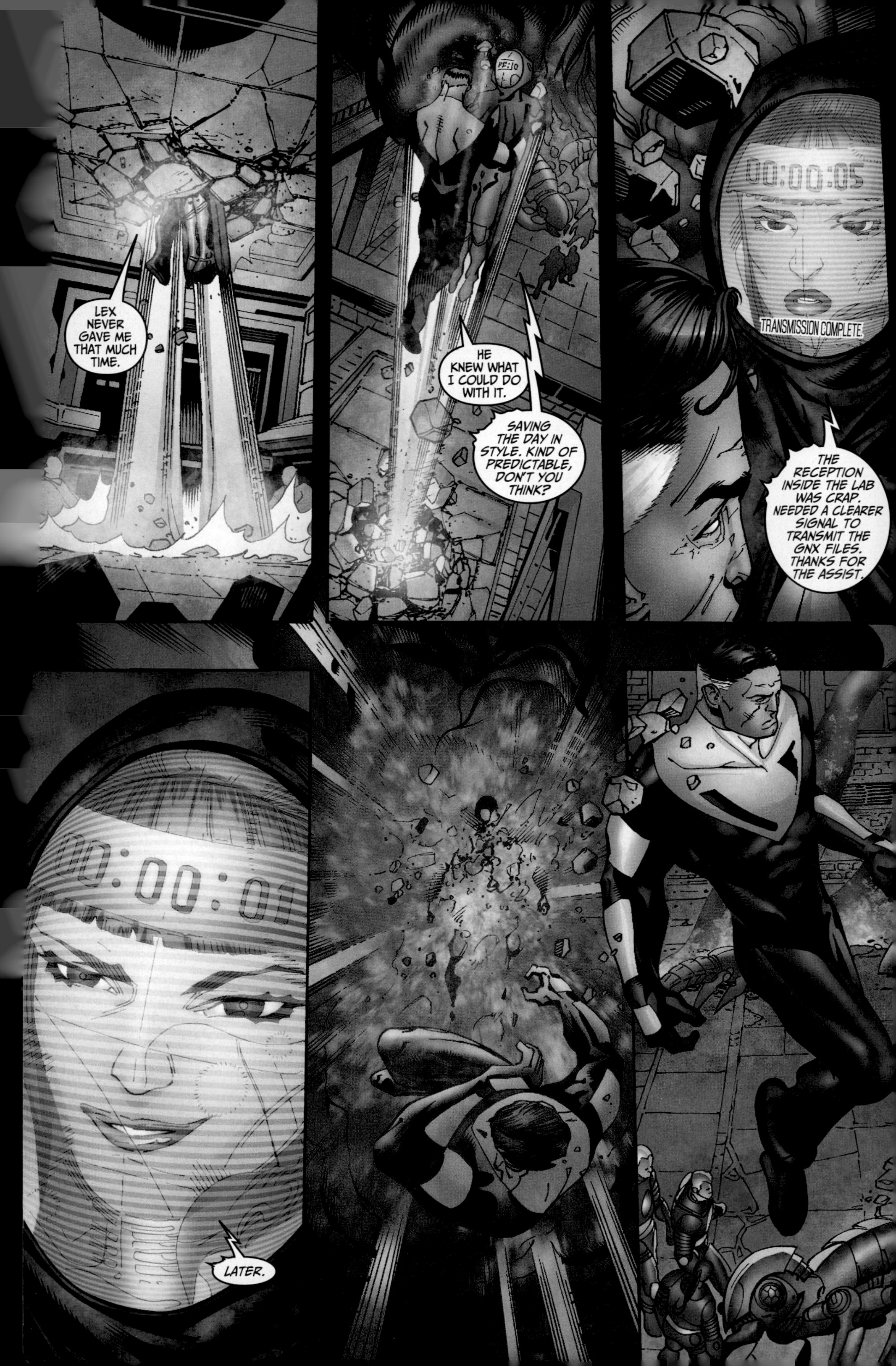
LEX NEVER GAVE ME THAT MUCH TIME.
HE KNEW WHAT I COULD DO WITH IT.
SAVING THE DAY IN STYLE. KIND OF PREDICTABLE, DON'T YOU THINK?
00:00:05
TRANSMISSION COMPLETE.
THE RECEPTION INSIDE THE LAB WAS CRAP. NEEDED A CLEARER SIGNAL TO TRANSMIT THE GNX FILES. THANKS FOR THE ASSIST.
00:00:01
LATER.

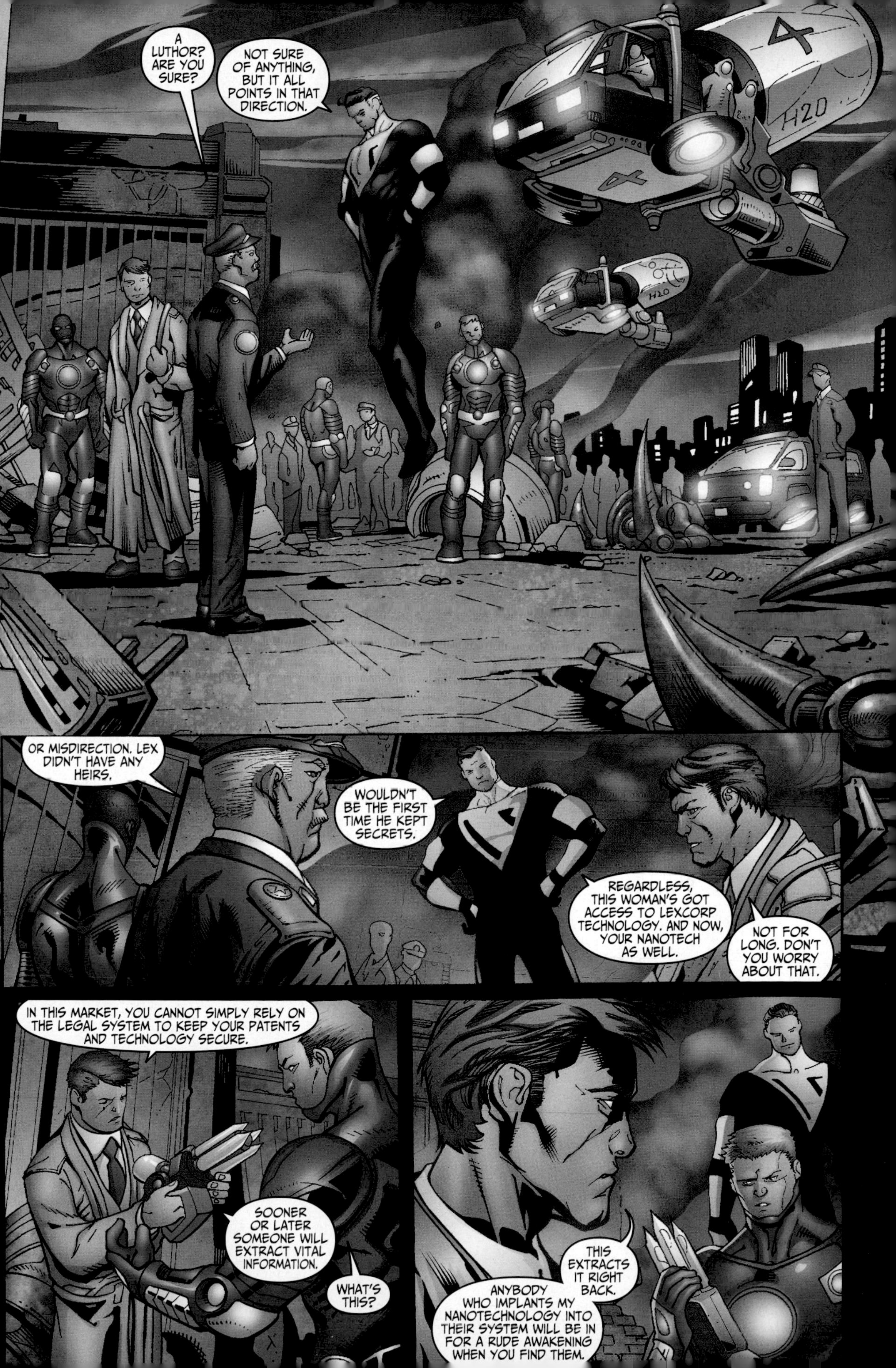
A LUTHOR? ARE YOU SURE?
NOT SURE OF ANYTHING, BUT IT ALL POINTS IN THAT DIRECTION.
OR MISDIRECTION. LEX DIDN'T HAVE ANY HEIRS.
WOULDN'T BE THE FIRST TIME HE KEPT SECRETS.
REGARDLESS, THIS WOMAN'S GOT ACCESS TO LEXCORP TECHNOLOGY. AND NOW, YOUR NANOTECH AS WELL.
NOT FOR LONG. DON'T YOU WORRY ABOUT THAT.
IN THIS MARKET, YOU CANNOT SIMPLY RELY ON THE LEGAL SYSTEM TO KEEP YOUR PATENTS AND TECHNOLOGY SECURE.
SOONER OR LATER SOMEONE WILL EXTRACT VITAL INFORMATION.
WHAT'S THIS?
THIS EXTRACTS IT RIGHT BACK.
ANYBODY WHO IMPLANTS MY NANOTECHNOLOGY INTO THEIR SYSTEM WILL BE IN FOR A RUDE AWAKENING WHEN YOU FIND THEM.

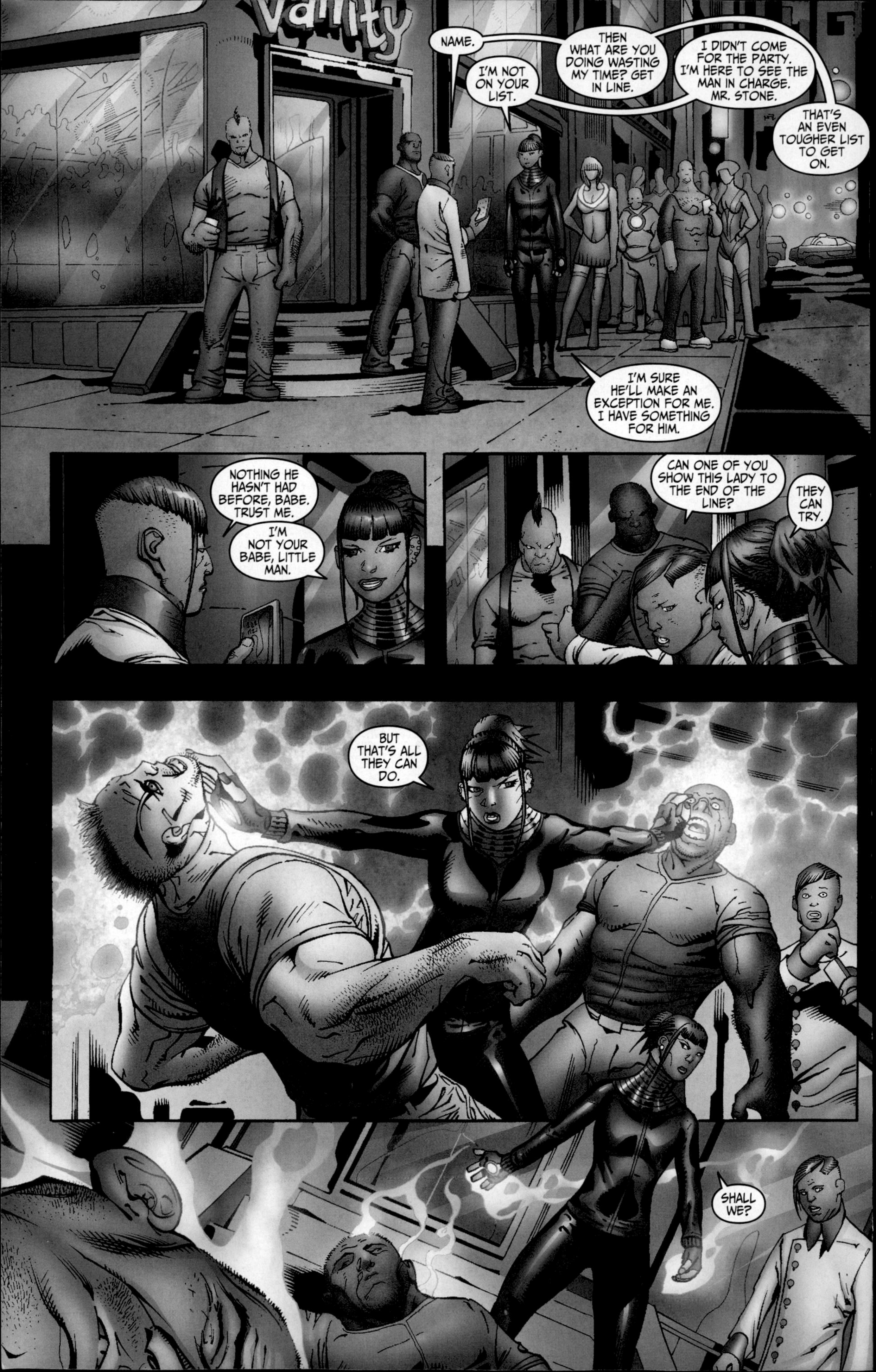
Vanity
NAME.
I'M NOT ON YOUR LIST.
THEN WHAT ARE YOU DOING WASTING MY TIME? GET IN LINE.
I DIDN'T COME FOR THE PARTY. I'M HERE TO SEE THE MAN IN CHARGE. MR. STONE.
THAT'S AN EVEN TOUGHER LIST TO GET ON.
I'M SURE HE'LL MAKE AN EXCEPTION FOR ME. I HAVE SOMETHING FOR HIM.
NOTHING HE HASN'T HAD BEFORE, BABE. TRUST ME.
I'M NOT YOUR BABE, LITTLE MAN.
CAN ONE OF YOU SHOW THIS LADY TO THE END OF THE LINE?
THEY CAN TRY.
BUT THAT'S ALL THEY CAN DO.
SHALL WE?

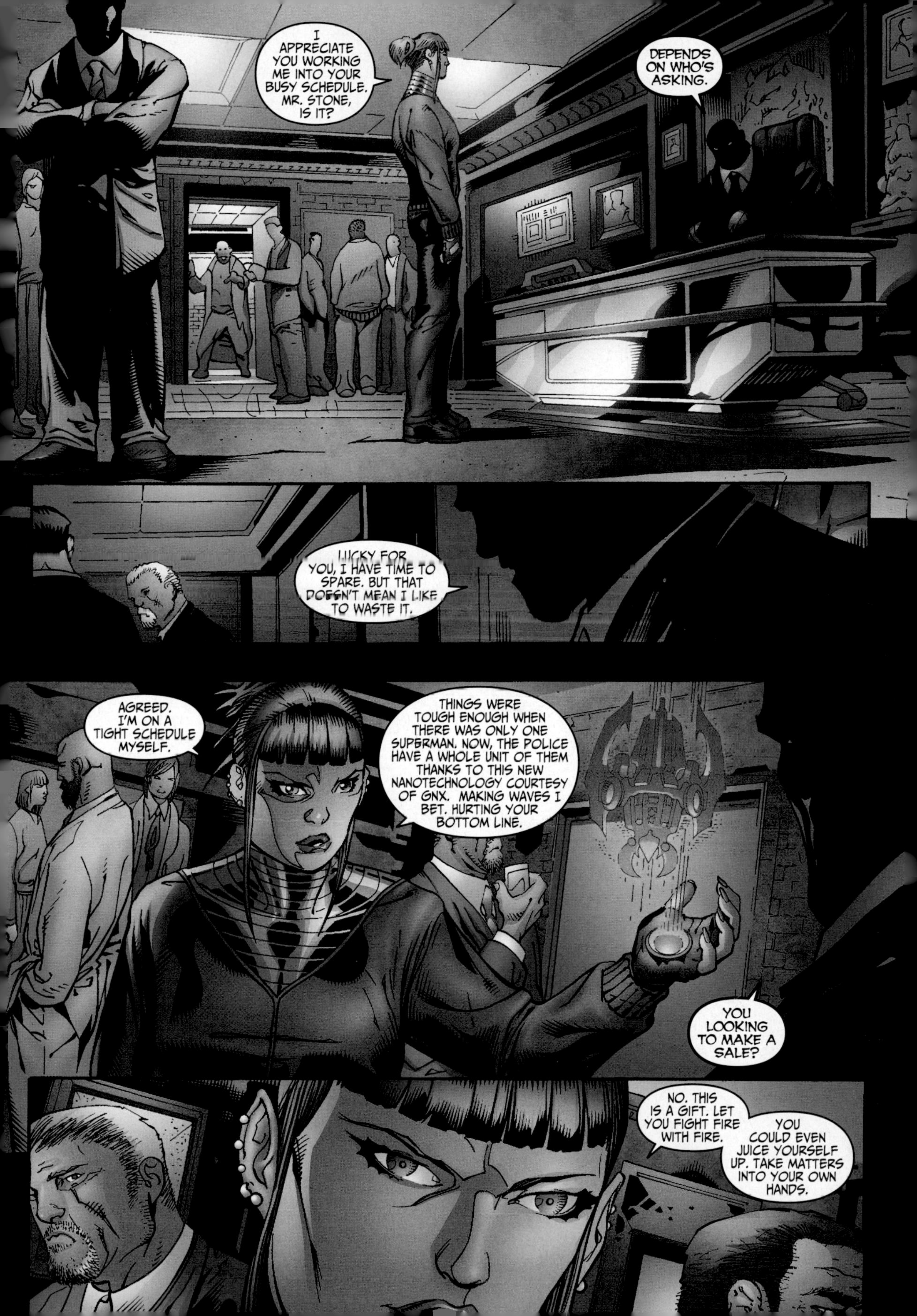
I APPRECIATE YOU WORKING ME INTO YOUR BUSY SCHEDULE. MR. STONE, IS IT?
DEPENDS ON WHO'S ASKING.
LUCKY FOR YOU, I HAVE TIME TO SPARE. BUT THAT DOESN'T MEAN I LIKE TO WASTE IT.
AGREED. I'M ON A TIGHT SCHEDULE MYSELF.
THINGS WERE TOUGH ENOUGH WHEN THERE WAS ONLY ONE SUPERMAN. NOW, THE POLICE HAVE A WHOLE UNIT OF THEM THANKS TO THIS NEW NANOTECHNOLOGY COURTESY OF GNX. MAKING WAVES I BET. HURTING YOUR BOTTOM LINE.
YOU LOOKING TO MAKE A SALE?
NO. THIS IS A GIFT. LET YOU FIGHT FIRE WITH FIRE.
YOU COULD EVEN JUICE YOURSELF UP. TAKE MATTERS INTO YOUR OWN HANDS.

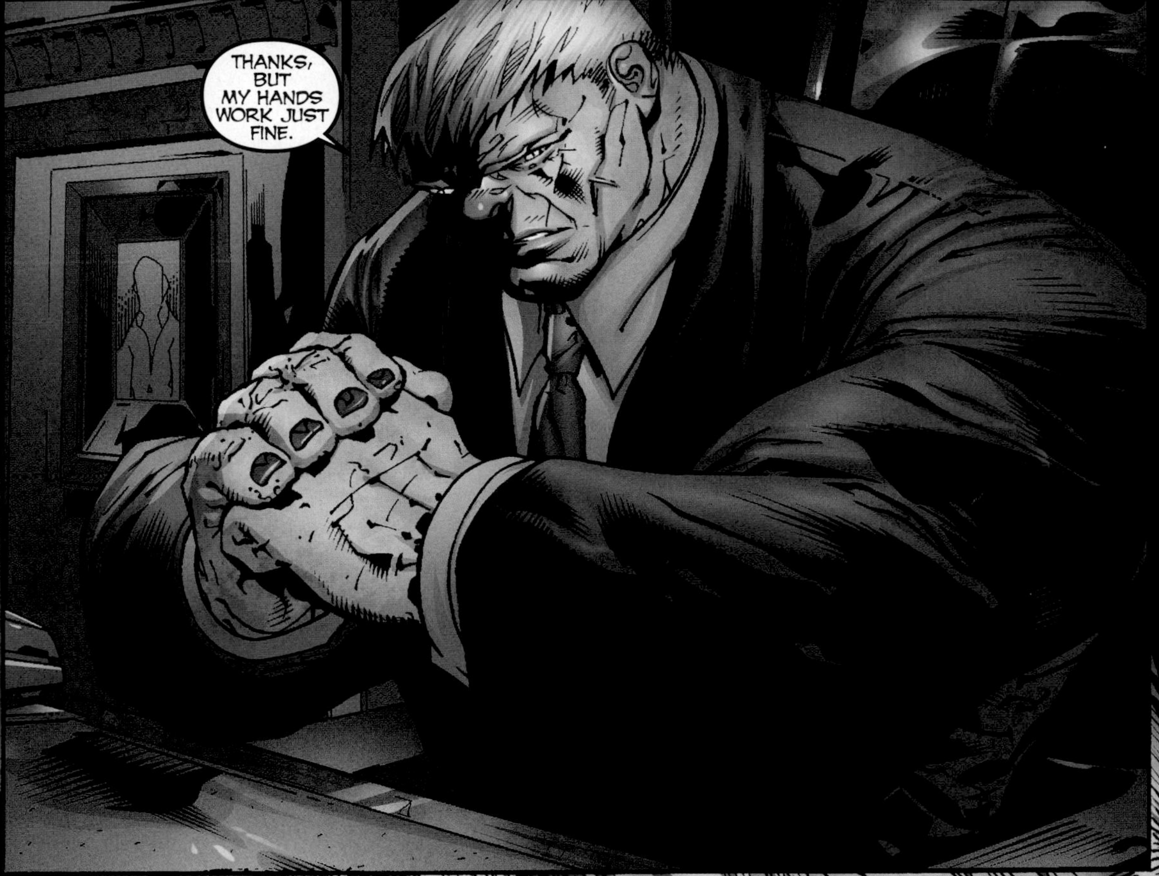
THANKS, BUT MY HANDS WORK JUST FINE.

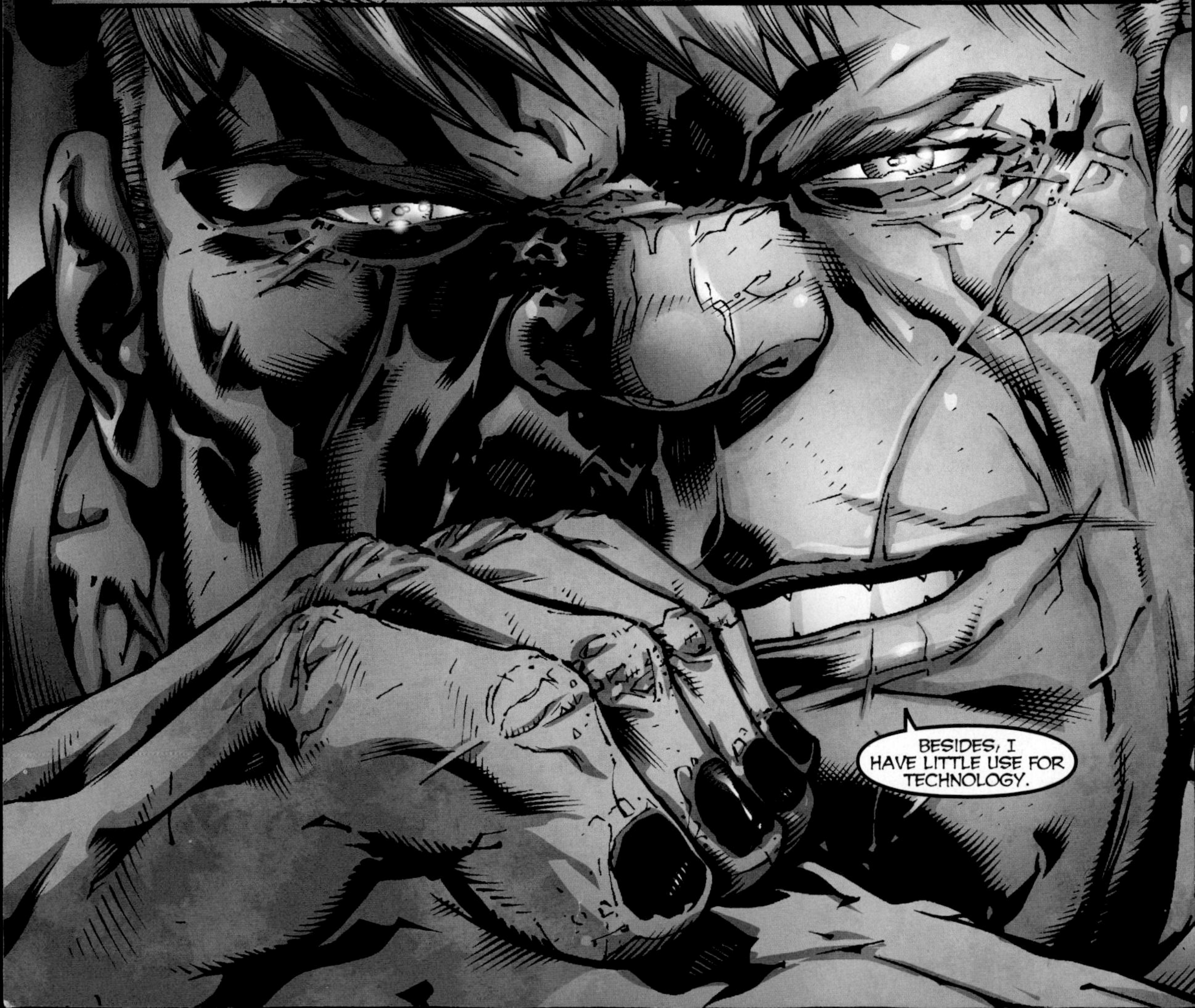
BESIDES, I HAVE LITTLE USE FOR TECHNOLOGY.

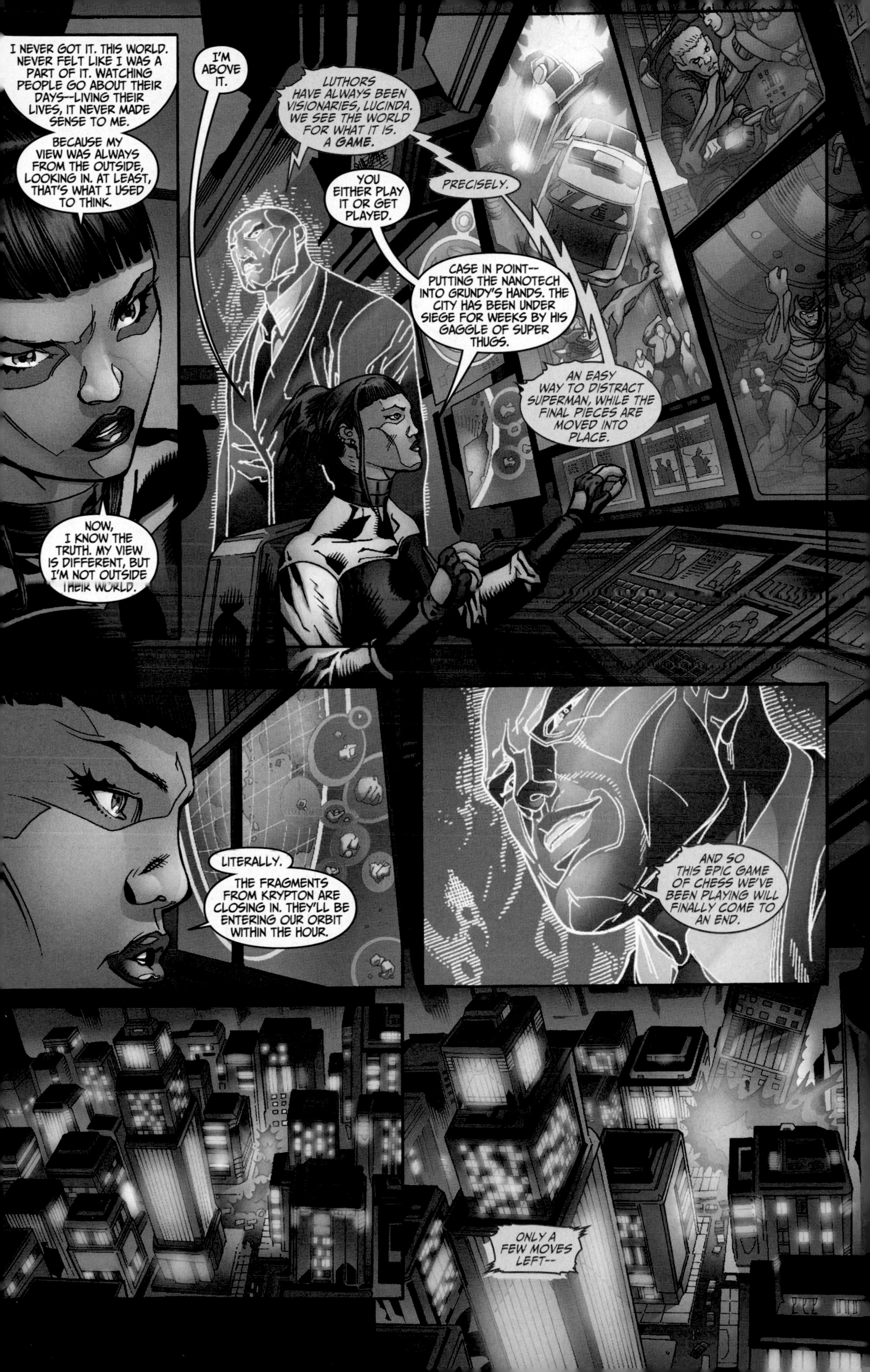
I NEVER GOT IT. THIS WORLD. NEVER FELT LIKE I WAS A PART OF IT. WATCHING PEOPLE GO ABOUT THEIR DAYS--LIVING THEIR LIVES, IT NEVER MADE SENSE TO ME.
BECAUSE MY VIEW WAS ALWAYS FROM THE OUTSIDE, LOOKING IN. AT LEAST, THAT'S WHAT I USED TO THINK.
I'M ABOVE IT.
LUTHORS HAVE ALWAYS BEEN VISIONARIES, LUCINDA. WE SEE THE WORLD FOR WHAT IT IS. A GAME.
YOU EITHER PLAY IT OR GET PLAYED.
PRECISELY.
CASE IN POINT-- PUTTING THE NANOTECH INTO GRUNDY'S HANDS. THE CITY HAS BEEN UNDER SIEGE FOR WEEKS BY HIS GAGGLE OF SUPER THUGS.
AN EASY WAY TO DISTRACT SUPERMAN, WHILE THE FINAL PIECES ARE MOVED INTO PLACE.
NOW, I KNOW THE TRUTH. MY VIEW IS DIFFERENT, BUT I'M NOT OUTSIDE THEIR WORLD.
LITERALLY.
THE FRAGMENTS FROM KRYPTON ARE CLOSING IN. THEY'LL BE ENTERING OUR ORBIT WITHIN THE HOUR.
AND SO THIS EPIC GAME OF CHESS WE'VE BEEN PLAYING WILL FINALLY COME TO AN END.
ONLY A FEW MOVES LEFT--

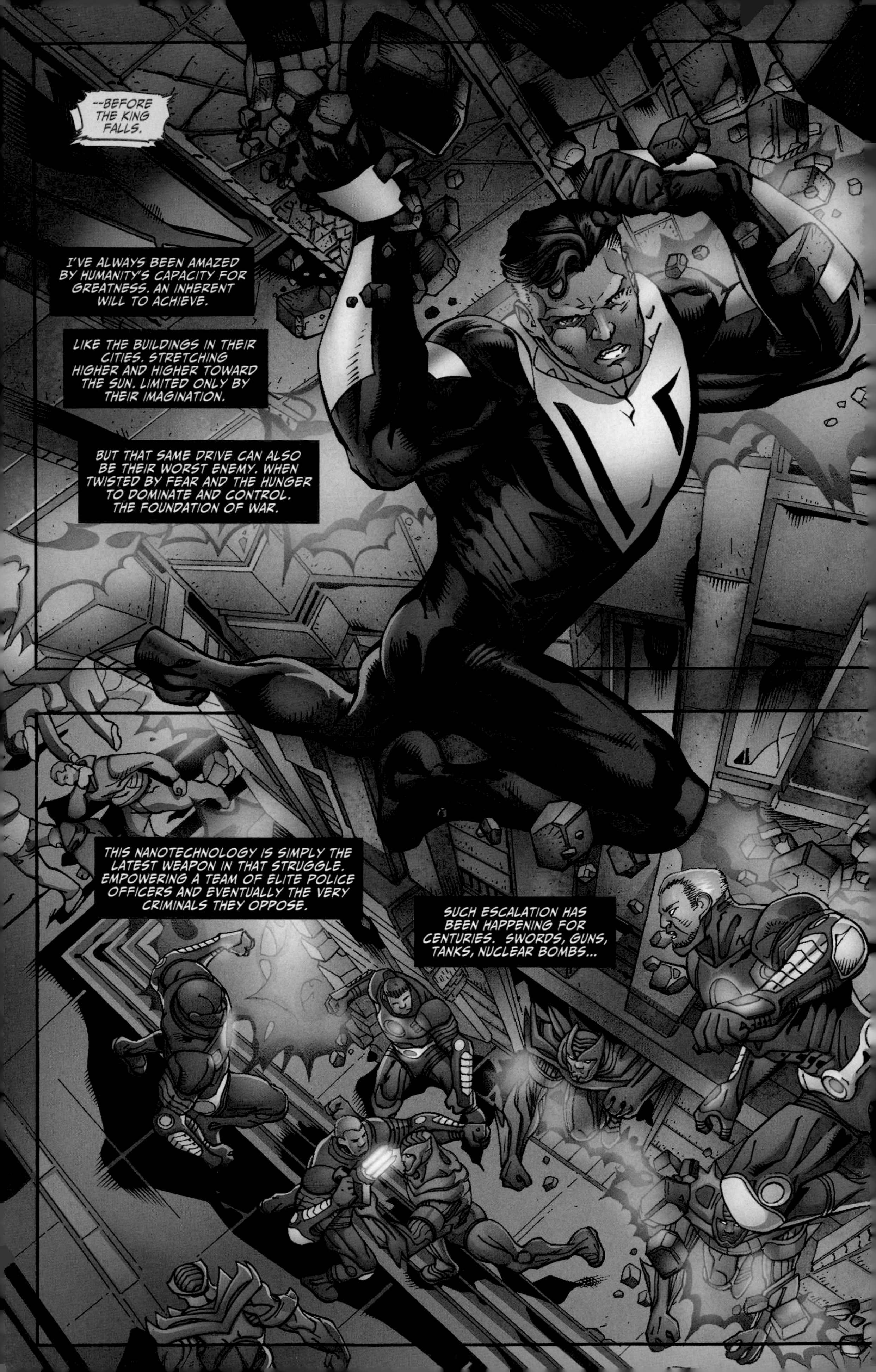
--BEFORE THE KING FALLS.
I'VE ALWAYS BEEN AMAZED BY HUMANITY'S CAPACITY FOR GREATNESS. AN INHERENT WILL TO ACHIEVE.
LIKE THE BUILDINGS IN THEIR CITIES. STRETCHING HIGHER AND HIGHER TOWARD THE SUN. LIMITED ONLY BY THEIR IMAGINATION.
BUT THAT SAME DRIVE CAN ALSO BE THEIR WORST ENEMY. WHEN TWISTED BY FEAR AND THE HUNGER TO DOMINATE AND CONTROL. THE FOUNDATION OF WAR.
THIS NANOTECHNOLOGY IS SIMPLY THE LATEST WEAPON IN THAT STRUGGLE. EMPOWERING A TEAM OF ELITE POLICE OFFICERS AND EVENTUALLY THE VERY CRIMINALS THEY OPPOSE.
SUCH ESCALATION HAS BEEN HAPPENING FOR CENTURIES. SWORDS, GUNS, TANKS, NUCLEAR BOMBS...

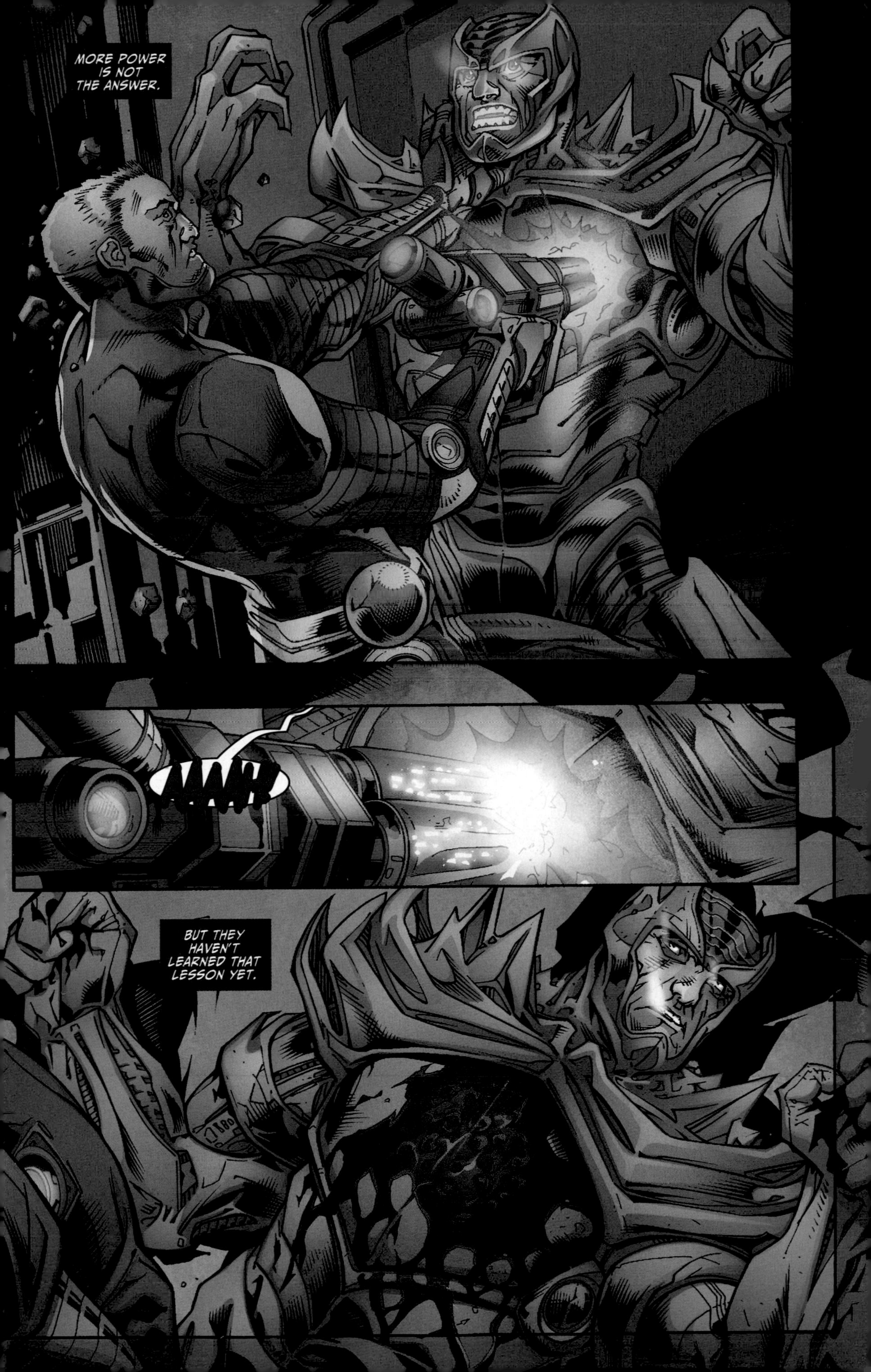
MORE POWER IS NOT THE ANSWER.
AAAH!
BUT THEY HAVEN'T LEARNED THAT LESSON YET.

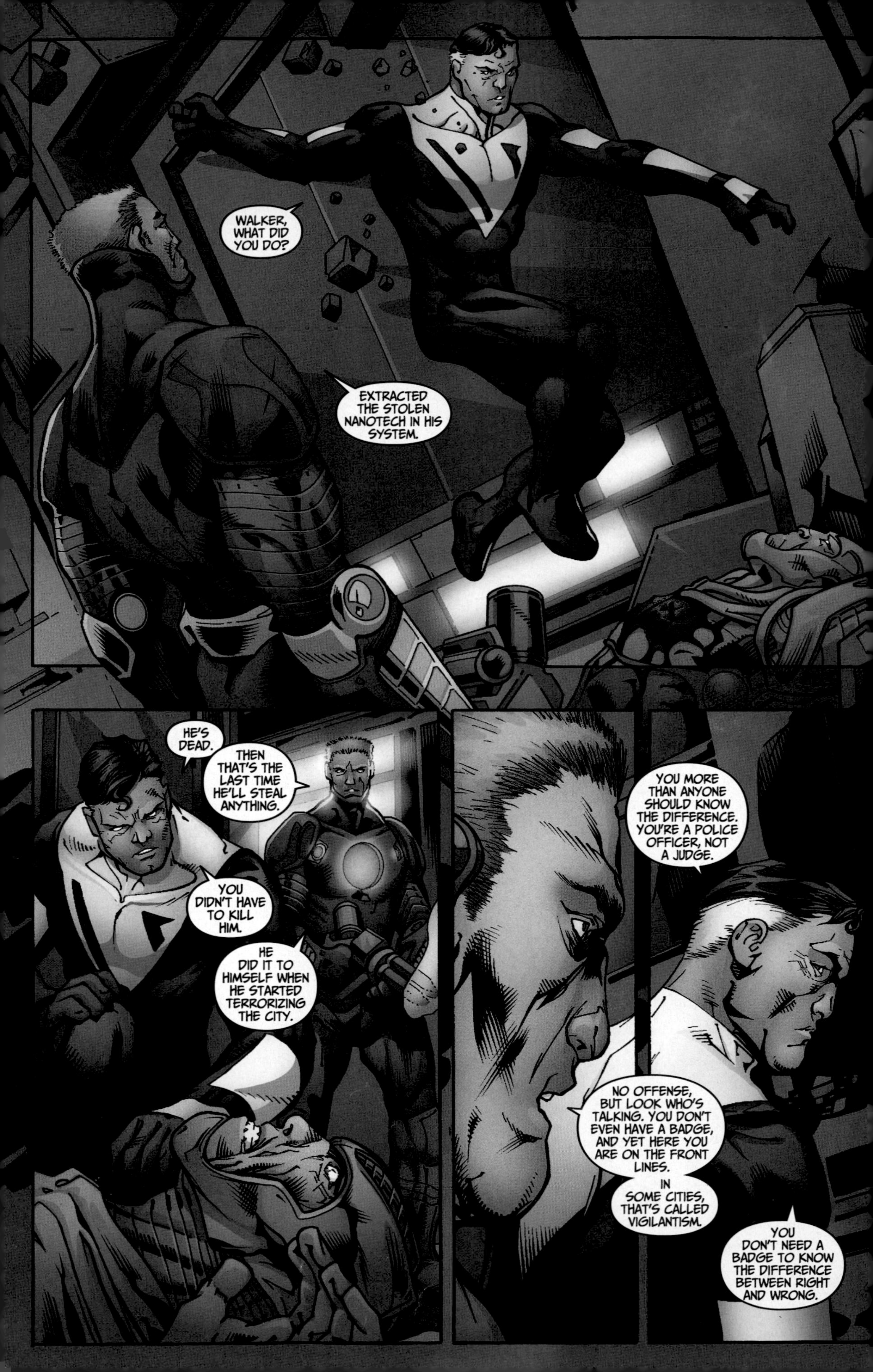
WALKER, WHAT DID YOU DO?
EXTRACTED THE STOLEN NANOTECH IN HIS SYSTEM.
HE'S DEAD.
THEN THAT'S THE LAST TIME HE'LL STEAL ANYTHING.
YOU DIDN'T HAVE TO KILL HIM.
HE DID IT TO HIMSELF WHEN HE STARTED TERRORIZING THE CITY.
YOU MORE THAN ANYONE SHOULD KNOW THE DIFFERENCE. YOU'RE A POLICE OFFICER, NOT A JUDGE.
NO OFFENSE, BUT LOOK WHO'S TALKING. YOU DON'T EVEN HAVE A BADGE, AND YET HERE YOU ARE ON THE FRONT LINES.
IN SOME CITIES, THAT'S CALLED VIGILANTISM.
YOU DON'T NEED A BADGE TO KNOW THE DIFFERENCE BETWEEN RIGHT AND WRONG.

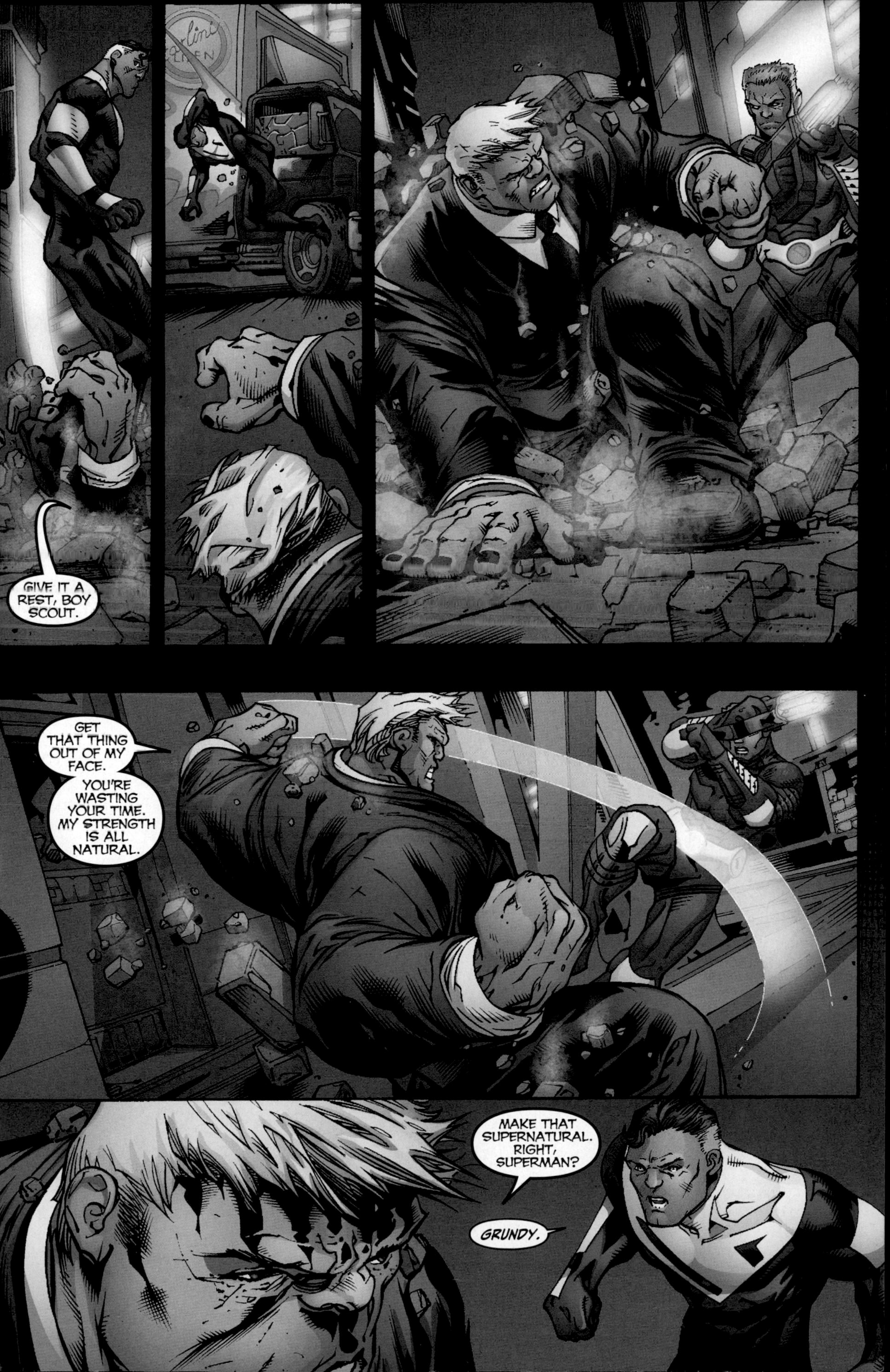
GIVE IT A REST, BOY SCOUT.
GET THAT THING OUT OF MY FACE.
YOU'RE WASTING YOUR TIME. MY STRENGTH IS ALL NATURAL.
MAKE THAT SUPERNATURAL. RIGHT, SUPERMAN?
GRUNDY.

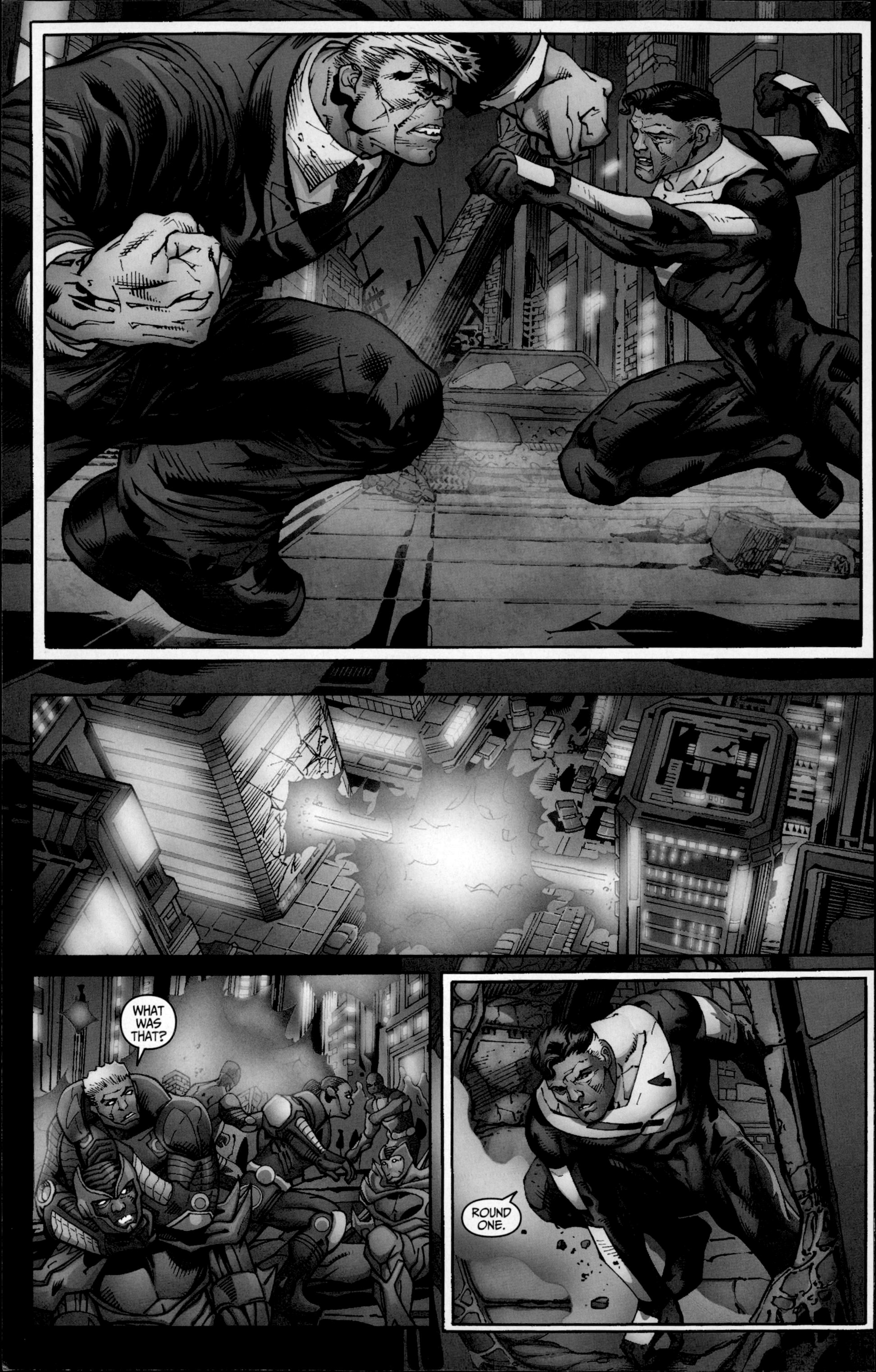
WHAT WAS THAT?
ROUND ONE.

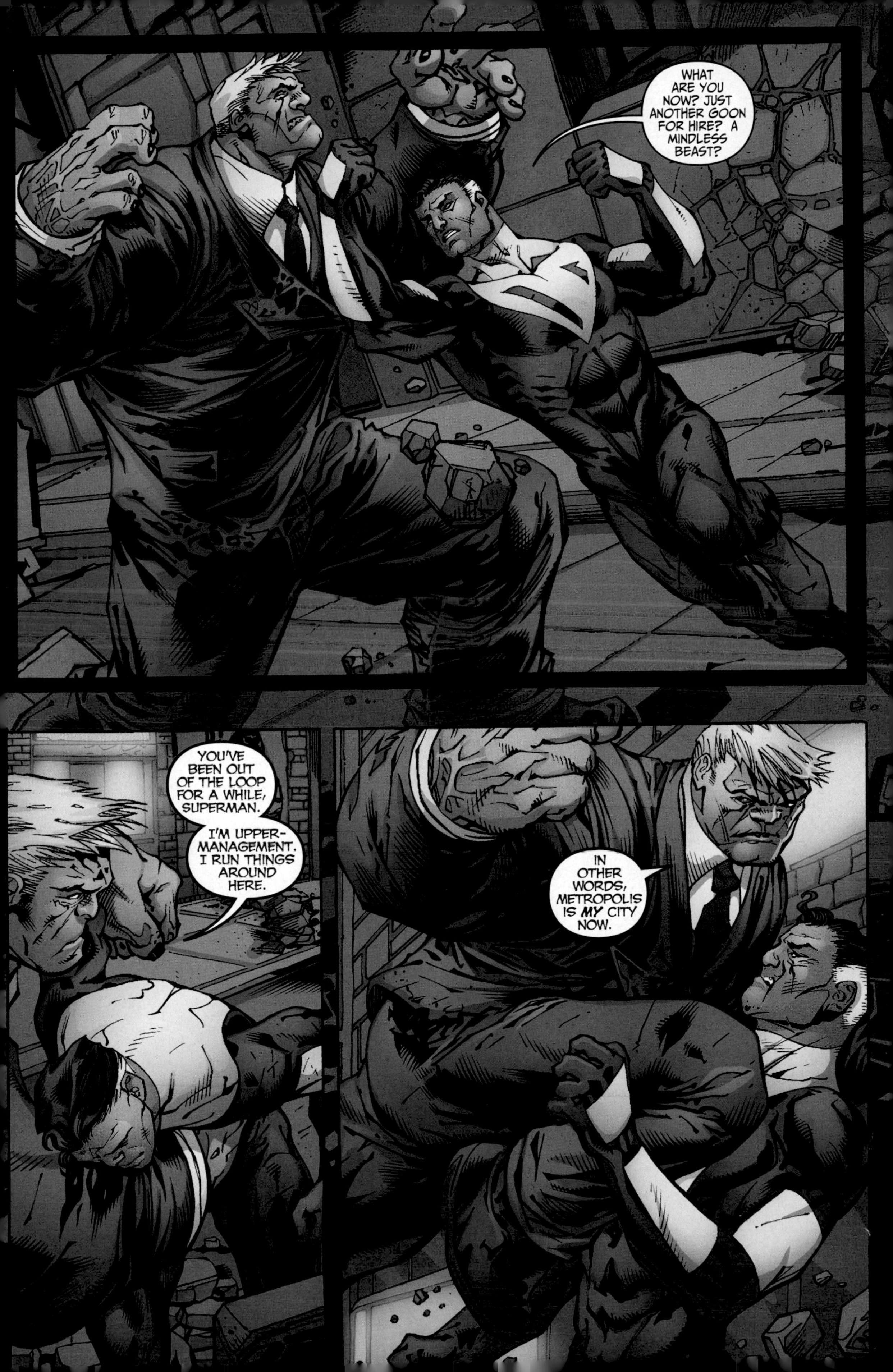
WHAT ARE YOU NOW? JUST ANOTHER GOON FOR HIRE? A MINDLESS BEAST?
YOU'VE BEEN OUT OF THE LOOP FOR A WHILE, SUPERMAN.
I'M UPPER-MANAGEMENT. I RUN THINGS AROUND HERE.
IN OTHER WORDS, METROPOLIS IS **MY** CITY NOW.

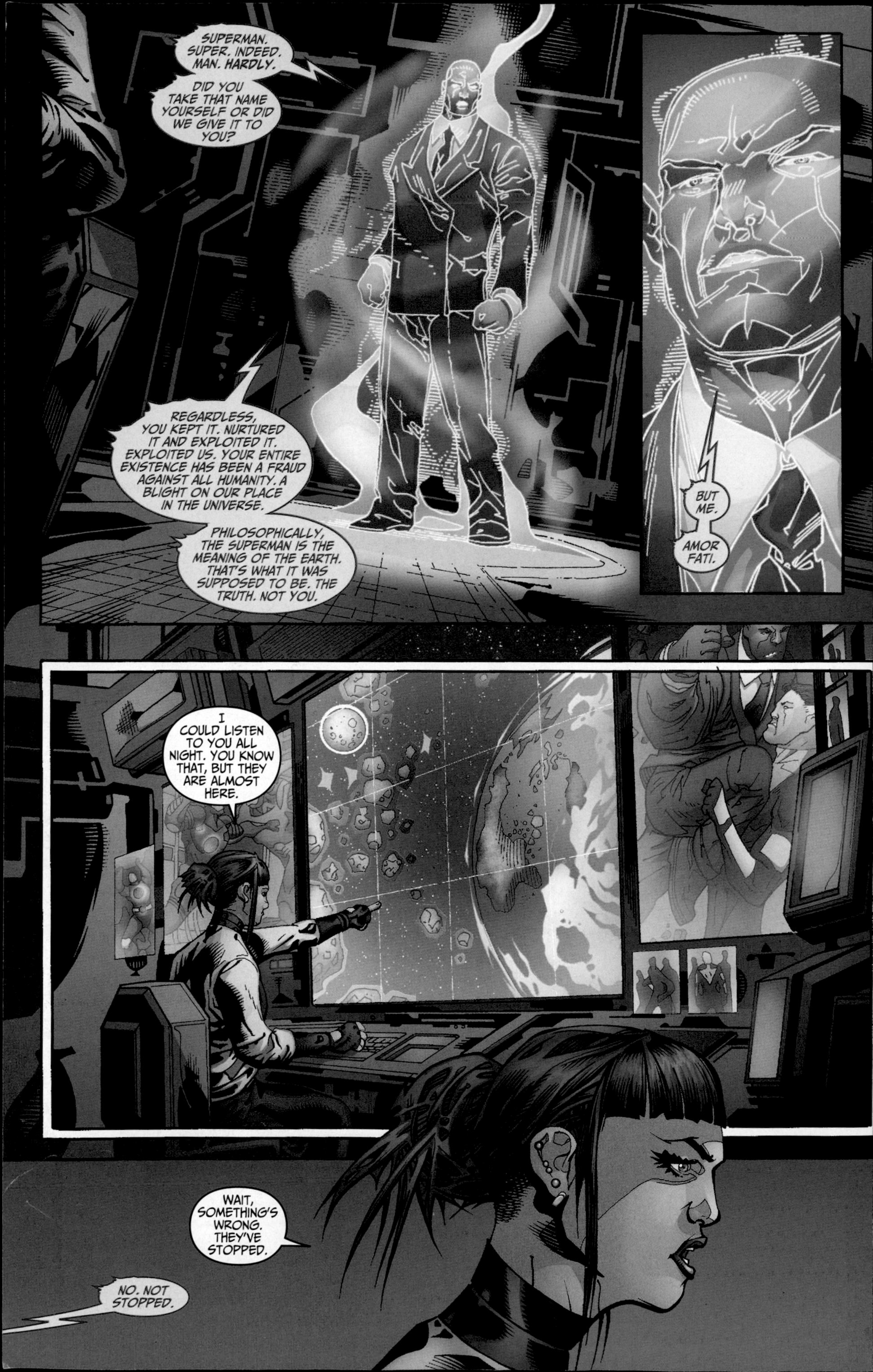
SUPERMAN. SUPER. INDEED. MAN. HARDLY.
DID YOU TAKE THAT NAME YOURSELF OR DID WE GIVE IT TO YOU?
REGARDLESS, YOU KEPT IT. NURTURED IT AND EXPLOITED IT. EXPLOITED US. YOUR ENTIRE EXISTENCE HAS BEEN A FRAUD AGAINST ALL HUMANITY. A BLIGHT ON OUR PLACE IN THE UNIVERSE.
PHILOSOPHICALLY, THE SUPERMAN IS THE MEANING OF THE EARTH. THAT'S WHAT IT WAS SUPPOSED TO BE. THE TRUTH. NOT YOU.
BUT ME.
AMOR FATI.
I COULD LISTEN TO YOU ALL NIGHT. YOU KNOW THAT, BUT THEY ARE ALMOST HERE.
WAIT, SOMETHING'S WRONG. THEY'VE STOPPED.
NO. NOT STOPPED.

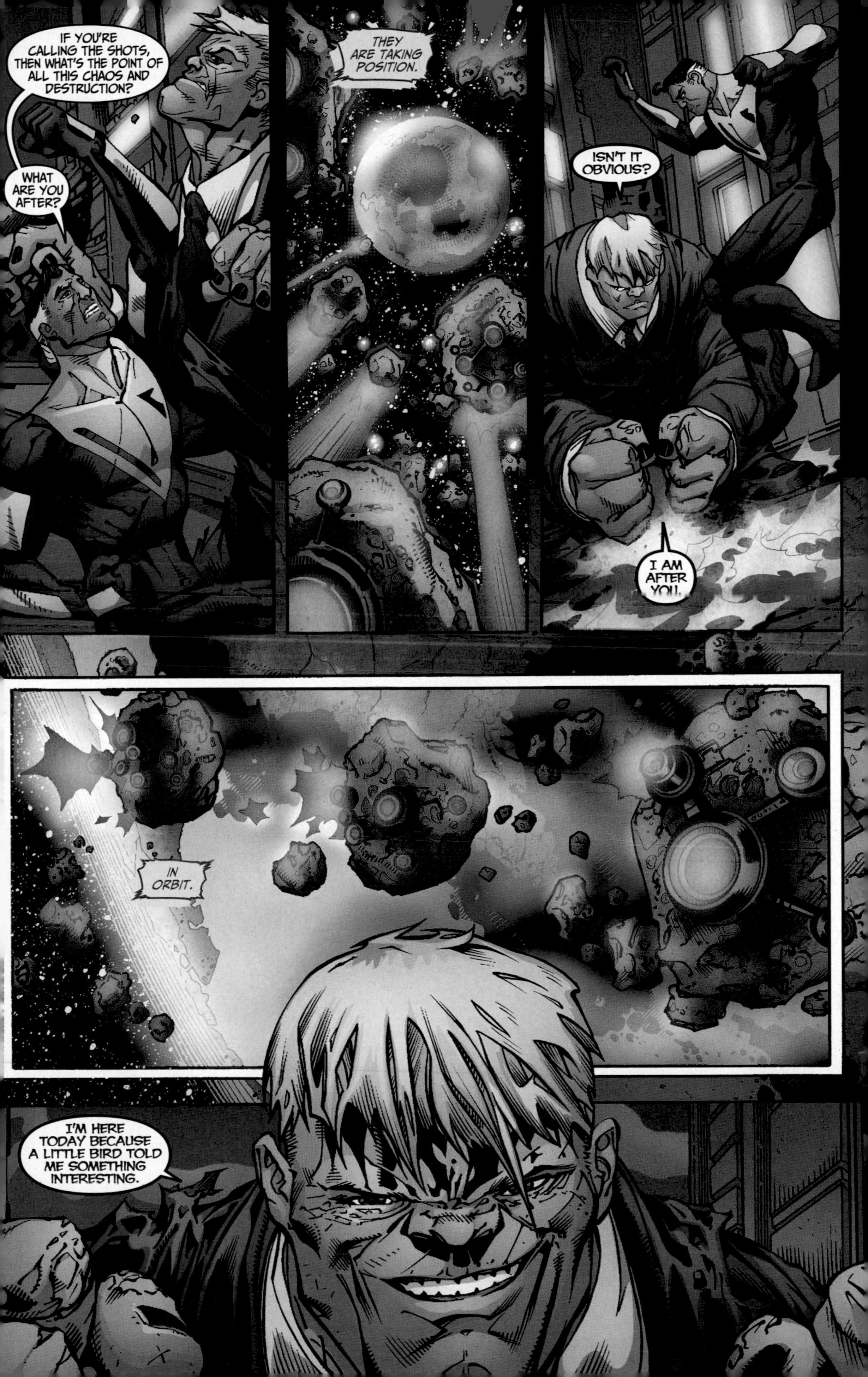
IF YOU'RE CALLING THE SHOTS, THEN WHAT'S THE POINT OF ALL THIS CHAOS AND DESTRUCTION?
WHAT ARE YOU AFTER?
THEY ARE TAKING POSITION.
ISN'T IT OBVIOUS?
I AM AFTER YOU.
IN ORBIT.
I'M HERE TODAY BECAUSE A LITTLE BIRD TOLD ME SOMETHING INTERESTING.

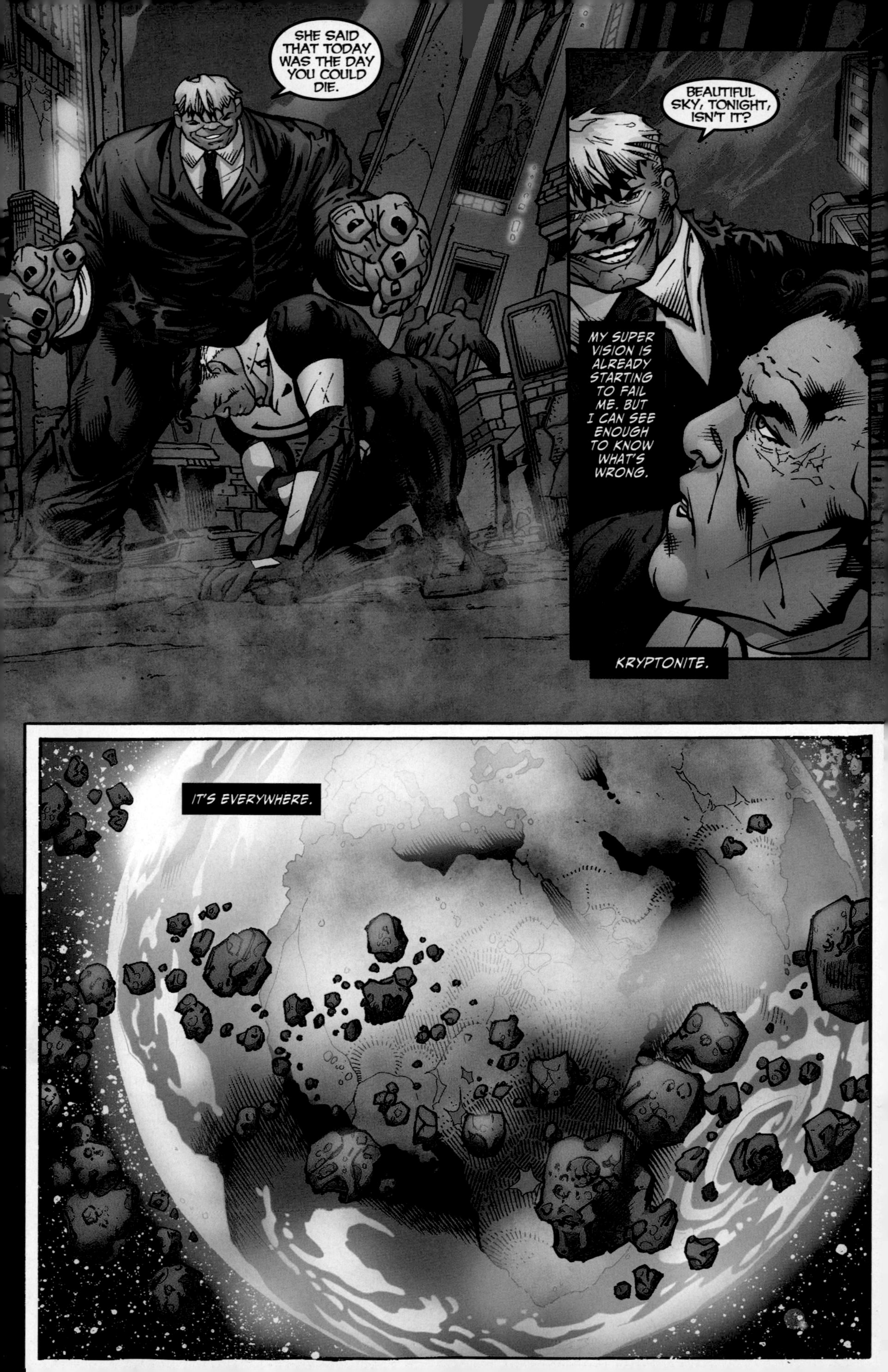
SHE SAID THAT TODAY WAS THE DAY YOU COULD DIE.
BEAUTIFUL SKY, TONIGHT, ISN'T IT?
MY SUPER VISION IS ALREADY STARTING TO FAIL ME. BUT I CAN SEE ENOUGH TO KNOW WHAT'S WRONG.
KRYPTONITE.
IT'S EVERYWHERE.

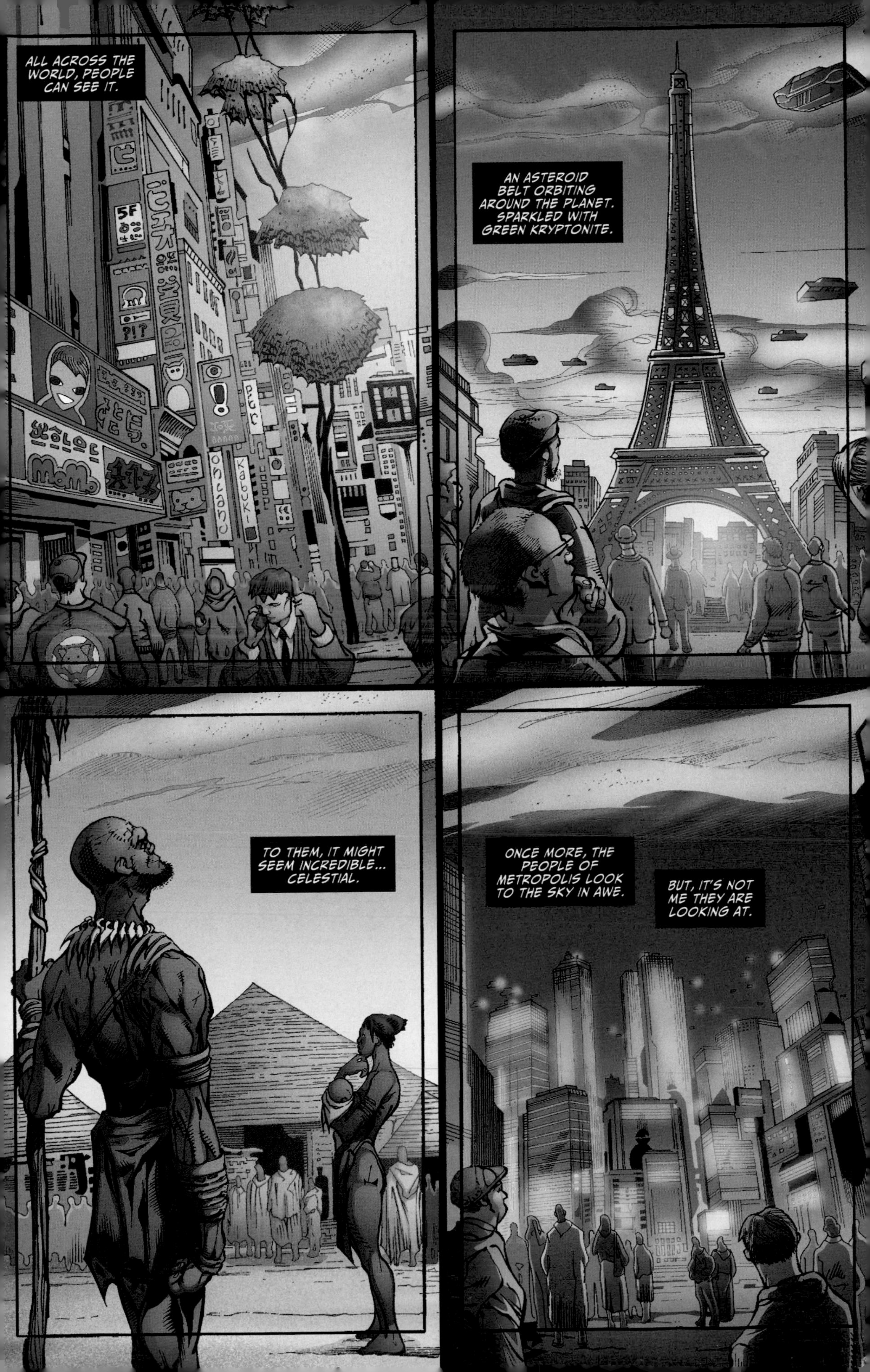
ALL ACROSS THE WORLD, PEOPLE CAN SEE IT.
AN ASTEROID BELT ORBITING AROUND THE PLANET. SPARKLED WITH GREEN KRYPTONITE.
TO THEM, IT MIGHT SEEM INCREDIBLE... CELESTIAL.
ONCE MORE, THE PEOPLE OF METROPOLIS LOOK TO THE SKY IN AWE.
BUT, IT'S NOT ME THEY ARE LOOKING AT.

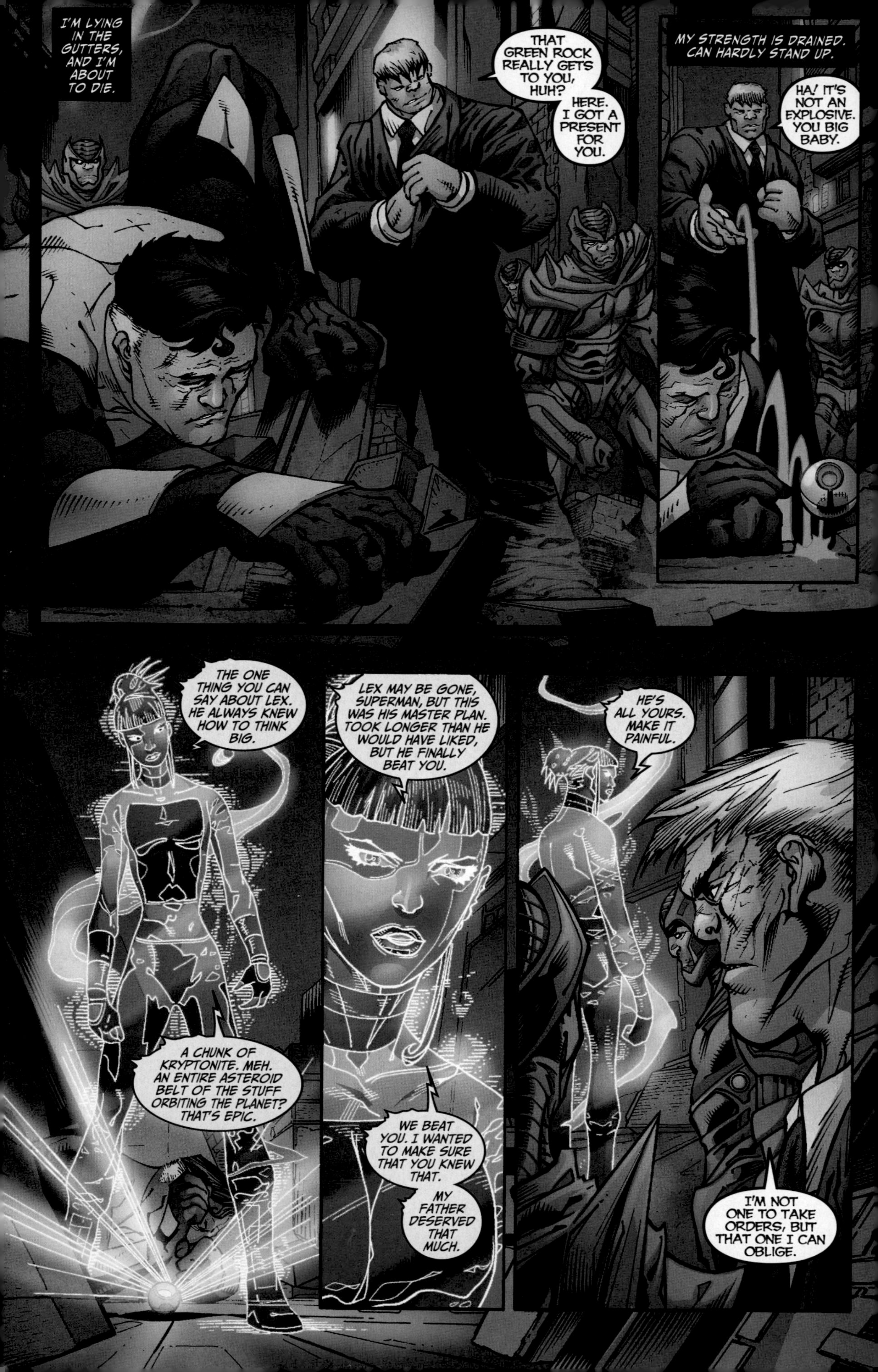
I'M LYING IN THE GUTTERS, AND I'M ABOUT TO DIE.
THAT GREEN ROCK REALLY GETS TO YOU, HUH?
HERE. I GOT A PRESENT FOR YOU.
MY STRENGTH IS DRAINED. CAN HARDLY STAND UP.
HA! IT'S NOT AN EXPLOSIVE. YOU BIG BABY.
THE ONE THING YOU CAN SAY ABOUT LEX. HE ALWAYS KNEW HOW TO THINK BIG.
A CHUNK OF KRYPTONITE. MEH. AN ENTIRE ASTEROID BELT OF THE STUFF ORBITING THE PLANET? THAT'S EPIC.
LEX MAY BE GONE, SUPERMAN, BUT THIS WAS HIS MASTER PLAN. TOOK LONGER THAN HE WOULD HAVE LIKED, BUT HE FINALLY BEAT YOU.
WE BEAT YOU. I WANTED TO MAKE SURE THAT YOU KNEW THAT.
MY FATHER DESERVED THAT MUCH.
HE'S ALL YOURS. MAKE IT PAINFUL.
I'M NOT ONE TO TAKE ORDERS, BUT THAT ONE I CAN OBLIGE.

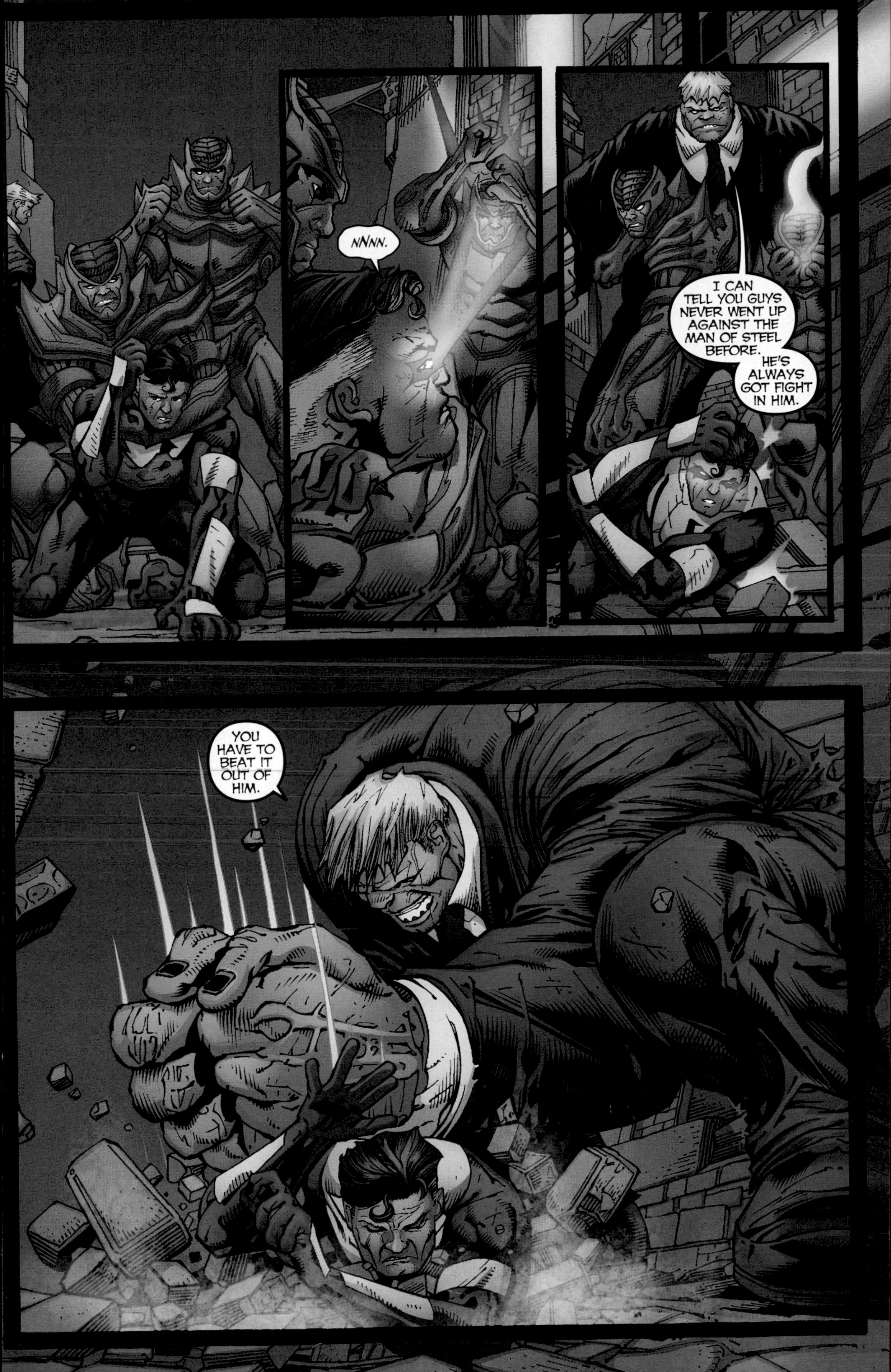
NNNN.
I CAN TELL YOU GUYS NEVER WENT UP AGAINST THE MAN OF STEEL BEFORE.
HE'S ALWAYS GOT FIGHT IN HIM.
YOU HAVE TO BEAT IT OUT OF HIM.

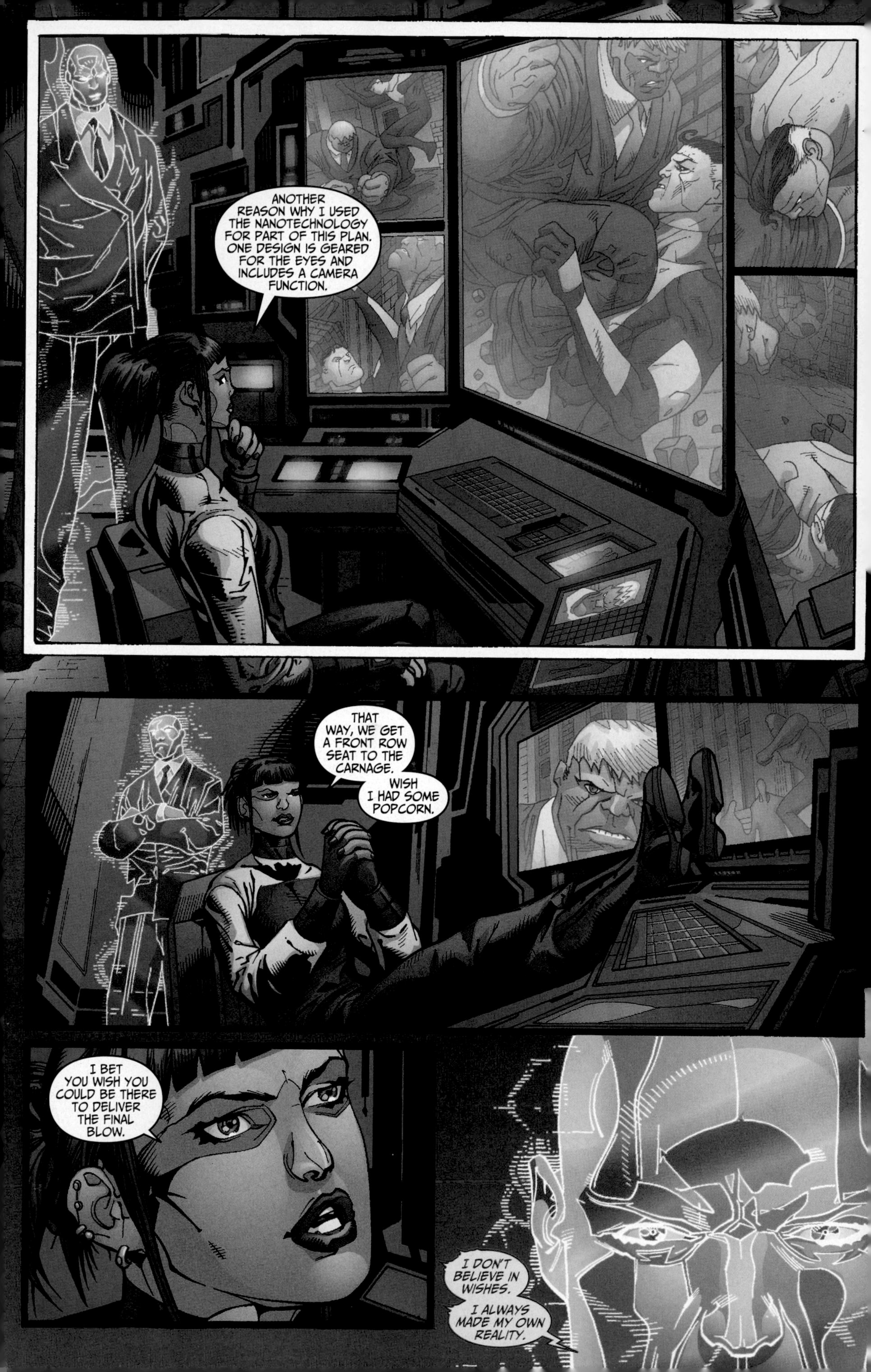
ANOTHER REASON WHY I USED THE NANOTECHNOLOGY FOR PART OF THIS PLAN. ONE DESIGN IS GEARED FOR THE EYES AND INCLUDES A CAMERA FUNCTION.
THAT WAY, WE GET A FRONT ROW SEAT TO THE CARNAGE.
WISH I HAD SOME POPCORN.
I BET YOU WISH YOU COULD BE THERE TO DELIVER THE FINAL BLOW.
I DON'T BELIEVE IN WISHES.
I ALWAYS MADE MY OWN REALITY.

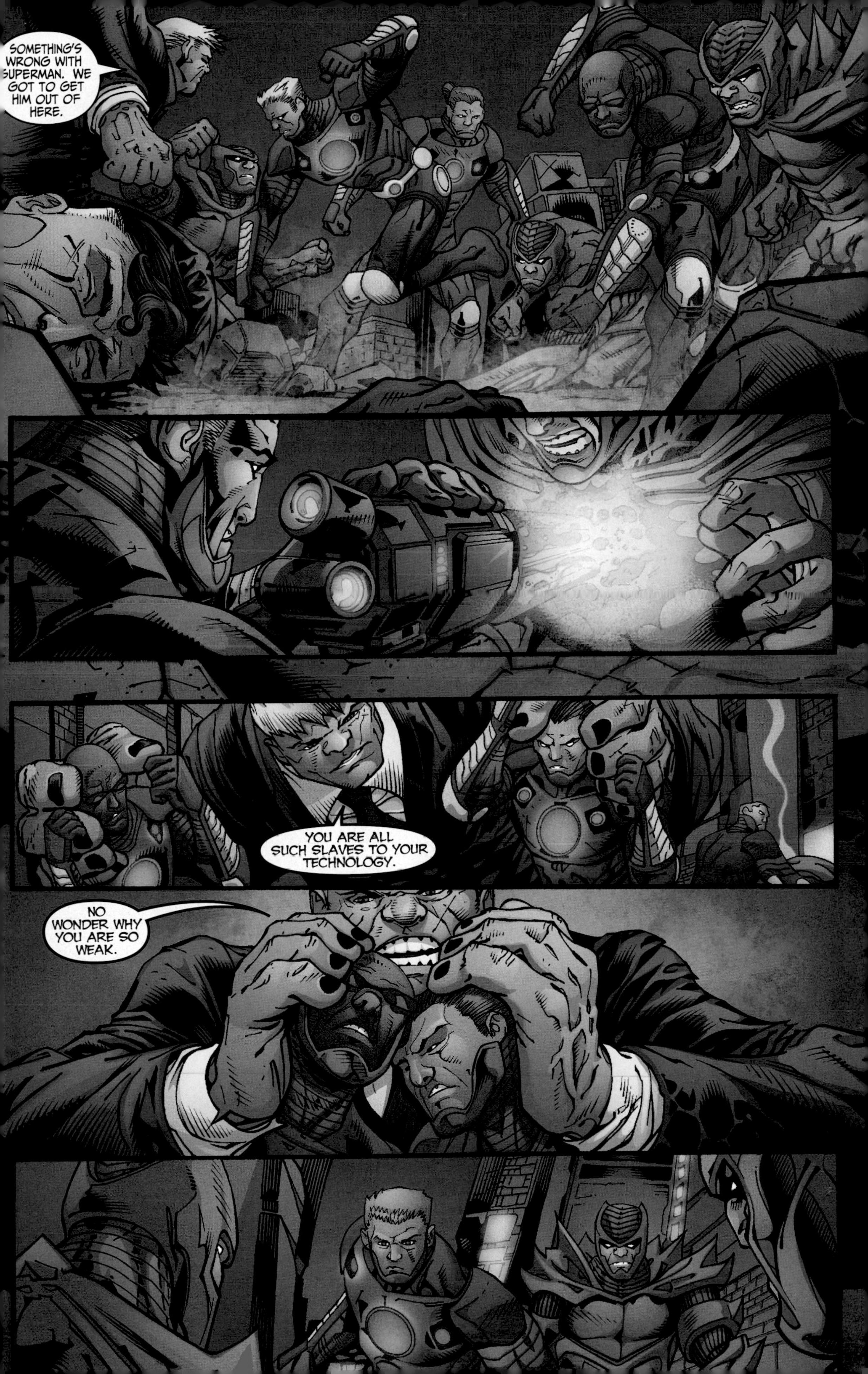
SOMETHING'S WRONG WITH SUPERMAN. WE GOT TO GET HIM OUT OF HERE.
YOU ARE ALL SUCH SLAVES TO YOUR TECHNOLOGY.
NO WONDER WHY YOU ARE SO WEAK.

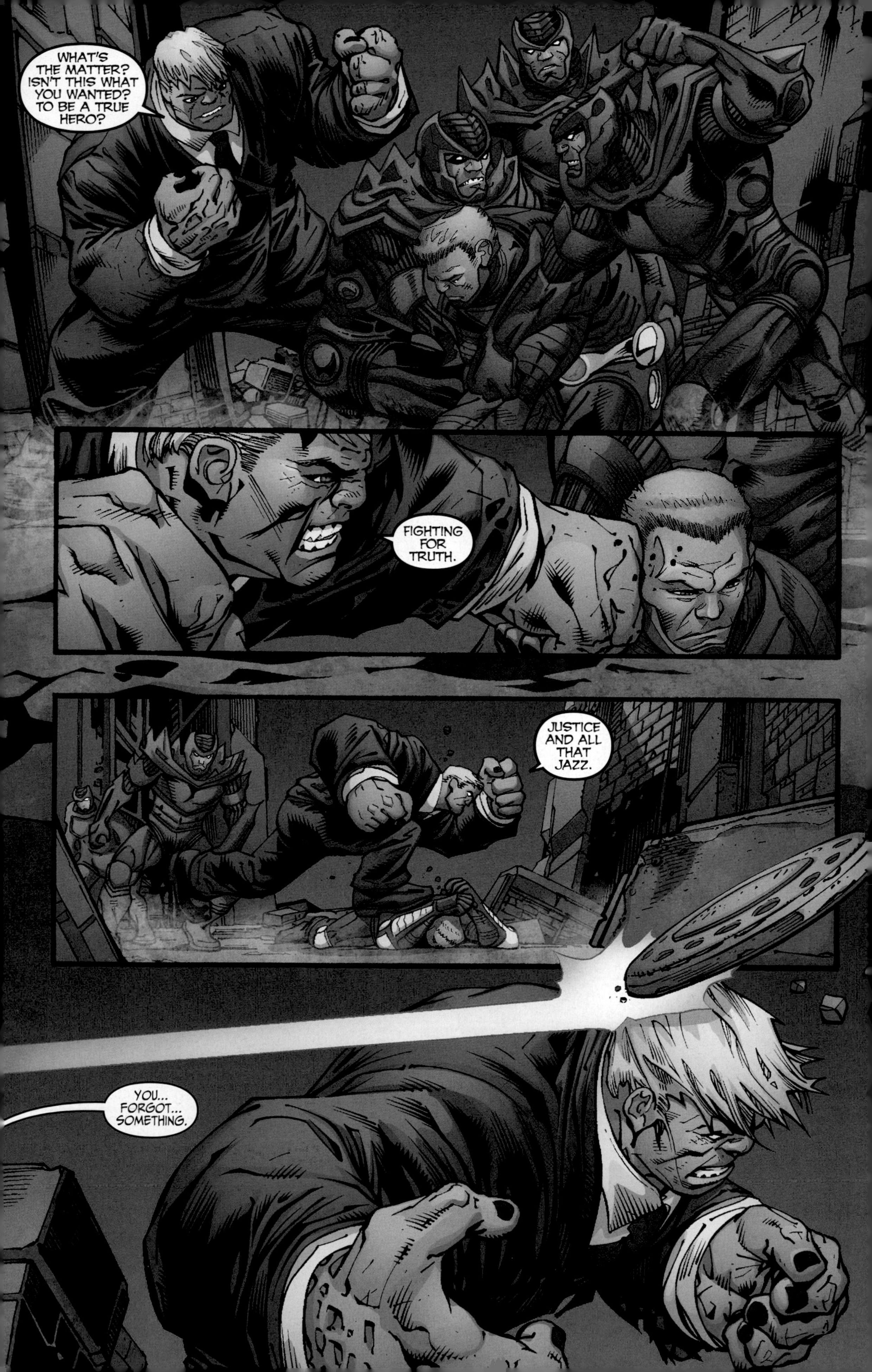
WHAT'S THE MATTER? ISN'T THIS WHAT YOU WANTED? TO BE A TRUE HERO?
FIGHTING FOR TRUTH.
JUSTICE AND ALL THAT JAZZ.
YOU... FORGOT... SOMETHING.

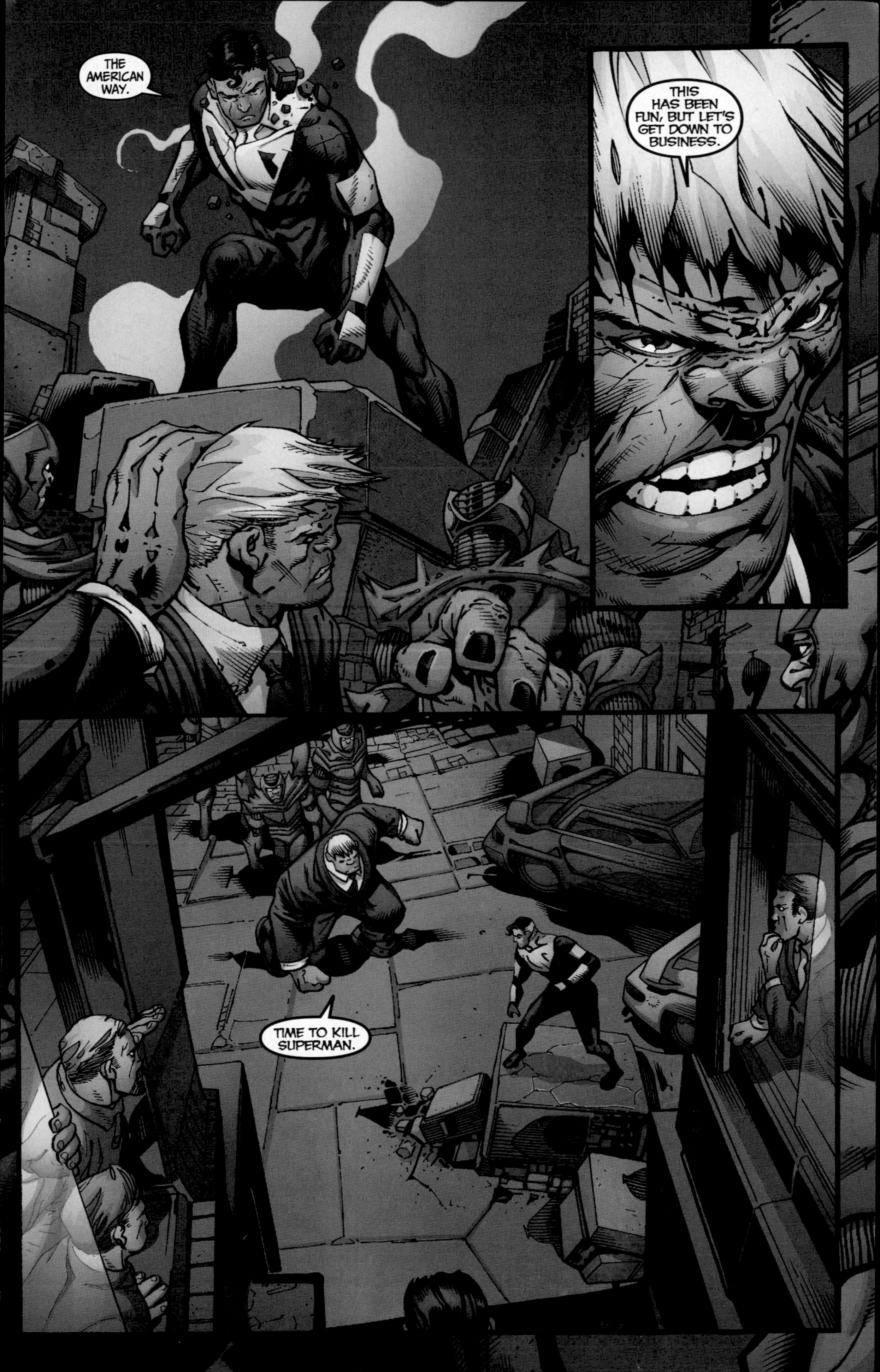
THE AMERICAN WAY.
THIS HAS BEEN FUN, BUT LET'S GET DOWN TO BUSINESS.
TIME TO KILL SUPERMAN.

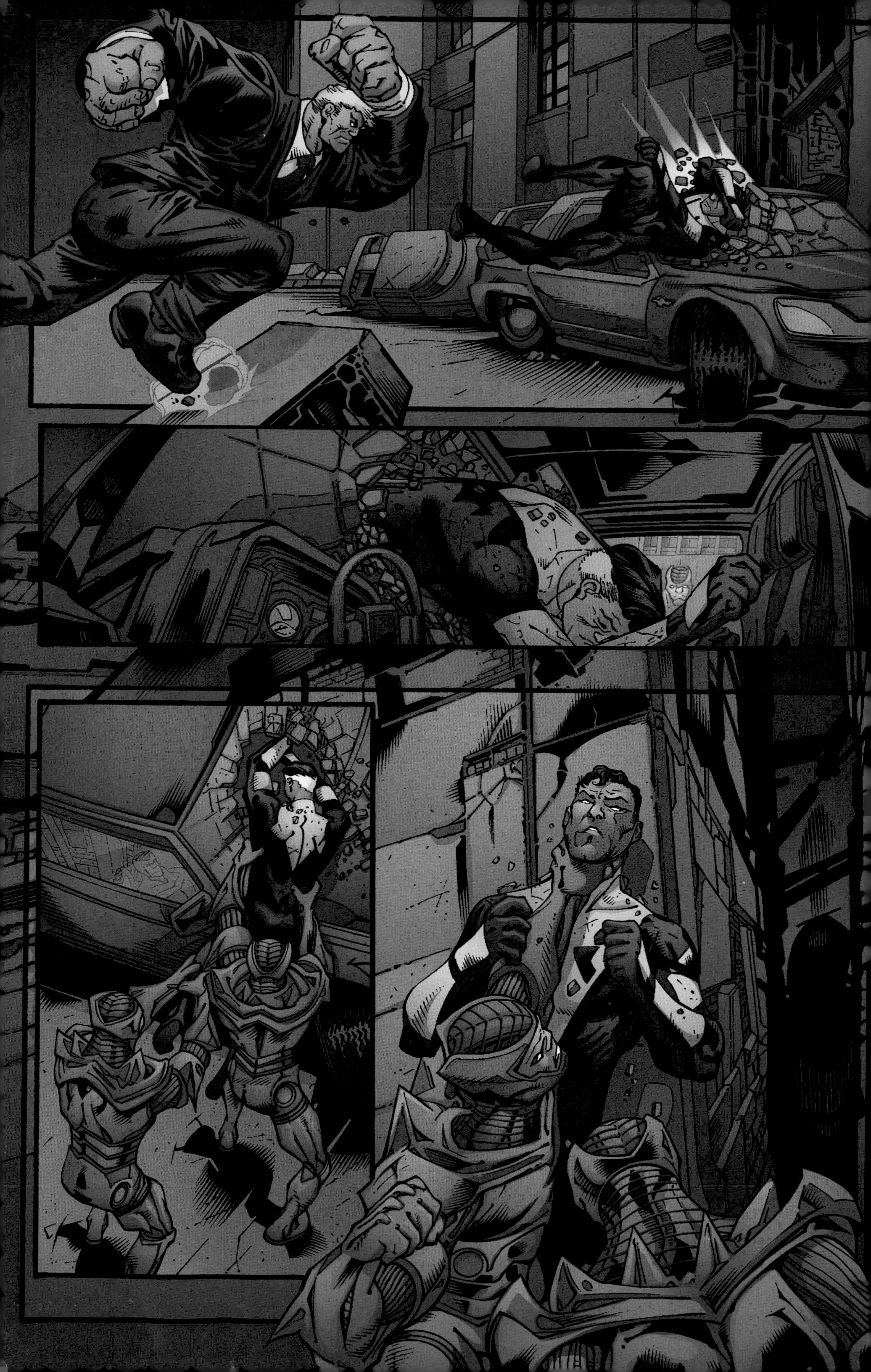

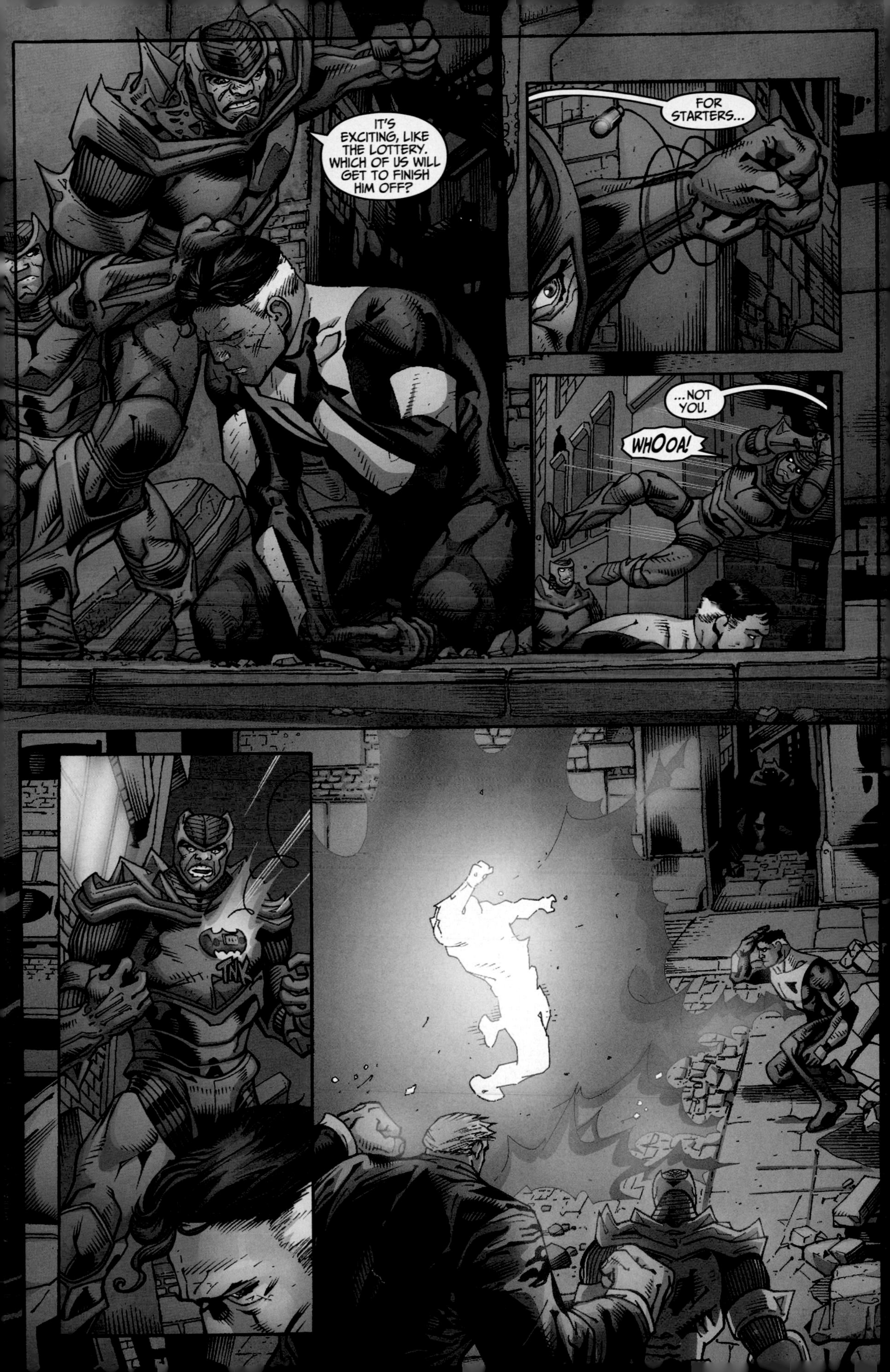
IT'S EXCITING, LIKE THE LOTTERY. WHICH OF US WILL GET TO FINISH HIM OFF?
FOR STARTERS...
...NOT YOU.
WHOOA!

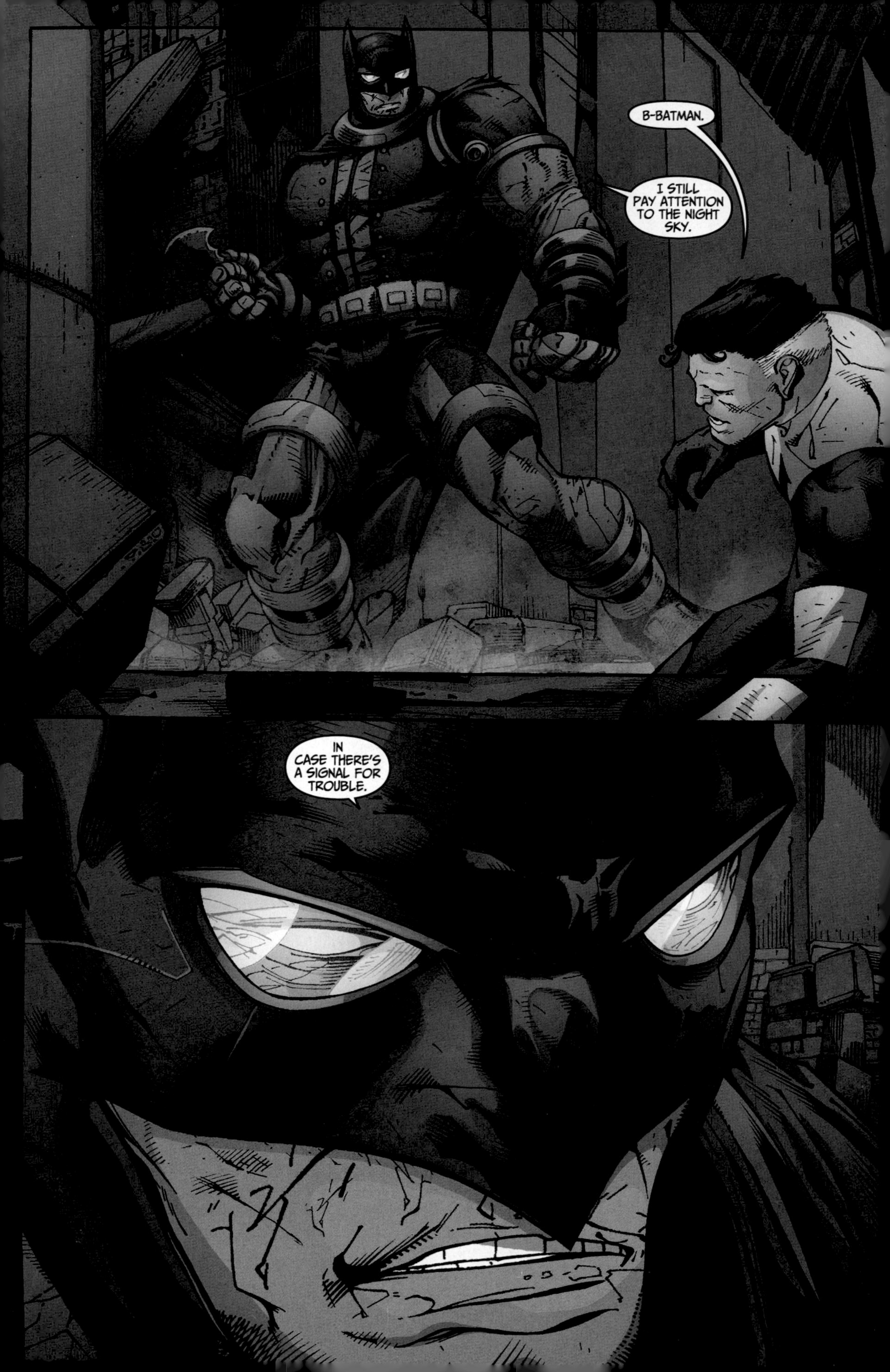
B-BATMAN.
I STILL PAY ATTENTION TO THE NIGHT SKY.
IN CASE THERE'S A SIGNAL FOR TROUBLE.

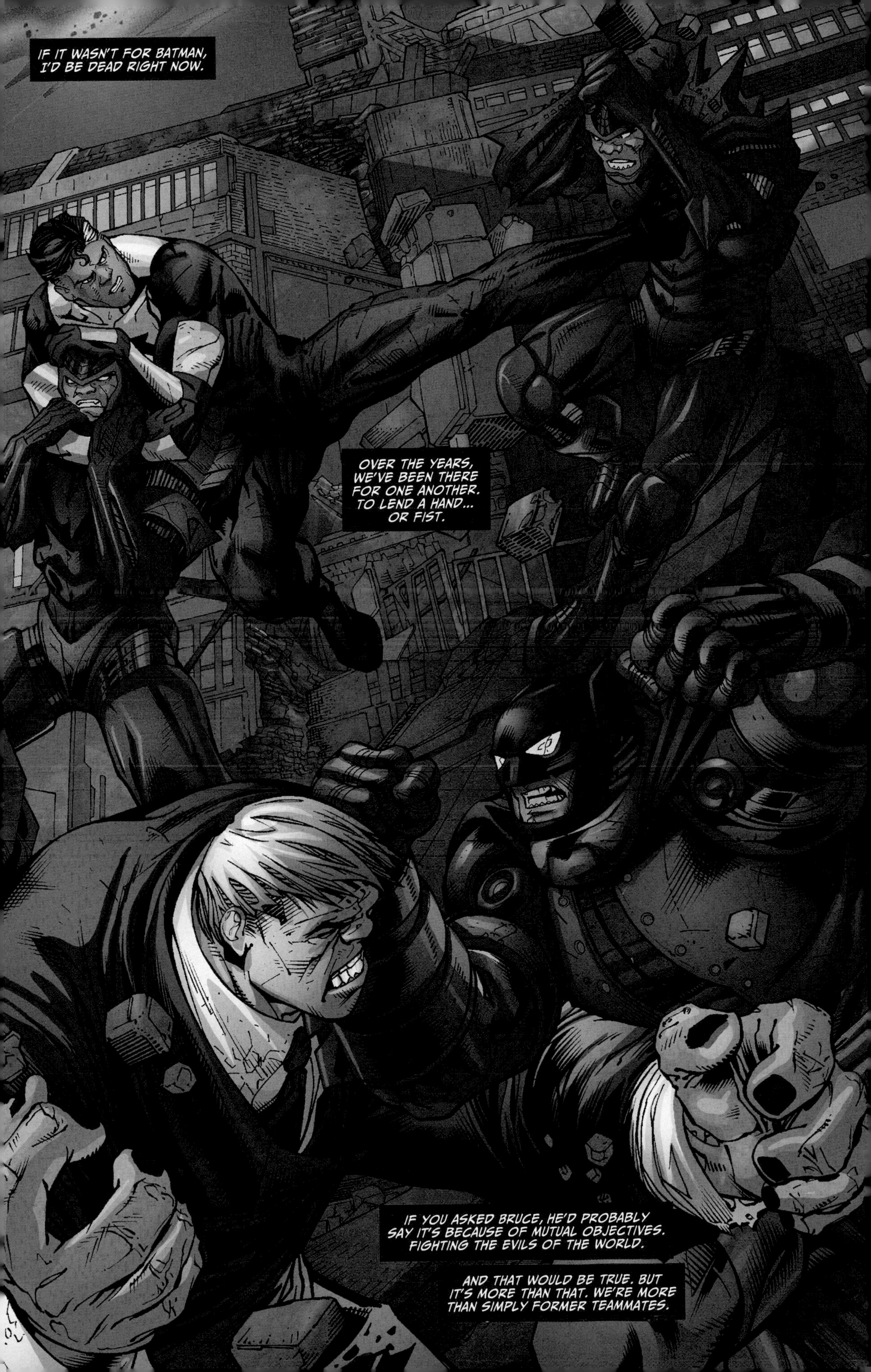
IF IT WASN'T FOR BATMAN, I'D BE DEAD RIGHT NOW.
OVER THE YEARS, WE'VE BEEN THERE FOR ONE ANOTHER. TO LEND A HAND... OR FIST.
IF YOU ASKED BRUCE, HE'D PROBABLY SAY IT'S BECAUSE OF MUTUAL OBJECTIVES. FIGHTING THE EVILS OF THE WORLD.
AND THAT WOULD BE TRUE. BUT IT'S MORE THAN THAT. WE'RE MORE THAN SIMPLY FORMER TEAMMATES.

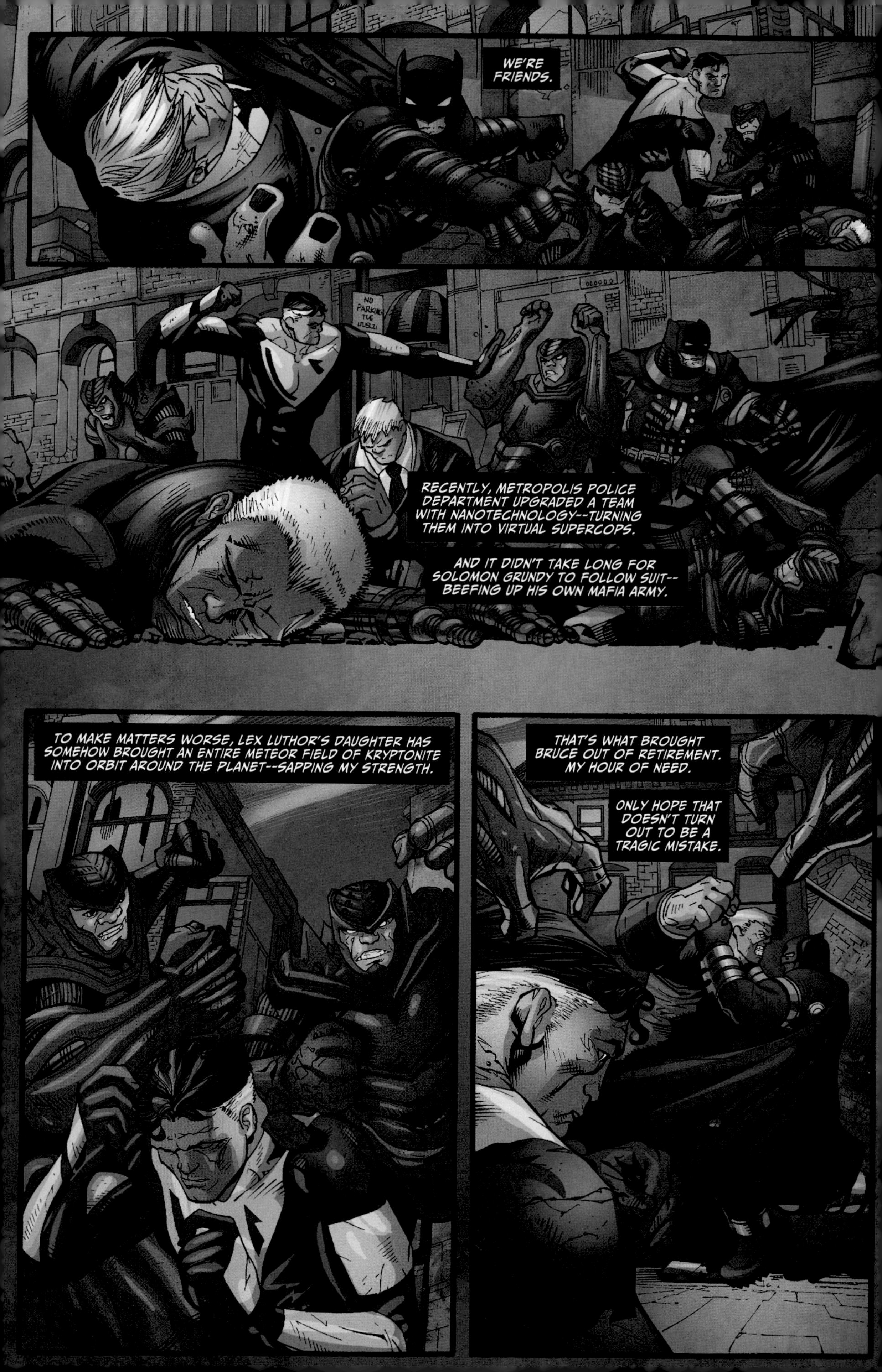
WE'RE FRIENDS.
NO PARKING
RECENTLY, METROPOLIS POLICE DEPARTMENT UPGRADED A TEAM WITH NANOTECHNOLOGY--TURNING THEM INTO VIRTUAL SUPERCOPS.
AND IT DIDN'T TAKE LONG FOR SOLOMON GRUNDY TO FOLLOW SUIT--BEEFING UP HIS OWN MAFIA ARMY.
TO MAKE MATTERS WORSE, LEX LUTHOR'S DAUGHTER HAS SOMEHOW BROUGHT AN ENTIRE METEOR FIELD OF KRYPTONITE INTO ORBIT AROUND THE PLANET--SAPPING MY STRENGTH.
THAT'S WHAT BROUGHT BRUCE OUT OF RETIREMENT. MY HOUR OF NEED.
ONLY HOPE THAT DOESN'T TURN OUT TO BE A TRAGIC MISTAKE.

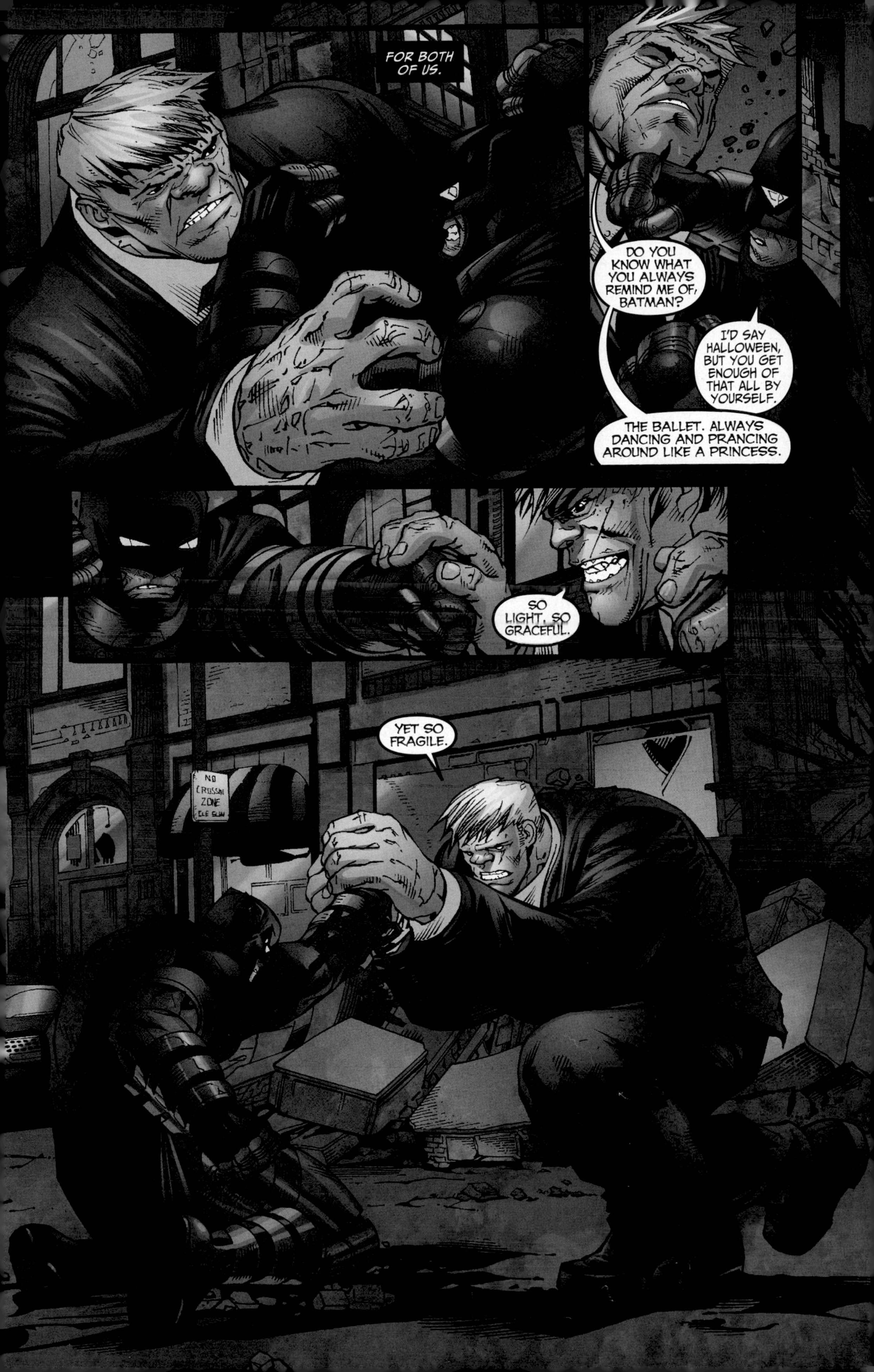
FOR BOTH OF US.
DO YOU KNOW WHAT YOU ALWAYS REMIND ME OF, BATMAN?
I'D SAY HALLOWEEN, BUT YOU GET ENOUGH OF THAT ALL BY YOURSELF.
THE BALLET. ALWAYS DANCING AND PRANCING AROUND LIKE A PRINCESS.
SO LIGHT, SO GRACEFUL.
YET SO FRAGILE.

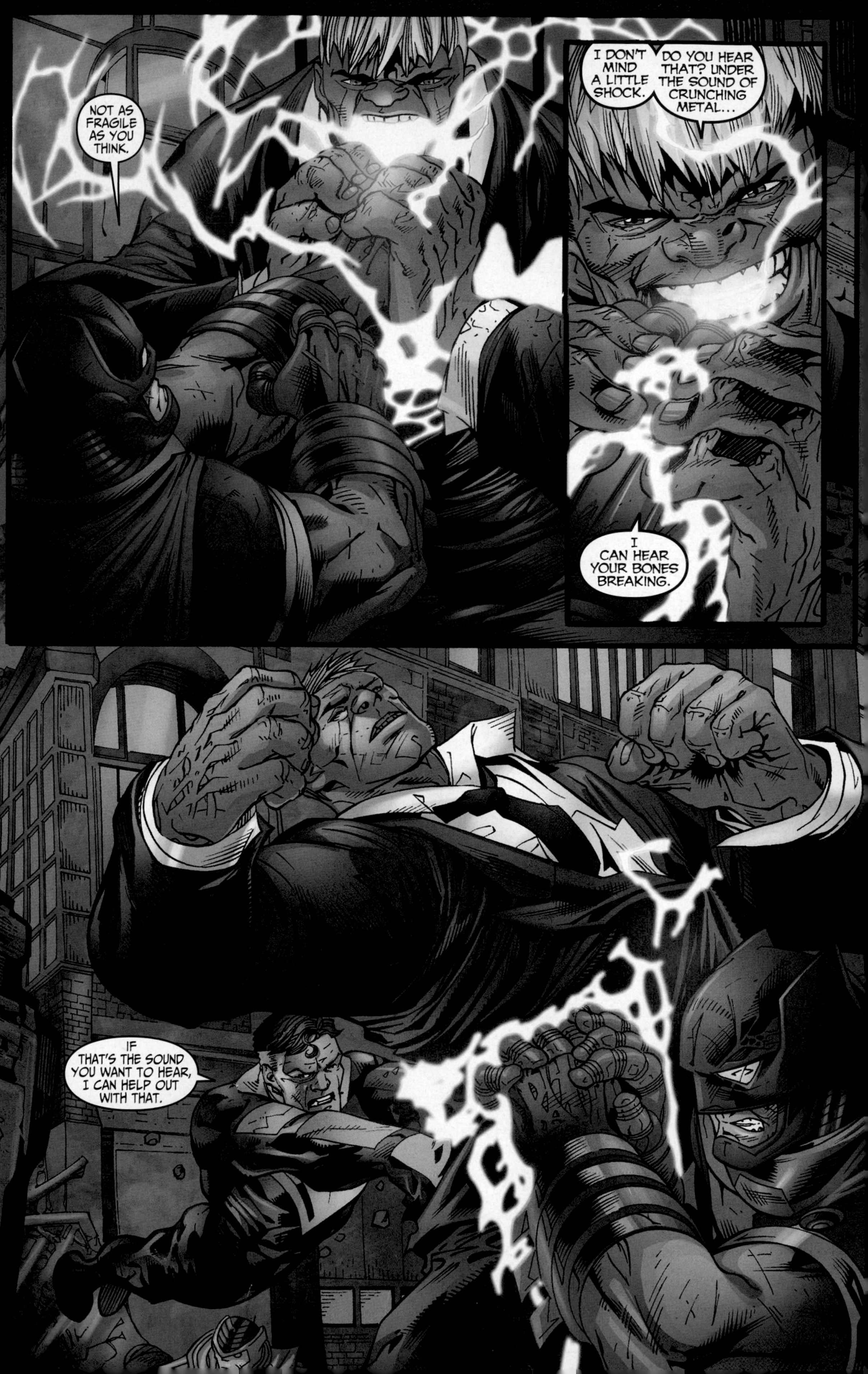
NOT AS FRAGILE AS YOU THINK.
I DON'T MIND A LITTLE SHOCK.
DO YOU HEAR THAT? UNDER THE SOUND OF CRUNCHING METAL...
I CAN HEAR YOUR BONES BREAKING.
IF THAT'S THE SOUND YOU WANT TO HEAR, I CAN HELP OUT WITH THAT.

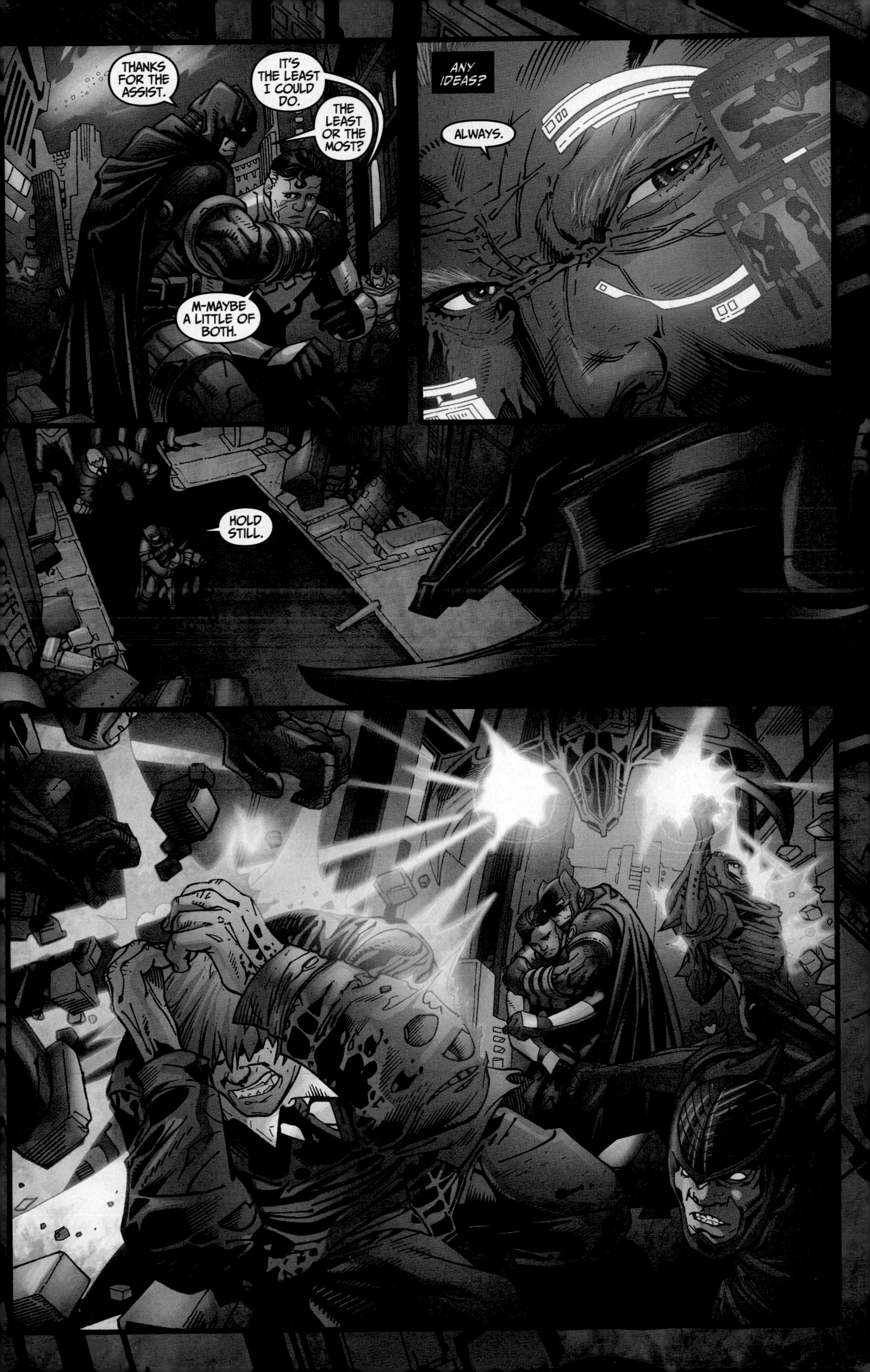
THANKS FOR THE ASSIST.
IT'S THE LEAST I COULD DO.
THE LEAST OR THE MOST?
M-MAYBE A LITTLE OF BOTH.
ANY IDEAS?
ALWAYS.
HOLD STILL.

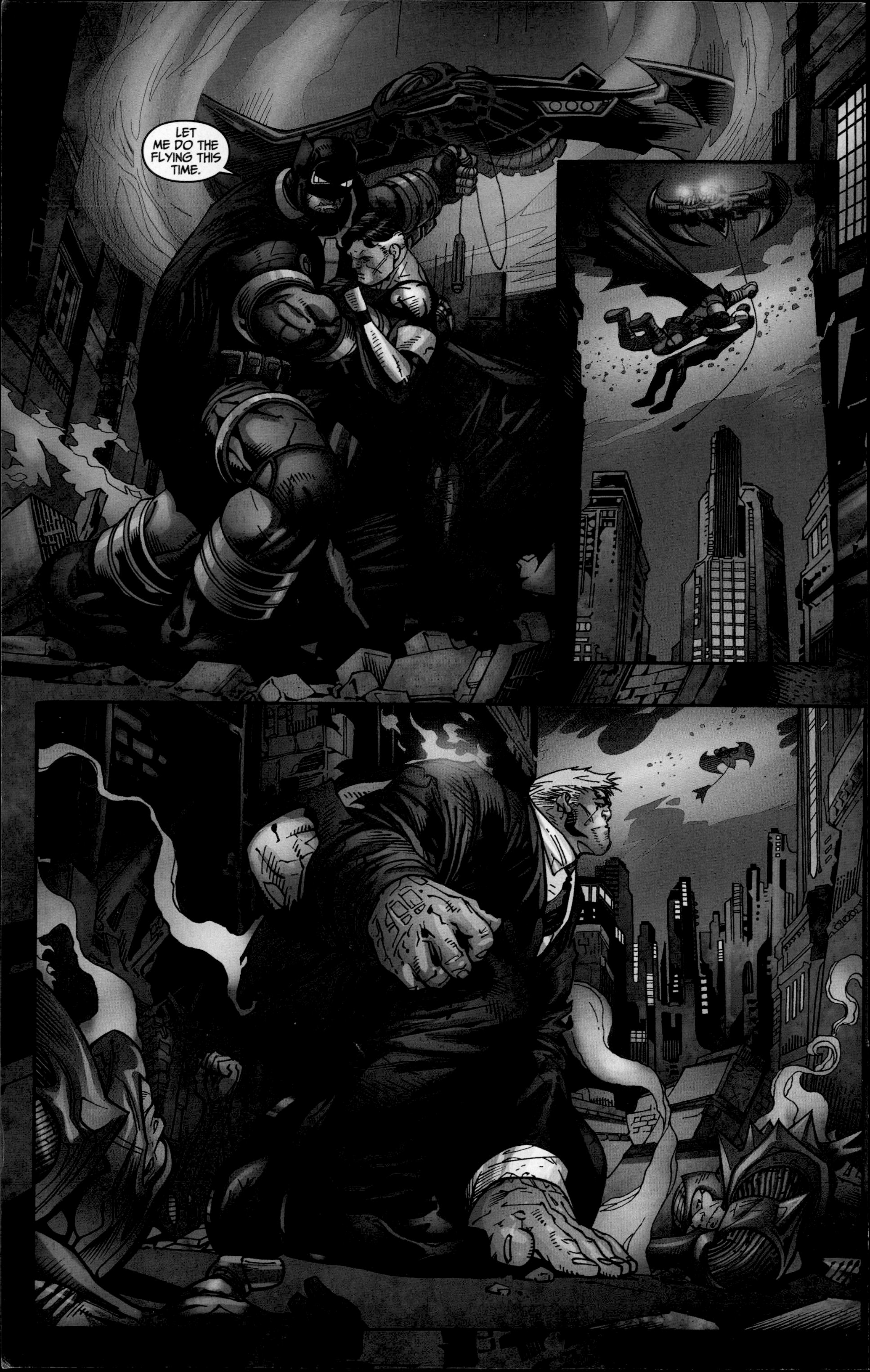
LET ME DO THE FLYING THIS TIME.

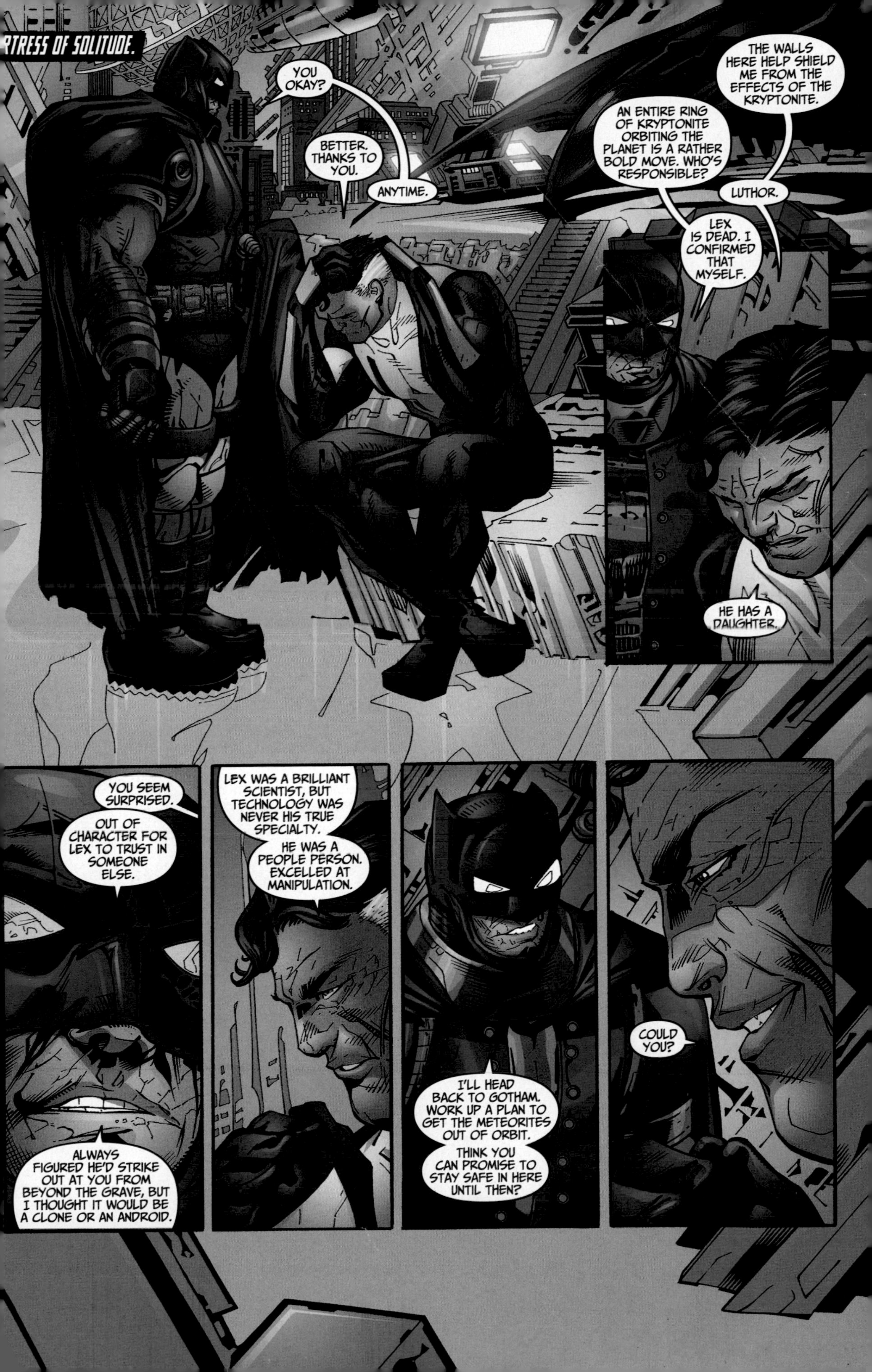
...RTRESS OF SOLITUDE.
YOU OKAY?
BETTER. THANKS TO YOU.
ANYTIME.
AN ENTIRE RING OF KRYPTONITE ORBITING THE PLANET IS A RATHER BOLD MOVE. WHO'S RESPONSIBLE?
THE WALLS HERE HELP SHIELD ME FROM THE EFFECTS OF THE KRYPTONITE.
LUTHOR.
LEX IS DEAD. I CONFIRMED THAT MYSELF.
HE HAS A DAUGHTER.
YOU SEEM SURPRISED.
OUT OF CHARACTER FOR LEX TO TRUST IN SOMEONE ELSE.
ALWAYS FIGURED HE'D STRIKE OUT AT YOU FROM BEYOND THE GRAVE, BUT I THOUGHT IT WOULD BE A CLONE OR AN ANDROID.
LEX WAS A BRILLIANT SCIENTIST, BUT TECHNOLOGY WAS NEVER HIS TRUE SPECIALTY.
HE WAS A PEOPLE PERSON. EXCELLED AT MANIPULATION.
I'LL HEAD BACK TO GOTHAM. WORK UP A PLAN TO GET THE METEORITES OUT OF ORBIT.
THINK YOU CAN PROMISE TO STAY SAFE IN HERE UNTIL THEN?
COULD YOU?

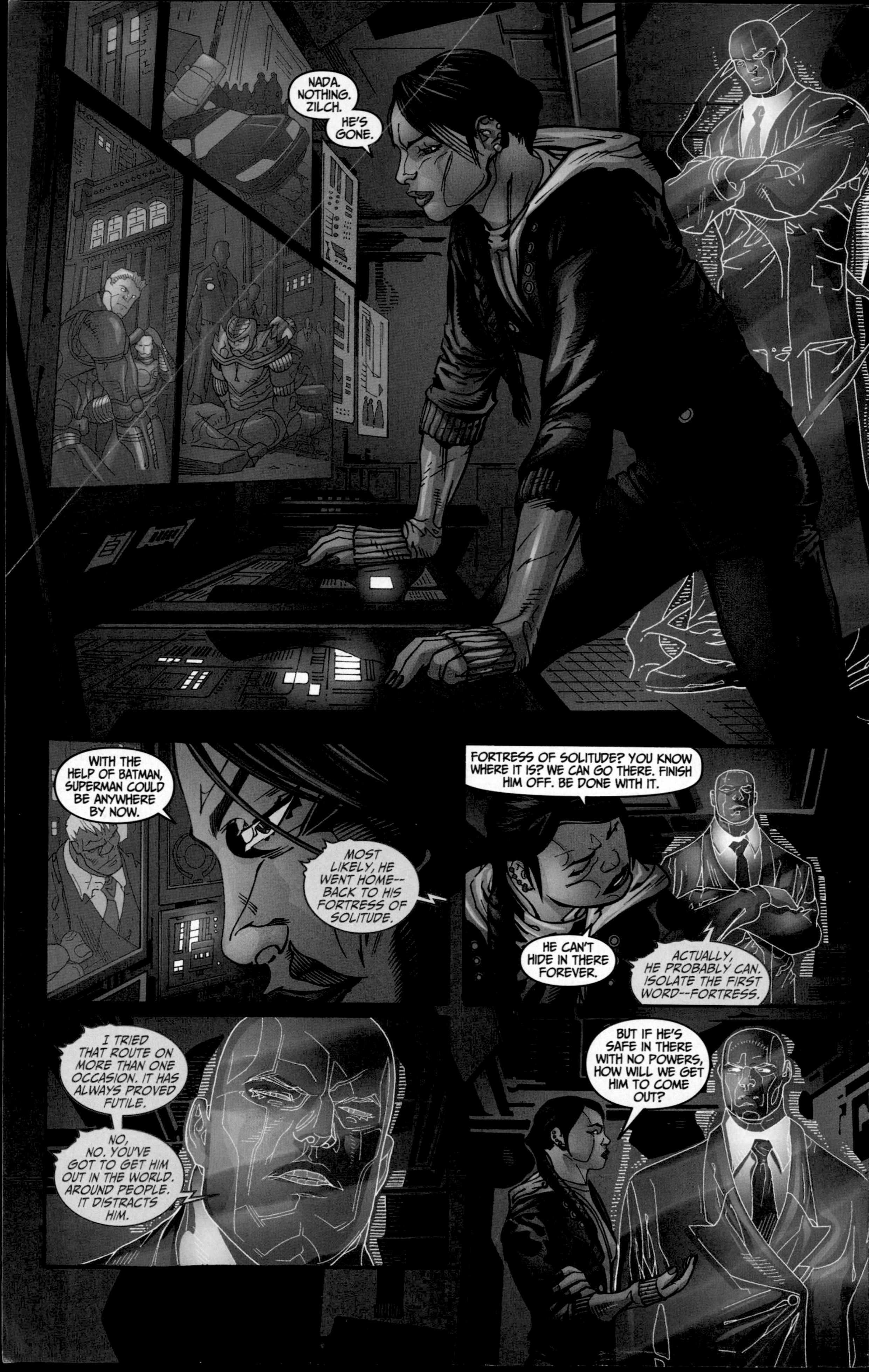
NADA. NOTHING. ZILCH.
HE'S GONE.
WITH THE HELP OF BATMAN, SUPERMAN COULD BE ANYWHERE BY NOW.
MOST LIKELY, HE WENT HOME--BACK TO HIS FORTRESS OF SOLITUDE.
FORTRESS OF SOLITUDE? YOU KNOW WHERE IT IS? WE CAN GO THERE. FINISH HIM OFF. BE DONE WITH IT.
HE CAN'T HIDE IN THERE FOREVER.
ACTUALLY, HE PROBABLY CAN. ISOLATE THE FIRST WORD--FORTRESS.
I TRIED THAT ROUTE ON MORE THAN ONE OCCASION. IT HAS ALWAYS PROVED FUTILE.
NO, NO. YOU'VE GOT TO GET HIM OUT IN THE WORLD. AROUND PEOPLE. IT DISTRACTS HIM.
BUT IF HE'S SAFE IN THERE WITH NO POWERS, HOW WILL WE GET HIM TO COME OUT?

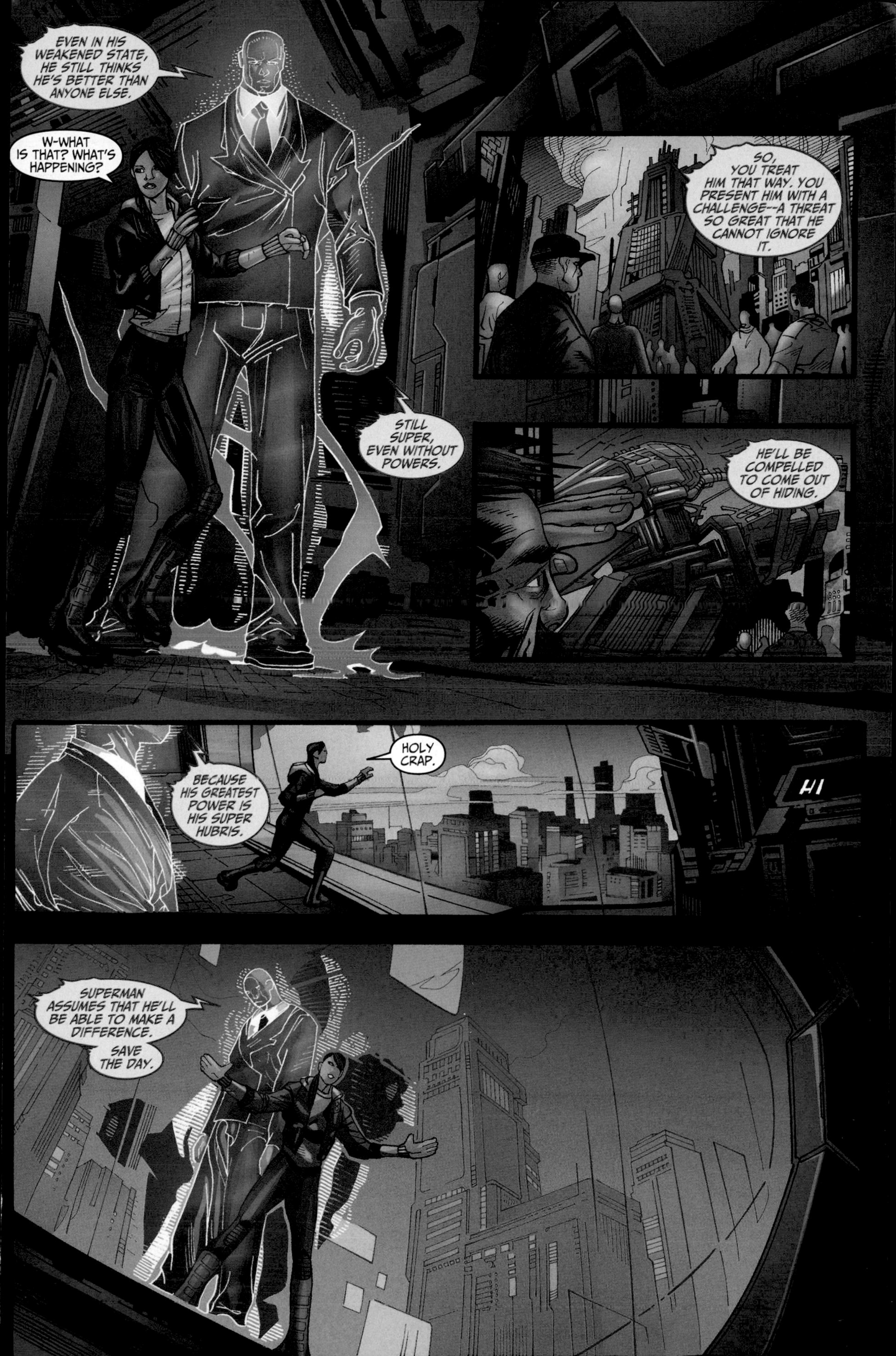
EVEN IN HIS WEAKENED STATE, HE STILL THINKS HE'S BETTER THAN ANYONE ELSE.
W-WHAT IS THAT? WHAT'S HAPPENING?
SO, YOU TREAT HIM THAT WAY. YOU PRESENT HIM WITH A CHALLENGE--A THREAT SO GREAT THAT HE CANNOT IGNORE IT.
STILL SUPER, EVEN WITHOUT POWERS.
HE'LL BE COMPELLED TO COME OUT OF HIDING.
BECAUSE HIS GREATEST POWER IS HIS SUPER HUBRIS.
HOLY CRAP.
HI
SUPERMAN ASSUMES THAT HE'LL BE ABLE TO MAKE A DIFFERENCE.
SAVE THE DAY.

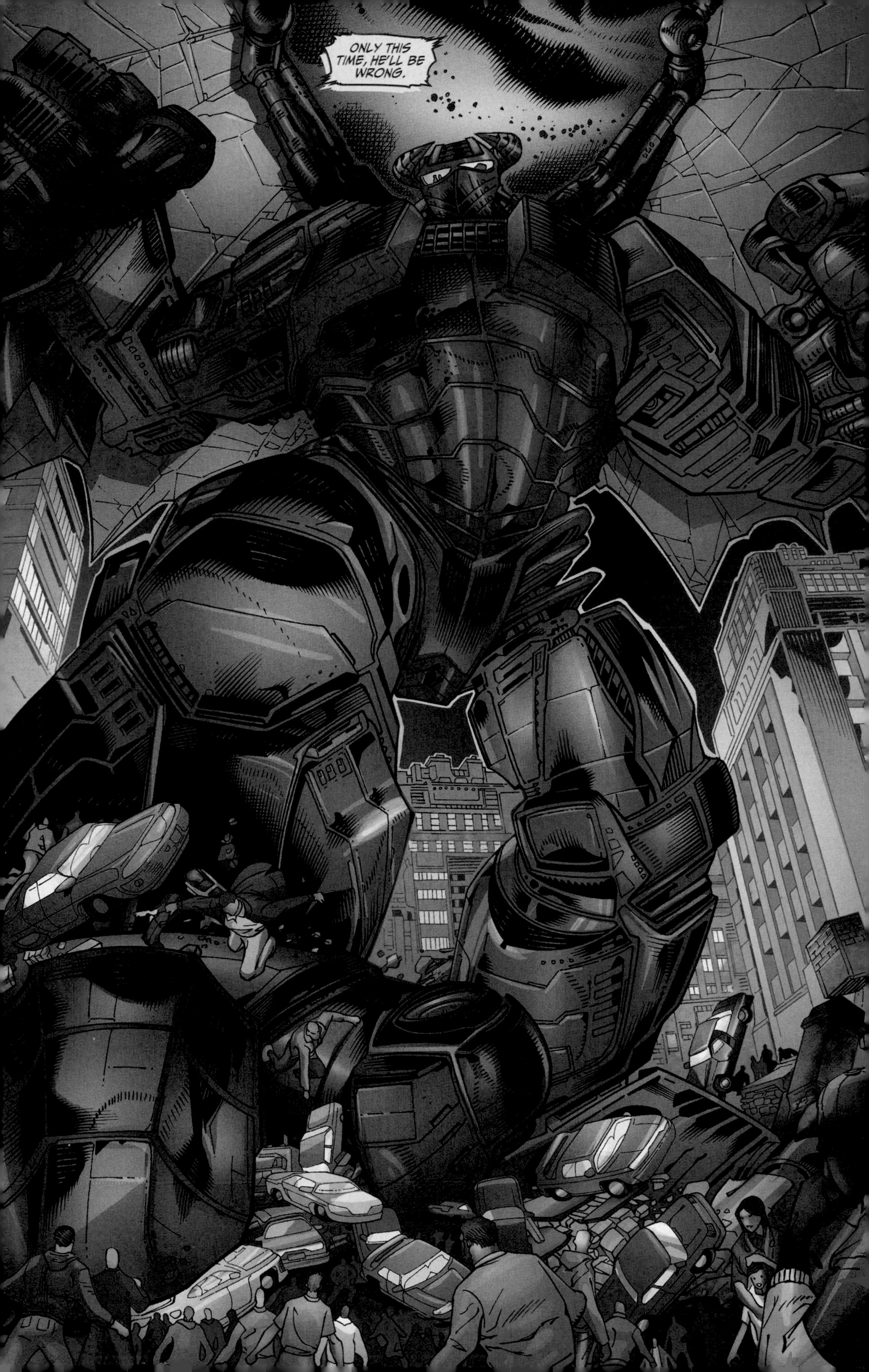
ONLY THIS TIME, HE'LL BE WRONG.

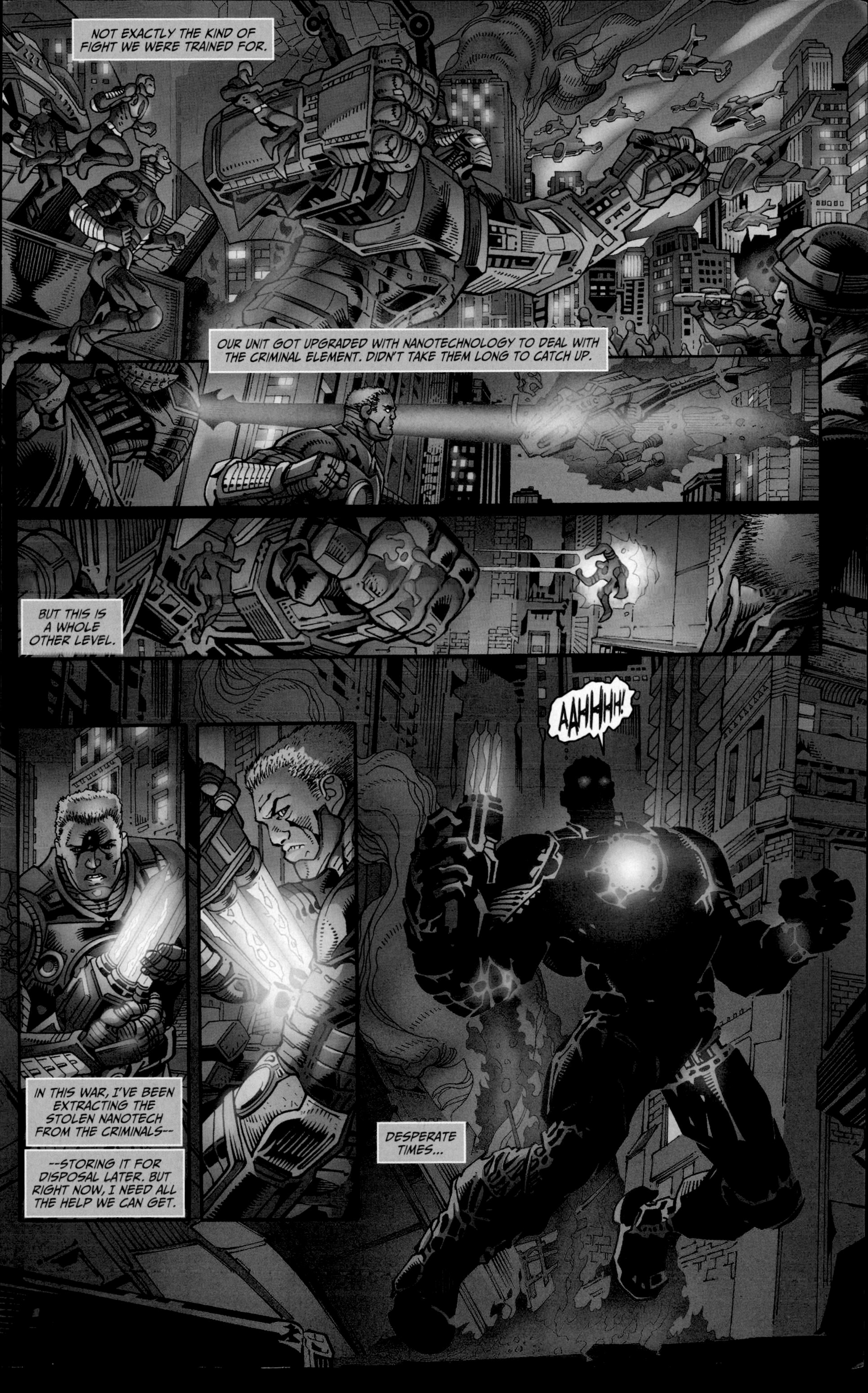
NOT EXACTLY THE KIND OF FIGHT WE WERE TRAINED FOR.
OUR UNIT GOT UPGRADED WITH NANOTECHNOLOGY TO DEAL WITH THE CRIMINAL ELEMENT. DIDN'T TAKE THEM LONG TO CATCH UP.
BUT THIS IS A WHOLE OTHER LEVEL.
AAHHHH!
IN THIS WAR, I'VE BEEN EXTRACTING THE STOLEN NANOTECH FROM THE CRIMINALS--
--STORING IT FOR DISPOSAL LATER. BUT RIGHT NOW, I NEED ALL THE HELP WE CAN GET.
DESPERATE TIMES...

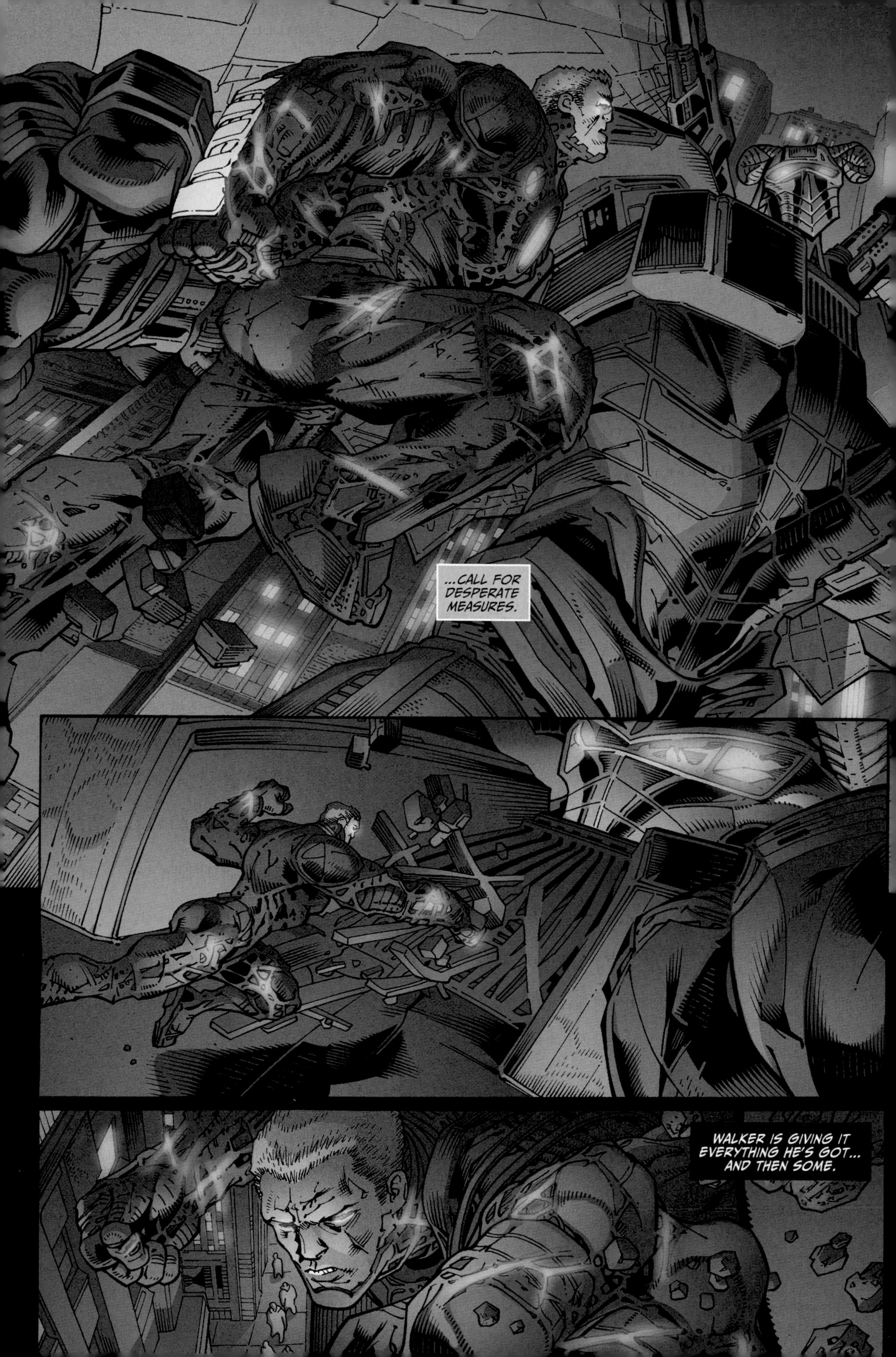
...CALL FOR DESPERATE MEASURES.
WALKER IS GIVING IT EVERYTHING HE'S GOT... AND THEN SOME.

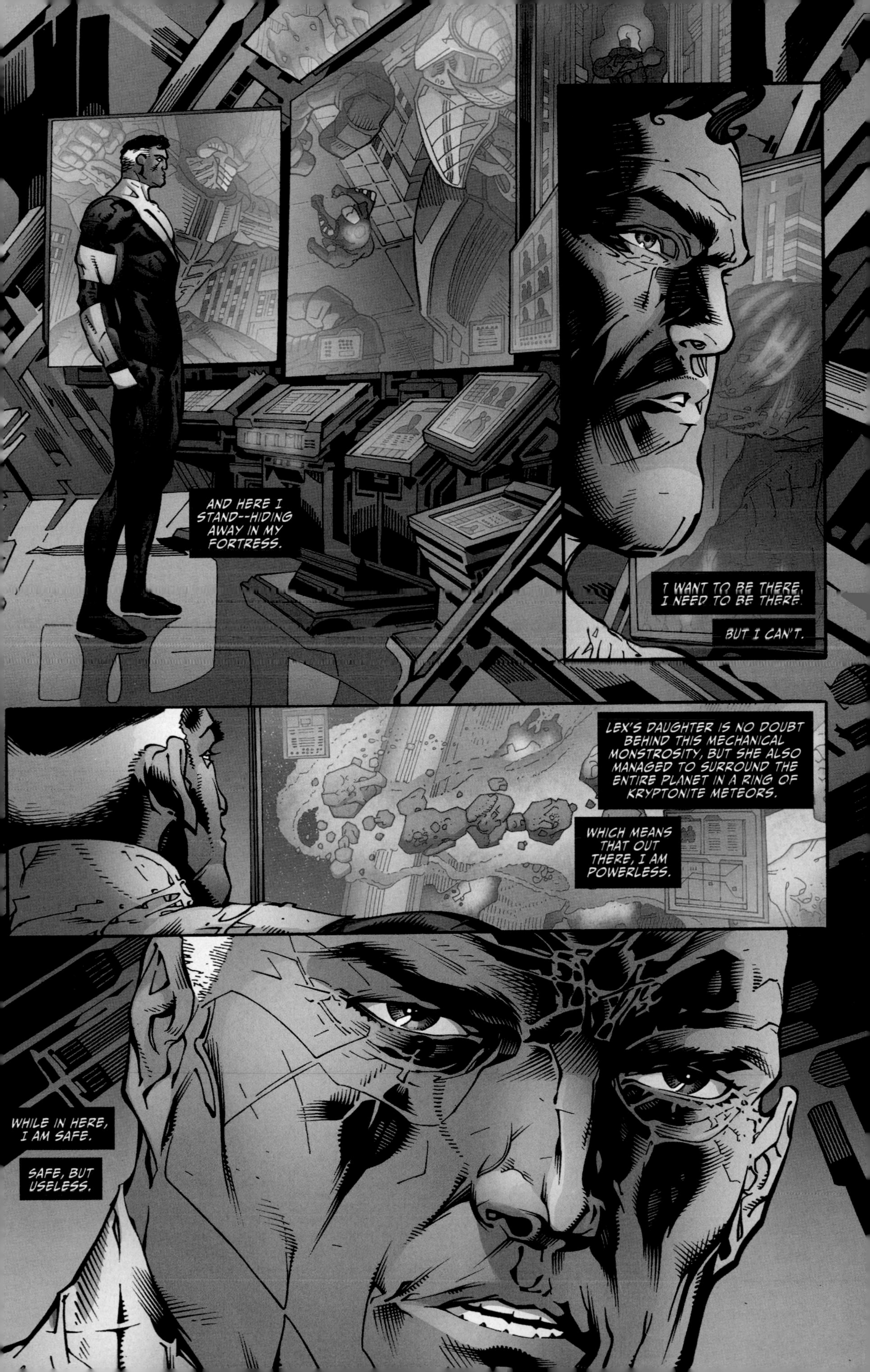
AND HERE I STAND--HIDING AWAY IN MY FORTRESS.
I WANT TO BE THERE. I NEED TO BE THERE.
BUT I CAN'T.
LEX'S DAUGHTER IS NO DOUBT BEHIND THIS MECHANICAL MONSTROSITY, BUT SHE ALSO MANAGED TO SURROUND THE ENTIRE PLANET IN A RING OF KRYPTONITE METEORS.
WHICH MEANS THAT OUT THERE, I AM POWERLESS.
WHILE IN HERE, I AM SAFE.
SAFE, BUT USELESS.

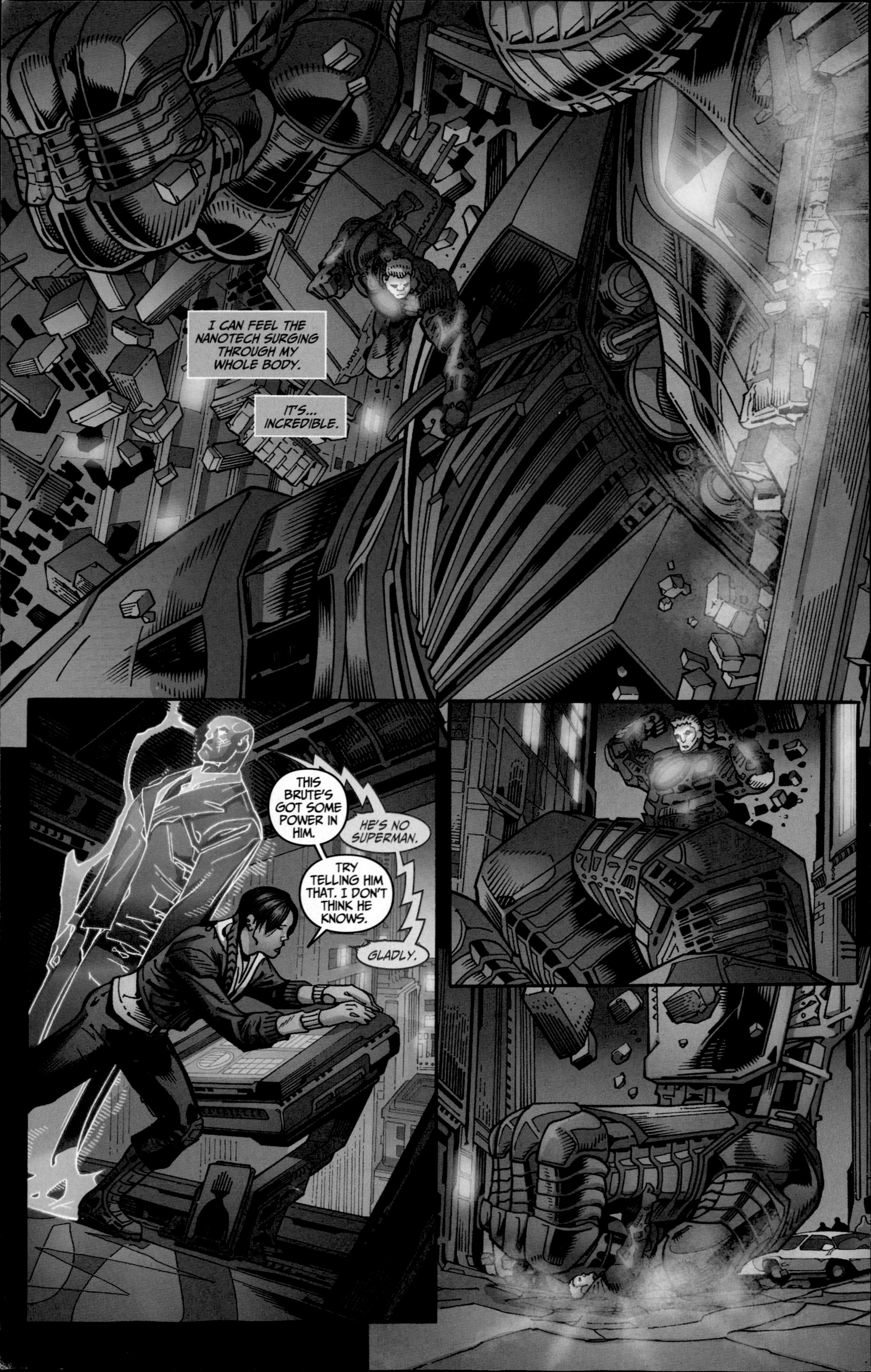
I CAN FEEL THE NANOTECH SURGING THROUGH MY WHOLE BODY.
IT'S... INCREDIBLE.
THIS BRUTE'S GOT SOME POWER IN HIM.
HE'S NO SUPERMAN.
TRY TELLING HIM THAT. I DON'T THINK HE KNOWS.
GLADLY.

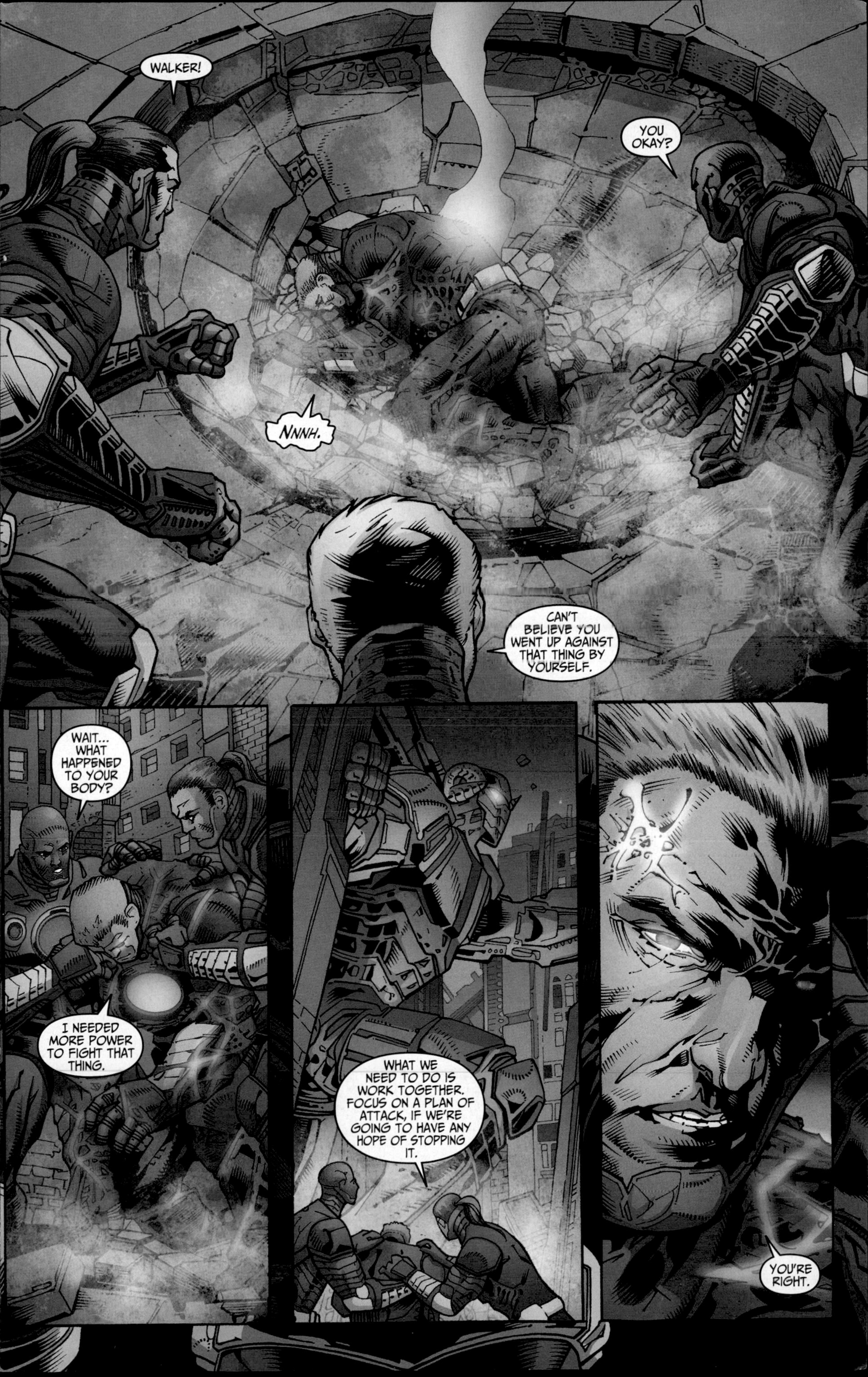
WALKER!
YOU OKAY?
NNNH.
CAN'T BELIEVE YOU WENT UP AGAINST THAT THING BY YOURSELF.
WAIT... WHAT HAPPENED TO YOUR BODY?
I NEEDED MORE POWER TO FIGHT THAT THING.
WHAT WE NEED TO DO IS WORK TOGETHER. FOCUS ON A PLAN OF ATTACK, IF WE'RE GOING TO HAVE ANY HOPE OF STOPPING IT.
YOU'RE RIGHT.

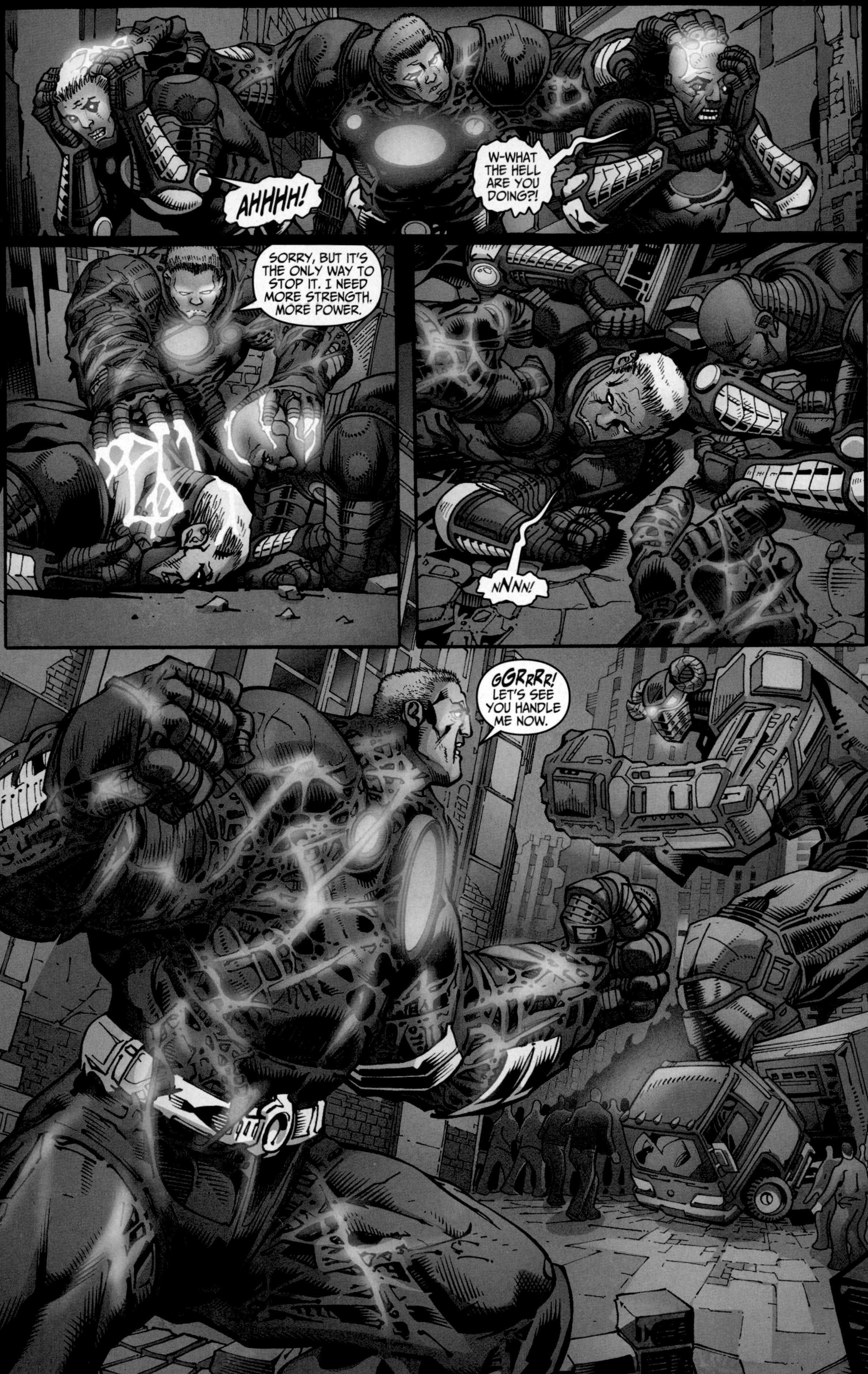
AHHHH!
W-WHAT THE HELL ARE YOU DOING?!
SORRY, BUT IT'S THE ONLY WAY TO STOP IT. I NEED MORE STRENGTH. MORE POWER.
NNNN!
GGRRRR! LET'S SEE YOU HANDLE ME NOW.

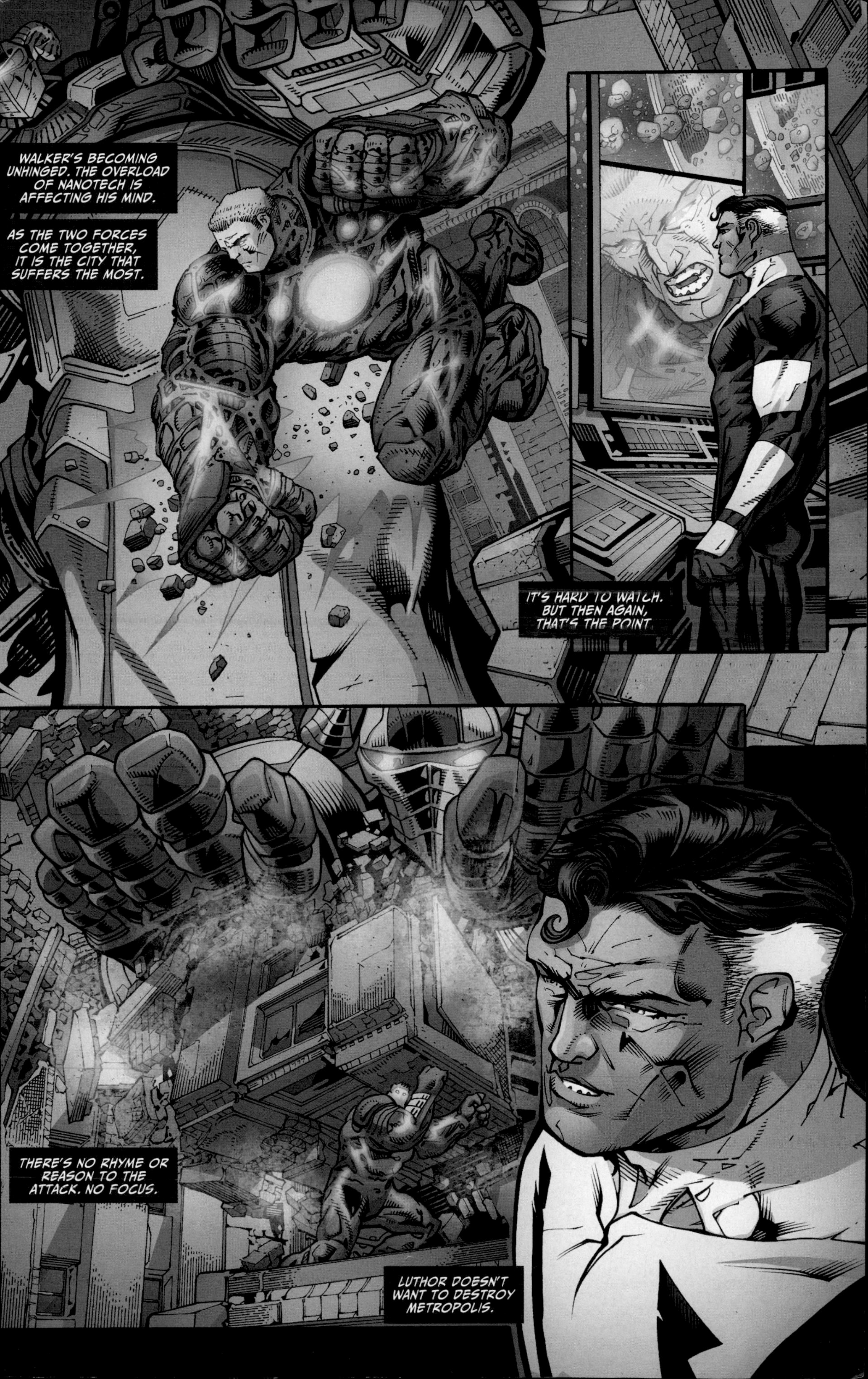
WALKER'S BECOMING UNHINGED. THE OVERLOAD OF NANOTECH IS AFFECTING HIS MIND.
AS THE TWO FORCES COME TOGETHER, IT IS THE CITY THAT SUFFERS THE MOST.
IT'S HARD TO WATCH. BUT THEN AGAIN, THAT'S THE POINT.
THERE'S NO RHYME OR REASON TO THE ATTACK. NO FOCUS.
LUTHOR DOESN'T WANT TO DESTROY METROPOLIS.

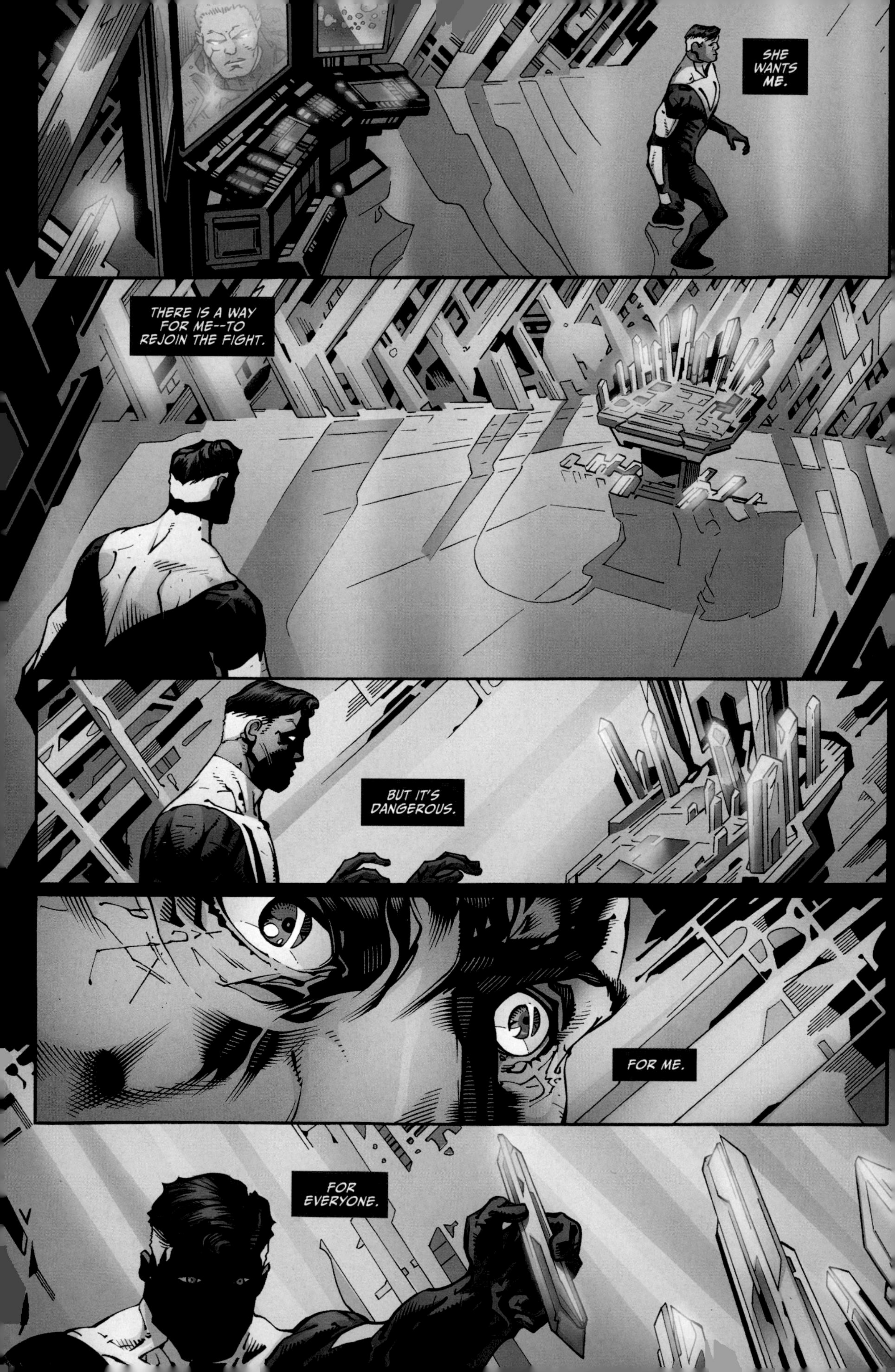
SHE WANTS ME.
THERE IS A WAY FOR ME--TO REJOIN THE FIGHT.
BUT IT'S DANGEROUS.
FOR ME.
FOR EVERYONE.

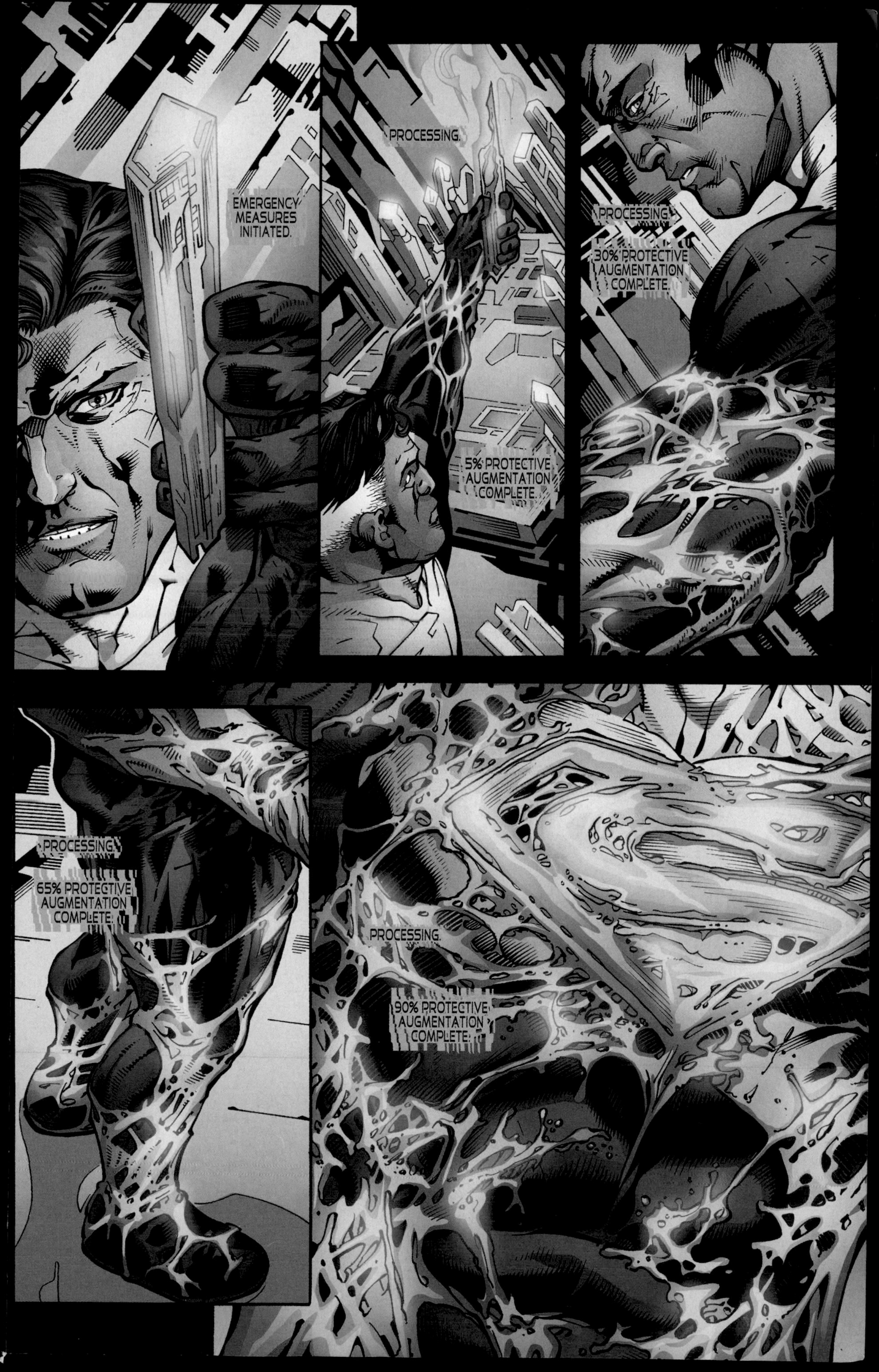
EMERGENCY MEASURES INITIATED.
PROCESSING.
5% PROTECTIVE AUGMENTATION COMPLETE.
PROCESSING.
30% PROTECTIVE AUGMENTATION COMPLETE.
PROCESSING.
65% PROTECTIVE AUGMENTATION COMPLETE.
PROCESSING.
90% PROTECTIVE AUGMENTATION COMPLETE.

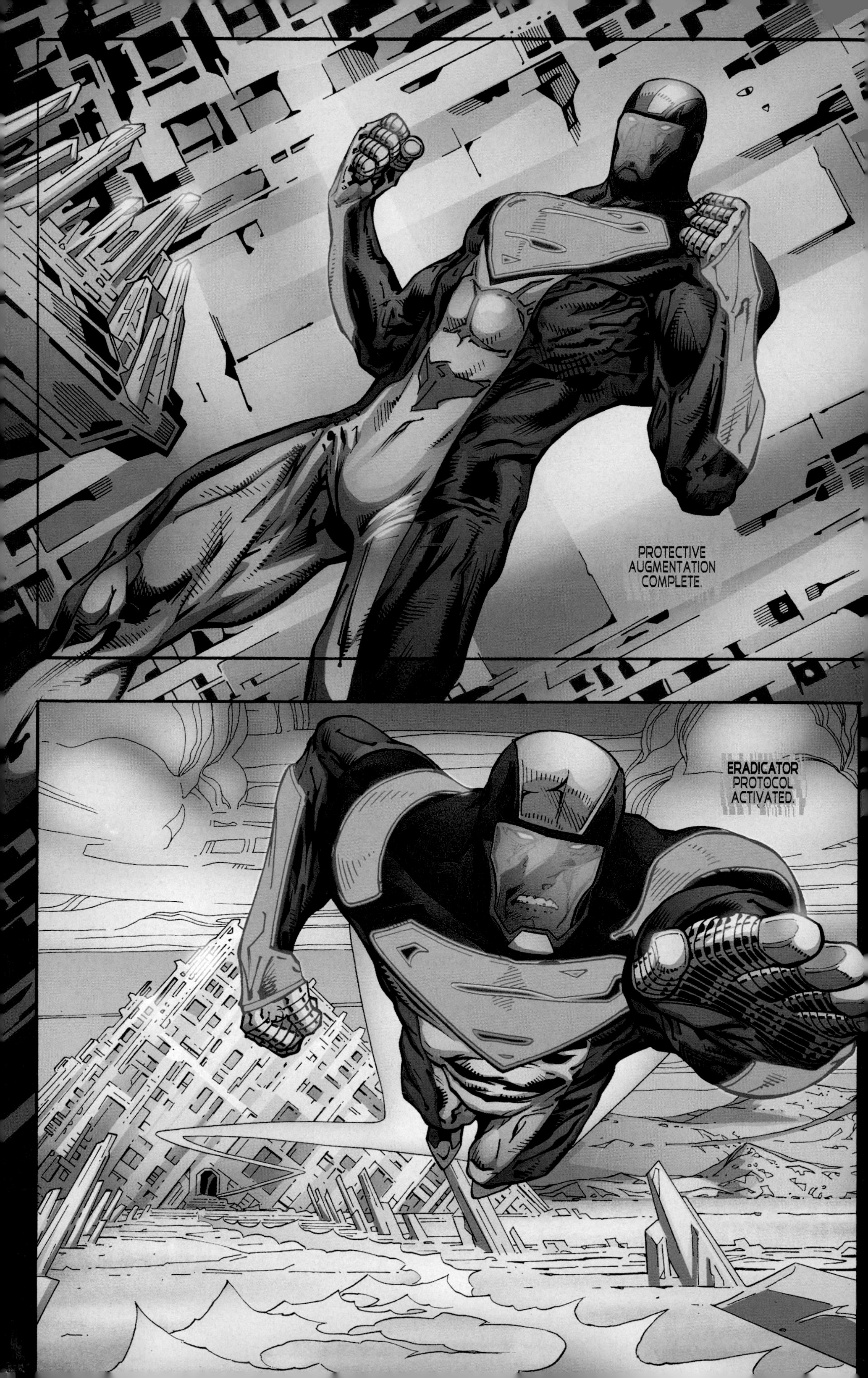
PROTECTIVE AUGMENTATION COMPLETE.
ERADICATOR PROTOCOL ACTIVATED.

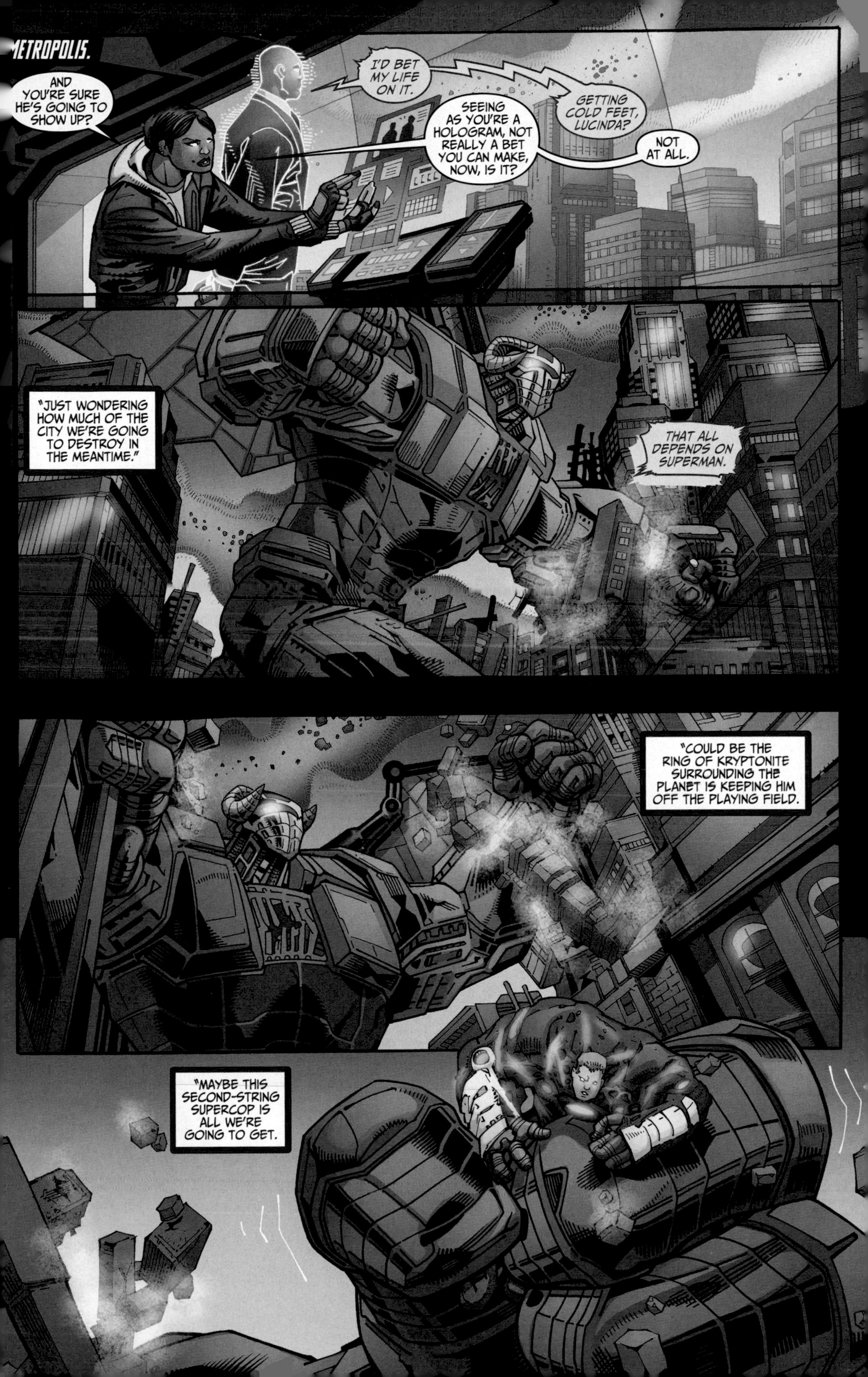
METROPOLIS.
AND YOU'RE SURE HE'S GOING TO SHOW UP?
I'D BET MY LIFE ON IT.
SEEING AS YOU'RE A HOLOGRAM, NOT REALLY A BET YOU CAN MAKE, NOW, IS IT?
GETTING COLD FEET, LUCINDA?
NOT AT ALL.
"JUST WONDERING HOW MUCH OF THE CITY WE'RE GOING TO DESTROY IN THE MEANTIME."
THAT ALL DEPENDS ON SUPERMAN.
"COULD BE THE RING OF KRYPTONITE SURROUNDING THE PLANET IS KEEPING HIM OFF THE PLAYING FIELD.
"MAYBE THIS SECOND-STRING SUPERCOP IS ALL WE'RE GOING TO GET.

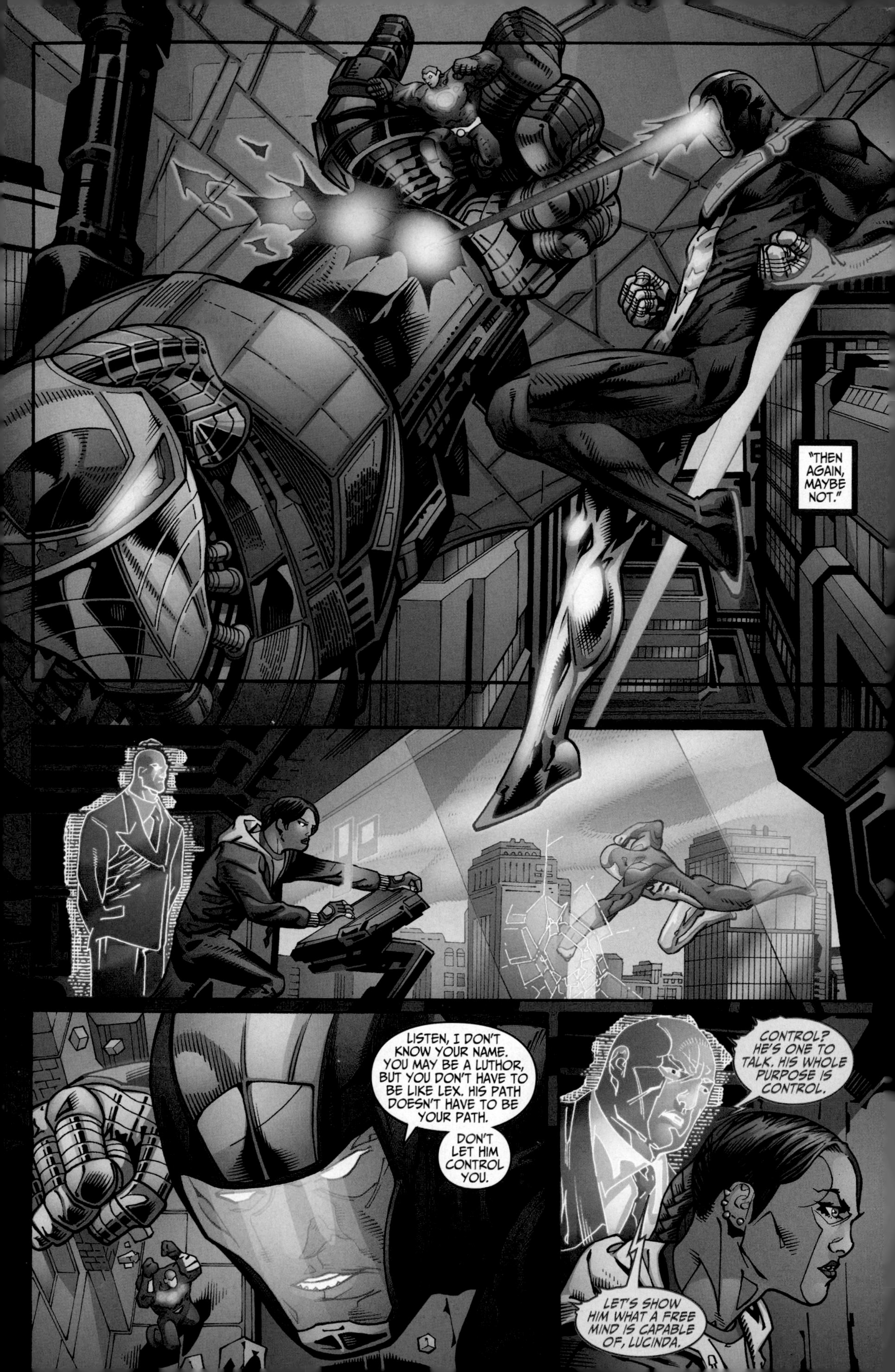
"THEN AGAIN, MAYBE NOT."
LISTEN, I DON'T KNOW YOUR NAME. YOU MAY BE A LUTHOR, BUT YOU DON'T HAVE TO BE LIKE LEX. HIS PATH DOESN'T HAVE TO BE YOUR PATH.
DON'T LET HIM CONTROL YOU.
CONTROL? HE'S ONE TO TALK. HIS WHOLE PURPOSE IS CONTROL.
LET'S SHOW HIM WHAT A FREE MIND IS CAPABLE OF, LUCINDA.

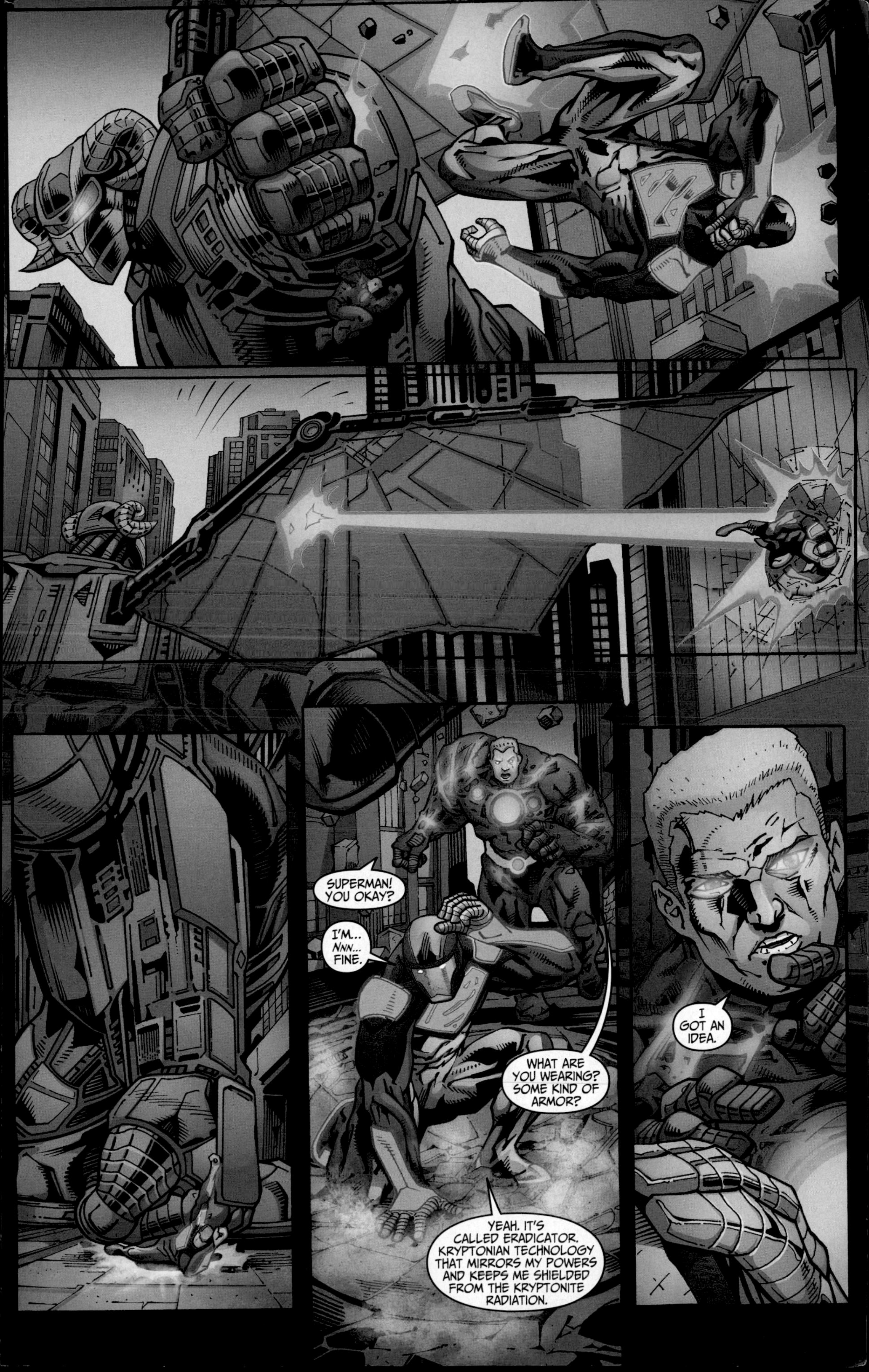
SUPERMAN! YOU OKAY?
I'M... NNN... FINE.
WHAT ARE YOU WEARING? SOME KIND OF ARMOR?
YEAH. IT'S CALLED ERADICATOR. KRYPTONIAN TECHNOLOGY THAT MIRRORS MY POWERS AND KEEPS ME SHIELDED FROM THE KRYPTONITE RADIATION.
I GOT AN IDEA.

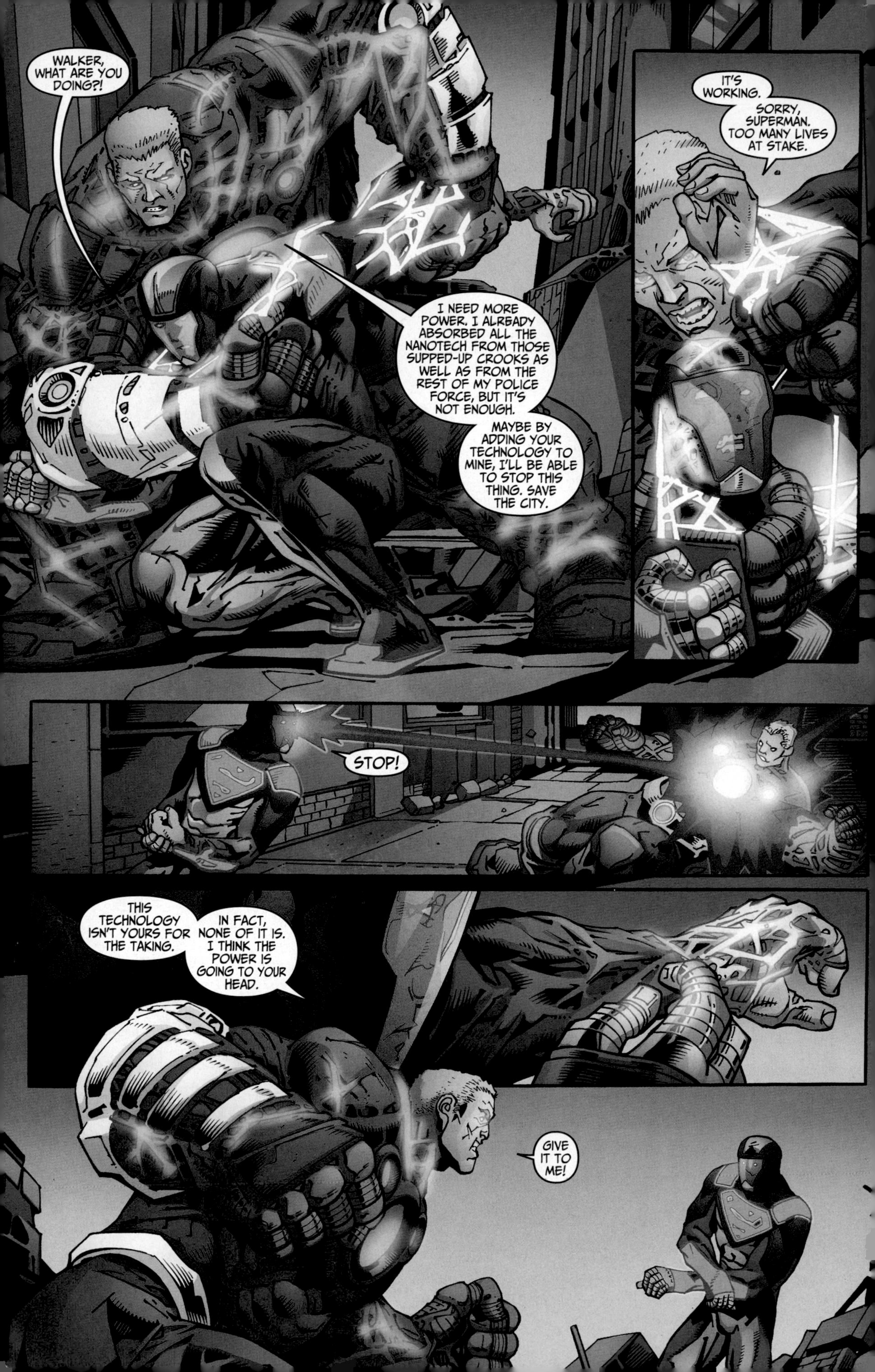
WALKER, WHAT ARE YOU DOING?!
I NEED MORE POWER. I ALREADY ABSORBED ALL THE NANOTECH FROM THOSE SUPPED-UP CROOKS AS WELL AS FROM THE REST OF MY POLICE FORCE, BUT IT'S NOT ENOUGH.
MAYBE BY ADDING YOUR TECHNOLOGY TO MINE, I'LL BE ABLE TO STOP THIS THING. SAVE THE CITY.
IT'S WORKING.
SORRY, SUPERMAN. TOO MANY LIVES AT STAKE.
STOP!
THIS TECHNOLOGY ISN'T YOURS FOR THE TAKING.
IN FACT, NONE OF IT IS. I THINK THE POWER IS GOING TO YOUR HEAD.
GIVE IT TO ME!

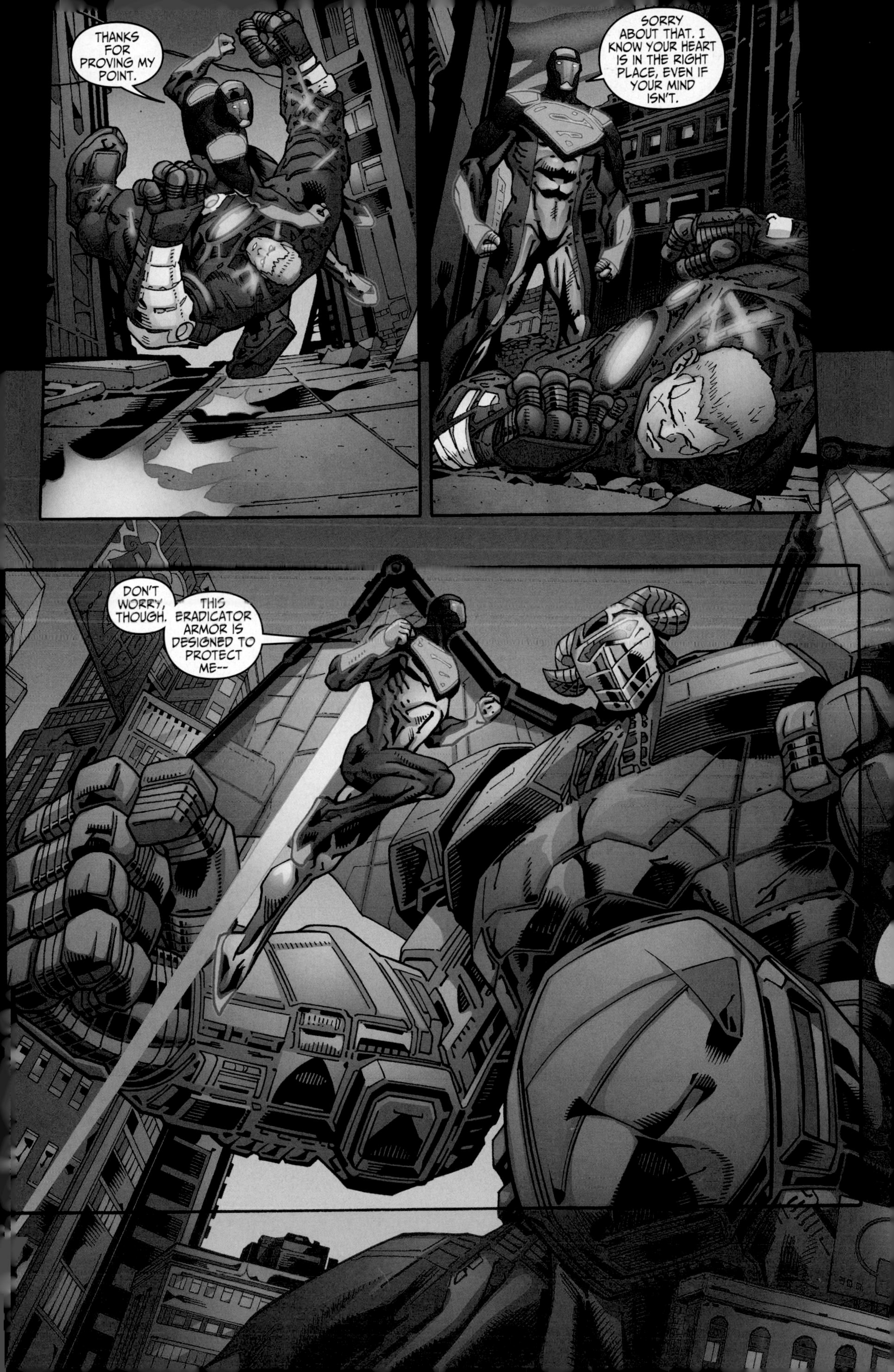
THANKS FOR PROVING MY POINT.
SORRY ABOUT THAT. I KNOW YOUR HEART IS IN THE RIGHT PLACE, EVEN IF YOUR MIND ISN'T.
DON'T WORRY, THOUGH.
THIS ERADICATOR ARMOR IS DESIGNED TO PROTECT ME--

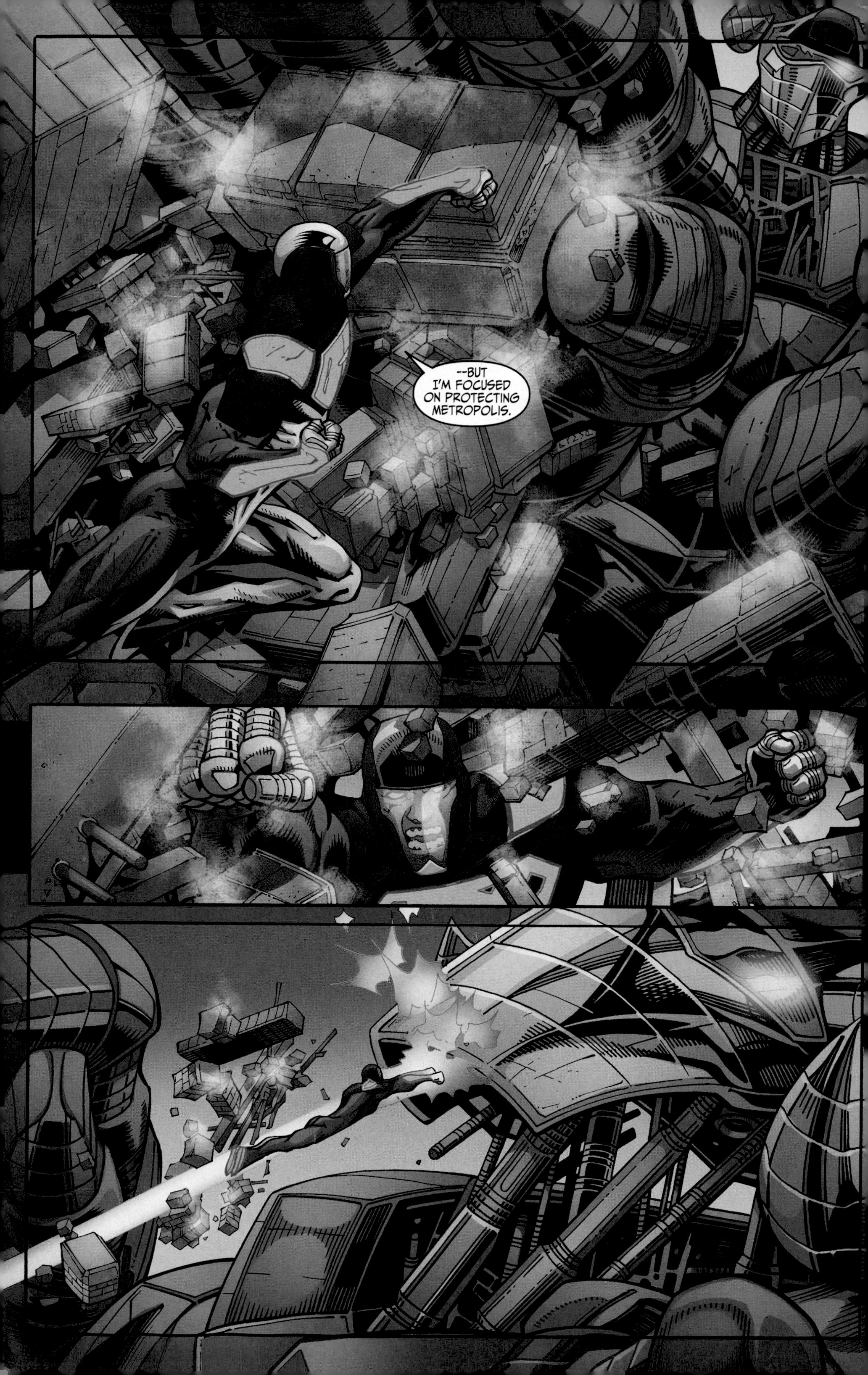
--BUT I'M FOCUSED ON PROTECTING METROPOLIS.

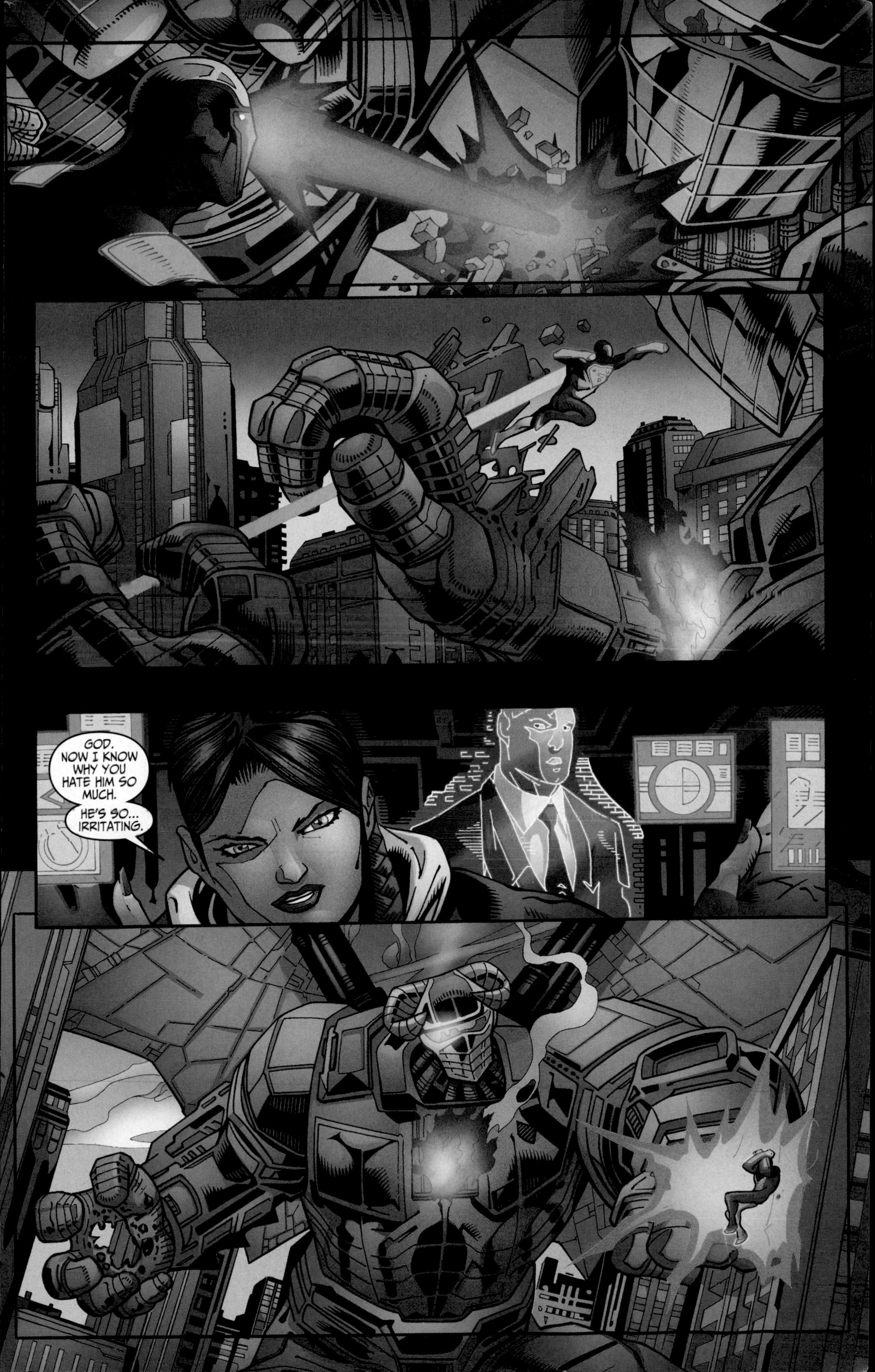
GOD. NOW I KNOW WHY YOU HATE HIM SO MUCH.
HE'S SO... IRRITATING.

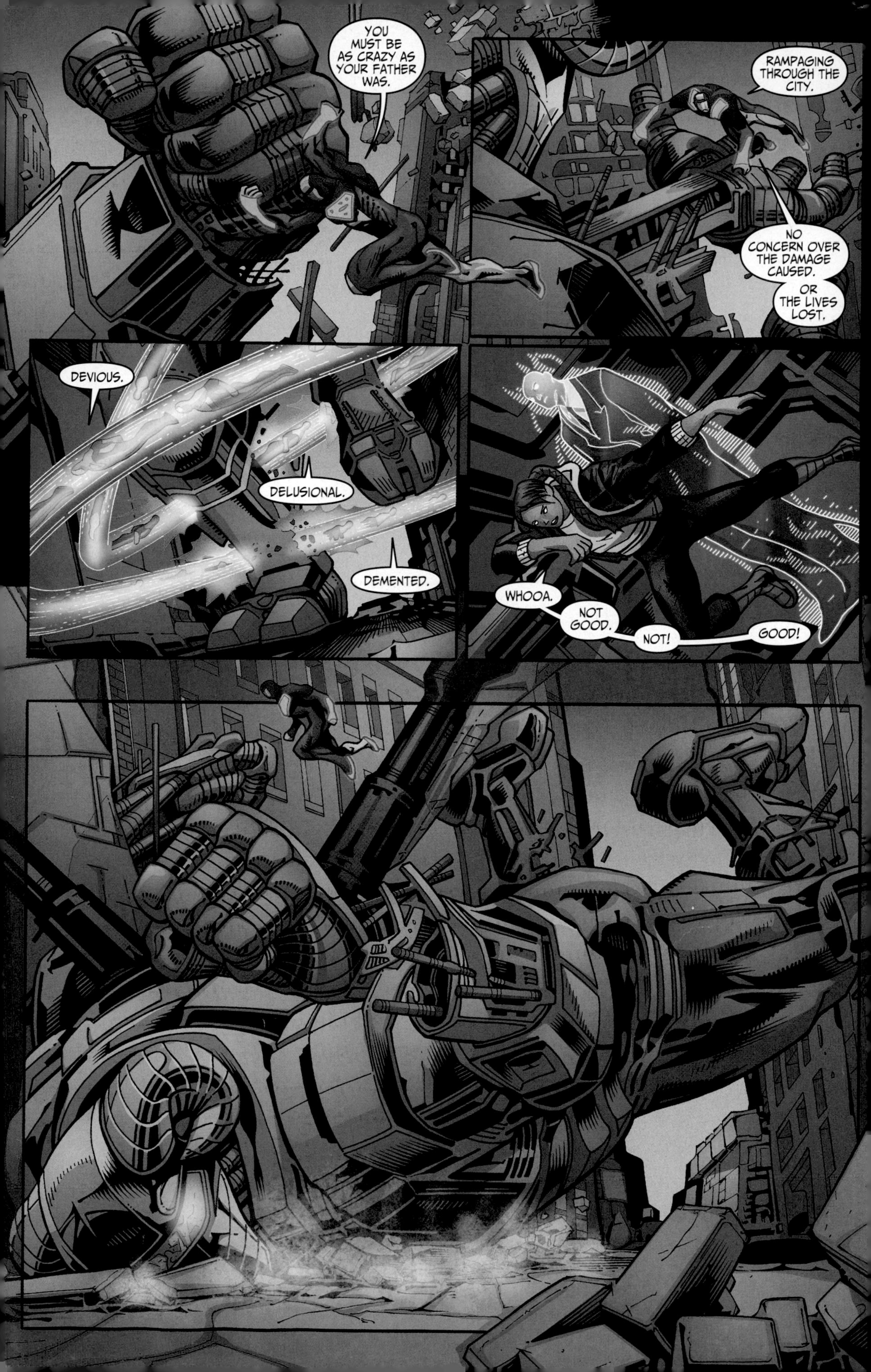
YOU MUST BE AS CRAZY AS YOUR FATHER WAS.
RAMPAGING THROUGH THE CITY.
NO CONCERN OVER THE DAMAGE CAUSED.
OR THE LIVES LOST.
DEVIOUS.
DELUSIONAL.
DEMENTED.
WHOOA.
NOT GOOD.
NOT!
GOOD!

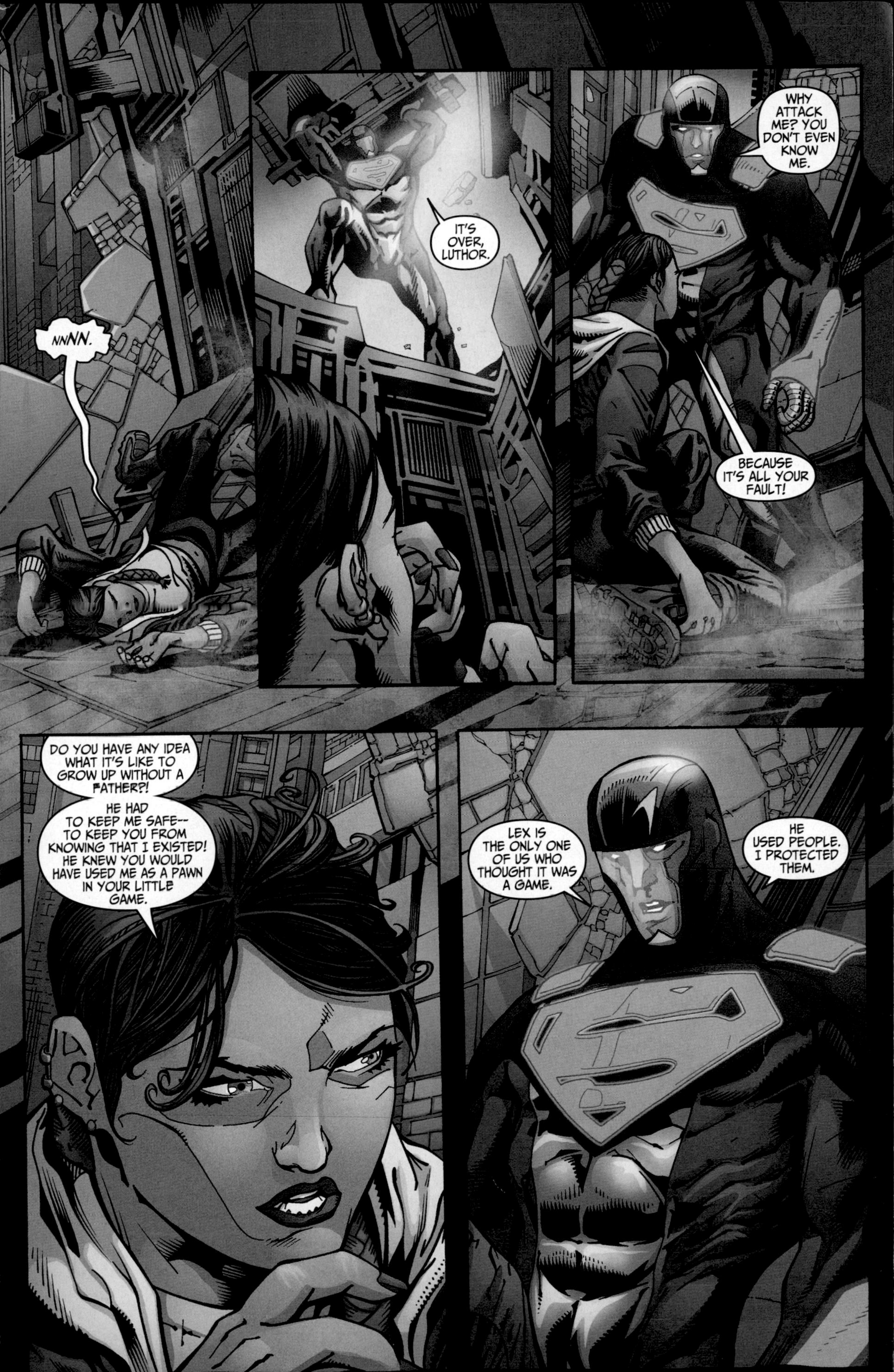
NNNN.
IT'S OVER, LUTHOR.
WHY ATTACK ME? YOU DON'T EVEN KNOW ME.
BECAUSE IT'S ALL YOUR FAULT!
DO YOU HAVE ANY IDEA WHAT IT'S LIKE TO GROW UP WITHOUT A FATHER?!
HE HAD TO KEEP ME SAFE-- TO KEEP YOU FROM KNOWING THAT I EXISTED! HE KNEW YOU WOULD HAVE USED ME AS A PAWN IN YOUR LITTLE GAME.
LEX IS THE ONLY ONE OF US WHO THOUGHT IT WAS A GAME.
HE USED PEOPLE. I PROTECTED THEM.

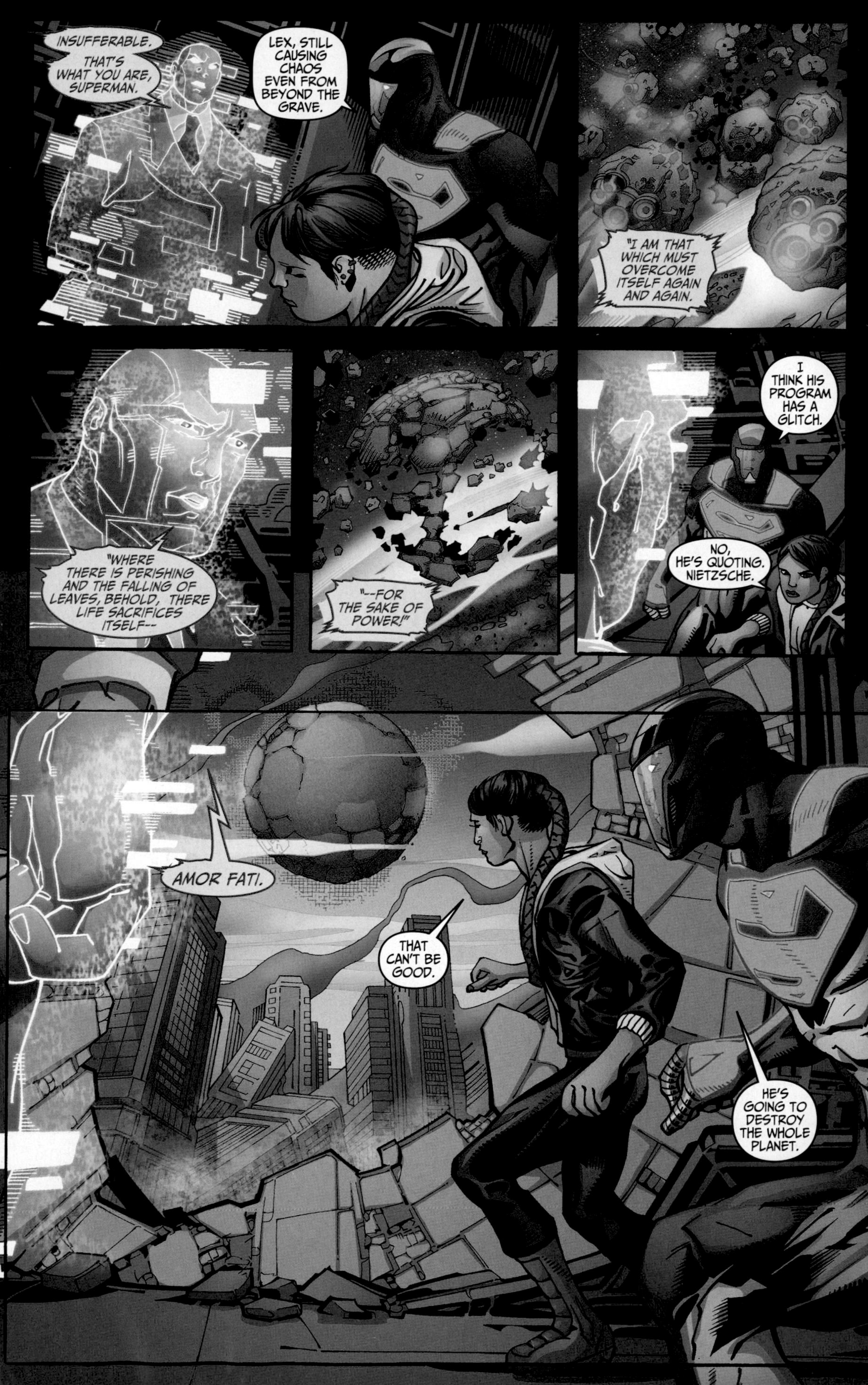
INSUFFERABLE. THAT'S WHAT YOU ARE, SUPERMAN.
LEX, STILL CAUSING CHAOS EVEN FROM BEYOND THE GRAVE.
"I AM THAT WHICH MUST OVERCOME ITSELF AGAIN AND AGAIN.
"WHERE THERE IS PERISHING AND THE FALLING OF LEAVES, BEHOLD, THERE LIFE SACRIFICES ITSELF--
"--FOR THE SAKE OF POWER!"
I THINK HIS PROGRAM HAS A GLITCH.
NO, HE'S QUOTING. NIETZSCHE.
AMOR FATI.
THAT CAN'T BE GOOD.
HE'S GOING TO DESTROY THE WHOLE PLANET.

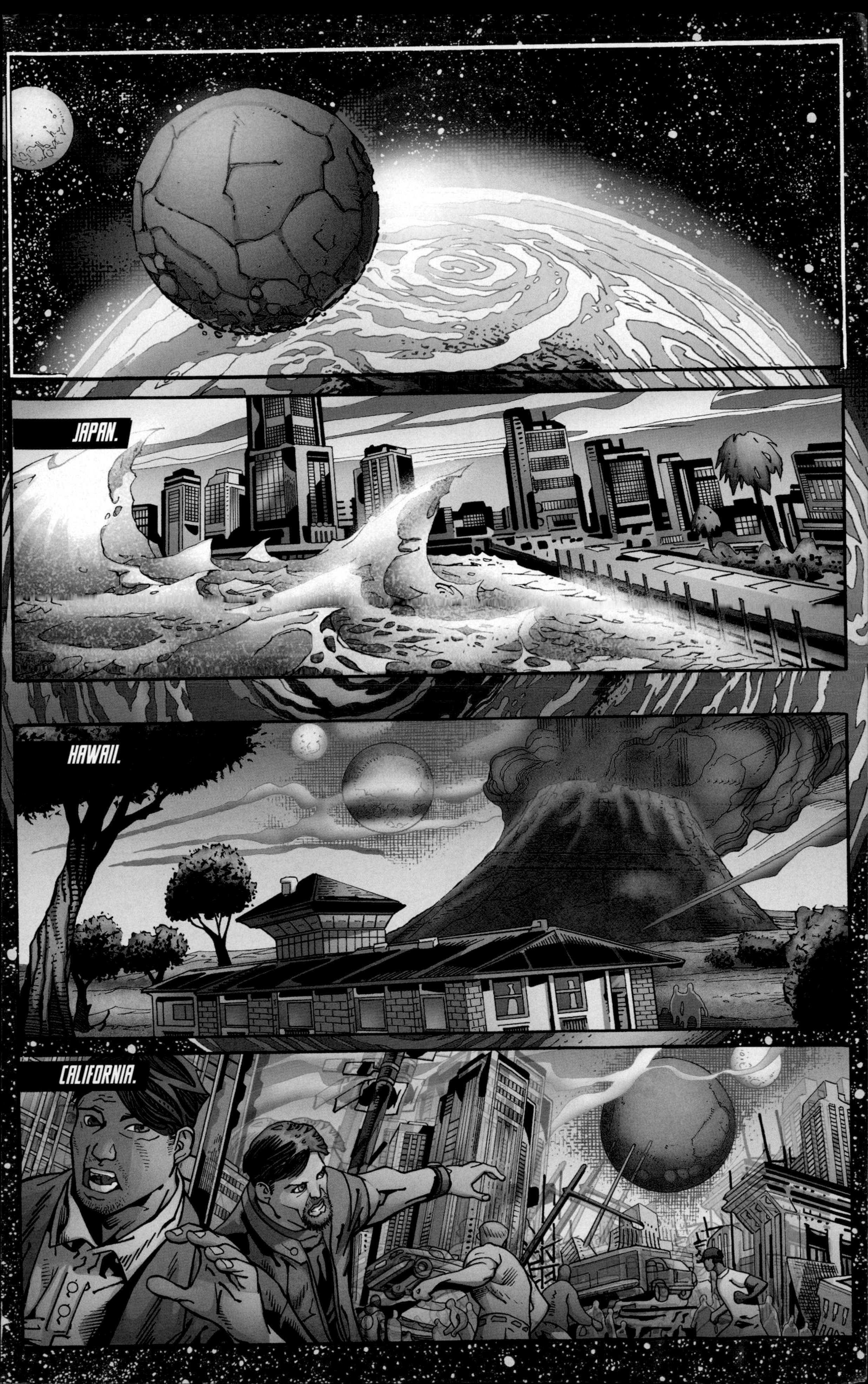
JAPAN.
HAWAII.
CALIFORNIA.

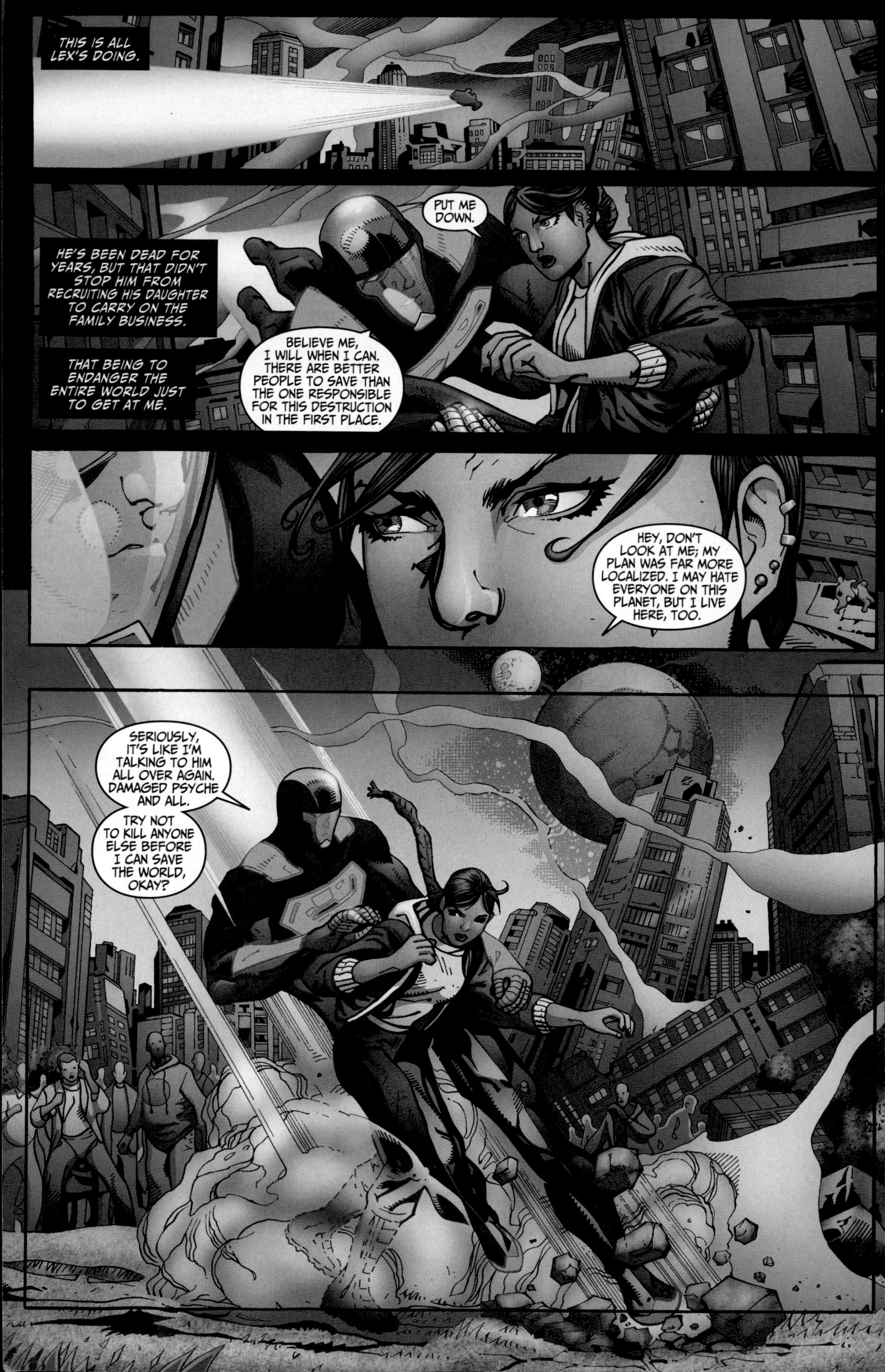
THIS IS ALL LEX'S DOING.
PUT ME DOWN.
HE'S BEEN DEAD FOR YEARS, BUT THAT DIDN'T STOP HIM FROM RECRUITING HIS DAUGHTER TO CARRY ON THE FAMILY BUSINESS.
THAT BEING TO ENDANGER THE ENTIRE WORLD JUST TO GET AT ME.
BELIEVE ME, I WILL WHEN I CAN. THERE ARE BETTER PEOPLE TO SAVE THAN THE ONE RESPONSIBLE FOR THIS DESTRUCTION IN THE FIRST PLACE.
HEY, DON'T LOOK AT ME; MY PLAN WAS FAR MORE LOCALIZED. I MAY HATE EVERYONE ON THIS PLANET, BUT I LIVE HERE, TOO.
SERIOUSLY, IT'S LIKE I'M TALKING TO HIM ALL OVER AGAIN. DAMAGED PSYCHE AND ALL.
TRY NOT TO KILL ANYONE ELSE BEFORE I CAN SAVE THE WORLD, OKAY?

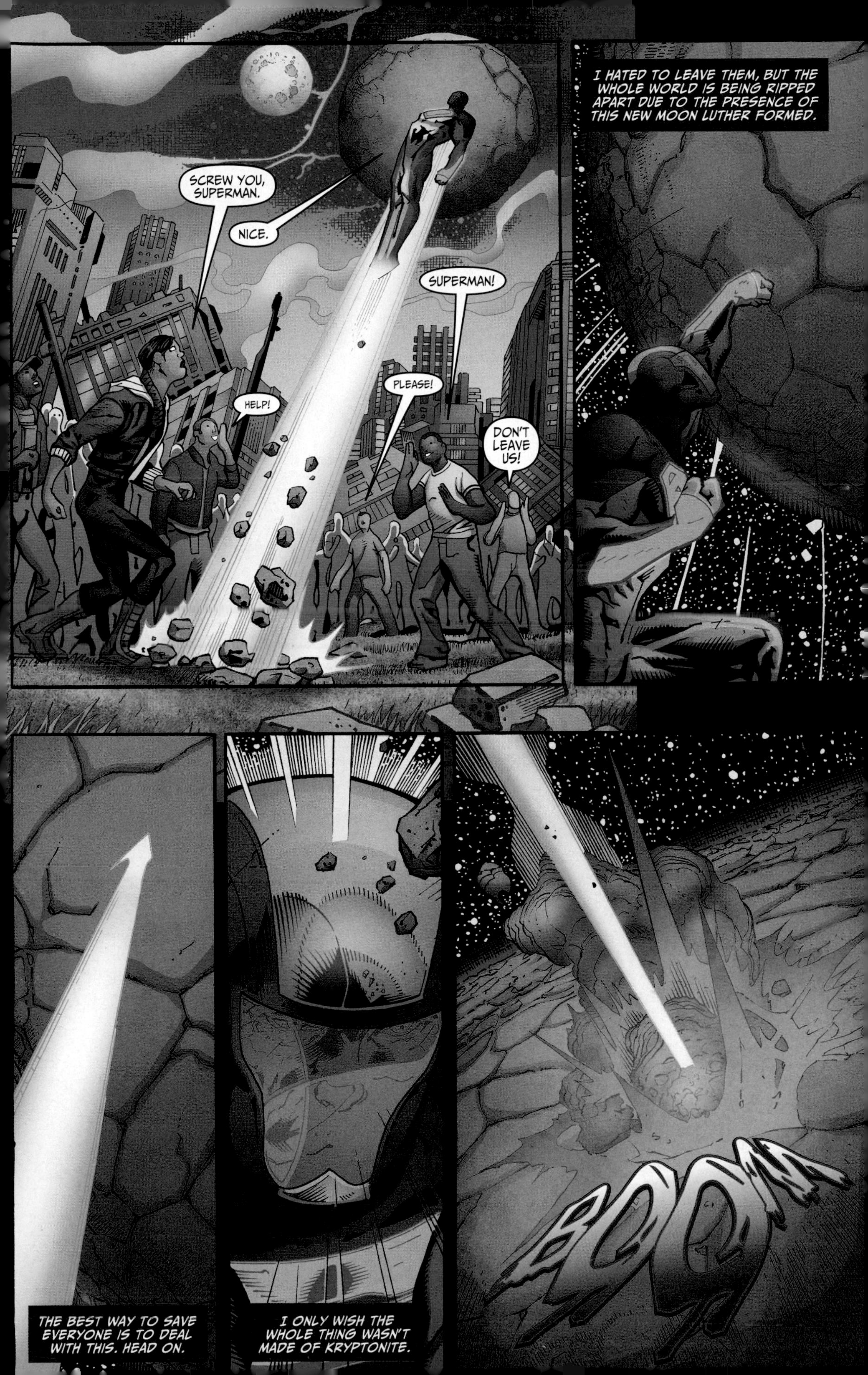
SCREW YOU, SUPERMAN.
NICE.
SUPERMAN!
HELP!
PLEASE!
DON'T LEAVE US!
I HATED TO LEAVE THEM, BUT THE WHOLE WORLD IS BEING RIPPED APART DUE TO THE PRESENCE OF THIS NEW MOON LUTHER FORMED.
THE BEST WAY TO SAVE EVERYONE IS TO DEAL WITH THIS. HEAD ON.
I ONLY WISH THE WHOLE THING WASN'T MADE OF KRYPTONITE.
BOOM

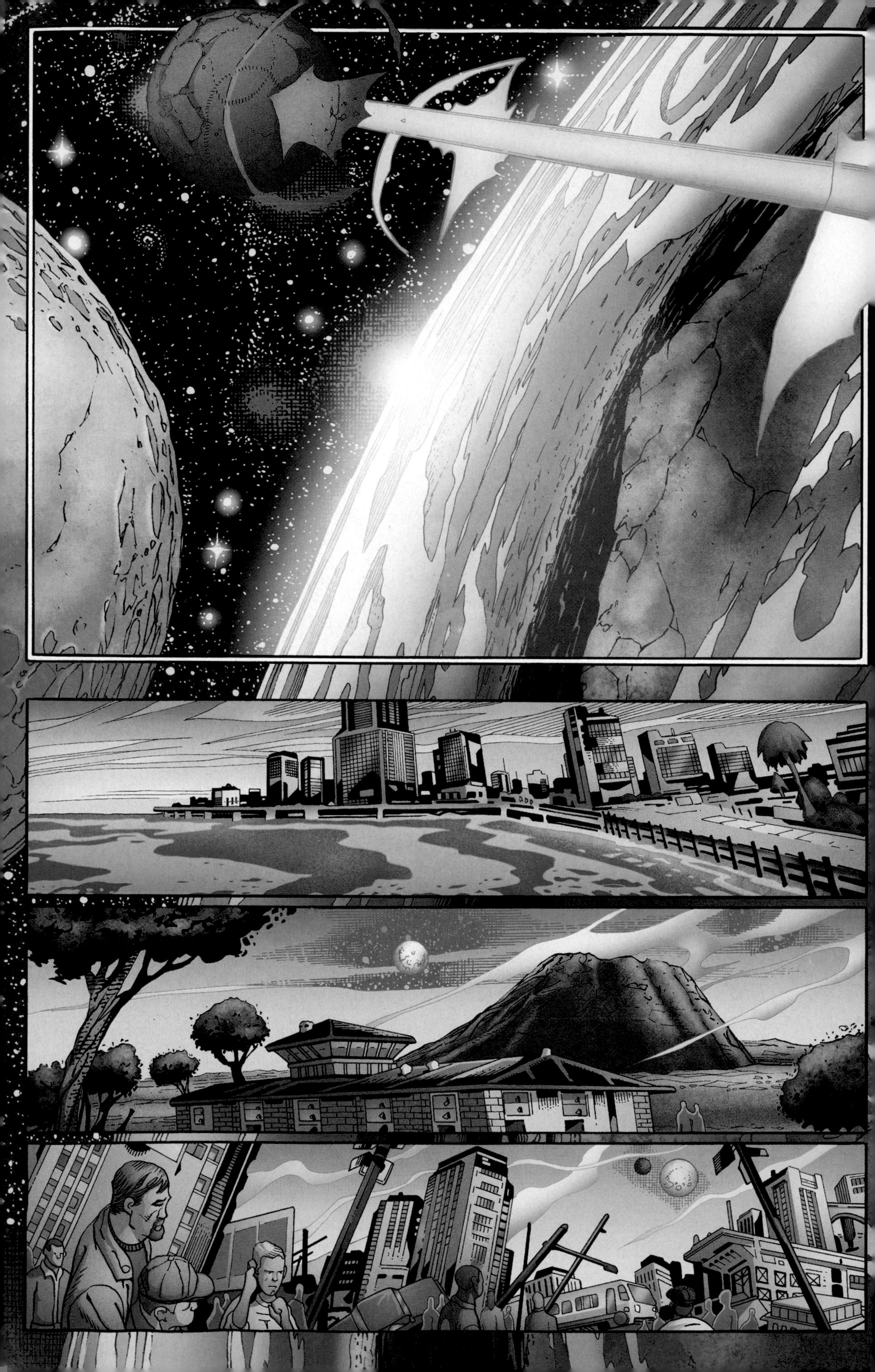

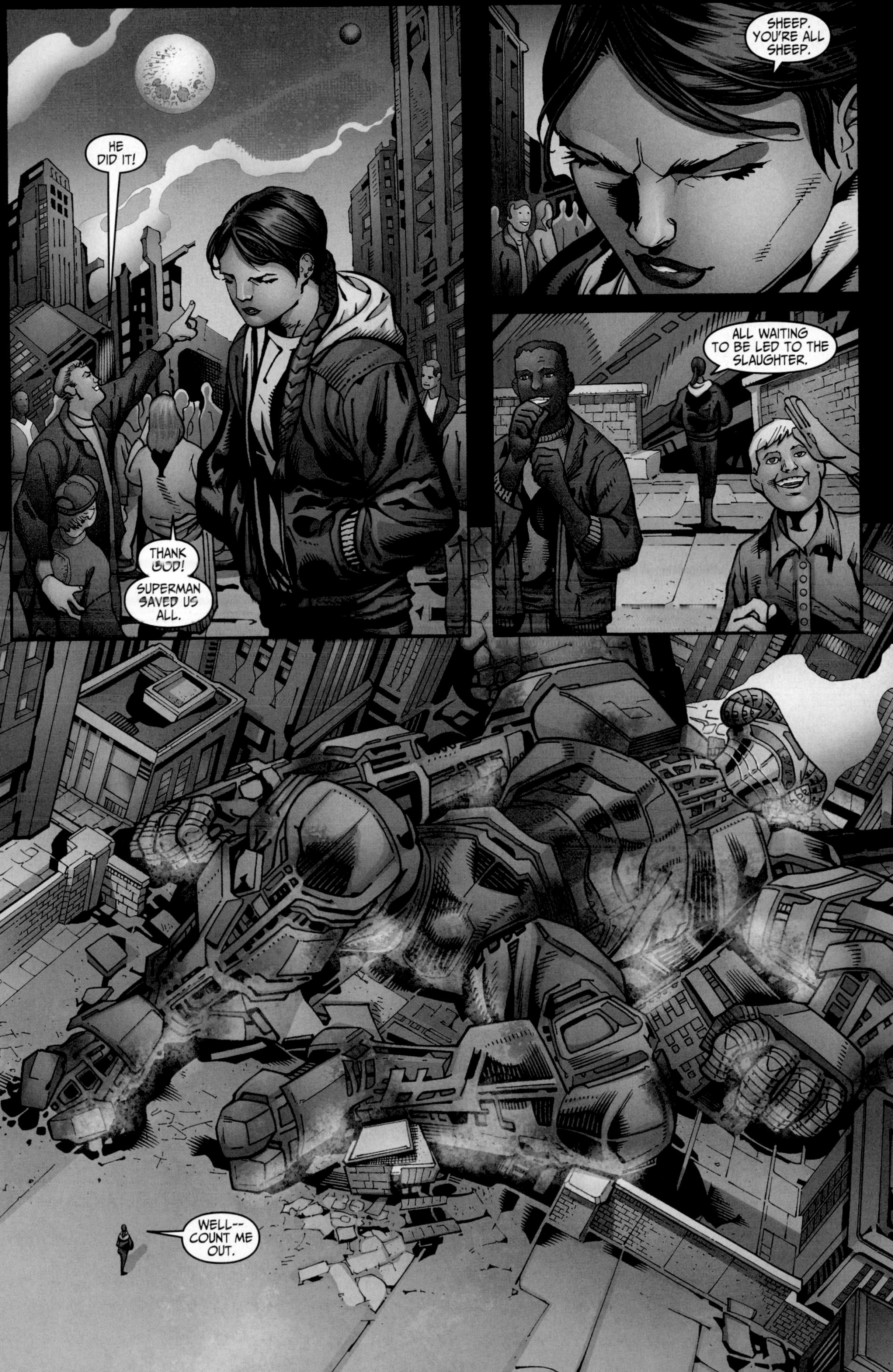
HE DID IT!
THANK GOD! SUPERMAN SAVED US ALL.
SHEEP. YOU'RE ALL SHEEP.
ALL WAITING TO BE LED TO THE SLAUGHTER.
WELL-- COUNT ME OUT.

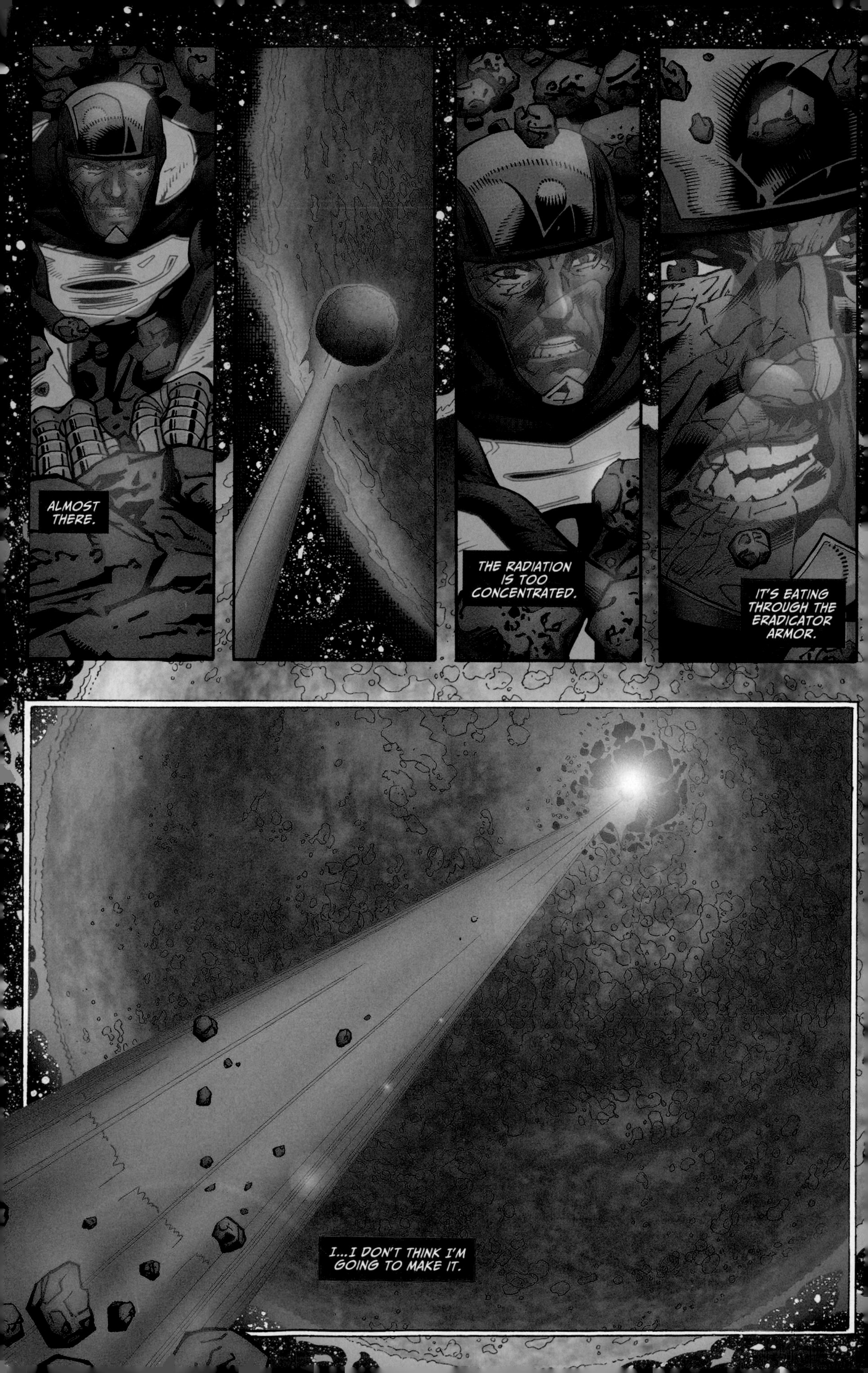
ALMOST THERE.
THE RADIATION IS TOO CONCENTRATED.
IT'S EATING THROUGH THE ERADICATOR ARMOR.
I...I DON'T THINK I'M GOING TO MAKE IT.

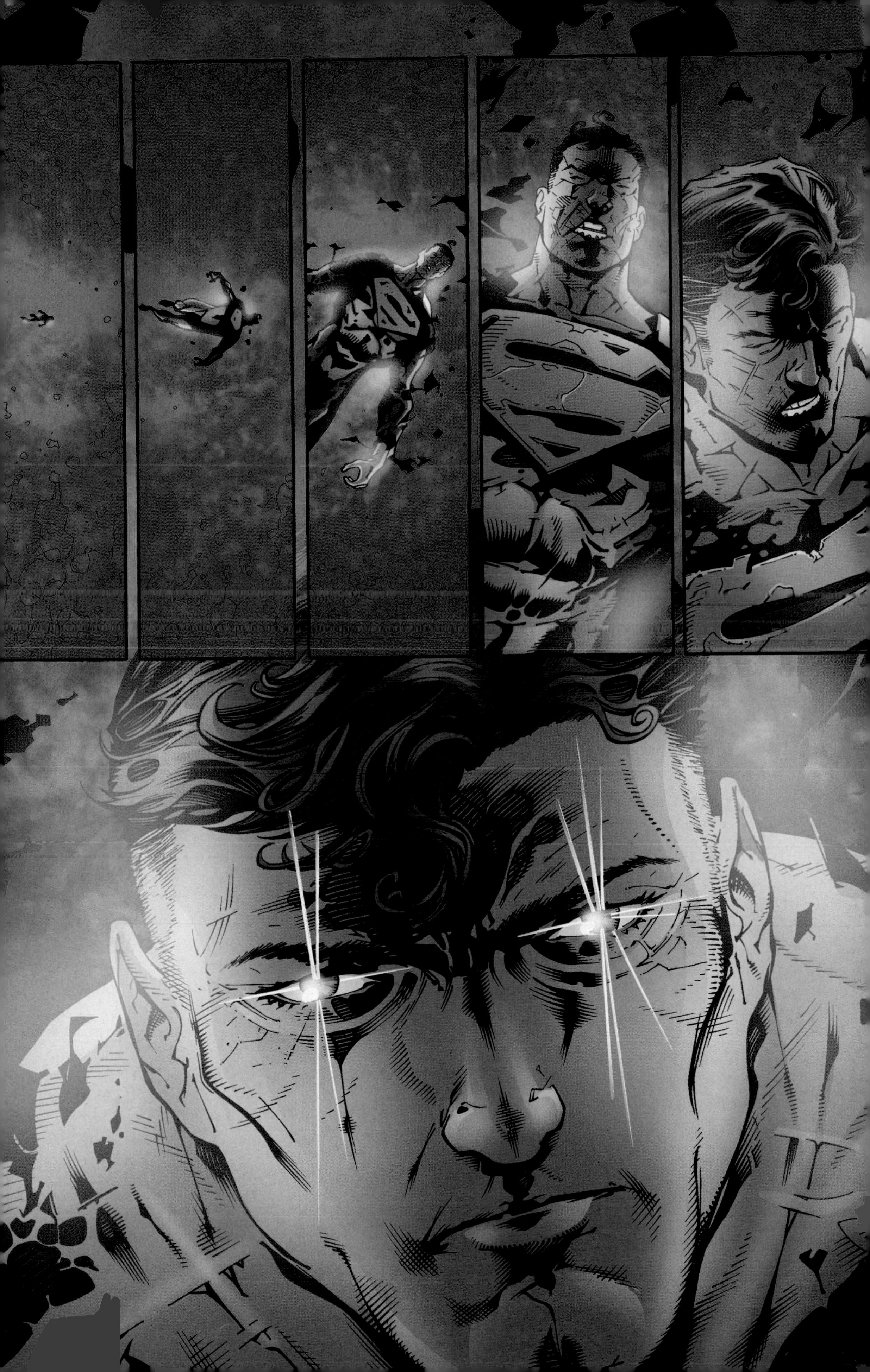

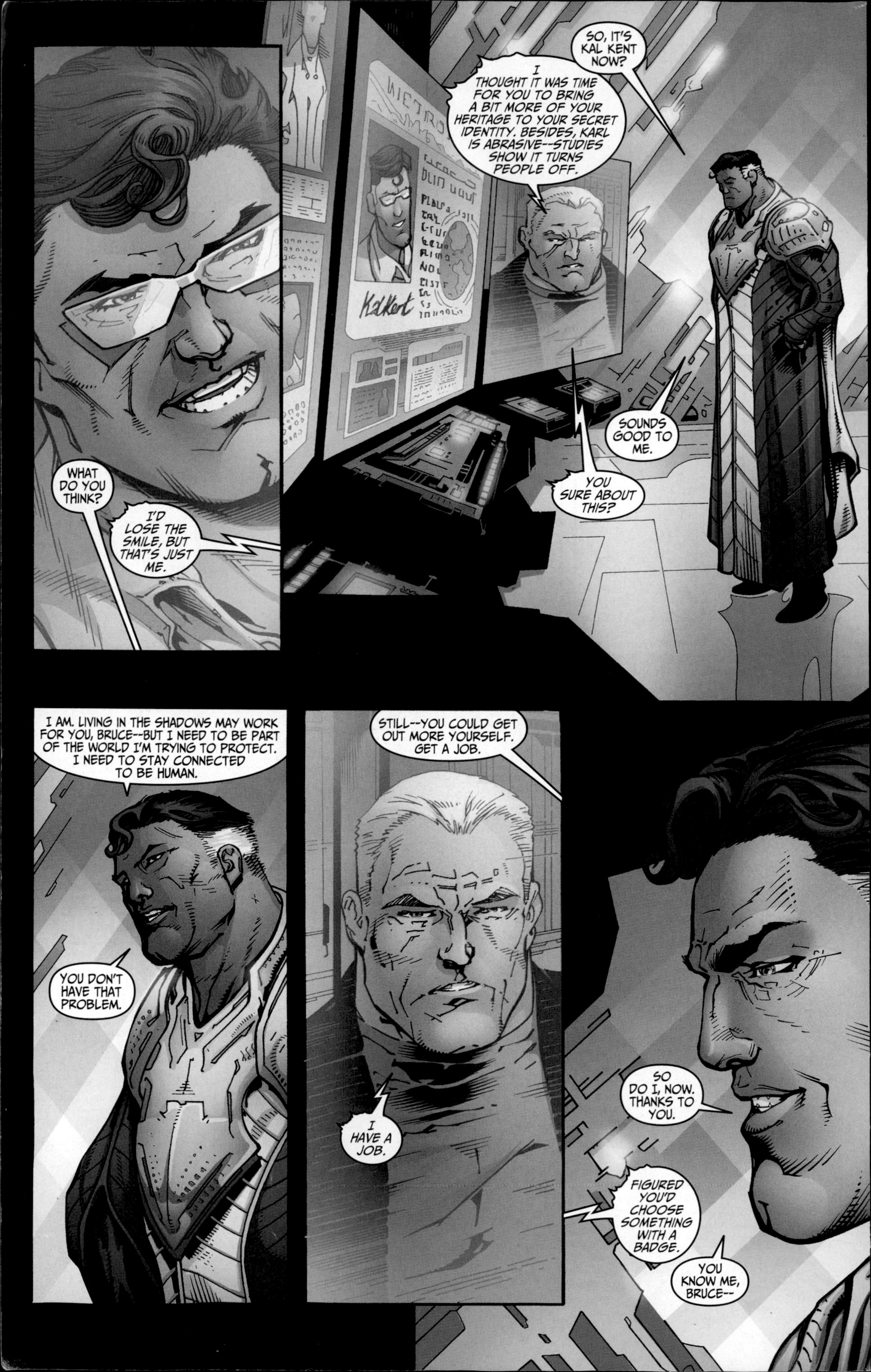
SO, IT'S KAL KENT NOW?
I THOUGHT IT WAS TIME FOR YOU TO BRING A BIT MORE OF YOUR HERITAGE TO YOUR SECRET IDENTITY. BESIDES, KARL IS ABRASIVE--STUDIES SHOW IT TURNS PEOPLE OFF.
SOUNDS GOOD TO ME.
YOU SURE ABOUT THIS?
WHAT DO YOU THINK?
I'D LOSE THE SMILE, BUT THAT'S JUST ME.
I AM. LIVING IN THE SHADOWS MAY WORK FOR YOU, BRUCE--BUT I NEED TO BE PART OF THE WORLD I'M TRYING TO PROTECT. I NEED TO STAY CONNECTED TO BE HUMAN.
YOU DON'T HAVE THAT PROBLEM.
STILL--YOU COULD GET OUT MORE YOURSELF. GET A JOB.
I HAVE A JOB.
SO DO I, NOW. THANKS TO YOU.
FIGURED YOU'D CHOOSE SOMETHING WITH A BADGE.
YOU KNOW ME, BRUCE--

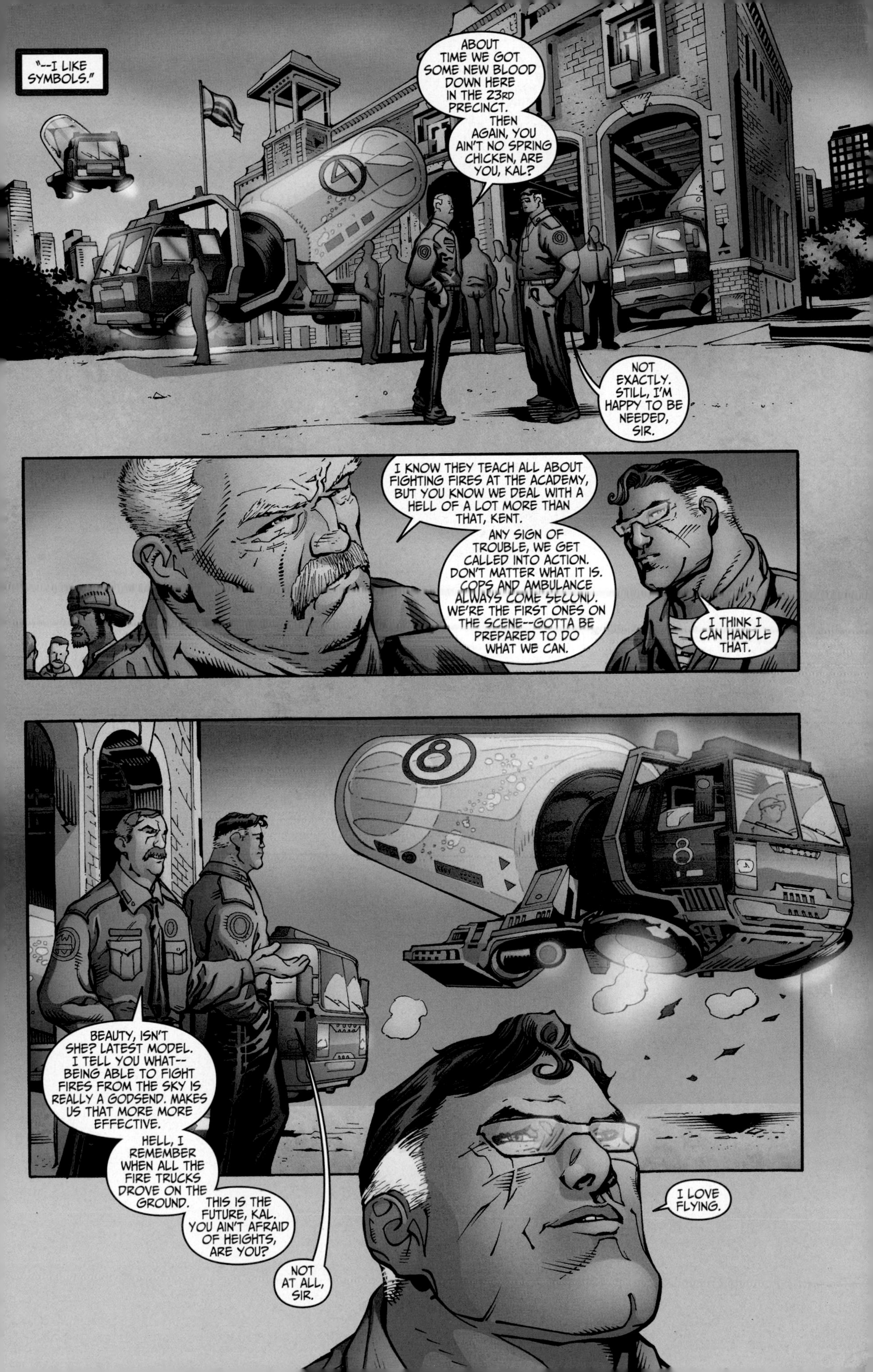
"--I LIKE SYMBOLS."
ABOUT TIME WE GOT SOME NEW BLOOD DOWN HERE IN THE 23RD PRECINCT.
THEN AGAIN, YOU AIN'T NO SPRING CHICKEN, ARE YOU, KAL?
NOT EXACTLY. STILL, I'M HAPPY TO BE NEEDED, SIR.
I KNOW THEY TEACH ALL ABOUT FIGHTING FIRES AT THE ACADEMY, BUT YOU KNOW WE DEAL WITH A HELL OF A LOT MORE THAN THAT, KENT.
ANY SIGN OF TROUBLE, WE GET CALLED INTO ACTION. DON'T MATTER WHAT IT IS. COPS AND AMBULANCE ALWAYS COME SECOND. WE'RE THE FIRST ONES ON THE SCENE--GOTTA BE PREPARED TO DO WHAT WE CAN.
I THINK I CAN HANDLE THAT.
BEAUTY, ISN'T SHE? LATEST MODEL. I TELL YOU WHAT--BEING ABLE TO FIGHT FIRES FROM THE SKY IS REALLY A GODSEND. MAKES US THAT MORE MORE EFFECTIVE.
HELL, I REMEMBER WHEN ALL THE FIRE TRUCKS DROVE ON THE GROUND.
THIS IS THE FUTURE, KAL. YOU AIN'T AFRAID OF HEIGHTS, ARE YOU?
NOT AT ALL, SIR.
I LOVE FLYING.

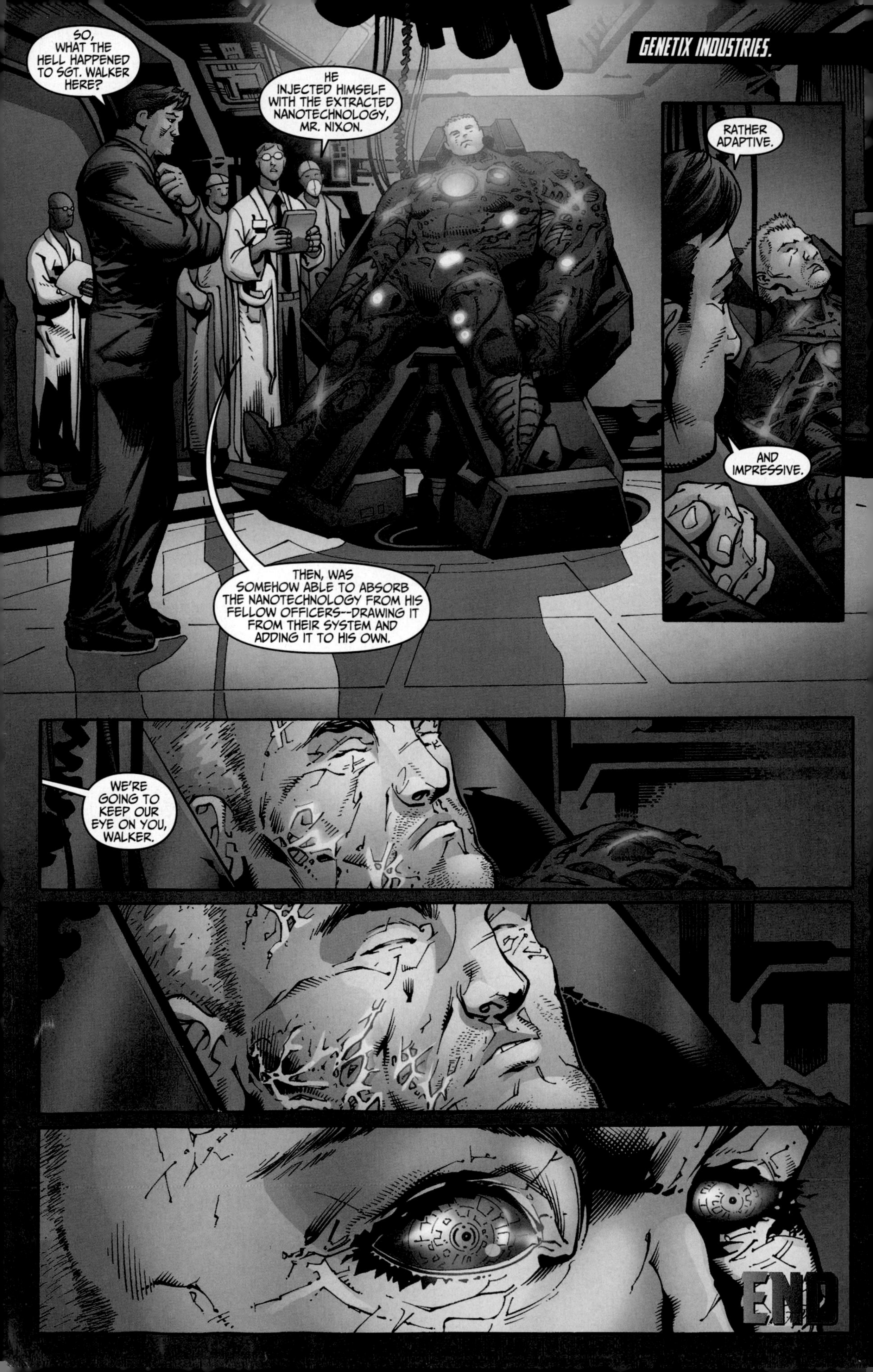
GENETIX INDUSTRIES.
SO, WHAT THE HELL HAPPENED TO SGT. WALKER HERE?
HE INJECTED HIMSELF WITH THE EXTRACTED NANOTECHNOLOGY, MR. NIXON.
THEN, WAS SOMEHOW ABLE TO ABSORB THE NANOTECHNOLOGY FROM HIS FELLOW OFFICERS--DRAWING IT FROM THEIR SYSTEM AND ADDING IT TO HIS OWN.
RATHER ADAPTIVE.
AND IMPRESSIVE.
WE'RE GOING TO KEEP OUR EYE ON YOU, WALKER.
END

SUPERMAN BEYOND #0

Variant cover by Ron Frenz & Sal Buscema

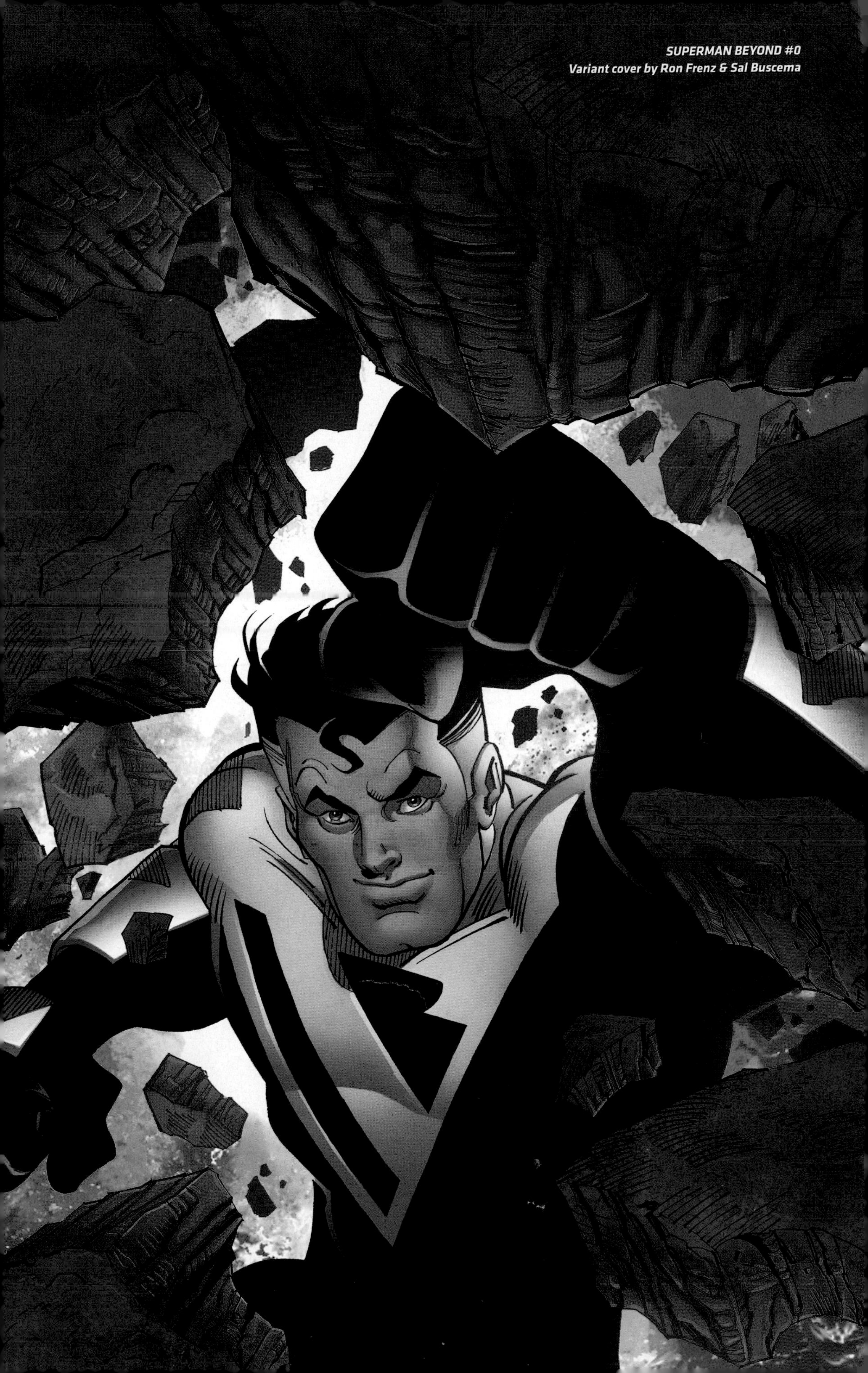

SUPERMAN BEYOND

Digital cover #2 by Howard Porter & John Livesay

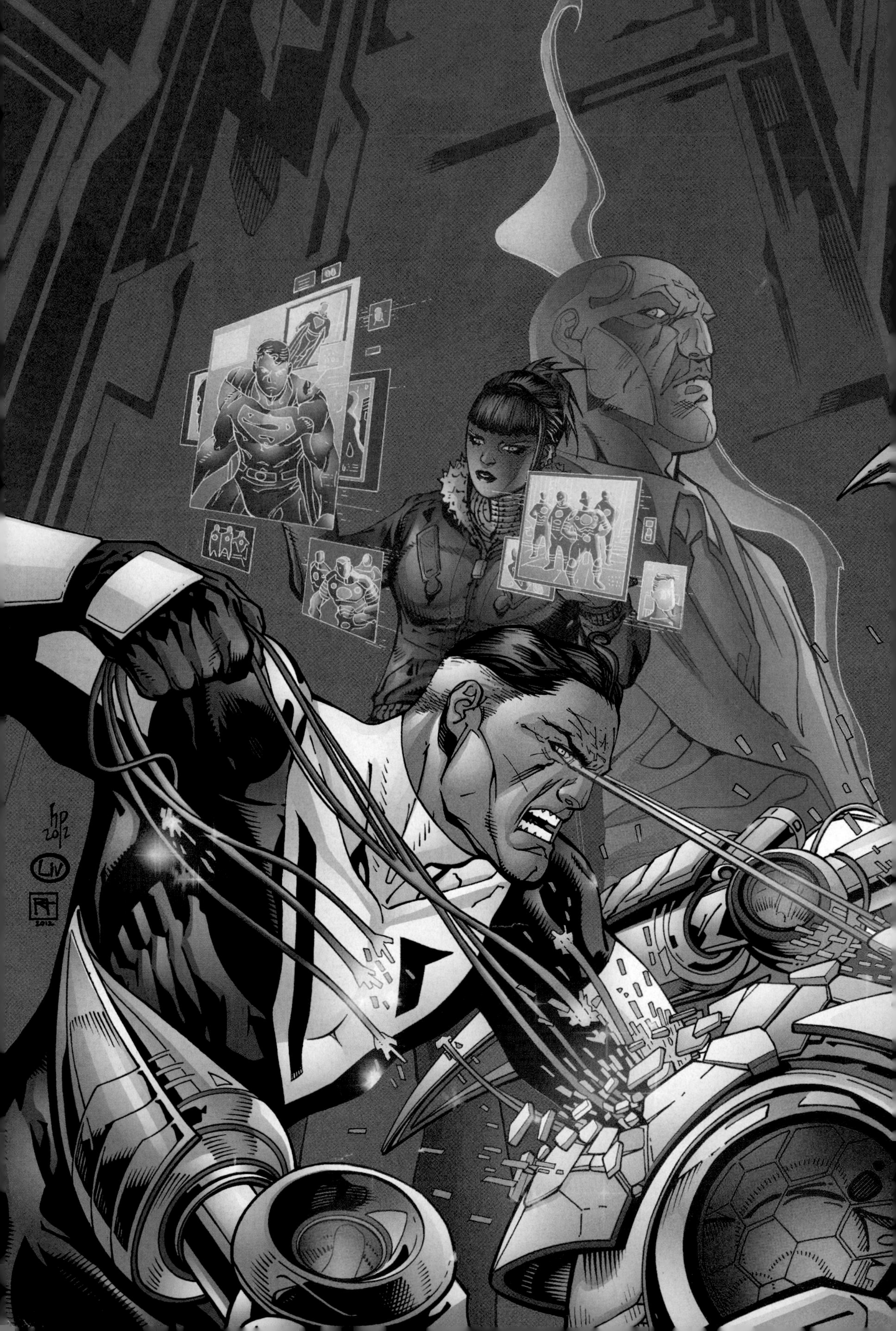

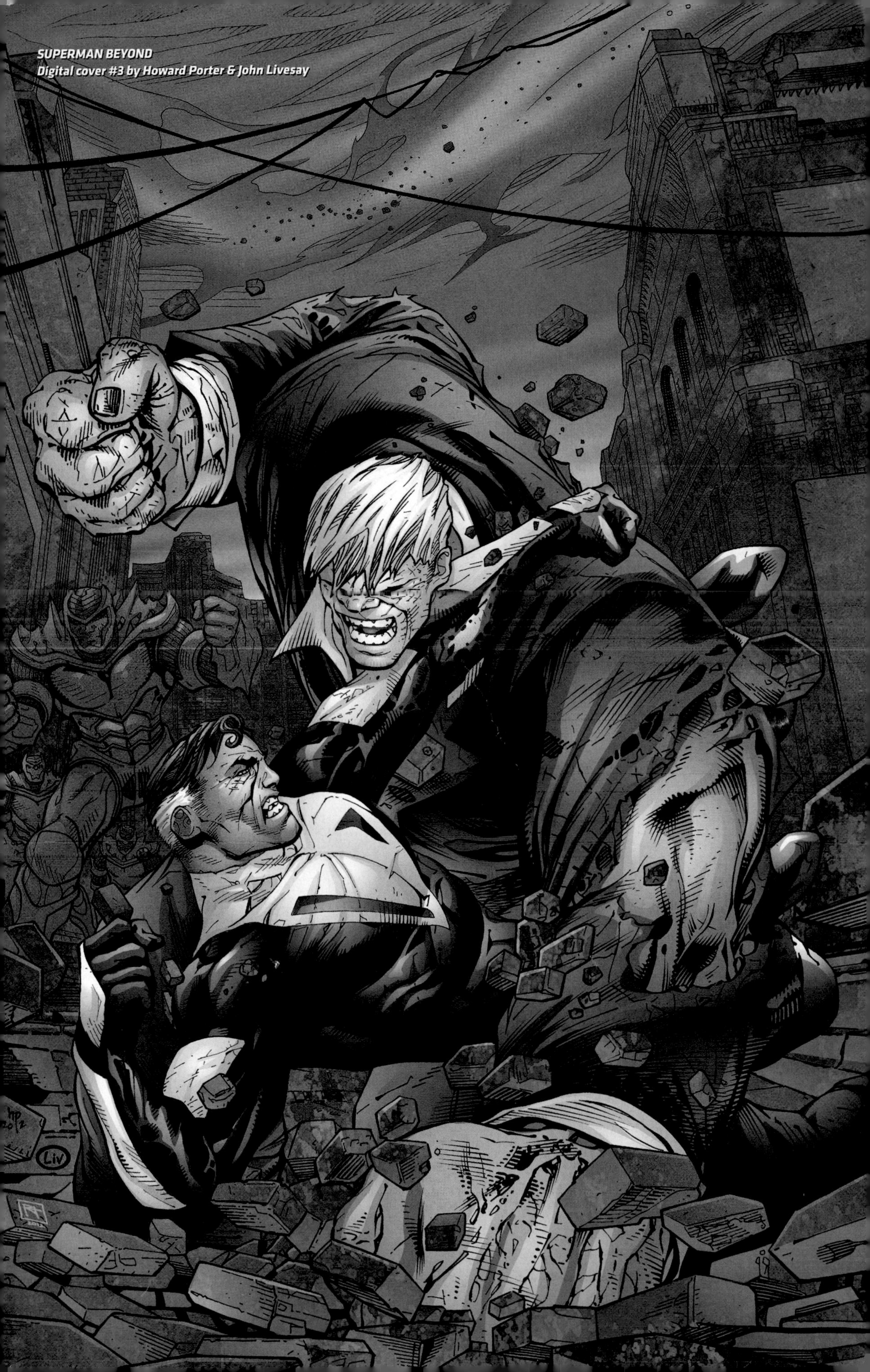

SUPERMAN BEYOND
Digital cover #3 by Howard Porter & John Livesay

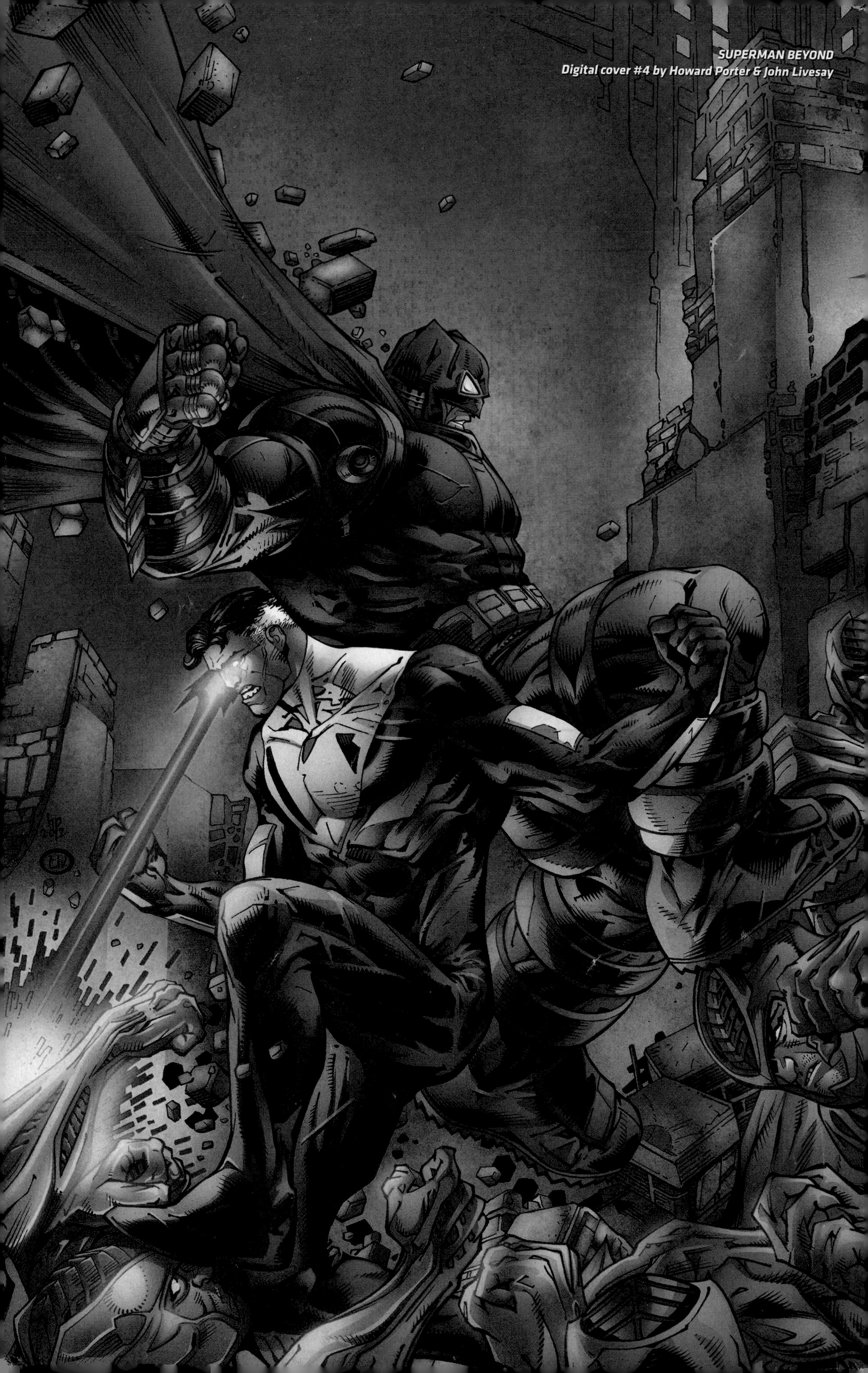

SUPERMAN BEYOND
Digital cover #4 by Howard Porter & John Livesay

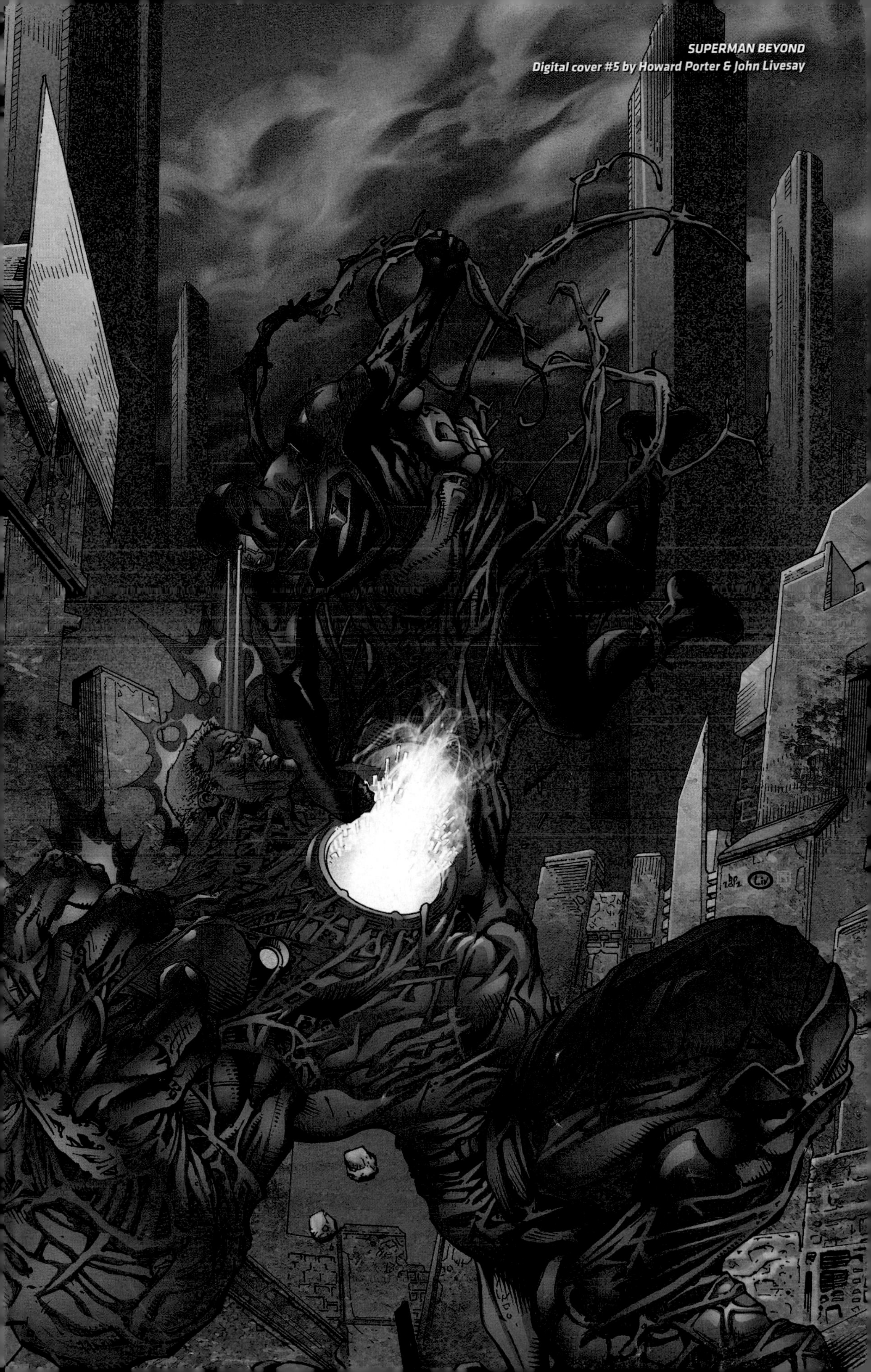

SUPERMAN BEYOND

Digital cover #5 by Howard Porter & John Livesay

SUPERMAN BEYOND layouts by Howard Porter

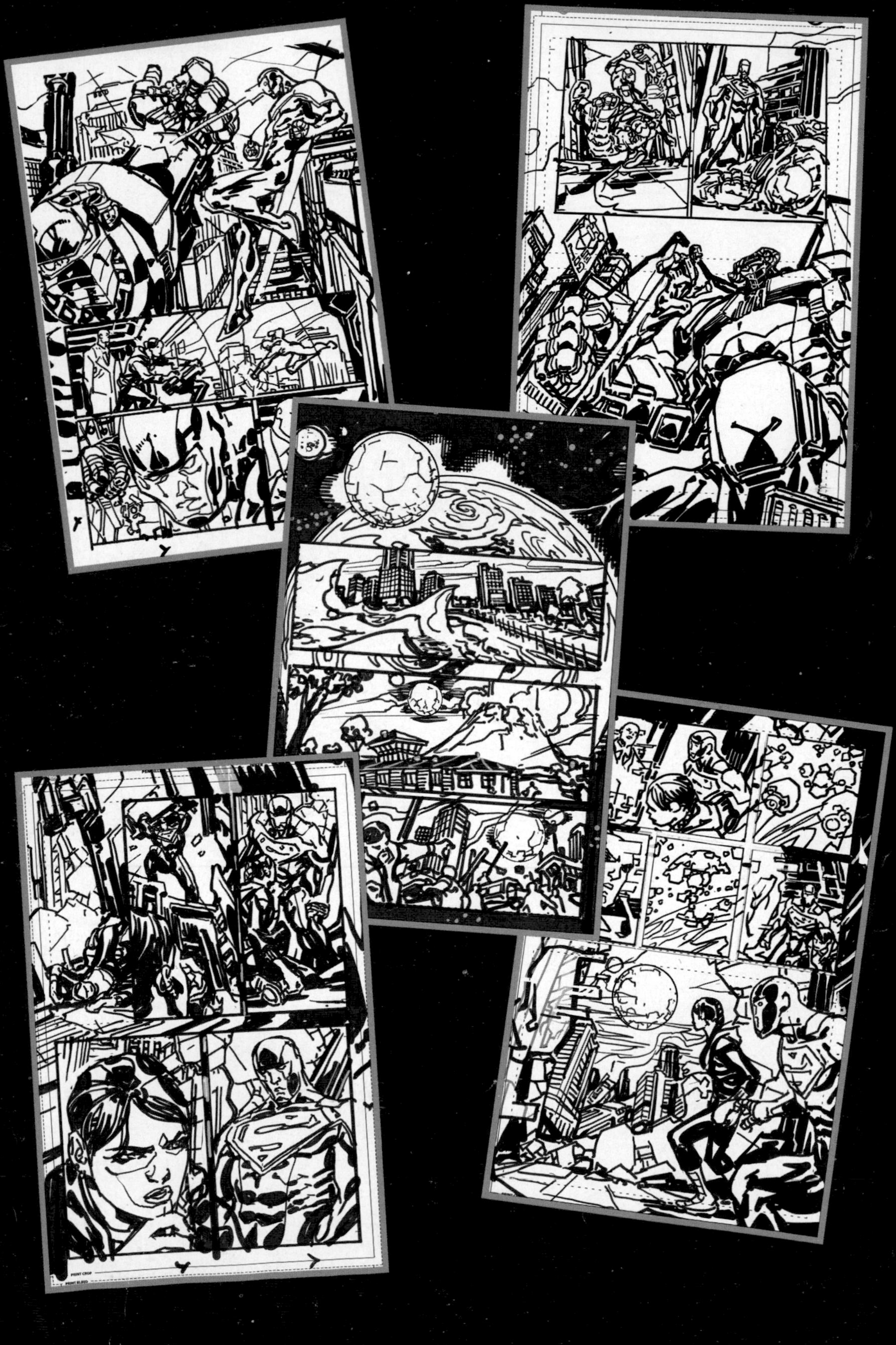